Reparative Craft

THEORY Q *A series edited by*
Lee Edelman, Benjamin Kahan, and Christina Sharpe

Reparative Craft

EVE KOSOFSKY SEDGWICK AS A TEXTILE ARTIST

JASON EDWARDS

Duke University Press Durham and London 2026

Printed in the United States of America on acid-free paper ∞
Project Editor: Lisa Lawley
Designed by Courtney Leigh Richardson
Typeset in Garamond Premier Pro, Ogg, and Proxima Nova
by Westchester Publishing Services

Library of Congress Cataloging-in-Publication Data
Names: Edwards, Jason, [date] author
Title: Reparative craft : Eve Kosofsky Sedgwick as a textile artist / Jason Edwards.
Other titles: Eve Kosofsky Sedgwick as a textile artist | Theory Q
Description: Durham : Duke University Press, 2026. | Series: Theory Q
Includes bibliographical references and index.
Identifiers: LCCN 2025040482 (print)
LCCN 2025040483 (ebook)
ISBN 9781478038856 paperback
ISBN 9781478033974 hardcover
ISBN 9781478062462 ebook
Subjects: LCSH: Sedgwick, Eve Kosofsky | Sedgwick, Eve Kosofsky—Criticism and interpretation | Textile artists—United States | Emotions in art | Art therapy | Breast cancer patients as artists—United States | Critical theory | Queer theory | LCGFT: Biographies
Classification: LCC NK3012.A3 S439 2026 (print) | LCC NK3012.A3 (ebook) | DDC 746.392092—dc23/eng/20260304
LC record available at https://lccn.loc.gov/2025040482
LC ebook record available at https://lccn.loc.gov/2025040483

Cover art: (*top*) Eve at Penland School of Craft; (*bottom*) Eve Kosofsky Sedgwick, untitled collage; both ca. 1996–99. Photographs by Kevin Ryan. Collection of H. A. Sedgwick. © H. A. Sedgwick

Death sets a Thing significant
The Eye had hurried by
Except a perished Creature
Entreat us tenderly
To ponder little Workmanships
In Crayon, or in Wool,
With "This was last Her fingers did"—
Industrious until—
The Thimble weighed too heavy—
The stitches stopped—by themselves—
And then 'twas put among the Dust
Upon the Closet shelves—

EMILY DICKINSON,
Poem J360/F640

CONTENTS

INTRODUCTION

Reparative Craft

Reading Reparatively, or Sedgwick's Textiles

Reparative Craft is the first monograph to explore Eve Kosofsky Sedgwick's work as a textile artist. An accomplished poet and paradigm-shifting literary critic primarily known for her work in queer and affect theory, Sedgwick also created textiles, which have proven to be of comparatively little interest, even to her admirers.[1] The book focuses on the period from roughly 1996 to 2003, in which she was working toward her most-cited monograph, *Touching Feeling: Affect, Pedagogy, Performativity* (2003). Following a discussion of her early patchwork experiments and brief, productive period as a weaver, the book examines in detail the four exhibitions Sedgwick took part in. These were an amateur group show featuring her earlier fabric collages, *Floating Columns* (1999–2000); and three solo shows, exhibited at North American campus galleries: *In the Bardo* (1999–2000); *Bodhisattva Fractal World* (2002); and *Works in Fiber, Paper, and Proust* (2005).[2]

In so doing, *Reparative Craft* represents a kind of retrospective catalog of Sedgwick's textiles. The book can be read in chronological order, or readers can dip into the individual entries in a sequence of their choosing, as a particular object or exhibition attracts their attention. From the start, then, *Reparative Craft* resists a developmental narrative, adopting, sympathetically, a *patchwork* aesthetic, a genre central to Sedgwick's textiles, as we shall see.[3]

The book also puts aside a more conventionally *argumentative* mode, in favor of something more *reparative*. Indeed, readers should note, from the outset, that *Reparative Craft* is not a work of literary/art *criticism*, bracketing throughout potential critiques of, for example, Sedgwick's Orientalism.[4] Instead, the book

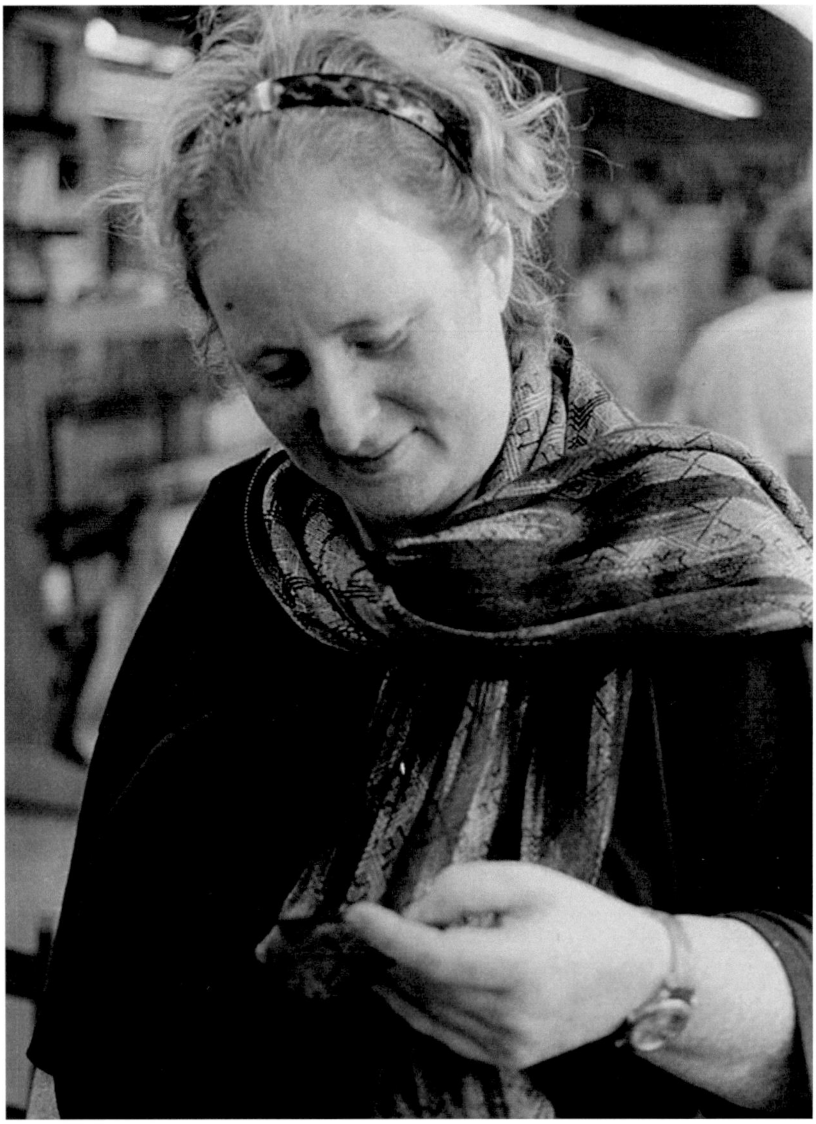

Figure I.1. Eve Kosofsky Sedgwick at the Penland School of Craft, ca. 1996–99. Photograph: H. A. Sedgwick. Collection of H. A. Sedgwick. © H. A. Sedgwick

engages with her textiles respectfully and compassionately, being more concerned with what we might learn from them, rather than imagining, *avant la lettre*, that we have something to teach them, from our arsenal of default critical positions.[5] As a result, *Reparative Craft* looks across at Sedgwick's textiles with wonder, rather than looking down on them with condescension.

In so doing, the book employs a *reparative* methodology, in Sedgwick's now famous, still little considered, terms. The book's founding premise is that her textiles represent her most sustained, useful example of reparative reading, because her artworks make repeated use of quotations from two literary sources. The first is Yoel Hoffmann's translations of Japanese haiku written by early modern Zen monks and poets on the verge of death, with Sedgwick usually incorporating the entire poem. Sedgwick's second key source is Marcel Proust's *In Search of Lost Time* (1913–27), in a range of English translations, from which she selects a number of single sentences, or a small number of successive sentences; rarely, however, as much as a paragraph.[6]

Rather than engaging with such literary sources in the familiar form of a critical essay, however, a genre Sedgwick continued to employ as she developed her craft practice, in her textiles she deployed quotations more as mantras, often in complex fonts and against colored or textured backgrounds. As such, Proust and Hoffmann represented text(ile)s that the artist, as well as her readers and spectators, could contemplate, *realize* in their minds, digest, and make nourishing use of; as Sedgwick herself seems to have done after her diagnosis with metastatic breast cancer in 1996, the moment at which her textile art practice began. (Sedgwick had been first diagnosed with breast cancer in 1990, undergoing a mastectomy and chemotherapy that year, before the cancer metastasized in her spine six years later.)[7]

In spite of the sustained literary-theoretical influence over the past twenty years of Sedgwick's *Touching Feeling*, and the number of so-called postcritical positions it inspired, the precise *reparative* methodology that she introduces there, that she employs in her textiles, and that I work with to engage sympathetically with them in this book, remains "little explored," even as it represents, in Sedgwick's view, the "heart of many histories of gay, lesbian, and queer," as well as trans, "intertextuality."[8] I add trans intertextuality here because, as we shall see, the iconography of many of her textiles centers on a bodhisattva, a Buddhist divinity who defers entering nirvana and returns to samsara, the endless cycle of karmic reincarnation, motivated by deep compassion, to help living beings achieve liberation from reincarnation. This idea of self-consciously selfless compassion, rather than egotistic criticism, is central to the reparative project, and to the affective motives of this book.

According to Sedgwick, the bodhisattva in question, Avalokiteshvara in the Indian Buddhist tradition, Kuanyin in the Chinese, was "usually portrayed as a man" up to "about the eighth century" in South Asia and then, "after about the twelfth," was "generally seen and known in female form" in East Asia, while the bodhisattva of the intervening centuries was "often much harder to classify in terms of gender." Discussing the bodhisattva, Sedgwick noted that her own "thought and hope" was that "even in the expression of a strong sensuality," Avalokiteshvara/Kuanyin did not need to be "shaped or perceived through the eyes of gender at all—not male, not female, not both male and female, and not neither male nor female."[9]

If Sedgwick's description circa 2007 emphasizes Kuanyin's freedom from the troubles of gendered embodiment, gender and its transformations remained central to a divinity who, iconographically and historically, began as an Indian man, Avalokiteshvara, before becoming a Chinese woman, Kuanyin, but who was able, throughout, to embody whichever gendered form was likely to prove most relationally skillful.

From as early as her 1977 narrative poem "Trace at 46," Sedgwick had been interested in ontologies "plaiting / together . . . lines female and male / and divine," divinities usually "referred to in the plural number."[10] In her 1985 essay "Up the Postern Stair: *Edwin Drood* and the Homophobia of Empire," however, Sedgwick argued that, too often, constructing a "position of apparent 'androgyny' or halfway-ness," while "pretending to share equally in the qualities of two symmetrically opposite groups, really manipulated the asymmetry of their status for personal advancement."[11]

But that 1985 argument was mostly unrepresentative of her wider thinking, which witnessed her frequent, controversial identification *as a gay man* rather than merely *with* gay men.[12] In 1997, meanwhile, as Sedgwick was beginning to engage deeply with textiles, she noted how honored she felt at being asked to "initiate a discussion of two papers" on trans issues at that year's Berkshire Conference of Women Historians, by Jack Halberstam and C. Jacob Hale, talks that "place[d] the very definition of 'woman' under the greatest conceivable pressure," and projects that collectively articulated subjectivities "that purposefully move[d] across the boundaries of gender."[13]

Sedgwick first introduced the idea of reparative reading in her fall 1996 introduction to the "Queerer than Fiction" special issue of *Studies in the Novel*, where she described as *camp* the reparative reading practice of many of her contributors.[14] Sedgwick then expanded on the idea in the introduction to her 1997 edited collection, *Novel Gazing: Queer Readings in Fiction*. The notion of reparative reading, however, received its best-known iteration in the conclusion to chapter 4 of *Touching Feeling*, "Paranoid and Reparative Reading, or, You're So Paranoid You Probably Think This Essay Is About You."[15] There, Sedgwick suggested that paranoid and reparative reading practices were often intwined, and in her textiles there are many moments when she continues to read "through paranoid lenses," employing the "x-ray gaze of the paranoid impulse" to see "through to [her own] unfleshed skeleton." More frequently, though, Sedgwick's reparative reading project in her patchworks is "additive and accretive." Indeed, patchwork was a form made up of many parts in complex interrelation through which Sedgwick sought to "assemble and confer plenitude on an object that [would] then have resources to offer" her own increasingly "inchoate self" in the context of a cancer treatment that ultimately proved "inadequate" and an illness that, in rezoning her own body into parts, and attacking them simultaneously and in succession, was "inimical" to her need for "nurture."[16]

Indeed, one might read Sedgwick's theorizations of camp in the mid-1990s, and the reparative reading practices that best responded to it, as an account of her aesthetic ambitions as a textile artist, a patchwork practice whose emergence coincided with the publication of the "Queerer than Fiction" essay in 1996, the year of Sedgwick's recurrence diagnosis. In addition, spectators might understand Sedgwick's textile practice as a resource-full attempt to model for her surviving readers and viewers what a reparative reading practice might look like should they themselves need one.

I make this claim because Sedgwick's patchworks, often employing literary quotations, as we have seen, alongside materials and visual iconography concerned with her embodied experience of metastatic breast cancer, articulate precisely her account of "classic camp performance" and of the reparative reading that did it justice. That is because her textiles, as well as my accounts of them, often represented "startling, juicy displays of excess erudition"; "passionate . . . antiquarianism"; a "prodigal production of alternative historiographies"; a "rich, highly interruptive affective variety"; a "disorienting juxtaposition of present with past, and popular with high culture"; an "irrepressible fascination with ventriloquistic experimentation," when it came to both Proust and her selected Japanese death poets; and an "'over'-attachment to fragmentary, marginal, waste or leftover products." Sedgwick's was a "sloppy craft," in a number of senses, as we shall see.[17] Sedgwick's frequently tacky or sticky reparative patchworks, often employing adhesives rather than embroidery, also visually register a "glue of surplus beauty," "surplus stylistic investment," in the form of the elaborate fonts she employed for the quotations, and the "unexplained wellings up" of parts that are "cement[ed] together and animate" the "amalgam of powerful part-objects."[18]

In this book I will "help . . . [my]self again and again" to Sedgwick's delicious, nutritious craft, to demonstrate that it is, in her words, "not only important but *possible* to find ways of attending to such reparative motives and personalities," to find ways of "develop[ing] and disseminat[ing] the richest reparative practices," even if I risk seeming "sappy, aestheticizing, defensive, anti-intellectual, or reactionary" in my often formalist, languorously ekphrastic, deeply interpretative, but never *critical*, reading and looking practices.[19] Indeed, I want the various readings and viewings contained within the book, taken together, to demonstrate Sedgwick's insistence that reparative readings are "no less acute than a paranoid position, no less realistic, no less attached to a project of survival," Sedgwick's and my own, modeling cumulatively, in the pages that follow, the "many ways selves and communities" can "succeed in extracting sustenance from the objects of a culture—even of a culture whose avowed desire has often been not to sustain them."[20]

To do so, *Reparative Craft* focuses on the range of textiles Sedgwick produced in the decade or so after her diagnosis with metastatic breast cancer in spring 1996. The book comprises six chapters in chronological order. The first half of the book examines her early textile experiments as well as a small amateur group show she took part in. The second part provides close readings of her three solo exhibitions: *In the Bardo* (1999–2000), *Bodhisattva Fractal World* (2002), and *Works in Fiber, Paper, and Proust* (2005). While my periodization acknowledges Sedgwick's diagnosis as, in some ways, radically interruptive, demarcating an extended "late" period of her life, *Reparative Craft* presumes a continuity of intentional idiom across her life and the different genres of her work, ranging from her better-known queer theoretical interventions, through her less well-known poetry, to her almost entirely ignored textiles.

If the book is, mostly, chronological, however, it isn't, as I have begun to suggest, meant to be teleological. We can certainly see Sedgwick getting more technically and conceptually accomplished as a craftsperson, but the book nonetheless honors her preference for a kaleidoscope of alternating Kleinian *positions* in any one reading, as well as across time, and her hostility to a Freudian maturational schema of *phases*.[21] In a late essay, "Reality and Realization" (1998), Sedgwick also suggested that reality and materiality were not "propositional," that they were "spatial as much as temporal."[22] The book is, therefore, ongoingly metamorphic, rather than axiomatic; restlessly performative, rather than argumentative; and unusually formalist and ekphrastic, rather than contextualizing, ideological, or cultural-historical. The book also fans out a wide range of readings *beside* one another, since, as Sedgwick noted, "the irreducible positionality of *beside*" offered "useful resistance" to binary, hierarchical, teleological thinking, comprising instead a "range of desiring, identifying, representing, repelling, paralleling, differentiating, rivaling, learning, twisting, mimicking, withdrawing, attracting, aggressing, warping, and other relation[s]."[23]

If the book's variety of chapter forms is generically unconventional, with later chapters resembling an exhibition catalog more than a literary theory

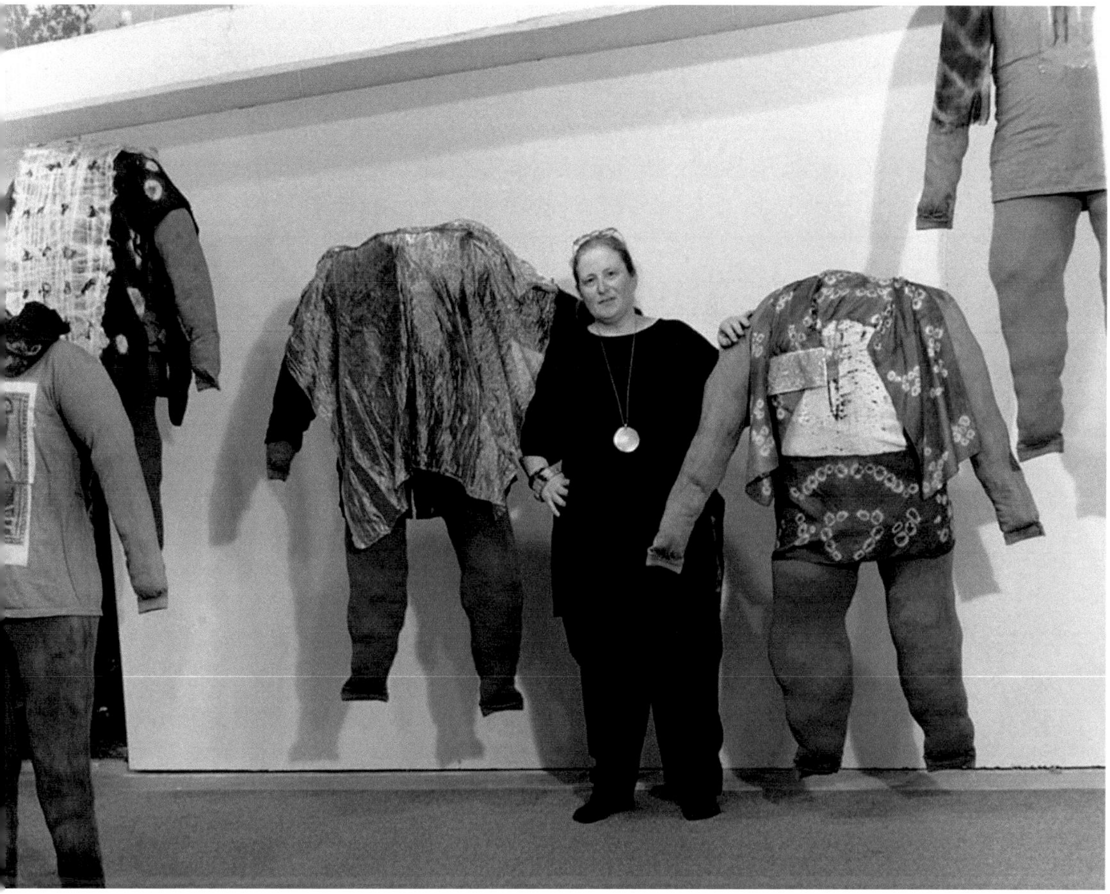

Figure I.2. Eve Kosofsky Sedgwick at the *In the Bardo* exhibition, 1999–2000. Photographer unknown. Collection of H. A. Sedgwick. © H. A. Sedgwick

monograph, I'm hoping that much else about it might productively unsettle readers' formal expectations: its maximalist *fat* bulk stretching minimalist attention spans; its repeated rhythm of returning to new objects akin to the spanking meters Sedgwick found so evocative, painful, and pleasurable. Indeed, the book presumes, throughout, a queer reader's paradigmatic interest in sexual language and perverse pornographic scenarios, particularly, in Sedgwick's case, the scenes of masturbation, anality, urethrality, and sadomasochism, with all their "plural possibilities" of "voyeurism, horror, *Schadenfreude*, disgust, or even compassion."[24]

Sedgwick's characteristic interests in these topoi were root deep and lifelong, although often controversial in and beyond her lifetime, with her circa 1989–90 essay "Jane Austen and the Masturbating Girl" notorious in Republican hack journalism "months before it was published" and singled out for ridicule, in one case, "before the essay was so much as *written*"; and with Sedgwick "considered more dangerous than Saddam Hussein," by some, in the early 1990s.[25] Indeed, my own first, life-changing encounter with Sedgwick in the flesh occurred in this period, while she was giving her similarly controversial essay "Is the Rectum Straight? Identification and Identity in *The Wings of the Dove*," which dilated on Henry James's sustained anality.[26] In addition, the publication of Sedgwick's 1996 edited collection of her friend Gary Fisher's S/M writing, *Gary in Your Pocket*, was, if anything, even more provocative for the way his texts frequently, performatively, coupled sexual and racial degradation.[27]

But as section II of Sedgwick's 1994 collection of poems, *Fat Art, Thin Art*, made clear, there was nothing new about her queer interests. Indeed, when it came to her lyric poetry, sadomasochism was, in many ways, its beating heart, in early poems, from the mid-1970s, including "Everything Always Distracts," "Sexual Hum," and "Sestina Lente," as well as in posthumously published poems, from the same period, including "Explicit" and "The Palimpsest"; interests that ran right up to the urethral and anal thematics of one of the last lyrics she published before her death, "Bathroom Song."[28]

If *Reparative Craft* is a queer book, it is also self-consciously interdisciplinary, straddling literary and craft theory, the product of my graduate training, as a literary close reader, and subsequent career, as a close looker, in art history. Taken as a whole, the book also articulates a queer phenomenology, suggesting that reading is a kind of looking, with a dense materiality of its own, and looking is as amenable to complex interpretation as the closest of readings.[29] That the book focuses on Sedgwick's amateur craft practice represents a particularly counterintuitive, canon-stretching evidence base from which to make such arguments. All the better!

In sum, *Reparative Craft* is, also perhaps, unusually descriptive, staying loyally, lovingly with its objects while promiscuously moving across lots of them. Sedgwick was aware of the resistance some readers had to such patient readings, noting in *Tendencies* that the "single most controversial thing" in several queer theory classes she taught was "*that they were literature courses*, that the path to every issue we discussed simply had to take the arduous defile through textual interpretation."[30] This was not, however, an ekphrastic approach Sedgwick herself resisted, quite the opposite. At one point in *Touching Feeling*, she acknowledged that "the pleasure of quoting Dickens threatens to take over my discussion."[31] I have a similarly endless pleasure in quoting Sedgwick.

In addition, *Reparative Craft* prides itself on being a piece of what Sedgwick characterized, in a lesser-known 1998 article, as "Experimental Critical Writing." The essay originated in a syllabus for a seminar Sedgwick was teaching, which sought to make the "ambitions of literary criticism become more expansive" at the "boundaries between genres, between 'critical' and 'creative' writing," as well as between "argumentation and performance," "individual and collaborative production," and "literary and non-literary texts," so as to "change the current profile of what is publishable in our profession," to "interrupt" the academy's "rather numbing" generic expectations, and to help further "overcome [readers'] inhibitions about experimentation."[32]

Following Sedgwick's lead, indeed writing as a paid-up member of the "Church of Sedgwick," I encourage spectators to "linger as long as they can" with the question of what the "ambition of this piece" of textile art is, focusing on novel answers that the "reader or even [artist] may not already know," mindful that "verbal meaning isn't the only or necessarily the most powerful form of meaning—even where words are involved." The book also ponders, as Sedgwick's students were encouraged to do, further questions: "What energies" does her work "tap into"? What happens when the "assignment of person changes" from "an 'I' . . . into a 'he' or 'she' or 'they', and/or vice versa"? And how and why does Sedgwick employ so many quotations? Indeed, Sedgwick's textiles center almost entirely on Proust, Japanese death haiku, and other assorted Buddhist texts, as we have begun to see, while parts of this book also wonder whether, as in "Walter Benjamin's fantasy," the "perfect book," or at least an interesting one, might "consist *exclusively* of quotations," "a fabric of quotations, a *catalogue raisonné* of quotations."[33]

As a self-conscious memorial, a hagiographic retrospective intellectual biography, *Reparative Craft* is also concerned, implicitly, throughout with "issues of representation and address that attach to the processes of loss and mourning," experimenting with what Sedgwick characterized as "obituary issues and impulses" within "historical or textual scholarship." In addition, just as Sedgwick's textiles move "back and forth between poetry and prose," between Proust and haiku, so the book shuttles freely across Sedgwick's better-known critical works and her less-known poems, the "unexpected *conjunction* of the forms" allowing us to do things that we "might not have been able to do using just one or the other," and exploring "the highly charged moments of switching back and forth" between different media. Again like the Sedgwick of "Teaching 'Experimental Critical Writing,'" *Reparative Craft* is interested in what she calls "the 'scrapbook' form" with its multiple "short sections, with frequent new beginnings,"

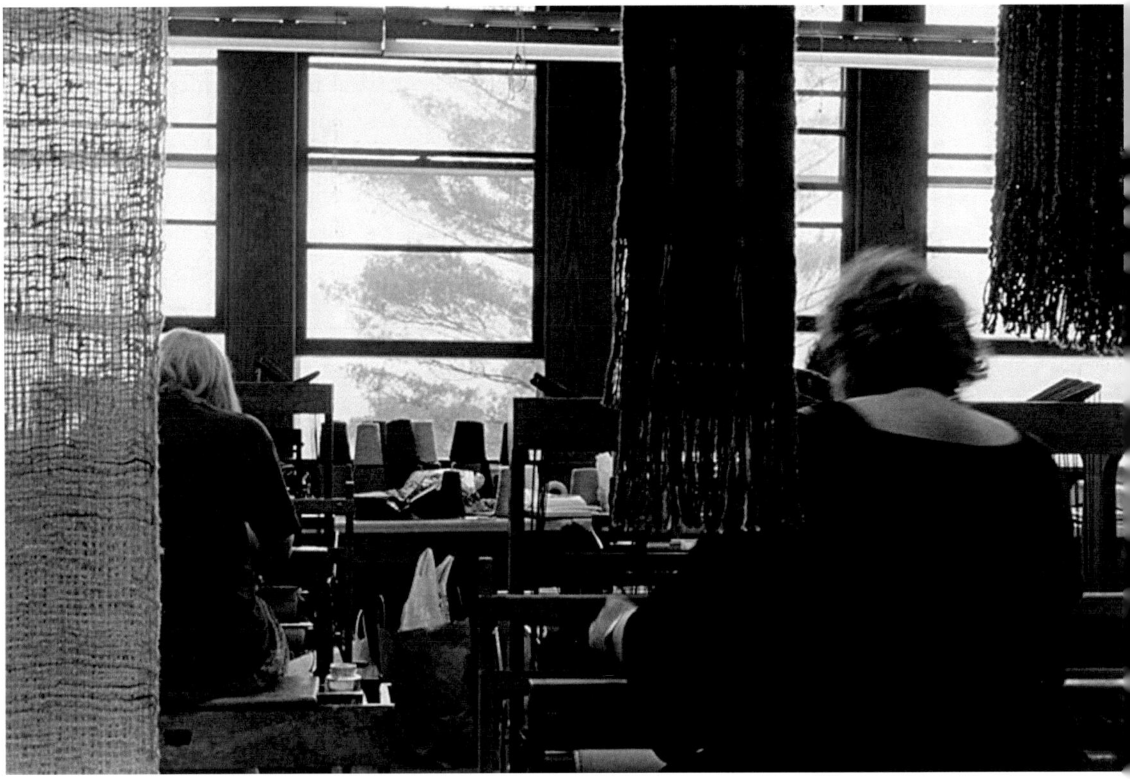

Figure I.3. Eve Kosofsky Sedgwick at the Penland School of Craft, ca. 1996–99. Photograph: H. A. Sedgwick. Collection of H. A. Sedgwick. © H. A. Sedgwick

and with the ongoing question of "how detachable" the parts are "from the overall structure"; a problematized relationship of parts and wholes evocative to an artist with metastatic breast cancer who is exploring the possibilities of patchwork, as we shall see.[34]

In her "Experimental Writing" class, Sedgwick additionally encouraged her students to think in the first person, to think how a "biographical study," like this one, might make "some interesting use of the fact that it is being written *by* somebody, as well as *about* somebody."[35] My own ambitions, here, however, chime more with Sedgwick's later, Buddhist interest in emptying out the first person, and in the desire she expressed, in an untitled poem from circa 1994, "to write" like her therapist "listen[ed]," hardly ever "offering back the face of my emotion, only, the face of [me] listening."[36]

Readers might also think about *Reparative Craft* as an example of *fat* criticism in celebration of what Sedgwick called *fat art* in the title of her first poetry collection, *Fat Art, Thin Art* (1994). While the book you are currently reading focuses on her textiles rather than her glass or ceramics, which remain little known, the volume provides layer on overlapping layer of analysis, self-consciously recalling a form Sedgwick deeply admired: the fat lists employed by her favorite, mid-twentieth-century affect theorist Silvan Tomkins.

Comparing Tomkins's lists to the "long sentences in Proust" she frequently quoted in her textiles, Sedgwick described how the items on Tomkins's lists gestured toward the "possibility of random, virtually infinite permutation, some of it trivial, some of it highly significant: the suggestion of sheer, unlimited extent mark[ing] the impress of radical contingency on the possible outcomes." And yet, she continued, "the items on the lists, far from random, are always carefully chosen to open and indicate new vistas."[37] I hope that the unusually many open-ended interpretations of Sedgwick's textiles that follow function in a similar way, opening multiple new avenues of interpretation and experience. The nourishing number and generative richness of those overlapping interpretations, and the textiles that inspired them, are one of the things that makes this book *fat*, a word that will recur frequently.[38]

As a self-assertive "fat woman," Sedgwick thought about fat art across her career. The unglossed phrase came from the end of her narrative poem "The Warm Decembers" (ca. 1980–86), which described "Two arts that feed as one. / Fat art, thin art."[39] She returned to the polyvalent, positive semiotics of fat in an essay coauthored with Michael Moon, "Divinity: A Dossier, a Performance Piece, a Little Understood Emotion" (ca. 1990), which thought about fat from several angles. As a whole, however, the essay challenged "offensive meanings" by celebrating the divinity of the "fat, beaming figure of the diva" as a fantasy alternate ideal body, which "never lost its representational magnetism," even as the essay differentiated the "gender specification, class complication, and racial bifurcation" of the semiotics of fat. Indeed, Sedgwick emphasized that in "*coming out as a fat woman*," within the context of a nascent "fat liberation movement," she wanted to make "clear to the people around [her] that their cultural meanings" would be "assaultive and diminishing to the degree that they are not fat-affirmative."[40]

Sedgwick returned to "The Uses of Being Fat" in a circa 1994 poem of the same name, collected in *Fat Art, Thin Art*, in which she revealed that she

> used to have a superstition that
> there was this use to being fat:
> no one I loved could come to harm
> enfolded in my touch—

that lot of me would blot it up,
the rattling chill, night sweat or terror.[41]

In the poem, Sedgwick's earlier sense of herself as a woman whose fat blotted up trouble is curtailed by "the rattling chill, night sweat or terror" of many of her friends living with AIDS, the poem's "night sweat" recalling Thom Gunn's then-recent 1992 collection of poems relating to the AIDS crisis, *The Man with the Night Sweats*. As I complete this book, I see now that *Reparative Craft* may have unconsciously, melancholically, believed something similar. In the parts written while Sedgwick was alive, I hoped that her inexhaustible creative energy could somehow defeat her terminal cancer. After her passing, I think I tried to endlessly remake her in my mind, even as other parts of me knew that I could never bring her back.

As a result of this realization, I want to conclude this introduction with a second, untitled poem from *Fat Art, Thin Art*: the untitled one beginning "One of us falls asleep on the other's shoulder." This describes how

An hour later when we peel apart:
in the fat of the shoulder, artful, improbable
brand, the double outside curve,
an ear.
For hours (shower, clothes) it doesn't fade.

Returning to this improbable aural imprinting, I realized that the decades of work that went into this book might have assumed the related form of a somehow listening fat shoulder, one imprinted by Sedgwick's artistry, endlessly open to her words, without ever quite realizing "how much mourning there already [was]" between her and me.[42]

I

THE FIRST FOUR PAGES OF A TEXTURE BOOK

(CA. 1996–99)

Getting Needled, or Some Bitching About Stitching

For a queer-feminist textile artist, Sedgwick was, perhaps, surprisingly disinterested in what Rozsika Parker famously characterized as the *subversive stitch*.[1] As *Epistemology of the Closet* (1990) argued, while Victorian embroidery answered to the "hungrily inventive raptness of the curious or subtle perceiving eye or brain," an exemplar of a desirably *fat art*, the "intricacy" of such "wrought" fabrics was usually fashioned by poorly paid, working-class British women or imported from South Asia, where indentured laborers earned even less.[2]

For Sedgwick, embroidery was, thus, a "monstrous," "strange," and "terrible" practice involving "tedious labor" and "sheer wastage of (typically female) eyesight," levied by men on women, by the upper classes on the lower, and by Europe on South Asia.[3] In addition, as we shall see, across her poetry and prose,

Sedgwick repeatedly bitched about the practice of needlework and, throughout her textiles, did not much incline to sewing or knitting needles, preferring the practice of gluing, a sewing machine, or a loom.

Sedgwick's aversion to needles bucked a trend in then-contemporary textiles, where stitch-and-bitch circles were increasingly fashionable. Although the phrase had circulated since World War II, the 2003 publication of Debbie Stoller's *Stitch 'n Bitch: The Knitter's Handbook* saw the idea become fashionable. Selling more than 200,000 copies in its first six months, Stoller's book led to the founding of numerous stitch-and-bitch circles across the globe, with four further volumes capitalizing on the craze.[4]

Sedgwick's aversion to needles, and preference for adhesion, when it came to sticking together her subsequent patchworks, perhaps derived from three sources. First, she was inspired by Walt Whitman's lifelong interest in the idea of queer *adhesion*.[5] Second, Sedgwick suffered from peripheral neuropathy, a side effect of her cancer drugs, which manifested as a painful tingling, a familiar pins-and-needles sensation in her hands and feet, making walking painful, difficult, and dangerous. Third, Sedgwick experienced repeated, arduous encounters with medical needles during her treatments. In 2006 she had a port inserted into a chest vein to enable the easier insertion of drugs into her body; a port vital given the way her chemotherapy made her veins narrower, more brittle, and difficult to access.

In *Fat Art, Thin Art* (1994), Sedgwick's first volume of poetry, she detailed her painful encounter with medical needles in an untitled poem:

> A scar, just a scar;
> I saw then
> how I would get to know the oncology nurses,
> when I was going to faint
> —and she was only needing to get some blood—
> and with her small severity we crossed the corridor
> to rows of curtained beds and whispering,
> her insistent with the needle, someone's soft tears
> and a far murmur that only barely
> wasn't my imagination, "spread your legs,"
> hearing which I knew
> someday soon I'd feel more nostalgia for this
> than for any school I'd been to.[6]

Punning on Freud's apocryphal statement that sometimes a cigar is just a cigar, and refusing its meaning-denying logic, the poem considers a scary, potentially scarring scene in which Sedgwick faints while a nurse tries to take her blood.[7] But while a scar represents a patch of injured skin that has healed over but lost the ability to respond to stimuli, the poem represents a condensed, clitoral point of retroactive, reparative arousal. But that is to get ahead of ourselves.

The poem first documents the anxiety, difficulty, and punishing discipline of having an unfamiliar nurse try to take blood, or, in the poem's idiom, "only needing to get some blood," with the words *needle* and *needling*, as well as *kneading*, hovering in the vicinity of *needing*. This was a needlessly sadistic procedure to be carried out with the same "small severity" with which Sedgwick was marched across the corridor to "rows of curtained beds," offering only the most minimal privacy, if the "whispering" is anything to go by, and a "far murmur" was audible. The nurse is "insistent with the needle," and Sedgwick feels anxious that she is "going to faint."

At this point, readers might predict the poem's reveal will be that "someone's soft tears" and the painful murmuring are Sedgwick's own; initially unrecognizable sounds indicative of her disorientation and need to put a distance between herself and her pain. But the poem's outcome is queerer, more reparative. The gynecological instruction "spread your legs," happening to a patient in a cubicle nearby, is "only barely" not Sedgwick's imagination, and after a dilating, enjambing line-length break in the poem, she acknowledges that, hearing the phrase, in the context of this painful, punishing institutional scenario, she knew she would "feel more nostalgia" and desire for the scene than "any school" she had been to. As readers learned, as early as Sedgwick's 1985 essay "A Poem Is Being Written," such scenes were the warp and weft of Sedgwick's fantasy life.[8]

Sedgwick returned to these needling scenes in her 1999 psychotherapeutic memoir, *A Dialogue on Love*. There, she told her therapist, Shannon Van Wey, whose capitalized notes make up much of the text, about her "bad veins" and how hard it was for a nurse to access them. Indeed, she recalled, with a sharp, new metaphor, that the nurse "had to play darts for a while" before Sedgwick informed her she was "about to faint."[9]

Toward the end of the memoir, however, Sedgwick described a second, more reparative set of initially painful needles. These are the "slippery pine needles" that mulched the "shrubby border between the two parking lots" close to Van Wey's office. As Sedgwick describes the scene, it was a therapy day, and she had gone to the practice where Van Wey worked early enough to cross the parking lot to ask someone at the nearby garage a question about her car. On the "unexpectedly steep," shrubby border between the practice and gas station, with its slippery pine needles, Sedgwick tumbled and almost fell, before proceeding with a "fat woman's / disavowing haste."[10]

So far, so familiar: Sedgwick's encounters with even pine needles are painful, disorienting, humiliating, and potentially injuring. After she had completed her garage errand, however, she spotted Van Wey on his way to meet her at the practice, looking thoughtful, oblivious to her presence, and moving with an enviably "calm buoyancy." More "alert to his surroundings" than Sedgwick had been, when he got "near the bottom of the shrubby border," he "gather[ed] up from the pavement the clumps of pine mulch" she had inadvertently "kicked down." Then, "bobbing up gently," he patted the pine needles back into place, his hands "smoothing" them in with the "other mulch."[11]

The "hidden treasure" of this "little, spied on / scene" became precious to Sedgwick; a condensed sweet to suck on; a little clitoral tender button that could be turned around in her fingers that made her smile; a "tight, light knot of space, time and seeing," precisely because Van Wey's environmental attention was *not* attention to her. Indeed, she felt relieved that he could repair her mistake, occupy the space she had been in, and encounter her ghost "without recognition."[12] Sedgwick's painful encounters with pins and needles could be repaired in her lifetime and would not outlive her. Despite everything, a reparative needlework perhaps remained possible.

Sedgwick's Kimono Collages

Sedgwick first traveled to Japan on a lecture trip in 2000, returning with a suitcase of vintage kimonos.[13] But kimonos had long played a part in her craft practice in the preceding years, appearing in three overlapping projects: as the backgrounds to some of her *Panda Alphabet Valentines* (ca. 1996), which I have discussed elsewhere; in the form of long horizontal wefts in some of Sedgwick's rag-work weavings, as we shall see; and in the project I discuss in this section, collaging together kimono swatches with the aid of silver embroidery.[14]

Sedgwick made four closely related kimono collages. None of the pieces has an obvious landscape or portrait orientation, and each can be rotated or circled by spectators until they find a viewing position that suits them. Each piece is roughly rectilinear, with the first three pieces more rectangular than square. Each collage contains six or seven patches of roughly cut, differently patterned kimono silk, with some recurring in more than one collage. Some scraps are laid horizontally; others, vertically. None of the individual fabric swatches is rectilinear. Instead, Sedgwick adopted a self-consciously *sloppy* cutting technique, queerly resisting *straight* edges and preferring, as in her poetry, ragged margins; her rough cutting led to visible fraying, further reducing the rectilinearity of the

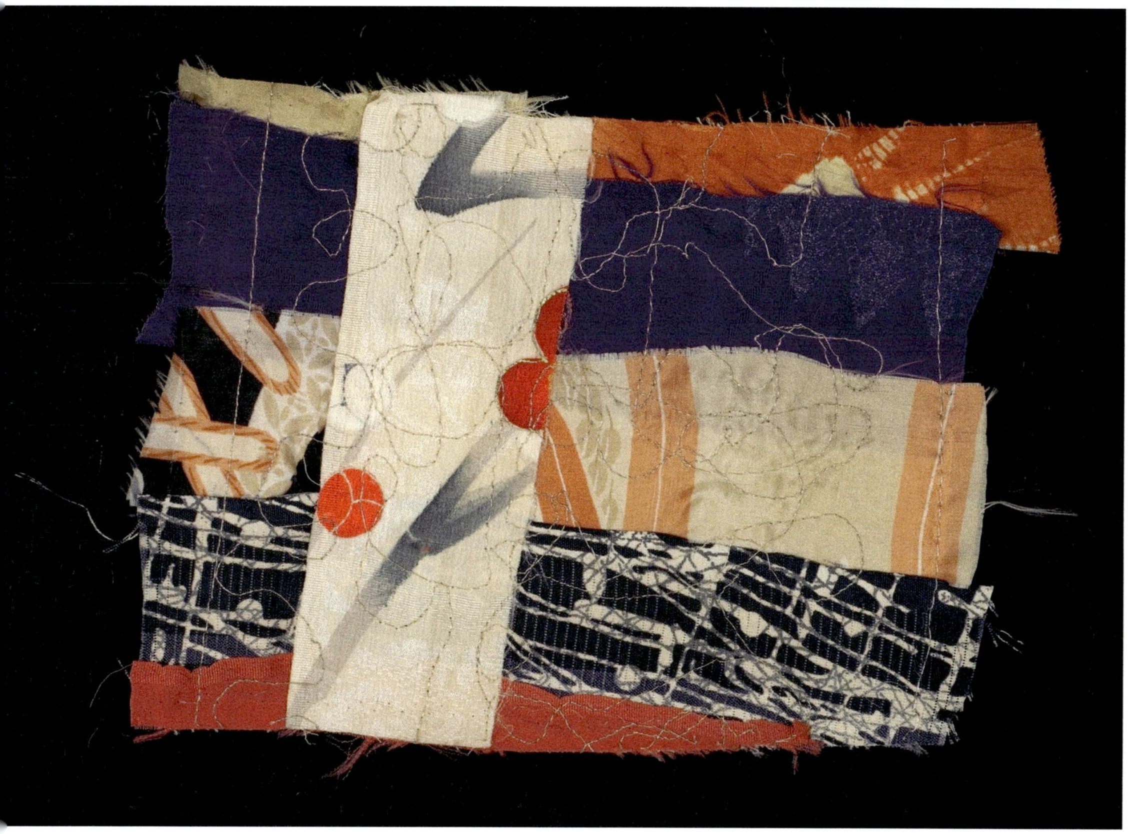

Figures 1.1–1.4. Eve Kosofsky Sedgwick, untitled collages, ca. 1996–99. Photograph: Kevin Ryan. Collection of H. A. Sedgwick. © H. A. Sedgwick

patches, with additional loose ends provided by the unsnipped tips of the silver stitching she employed for structural and decorative purposes.

In almost all the cases, the uppermost piece or pieces of kimono silk are layered over the others in a perpendicular orientation. These upper pieces extend from one end of the collage to the other, providing binding structural, spine-like support, except for the third collage, where the uppermost piece extends nearly, but not quite, from right to left, while the lower piece floats internally free. These structural elements anticipate the title of Sedgwick's first exhibition, *Floating Columns*, and reflect the increasingly fragile state of her own dissolving spine, risking leaving individual vertebrae floating untethered.

Viewers might also think about the four pieces' overall aesthetic as *queer*, by Sedgwick's famous 1993 definition, in *Tendencies*, if one of the things *queer* can refer to is the "open mesh of possibilities, gaps, overlaps, dissonances, lapses

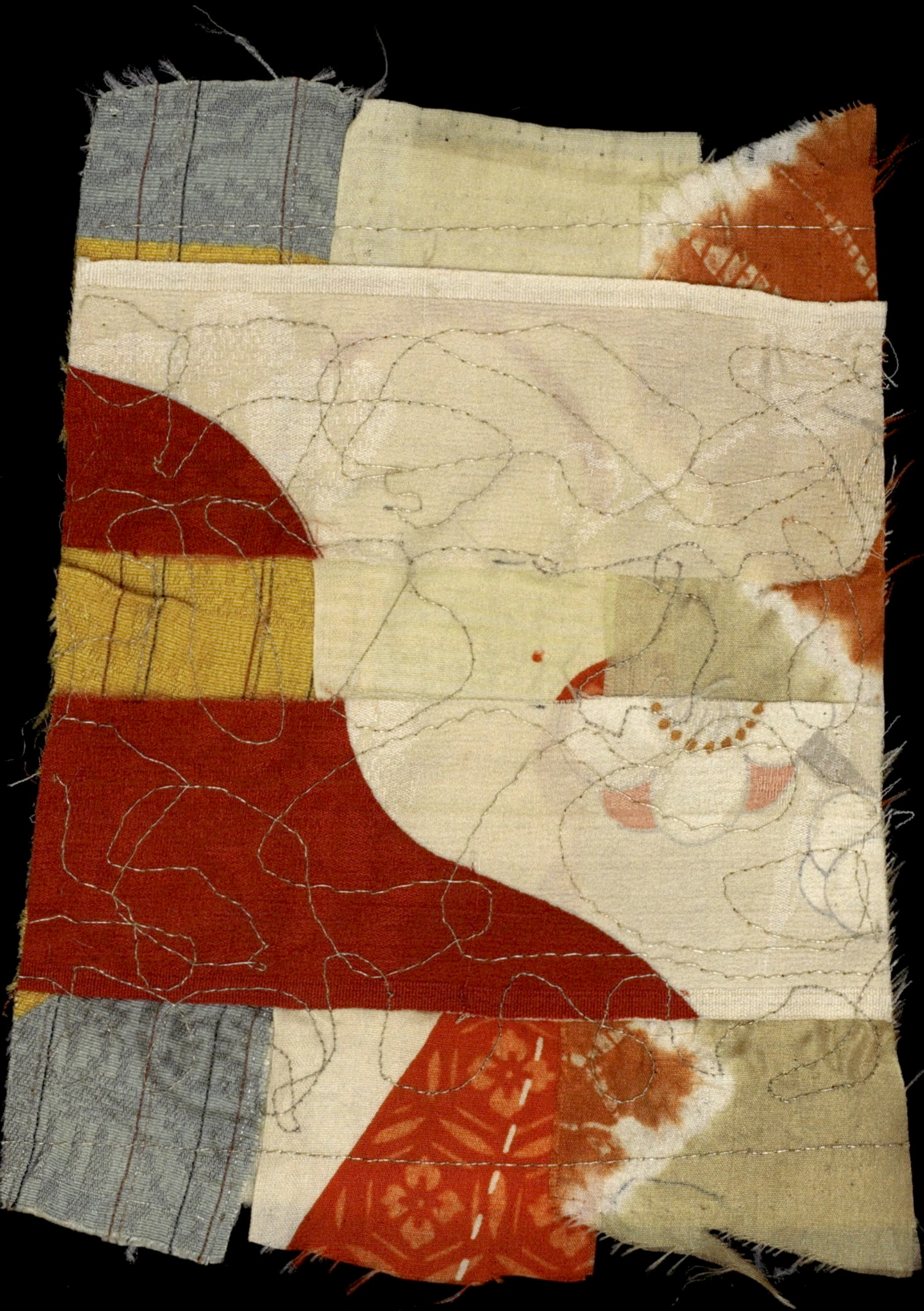

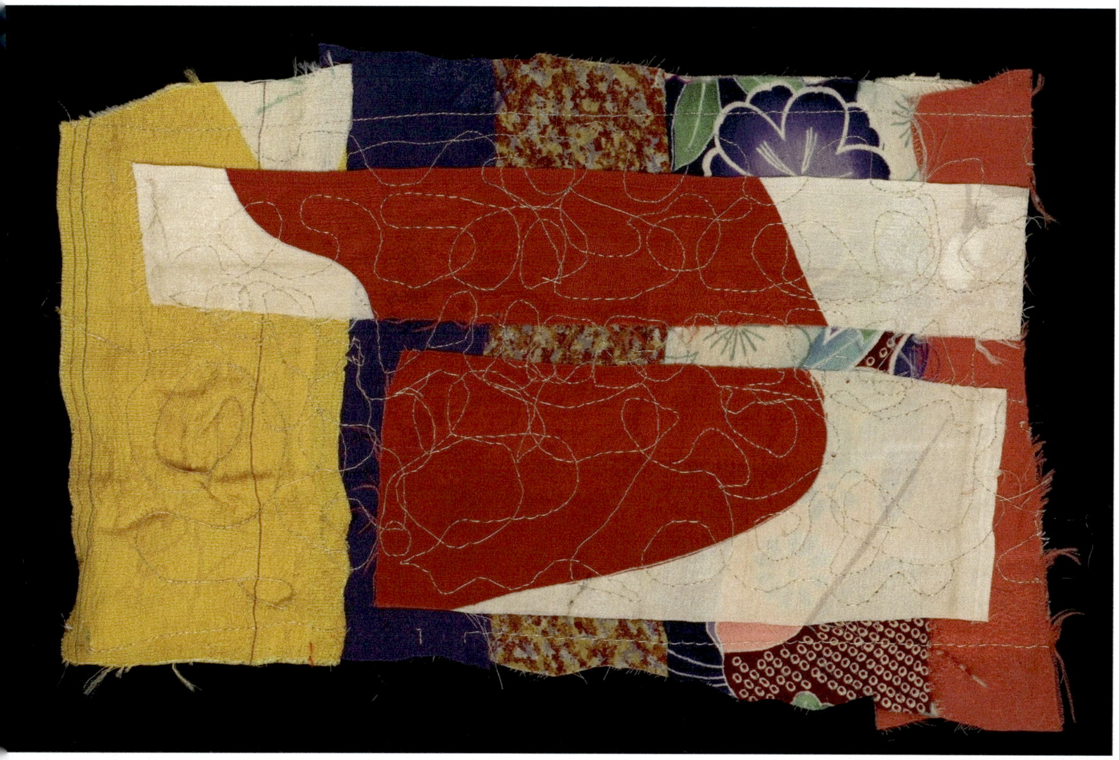

and excesses of meaning when the constituent elements . . . aren't made or *can't be* made to signify monolithically."[15] Because of Sedgwick's sloppy cutting and indifference to tailored hemming, many of the swatches fray to an open mesh of possibilities. Gaps are formed in many of the patterns both when overlain by another silk swatch and when cut in nonrectilinear ways, leaving viewers to complete the patterns in their minds.

Collage is also always about overlaps, and Sedgwick lays various swatches of colored, textured, and patterned kimono silk first next to each other in a chosen but usually difficult-to-rationalize, and thus interruptive, dissonant sequence; and then either over or under the adjacent piece or pieces. In addition, spectators might think about the various visible threads at the frayed edges as lapses or excesses of structure, decoration, and meaning, with these various effects resulting in ragged, nonrectilinear, multipiece and multistranded collage that is not designed to be, and cannot be made to signify monolithically, in a single gestalt.

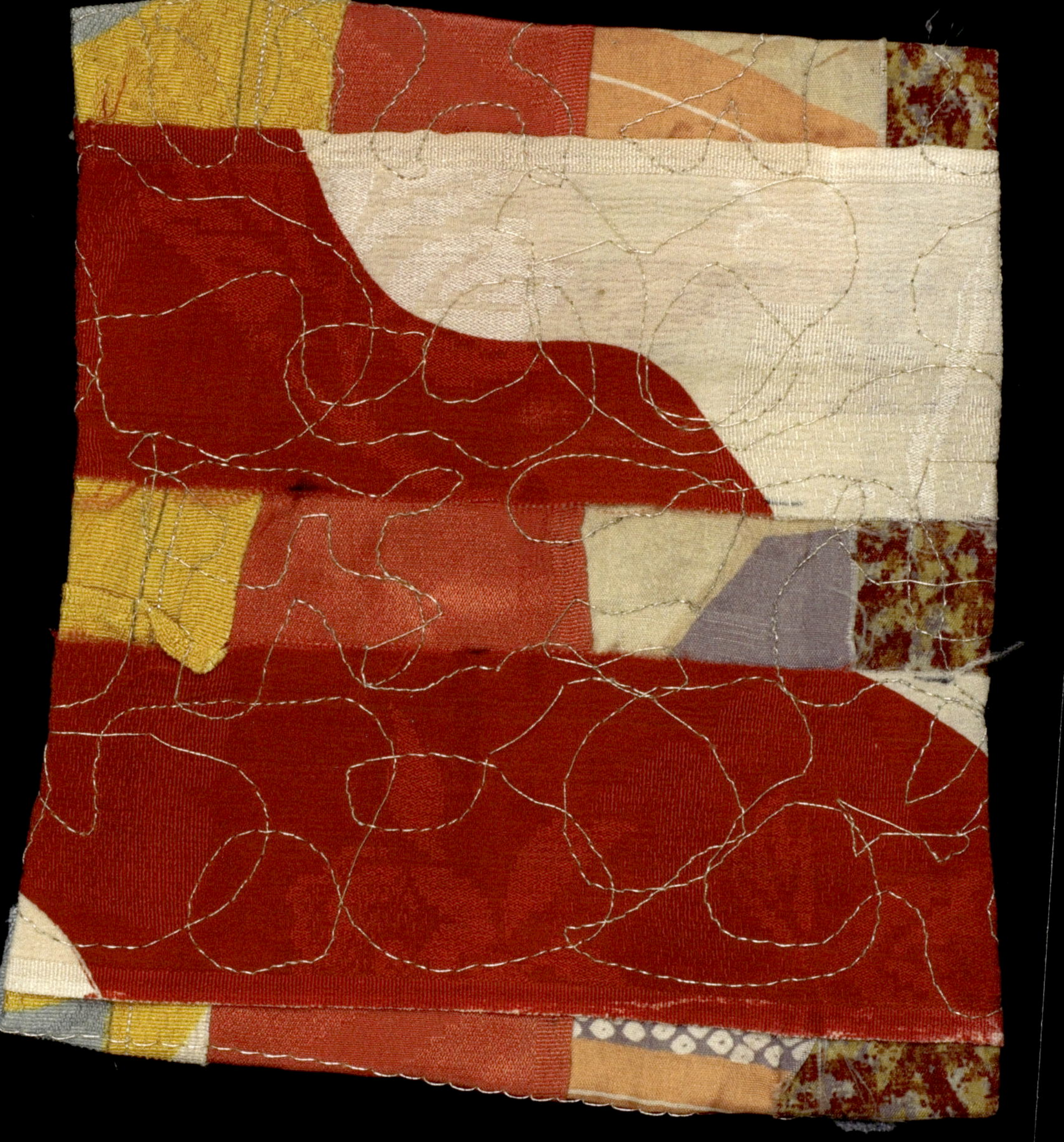

Perhaps the most striking and difficult-to-rationalize aspect of the collages is their emphatic, difficult-to-follow silver embroidery. This uncharacteristic, minute stitchery functions like a textile *kintsugi*, with silver thread replacing gold leaf to suture together the broken fragments, with the difference that whereas, in *kintsugi* ceramics, the pieces originally formed a cohesive whole, in Sedgwick's patchworks the patches derive from multiple, separate sources and form a new, still various object.[16]

As such, the collages are *reparative*, by Sedgwick's definition. They are "additive and accretive," and, in the context of a medical culture that was "inadequate" to her "nurture," especially when it came to needles, spectators might perceive these collages wanting to "assemble and confer plenitude" on a needlework practice that "will then have resources to offer to an inchoate self." The ragged kimono patchworks also clearly involve "the 'over'-attachment to fragmentary, marginal, waste, or leftover products," whose structure offers a "disorienting juxtaposition" of elements and a "rich, highly interruptive affective" and decorative variety, all bound together with a "glue of surplus beauty" and "unexplained upwellings" of swatches, cemented together and animating an "amalgam of part objects."[17]

In addition, the pieces are obviously "attached to a project of survival," with Sedgwick turning to textile practice at the point she was diagnosed with metastatic cancer.[18] The collages also bear a close relationship to Van Wey's capitalized noting, in *A Dialogue on Love*, of Sedgwick's interest in "SILK WORK" and the "TREASURE[D] SCRAPS OF SILK" she employed in the service of a project of "TURNING FABRIC INTO OTHER FABRIC." This recalled her "CHILDHOOD BLANKET WITH THE SATIN BINDING," its sheen evoked by the collage's shiny silver embroidery. The kimono collages also respond to ideas of "SKIN HUNGER," to Sedgwick's and her family's "FASCINATION" with "HOW SILKY" her "SKIN WAS," the "DOWNSIDE" being that she became "AN OBJECT FOR OTHERS TO SATISFY THEIR TOUCH NEEDS, NOT MINE." This sense of impingement is, perhaps, registered by the way the embroidery stitches permanently puncture the silk scraps beneath.[19]

In three of the montages, the easiest row of stitches to rationalize is that providing a framing, rectilinear, structural, more or less straight edge running the length of the piece, although not necessarily the longest length, uniting the patches together, in a similar way to how the uppermost patches, laid and glued at a ninety-degree angle to the rest, work to anchor the whole. In the first and second collages, Sedgwick sews more or less straight along the shorter edges; in the third collage, she sews straight along the longer edges; while the fourth comes closest to a hem, with the stitching running not across the upper surface but along its sides. While Sedgwick is keen to provide some rectilinear structure, she does not include a structural backing panel; a further allusion, perhaps, to her crumbling spine.

Occasionally, Sedgwick's *backstitches*, another resonant word in her metastatic context, interact more closely with the patterns on the kimono swatches below. In the first piece, the overall appearance of Sedgwick's stitches echoes the loopy white-on-black linear pattern of one of the pieces of underlying kimono silk; and, on a second scrap, some of the individual stitches trace the outlines of the red half circles of the berry motif.

In the second example, Sedgwick employs as one of her kimono swatches, at bottom center, a piece of silk with an orange floral pattern made with the *shibori*, or tie-dye, technique, in which a running stitch had been added to the fabric, acting as a resist during the dyeing, leaving six bleached stitchlike marks on its surface, which interact with the backstitches above. The actual stitches *on* the surface alongside the ghost of the *shibori* stitches *within* the pattern provide a further, fractal *two-and-a-half dimensionality* to the whole; a dimensionality that would be increasingly important to Sedgwick, as we shall see. In the second collage, Sedgwick also employs, on the left, a swatch of kimono silk with vertical lines of stitching within it; a vertically stitched striped piece is also present in the third example.

But most of the stitching, while providing binding, functions less like a rectilinear frame, or pattern outline, and more like a random, looping line that interrupts the kimono patterns, providing a further, democratizing embroidery layer *across* the more hierarchically layered swatches of kimono silk. The twining lines, made up of individual line-like backstitches, often cross themselves, providing multiple junctions in the network. This is a journey that can be traced visually or by hand only with some care, close-up.[20]

In addition, the collages recall further details from Van Wey's account of Sedgwick's "SILK WORK." They evoke the close connection, in her mind, between silk and "DROOL" on her brother's childhood pillow. They suggest the masturbatory residue of the Kosofsky children allowed to "DEVELOP AUTONOMOUS RESOURCES" when it came to their bodies, with the overlapping patches of silk having a strongly multilayered, epidermal character. In addition, if somehow "SILK AND SHIT GO TOGETHER," for Sedgwick, spectators might think about her random embroidery trails as the shit-like excreta of slug and snail trails, and the silk scraps beneath as a parallel form of substance extruded from silkworms, an anal aesthetic notoriously central to Sedgwick's literary criticism.[21]

In *Learning to Weave* (1995), a how-to book in Sedgwick's collection, Deborah Chandler noted that unlike other protein fibers, silk is "an extrusion, not a growing hair." The "finest, most lustrous silk" is made from "reeled silk," obtained by "unwinding silk cocoons"; lesser-quality silk is "spun from broken or cut pieces, taken from damaged cocoons (such as the ones from which the moths have emerged)." In its "natural state," the "two basic colors of silk" are white and golden; with white silk "finer and softer," and golden "coarser, stronger, and less expensive," but with individual strands dependent, for their consistency, on the silkworm's diet.[22] As such, Chandler's account, as well as Sedgwick's use of silk scraps and her snail-trail embroidery, help make sense of Van Wey's notation that, for Sedgwick, silk was associated with "WASTE PRODUCTS."[23]

Also close to Sedgwick's mournful, queer aesthetic in the collages was Jacques Derrida's 1996 essay, "A Silkworm of One's Own (Points of View Stitched on the Other Veil)," first published around the time she was working on the patchworks.[24] In Derrida's bardo-like essay, written "before it's too late" and before he had to "stop writing," he profoundly identified with a "mortally wounded animal," the silkworm, and similarly focused on a "childhood memory" of silk; what Derrida called the "*metis* of weaving-unweaving." Derrida's idiom frequently parallels Sedgwick's. Like Derrida, Sedgwick employed originally woven silk scraps, in the form of kimono fragments, that she had cut from larger garments and woven together in a warp and weft–like structure that she allowed to fray at the edges, a further act of unweaving. This represented, in Derrida's words, a kind of "shroud" or "winding sheet," in terms of the tragic cocoon origin of the silk, killing the silkworm in the process, and in terms of Sedgwick, surrounding her by-then terminally ill body with comforting fabrics, mindful that while she didn't want to "lose the thread," there were many unraveling fibers within her, and that, at some point, she, too, would "have to give up touching as much as seeing," saying, and sewing.[25]

But if Sedgwick's kimonos were not fashioned from reeled silk, obtained by unwinding silk cocoons, killing the silkworms, but from the cheaper variety taken from damaged cocoons, from which the moths had already emerged, she might, conversely, have been thinking about the life of the silkworm as, in Derrida's terms, an "event of quasi-resurrection." That is because silkworms undergo an unwilled, almost unimaginable metamorphosis from worm to moth, perhaps encouraging Sedgwick to imagine her unwilled metastatic metamorphosis as not necessarily from a more to a less beautiful or mobile state, even if she would, ultimately, lose the ability to walk toward the end of her life. Indeed, Derrida encourages viewers to understand Sedgwick's collages as autobiographical, since there was a revealing homophonic pun, in French, on the words "*soi* [self] and *soie* [silk]," to which we shall return.[26]

Indeed, for Derrida, as for Sedgwick, the silkworm was an evocative totem animal because it emblematized both mortality and metamorphic possibility. As Derrida noted, there was no conventional way to refer to the silkworm during the first stage of its life, before it became a moth: We "*sometimes say the worm, sometimes the caterpillar*." And, for Derrida, and perhaps Sedgwick, that it was "*impossible to discern a sex*" was, as in the case of the bodhisattva Kuanyin, surely part of its appeal.[27] Indeed, for Derrida and Sedgwick, there was something queer about the silkworm, not just because it was difficult to gender, but because silk, its bodily product, was erotically evocative.

For example, Derrida spent much time, as a child and in the essay, pondering "*the orifice you had to imagine to be at the origin of . . . silk, this milk become thread, this filament prolonging the . . . body and remaining attached to it for a certain length of time: the extruded saliva of a very fine sperm, shiny, gleaming, the miracle of a feminine ejaculation*." And, for Derrida, the silkworm's extruding orifice was as much "*labial or salivary*" as "*rectal*," while the silkworm evoked a "*little fantasy of a penis*," whether in "*erection or detumescence*." In addition, if, for Sedgwick, silk was identified with her brother's drool, for Derrida the silkworm similarly "*dribbled*." Derrida's description of the silk moth "*coming out*" of its cocoon, meanwhile, encourages readers to think about the silkworm's life cycle as a kind of ontology of the closet, a willed late-life, late-style metamorphosis; a reparatively *positive*, unpredictable biological transformation again resonant with Sedgwick's metastatic cancer, an idea to which we shall repeatedly return.[28]

Sedgwick's technique of embroidered kimono scraps also recalls the traditional Japanese stitching technique of *sashiko*, a practice of patchworking old clothes together to make a new garment.[29] Indeed, as Kumiko Sudo documents, *sashiko* represented part of a much broader patchwork culture that, within Shinto-influenced Japan, had "practical, religious, and aesthetic" resonances, such that "all things, including cloth," were believed to possess a spirit, so that "prolonging the life of an old fabric" by "salvaging scraps to use in patchwork" was a "spiritual exercise." Japanese Buddhism similarly employed patchwork robes, the *Sakiori*, "often made from shredded kimono or other recycled garments," as "fine offerings in Buddhist temples."[30]

Sedgwick's recontextualization of kimono fabric also drew on a longer Japanese tradition in which kimonos were frequently "redyed, once or twice during the lifetime of the owners and sometimes after their deaths," to make them "more appropriate for the wearers as they reach[ed] different stages in their lives"; as well as "restyled to keep them current." Kimonos were also "redyed if they had lost their magnificent original colours or were badly stained"; and cut and retailored into "children's kimonos," usually "within a family," since most Japanese people preferred "not to buy or wear used kimonos with another person's karma attached to them."[31] Sedgwick, by contrast, was very interested in quotation, in imaginatively inhabiting another person's karmic identity.

Meanwhile, Sedgwick's taste for kimono patterns featuring bamboo, a symbol of longevity, and flowers, a symbol of brevity, also seems closely related to her preoccupation with mortality.[32] And were we able to establish whether her swatches had been dyed "after being woven" or "prior to the weaving of the cloth," we might understand better whether she was thinking more about the literal and metaphoric resonance of the idea of "*atozome* ('after dyeing')" or "*sakizome* ('before dyeing')." But, given the complexity of the patterns on the majority of her swatches, in comparison to single color-saturated yarn-dyed fabrics, it would appear that the bardo of the afterlife was more on her mind.[33] With that in mind, Sedgwick's early kimono collages may represent the first four pages of the "TEXTURE BOOK" she described in *Dialogue*, which "WOULDN'T NEED A FIRST PERSON AT ALL," her swatches of kimono silk far removed from the individually tailored kimonos traditionally worn in Japan.[34]

She Had Mixed Feelings About the Quilt

Given their patchwork idiom, Sedgwick's silk collages inevitably recall the NAMES AIDS memorial quilt, the exemplar of queer textiles to date, for obvious reasons.[35] Sedgwick discussed her response to the quilt in her 1992 essay "White Glasses," contextualizing it within a broader discussion of the "powerfully performative rhetorical force of obituaries and memorials" more generally, from the perspective of a person then recently diagnosed with terminal cancer, who had a lifelong "morbid" fascination with such forms, inclined to propel herself into "all the positions around every obituary" with the "whole force" of her imagination.[36]

In the essay, Sedgwick acknowledged that her most powerful fear was less dying young and more "losing the people" who made her want to live; the "most compelling thing about obituaries" being "how openly they rupture[d] the conventional relations of person and of address."[37] Sedgwick focused on three spaces of obituary encounter: the tombstone, the *New York Times*, and the "panels on panels on panels" of the quilt, whose "voice speaks impossibly to whom?"[38]

Exploring how the quilt represented a complex, queer speech act without a straightforward speaker or audience, she described how its spectators were "wrung, whirlpooled, turned inside out" by its obituary relation. Her metaphor consciously alludes to the quilt's multitextile form, as its spectators are mimetically reduced to fabric, soaked with tears, thrashed about, deformed in the wash.[39]

For Sedgwick, the quilt's identificatory call-and-response process was also economic in character, and certainly derivative of its sources, as she pondered, "From where" was the quilt's "rhetorical power borrowed, and how and to whom [was] it to be repaid?" She then quoted, without speech marks, as if in her own voice, three texts from the quilt: "We miss you. Remember me. She hated to say goodbye"; the first and third presumably deriving from survivors, the second originating in the body of a person with AIDS, but all inflected through Sedgwick. "Participating in these speech acts," she continued, "we hardly know whether to be interpolated as survivors, bereft; as witnesses or even judges; or as the very dead."[40]

To think further about the quilt's status and efficacy, Sedgwick described how she looked at her photographs from the 1987 gay and lesbian march on Washington, where the quilt was first laid out on the National Mall, and saw, in the snapshots, her friend the poet and queer theorist Michael Lynch, to whom "White Glasses" was addressed, "across a distance, white glasses blazing, looking young and forlorn with no mustache," only weeks after "Bill's sudden death."[41] And "in the panels of the quilt," she could "see that anyone, living or dead, may occupy the position of the speaker, the spoken to, the spoken about." She then included, as indented quotations, some further quote- and double-quote-marked text from the "fabric squares," suggesting a characteristic Russian-doll-like layering of the reader's attention, down through Sedgwick's voice to the people fashioning the quilt, themselves quoting the words of the person commemorated, sometimes signaling their quotations with quotation marks, as in the case of Frederick Abrams, sometimes not, in the case of Michel Foucault.

> "Love you! Kelly."
> "Frederick Abrams. 'Such drama.'"
> "Roy Cohn. Bully. Coward. Victim."
> "Michel Foucault. Where there is power, there is resistance . . . a plurality of resistances . . . spread over time and space . . . It is doubtless the strategic codification of these resistances that makes a revolution possible."
> "For our little brother, David Lee."
> "Sweet dreams."
> "Hug me."[42]

The panels Sedgwick singled out were not immediately adjacent on the quilt, nor the only ones she photographed. They also involved some famous individuals, including one of her theoretical heroes, Foucault; and one person about whom she had more mixed feelings, the "poisonous Roy Cohn," the "poisonous coverage" of whose then-recent AIDS-related death she publicly critiqued in *Epistemology of the Closet.*[43] In addition, Sedgwick might have been thinking of her own "little brother," David, in the panel for David Lee; and of the comforting qualities of American patchwork quilts in the wish for "sweet dreams" and the infantile, tactile, maybe prophylactic, comfort of a padded hug; an idea she returned to in her poem "The Uses of Being Fat" (ca. 1994) as we have seen.[44] Readers might recognize, too, in the long quotation from Foucault an account of the quilt itself as a form of Foucauldian "resistance"; indeed, in its patchwork form, a "plurality of resistances," spread out, reverentially, "over time" and, pointedly, over the space of the Mall, to resist the then American government's genocidal indifference to the AIDS pandemic.[45]

Sedgwick further emphasized the quilt's material, Victorian industrial scale, and handcrafted qualities, as a colossal, machine-woven, patchwork form, when she discussed how this "fractured and *therefore* militant body of queer rebellion" had been "churned out of the mill of identities crossed by desires crossed by identifications"; the quilt militant perhaps because its multiform represented so many different types of people, lined up, uniformly and squarely, like a rebellious army.[46]

But Sedgwick's sense of the *fractured* body of militant queer resistance went deeper than her response to the quilt's patchwork aesthetic, drawing on her experience of the difficult project of that rebellion, after she and an unnamed ACT UP friend had gone to do "some fence-mending with the local Names Project Committee"—a committee "monopolizing, for no purpose more liberatory than memorializing and consolation, the energies and money of a lot of the A-list of North Carolina gays," for which Sedgwick and her allies thought ACT UP might find "considerably more telling uses."[47]

At the end of the meeting, Sedgwick recalled, with a tacit nod to the Gettysburg Address, that the "unctuous guy who was chairing" announced that "to remind ourselves what the committee was all about, and to rededicate ourselves to our (or its) purposes, he and some other people were going to unfold, in the lobby of the building, the latest of the big quilt panels that had passed through their hands—for us to view." "I had to do it," the coerced Sedgwick noted, but "I didn't want to." That was because the quilt "wrings me out, as it does any viewer," further suggesting the quilt's ability to transform its audience mimetically into fabric, "in a way that I don't always want to be available to." This was especially so, at the moment Sedgwick was recalling, because somebody she loved very much was "barely hanging on and wasn't sure he wanted to," and because she was "very angry with the project, and its nostalgic ideology and no politics, with its big, ever-growing, and sometimes obstructive niche in the ecology of gay organizing and self-formation."[48]

So Sedgwick "truculently and furiously" perused the "random patchwork of other people's mourning," as it unfolded, "daring it to make [her] cry" even though she felt she "would be lost if [she] started crying." A "now too familiar topoi" of "terrible losses" unfurled before her, she documented, of "appliquéd rainbows, teddy bears, photographs, baby blocks, 501 jeans; the first-person utterance of survivors," and "the awful first-person utterance attributed to the dead." These were the kinds of idioms that had gotten Sedgwick's attention on the Washington march, whose photographs similarly include a couple of images of panda bears. Such idioms also clearly represent substrates in her later textile practice. They took the form of the soft toy pandas she included in her *Panda Alphabet Valentines*; the pastel rainbow appliqués she incorporated, as we shall see, in her collage *Reality Is Flowerlike*; and the body scans and other photographs she employed across *Floating Columns* and *Bodhisattva Fractal World*. In addition, Sedgwick's later, sustained experimentation with indigo-dyed cotton, as we shall see, recalls the quilt's 501s as well as Derek Jarman's 1993 film *Blue*, a second, influential meditation on the AIDS crisis and the filmmaker's own HIV diagnosis.[49]

In the winter of 1987, however, forced again to face the quilt, Sedgwick recalled feeling "somewhat desperate," even though she hoped that she "knew and could at that moment resist it all." But, as it turned out, "the square" she had "no way of dealing with was the one appliquéd with SILENCE = DEATH and ACT UP T-shirts: not because of them, but because of the unplaceable, unassuageable voice of its lettering, which said starkly: 'HE HATED THE QUILT'"; capital lettering Sedgwick repeatedly employed in *A Dialogue on Love* and across her subsequent textile practice, as we shall see.[50]

Looking back, Sedgwick didn't know whether her "tears and bile were finally those of rage, surrender, envious exultation, or absolute hopelessness." She also didn't know "whose powerful voices" she was "hearing or which were triumphing: the heroic and now immortalized refusal of the dead man," or "the—what?" since she didn't "know how to begin to characterize the possible tones—of the survivors who honored him and by the same gesture surrendered him up to what he hated." Nevertheless, she was deeply moved by the "ravenously denuding, homogenizing, relentlessly anthropomorphizing and yet relentlessly disorienting abyssal voice of the obituary imperative," the "implacably inclusive format of memorial relation and address."[51]

Gary in Her Patchwork

With the quilt in mind, Sedgwick's nameless, textless, and untitled kimono patchworks look more poignant, resistant, modest, silent, melancholic, mournful, fractional, impersonal, yet still unavoidably relational, recalling most intimately, perhaps, the idiom of her friend and student, the African American writer and poet Gary Fisher, whom she first met after he was diagnosed with HIV. In particular, the collages remember the painting Sedgwick owned and selected for the front cover of her posthumous collection of Fisher's writings, *Gary in Your Pocket*, first published in 1996, around the time that she was likely at work on the collages.[52]

For example, in her first panel, the lower pink and upper purple swatches echo the positioning of the related colors in Fisher's watercolor, the white text running down the left of the volume recalled by the white swatch running down the patchwork's left. In Sedgwick's second panel, the upper-left light blue swatch, the mid-left horizontal orange patch, and the lower-right buff swatch, especially as juxtaposed with the red patches emerging from the left, again all recall the upper gray-blue and lower green background of the watercolor and the phallic red patch entering from the right and meeting a similarly suggestive patch of orange coming from the left. In the third patchwork, the purple flower at top right and the vertical purple swatch running down the mid-left similarly recall the purple fishlike form at the top right of the cover. Finally, the fourth panel's top-left yellow swatch recalls the watercolor's bottom-right golden-yellow leaf.

Sedgwick did not carry Fisher only in her memory, as she continued to face her mortality around 1996, the year in which *Gary in Your Pocket* was published; his ghostly idiom haunted her patchworks as, "almost every night," she "dreamed, not *of* Gary, but *as* him," moving through the world "clothed in the restless, elastic skin of his beautiful idiom," the "very warp and woof" of his syntax recalled in her restless, elastic embroidery. Reflecting on the experience of Fisher's passing, Sedgwick acknowledged that, in posthumously publishing him, she didn't know whether it had been "more a way of mourning or of failing to mourn; of growing steeped in, or refusing the news of [Fisher's] death." Speaking for myself, and after working on this book for nearly twenty years, I similarly have little idea whether *Reparative Craft* represents a way of mournfully coming to terms with Sedgwick's death or stubbornly refusing to. All I

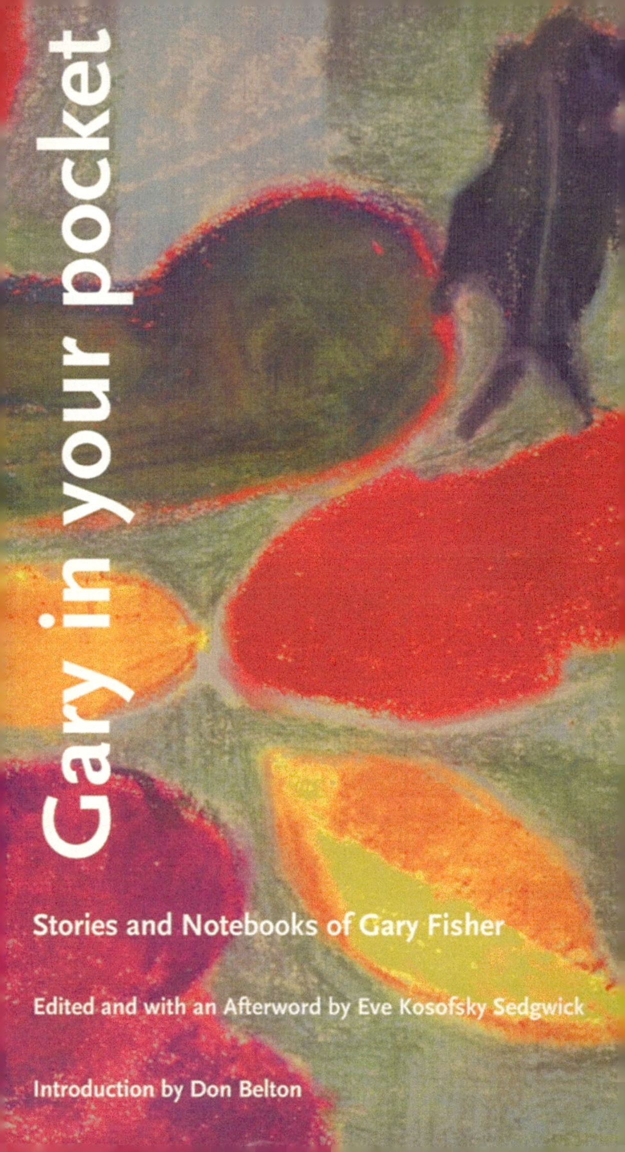

Gary in your pocket

Stories and Notebooks of Gary Fisher

Edited and with an Afterword by Eve Kosofsky Sedgwick

Introduction by Don Belton

know is that, like Fisher's, Sedgwick's reparative craft practice represents an "idiom that longs to traverse and be held in the minds of many people who never knew [her] in another form."[53]

While there may be a risk of overreading Sedgwick's early collages, amateur experiments with embroidered patchworks that she at least initially experienced as radically divorced from, as an adulterous escape from, her queer theoretical work, it is clear from contextualizing her early patchworks in relation to her diagnosis by then with metastatic cancer and her wider writerly corpus that many of her long-term key concerns chromatically saturated, animated, underpinned, and were stitched into her interest in silk and patchwork: silk as somehow simultaneously skin, spit, and shit; as an adult equivalent of a childhood comfort blanket; as a winding sheet in which to die and a metamorphic closet from which to come out; and, seen through white glasses, patchwork as a way of melancholically engaging with, and militantly refusing to cede exclusive ground, to the NAMES quilt. Silk work also as a way of grieving, and refusing to grieve, her friends Michael Lynch and Gary Fisher, who passed away from HIV/AIDS shortly before she began her textiles.

Having considered Sedgwick's early embroidered patchworks from various reparative perspectives, in the next chapter I turn to her simultaneously emerging interest in weaving, arguing that if many of Sedgwick's subsequent textiles incorporating text represent forms of reparative reading, her weavings form parallel, *cybernetic* exemplars of a second essay from *Touching Feeling*, "Shame in the Cybernetic Fold," cowritten with Adam Frank.[54] Like "Paranoid and Reparative Reading," the essay on shame originated in the mid-1990s, initially as a stand-alone article in the winter 1995 issue of *Critical Inquiry* and then as the introduction to Sedgwick and Frank's 1995 collection, *Shame and Its Sisters: A Silvan Tomkins Reader*, published around the same mid-1990s moment at which Sedgwick turned from patchwork to the loom.

2

A WEFT IS BEING BEATEN, OR WEAVING IN THE CYBERNETIC FOLD

(CA. 1996–99)

A Woven Thing with Just a Woven Depth, or Kimo-Therapy

In an early 1973 poem, "An Essay on the Picture Plane," Sedgwick meditated on the play between two and three dimensions in single-point perspectival painting and between painterly figuration and the woven ground of the canvas. She noted how, with an artist's first mark—the first "horizontal stroke"—the canvas dissolved, and a horizon appeared. At "a stroke," there was the "distance" of landscape, between viewer and horizon, established by the semiotically minimal, diacritical difference between the mark and ground.[1] At first glance, Sedgwick's language appears gentle, tactile, as if the artist stroked the canvas through the soft, fibrous paint-laden brush. But Sedgwick's noun, *stroke* also recalls experiencing a stroke of genius or having a stroke, as if the artist's conscious individuality was shockingly dissolved into the painterly medium or canvas ground, signaling the death of the author.

Sedgwick then brings the viewer into the scene, "absent both from the horizon," as far from the spectator as a horizontal mark could be, and "the fabric itself," which is "too articulate." Employing another S/M idiom common to her accounts of medium and genre, she also notes that the canvas is "stretched," "stretching clear to the edges, and immobile"; a tableau of the immobilized, dilated body, familiar from "A Poem Is Being Written," as we have seen. But after thinking about their "confusing purchase on the space" of the canvas, a queer locus of "fears, inflictions, and ambitions," viewers might be grateful for some relief, that the canvas, beyond Sedgwick's idiomatic, perverse formalism, might sometimes "resolve . . . / as a woven thing with just a woven depth."[2]

A related scene occurs in Sedgwick's circa 2006 essay on her own artistic practice, "Making Things, Practicing Emptiness," which documented how although she had "always loved textiles," "something different" was happening around age forty-six, which is to say, around 1996, "something . . . kept kidnapping [her] from [her] teaching and writing tasks and pinning [her] to [her] kitchen table." What made this S/M textile scene novel was that Sedgwick had "given up the pretext of self-ornamentation," to which her "love of textiles had always clung." Indeed, she documented that she "had all these gorgeous silk clothes" she had "bought or made but never ever wore," when she realized that to tie her "acute sense of beauty" to the project of making herself beautiful was a "mug's game." In its place, the "notion of a visual or tactile beauty that might be impersonal, dislinked from the need to present a first-person self" came as "late news. But exciting!" Suddenly, her "fingers were very, very hungry to be handling a reality, a beauty, that wasn't [her]self, wasn't any self, and didn't want to be."[3]

Here, readers encounter a complex, characteristic Sedgwickian scene where she enjoys being perversely subjected to and lost in a medium that is also a reparatively *fat* medium, addressing a hunger, nourishing her hungry fingers. Immediately dividing these two quotations, in the essay, are three illustrations. The first, a woven wall hanging, supports her assertion that she abandoned self-adornment as a motive for her textile practice. The second, however, reveals a scarf she had earlier sported in the *New York Times*, to celebrate her appointment at CUNY.[4]

Taking Sedgwick's weavings seriously, then, requires spectators to consider them as a "woven thing, with just a woven depth," and as potential exhibits bound up with her queer idiom.

For example, viewers might think further about the relationship between Sedgwick's kimono source material in many of her weavings, which we encountered in

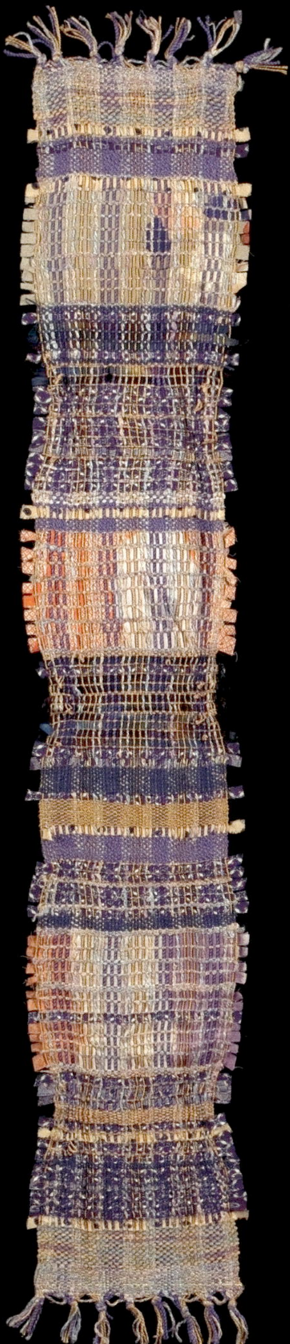

Figure 2.1. Eve Kosofsky Sedgwick, weaving, ca. 1996–99. Photograph: Kevin Ryan. Collection of H. A. Sedgwick. © H. A. Sedgwick

collage form in chapter 1, and Gary Fisher's sadomasochism, an eroticism that he shared with Sedgwick and that bound them together. In a note from Fisher to Sedgwick quoted in her afterword to *Gary in Your Pocket*, he described how he had "had a small battle with KS," by which he meant Kaposi's sarcoma, a rare form of cancer affecting people with HIV, causing abnormal tissue to grow below the skin. But KS also represents Sedgwick's last two initials. In addition, Fisher documented how "the kimo" he had, to treat the sarcoma, made him "ill even at such low dosages," causing him to want to talk to Sedgwick, who was "in the middle of chemotherapy" herself following her cancer diagnosis.[5] I draw attention to the passage less because it reveals Fisher's characteristically sadomasochistic relation to Sedgwick than because of that resonant word *kimo*, short for *chemotherapy* and an abbreviated form of *kimono*, as if Fisher, like Sedgwick, chopped up kimonos as part of a reparative response to his cancer.[6]

Weaving in the Cybernetic Fold

Perhaps the most conceptual way of contextualizing Sedgwick's weavings is by juxtaposing them with the essay she cowrote with Adam Frank circa 1995, "Shame in the Cybernetic Fold." At first, the essay might seem far removed, introducing as it does the work of affect theorist Silvan Tomkins. Within it, Sedgwick and Frank attempt to critique and aerate, with some new possibilities, the "routinizing critical projects of applied theory," desiring to do greater justice to difference, contingency, and the possibility of change. And yet the early assertion that human language may not "offer the most productive" model for their project might give us pause. After all, what could be more emblematic than weaving, with its weft threads moving under, then over, the next available warps, of the "structuralist reliance on symbolization through binary pairings of elements, defined in diacritical relation to one another," that had "not only survived the structuralist moment" but "been propagated even more broadly through varied and unresting critique"? This was a critique that, like a good weaving, perhaps, "reproduce[d] and popularize[d] the *structure*," even as it complicated an "understanding of the *workings*, of the binarisms."[7]

But like Sedgwick and Frank's readings of Tomkins, her weavings may have had a *reparative*, as well as conceptual, function at this moment in her life. In the photograph that graces the cover of this book, Sedgwick is seen barefoot at a loom, absorbed, with her left foot pressing the treadle to raise or lower the alternating warp threads and her hands throwing the shuttle that carries the weft across them, apparently oblivious to being photographed.

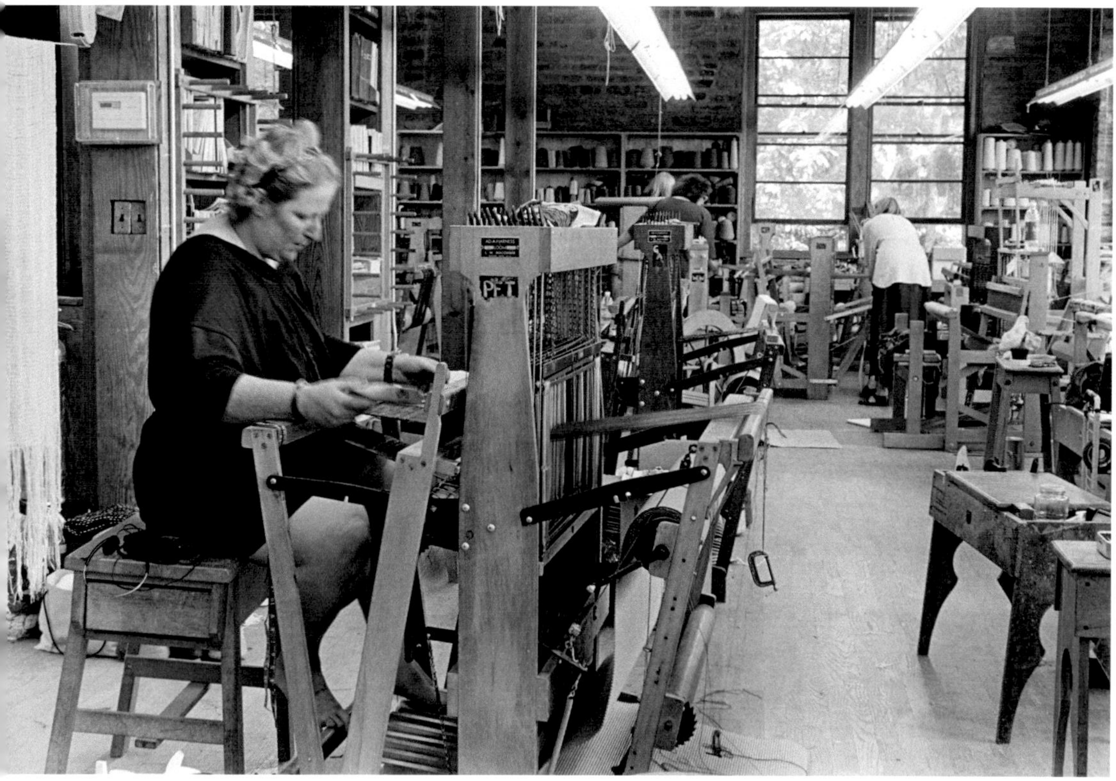

Figure 2.2. Eve Kosofsky Sedgwick working at a floor loom at the Penland School of Craft, ca. 1996–99. Photograph: H. A. Sedgwick, rephotographed in frame by Kevin Ryan. Collection of H. A. Sedgwick. © H. A. Sedgwick

Her posture recalls the attitude of shame, meditation, and reading. Like all three, in Sedgwick's account, her absorption here has a similar "force-field creating power" and represents an interaction with the world, as well as withdrawal from it. Like the absorbed reader, the photograph suggests the "kind of skin that sheer textu[r]al attention can *weave* around a [weaving] body" and registers as extroversion as much as introversion, as a public statement as much as a private absorption. The "additional skin shimmering as if shrink-wrapped around" Sedgwick's body and the loom "sharply and sheerly delineates the conjunction or composition, making figural not escape or detachment but attention, interest." Or at least it sharply delineates when it comes to certain details but blurrily depicts Sedgwick's hands and head in motion. Indeed, viewers might think about the shimmering skin of absorption in relation both to Sedgwick at work and to the silk scarf she was making, once it was complete and could be worn.[8]

But why was Sedgwick as "excited and calmed, inspired and contented," by her weaving as she and Frank were by Tomkins's writing? (see figure 2.1). Like Tomkins's style, viewers might think of Sedgwick's weaving as a kind of "sampling" or "listing the possible." It was sampling in the sense that she employed swatches of kimono fabric for her wefts and in the way she employed different textiles to explore numerous possible variants within the geometric parameters of her warp and weft. Spectators might also note how just as certain "phrases, sentences, sometimes whole paragraphs repeat" in Tomkins's writing, so Sedgwick's warp employs predominantly gold and purple threads, which recur repeatedly, in pairs or threes, across the weft, although interrupted there by lone aqua and pink threads. And just as Tomkins's "pages are taken up with sentences syntactically resembling one another," so there are page-like structures in the weft, in the eight rows of the middle diamond-printed salmon section, where she employs continuously the same kimono silk scraps in sequence. In addition, viewers might think about the predictably alternating warp and weft as a parallel to the way Tomkins employed "multiple, overlapping voices to attenuate terror" and "burn out" "fear response[s]."[9] Weaving's overall rectilinearity, meanwhile, resembles a page or a centered poem with ragged left and right edges.

But, like Tomkins's writings, Sedgwick's weavings are never entirely, predictably *systematic* as she employs a carefully calibrated heterogeneousness; what she and Frank characterize as the "alchemy of the contingent." Looking at the warp threads Sedgwick employs, the most obvious system seems to be alternating rows of gold and purple fibers, intermixed with blue/pink threads, but because of their twisted fibers, these blue/pink braids sometimes register as blue and sometimes as pink. Similarly, Sedgwick utilizes a near-vertical bilateral symmetry for her threads, up until the middle, where she provides an exception. As such, and like Tomkins, the "highest interest" of taxonomies of the *mostly symmetrical* is in their "making grounds for disconfirmation and surprise" and their "resistance to teleological presumptions," at the "grossest" levels, in terms of the broader patches of kimono silk or matching warp wool threads that make up the weft at those moments when the weft is also wool, and at the "finest levels" of individual warps, depending on whether there is a predominance of blue or pink threads in the braided threads.[10]

Spectators might also think about Sedgwick's weaving as concerned with "cybernetics and systems theory" in terms of the "highly complex, . . . explicit layering of biological and machine models" involved in her working at the loom, in which the "very concept 'machine' was a complex one." After all, loom weaving might be described as a "complex interleaving of endogenous and exogenous, perceptual, proprioceptive, and interpretive—causes, effects, feedbacks,

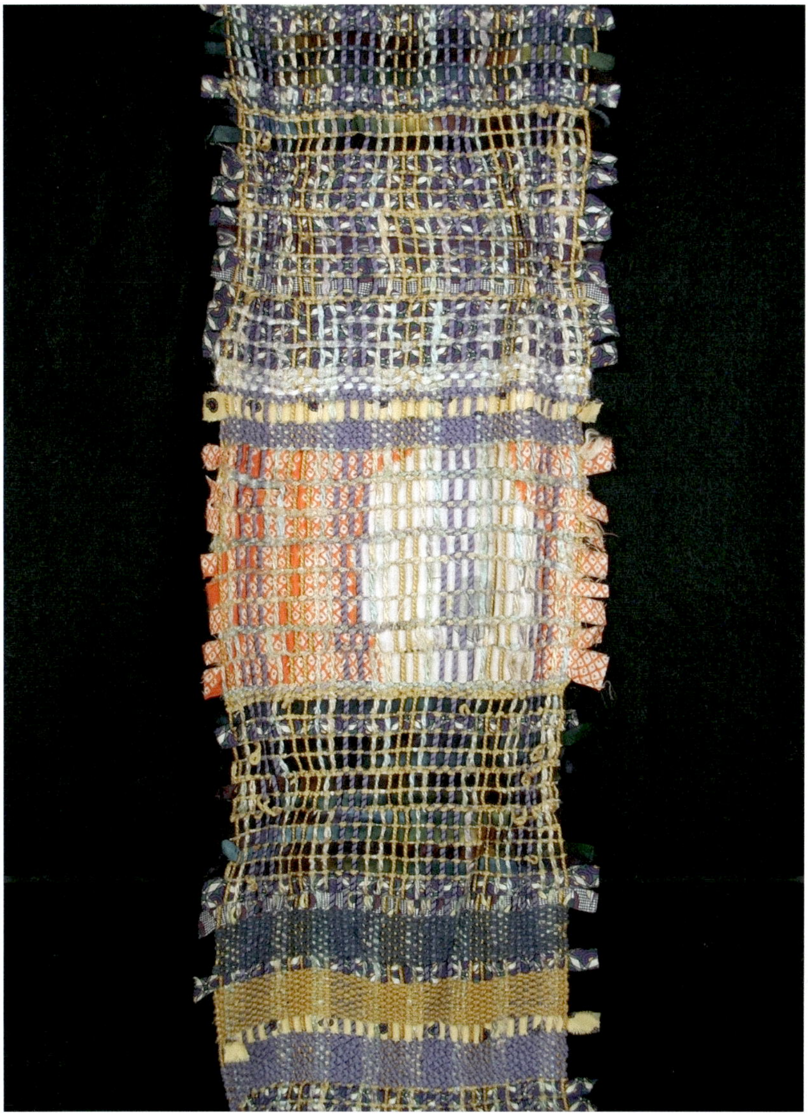

Figure 2.3. Eve Kosofsky Sedgwick, weaving (detail of figure 2.1), ca. 1996–99. Photograph: Kevin Ryan. Collection of H. A. Sedgwick. © H. A. Sedgwick

motives, long-term states such as moods and theories, along with distinct transitory physical . . . events."[11]

To be a proficient weaver, Sedgwick had to master certain mechanical processes: the pushing down of treadles with her feet to raise and lower the alternating warp to allow her to float her waddle of wefts through, risking reducing her to being, if not quite a machine, then a mechanical operative. But depending on the amount of pressure she applied with her foot to the paddle, the warp would rise higher or lower, get tighter or looser, offering her possibilities for idiomatic creases and kinks, rather than a uniform flat surface, that a machine alone could not achieve. As such, Sedgwick and her loom, like the machines and minds in cybernetic theory, worked across a spectrum of varying "degrees of independence, dependence, interdependence, and control and transformation of one by the other."

What is perhaps *most* cybernetic about Sedgwick's weaving, however, was the way that rather than modeling a predictable binary model of "two possibilities," labeled "Express or Repress," "potent/impotent," or the "subversive versus the hegemonic, resistance versus power," as the wefts moved over and under the visibly expressed or repressed warps, her weavings also modeled the "great conceptual value," when it came to challenging binary thinking, of the "habit of layering digital (on/off) with analog (graduated and/or multiply differentiated) representational models," where the analog models offered "a multiplication" of options but a "finite and concrete multiplication."[12]

After all, according to Frank and Sedgwick, the great conceptual value of cybernetic thinking was the way it offered a "heterogeneous mixture" of, and "constant switching" between, "digitally structured [and] analogically structured representational mechanisms." The former could be codified by the alternating idea of 1/0, and in the case of weavings by the alternating, raised and lowered, "leapfrog[ging] and "interleav[ing]" warp and weft patterning, required to be "represented, necessarily, analogically, via graph or map."[13] Which is to say that viewers might, at first, be inclined to interpret Sedgwick's weavings in structuralist terms, as an aestheticizing equivalent to her and Frank's desire to "describe structuralism, not as *that mistaken thing that happened before poststructuralism but fortunately led directly to it,* but rather as part of a rich intellectual ecology, a Gestalt (including systems theory) that allowed it to mean more different and more interesting things than have survived its sleek trajectory into poststructuralism." As such, in her weaving Sedgwick continued her career-long practice of showing how binary oppositions, the warp and the weft, worked in practice and, often, failed to work, perhaps explaining her queer preference for weavings that refused the conventions of strict rectilinearity and that had considerable flexibility. Indeed, the binary character of the warp and weft clearly appealed to a Sedgwick not averse, across her career, to axiomatic and diagrammatic pronouncements, "imagined with a structural elegance," as well as an interest in the "conceptual economy of means and modeling."[14]

But Sedgwick was also interested in what she called more or less "minimal and apparently nonsignifying grammatical differentiations," or "nonce taxonomies," descriptions and *weak* theories that could not be generalized beyond a single, complex case.[15] Her weavings again capture a productive middle ground. In them, she gestured toward the "possibility of random, virtually infinite permutation, some of it trivial, some of it highly significant," when it came to which colors or fibers she employed. These offered the "suggestion of sheer, unlimited extent" and the "impress of a radical contingency on the possible outcomes." But, given her almost, but not quite bilateral symmetry, her choices were "far from random" and "always carefully chosen to open and indicate new vistas, to represent new *kinds* of possible entailments involved in any generalization." As a result, her weavings simultaneously undo existing and suggest "new taxonomical work," giving viewers practice in "ever more imaginatively and profoundly" engaging with the "local possibilities of an individual psyche."[16]

256k Shades of Gray, or Sedgwick's Modernism

When it came to the desirable "many-valuedness" of analogical systems that referred to "*more than two* but . . . *finitely-many* values or dimensions," with the possibilities for "infinite gradations along the finitely specified dimensions," Frank and Sedgwick acknowledged it was "hard to hold on to the concept of eight or thirteen (and yet not infinite) *different kinds of* . . . anything important without having a biological model somewhere in the vicinity." They also suggested that "capitalist rationalism," of the kind that led to the invention of the Jacquard loom in 1801, was, among other reasons, to blame for evacuating the "conceptual space between 2 and infinity."[17]

To give readers a better imaginative sense of that difficult "analogical realm" of "*finitely multiple qualitative differences*," Frank and Sedgwick turned to the visual arts and color theory. They noted that, however good deconstruction was at articulating the complexities of how binary systems worked, it was like a scanner or copier. It could "reproduce any work of art in 256,000 shades of gray," but "however infinitesimally subtle its discriminations may be," there were "crucial knowledges it simply cannot transmit unless it is equipped to deal with the coarsely reductive possibility that red is different from yellow is different again from blue."[18]

Sedgwick and Frank then twice pointed to the "necessarily analog models of the color wheel" as a resource for thinking about more multivectored analogical analysis. Sedgwick's weaving employs pretty much all the colors from the spectrum: red, red orange, orange, yellow orange, blue green, blue, blue violet, violet, and red violet, lacking only primary red, yellow, yellow green, and primary green. She is particularly fond, however, of Proustian secondary hues, to which we shall return, not quite on the wheel, such as salmon pink and gold, employing her "nine" or so "distinctive and irreducible" components in a range of hard-to-predict, but not impossible-to-systematize, ways.[19]

So far, my reading of Sedgwick's weavings might be understood as what she and Frank describe as the ordinary art historian's "lover's discourse"; the desire to propagate "nodes of reception for what [I] take to be an unfamiliar and highly exciting set of moves and tonalities."[20] But in paralleling Sedgwick's weavings to her and Frank's thinking on the cybernetic fold, there is a risk of reducing her weavings to their mathematical drafts and making them sound like an abstract modernist grid, or like the earlier, still apparently paradigmatic rectilinear and architectonic weavings of early twentieth-century Bauhaus artist Anni Albers.[21]

Perhaps the most famous account of such mathematical grids is Rosalind Krauss's 1979 *October* article, which argued that the grid was "emblematic of the modernist ambition within the visual arts" and a form that announced "modern art's will to silence" and "hostility to literature," "narrative," and "discourse." This was a job it had done with "striking efficiency."[22] At first reading, Krauss's claims chime, perhaps, with Sedgwick's larger "MANIA FOR MAKING UNSPEAKABLE" objects—which is to say, unspeaking as well as shameful, queer objects—and her account of her weaving as a "TEXTURE BOOK" that "WOULDN'T NEED A FIRST PERSON AT ALL"; a model of weaving as a woven thing with just a woven depth.[23]

Krauss's remarks on the ways grids "unravel through time," meanwhile, and encouragement to read girds centrifugally and centripetally inspires spectators to think about the loose warp threads at either end of Sedgwick's weaving and the similar loose ends of her kimono swatches. According to Krauss, a centrifugal reading "operates from the work of art outward, compelling our acknowledgement of a world beyond the frame." Here, viewers might think about Sedgwick's loose warps, knotted into place but free to move beyond the knot, as less subject to alternating, subjugating patterning constraint. As such, they represent weaving's queer horizon, if one of the things *queer* refers to, according to Sedgwick, was the "open mesh of possibilities, gaps, overlaps, dissonances and resonances, lapses and excesses of meaning when the constituent elements of something," say a warp and weft, "aren't made (or *can't be* made) to add up" to a rectilinear, straight whole.[24]

Something similar happens with Sedgwick's kimono wefts. Some of these, as in the case of the blue and purple patches, fold back on themselves, to form another row, while others, in the case of the salmon pink scraps, are single-row elements that extend into space, where they might fray, at either end. But if Krauss's centrifugal reading might understand those threads as a fraying queer margin, a centripetal reading would interpret them as increasingly constrained and subordinated within order, pattern, and structure, depending on whether spectators prefer the idea of normativity as endlessly structuring or queer as open-endedly troubling.

Krauss's influential masculinist-modernist accounts of the grid, extending from the visual arts to the "three-dimensional grid" and out to music and dance, do not, however, include weaving, even if she repeatedly employed textile metaphors. For example, she noted the way in which, read centrifugally, the grid "extended, in all directions, to infinity," with the result that any artwork employing a grid appeared as a "mere fragment, a tiny piece arbitrarily cropped from an infinitely larger fabric." Read centripetally, the opposite was true, and "concentrating on the surface of the work as something complete and internally organized" tended to "dematerialize that surface."[25]

But what if viewers *rematerialized* Sedgwick's weavings and thought further about the kimonos she employed, refusing the move she and Frank made, toward the end of their essay, where they acknowledge they had deferred, specifically, a "cross-cultural perspective"?[26]

"Keep Talking While I Change . . . ," or Sedgwick's Merrillian Weaving

In *A Dialogue on Love*, around the time of the 1995 death of James Merrill, one of Sedgwick's favorite poets, she and her therapist, Shannon Van Wey, talked about Merrill's 1976 poem "The Kimono," quoting the final three lines:

> Keep talking while I change into
> The pattern of a stream
> Bordered with rushes white on blue.[27]

The poem describes its speaker's return from a "lovers' lane," his hair "white as snow," leaving uncertain whether from winter weather or age. He has "seen[,] like seasons come and go," a range of emotions, "joy, incomprehension, pain," and has returned home again, to his open relationship, "frozen half dead" by a route the speaker's interlocutor, and probable lover, knows only too well. The patient lover hides a smile and quotes a text, noting how "Desires ungratified / Persist from one life to the next," in a form like "blueprints"; an idiom Sedgwick was profoundly interested in, as we shall see.[28] Merrill and his partner then reflect on how, each year, snow would melt, and winter would become April, when there would be a "bubble-gleam" and "sudden beam" of sunshine. In the poem, then, time is cyclic, and during changes, some things persist, across the seasons and *bardo*s between lives. The only thing to do is to embrace the changes and rhythms, to dress oneself up in an appropriate kimono, blueprinted with the "pattern of a stream / Bordered with rushes white on blue."

A second kimono appears in the final poem of "Prose of Departure," Merrill's *haibun* travelogue that inspired the similarly part-prose, part-haiku format of *Dialogue*. In Merrill's 1988 poem "In the Shop," readers find the same pair of lovers offered "the most fabulous kimono of all: dark, dark purple traversed by a winding, starry path," causing Merrill's partner to wonder, "To what function, dear heart, could it possibly be worn by the likes of—" Finishing the sentence with a buried "us," Merrill says, "Hush. Give me your hand."

At the end of the trip, with so many of their friends lost to AIDS, Merrill asks, Why not buy it? Alluding to the *shibori* tie-dye technique Sedgwick so loved, as we shall see, the passage continues:

> Dyeing. A homophone deepens the trope. Surrendering to earth's colors, shall we not *be* earth before we know it? Venerated therefore is the skill which, prior to immersion, inflicts upon a sacrificial length of crepe de Chine certain intricate knottings no hue can touch. So that one fine day, painstakingly unbound, this terminal gooseflesh, the fable's whole eccentric
>
> star-puckered moral—
> white, never-to-blossom buds
> of the mountain laurel—
>
> may be read as having emerged triumphant from the vats of night.[29]

If "The Kimono" speaks of resurrection and the persistence of characteristics, desires, and experiences beyond the bardo, "In the Shop" focuses on a homophone to which we have already drawn attention, *dyeing* and *dying*. Given the context, readers might suspect, from what's said and what's not, that the lover living with HIV is buying the kimono as a burial shroud. Before long, he, too, will be "surrendering to earth's colors" and shall "*be* earth." What, then, wonders Merrill, as Sedgwick was to ponder herself, to do in the bardo between diagnosis and death? An answer they shared was to venerate the skill of the *shibori* artist who made kimono patterns, who tied intricate knots around crepe de chine before immersing it into the dye vat, making patterns no hue could touch, in the sense both of their being preserved from dyeing by the knots and of their superlative quality. The *shibori* pattern represents, then, an image of what might remain of Merrill and his lover having "emerged triumphant from the vats of night," and of what did not have time to flower into expression: the (suggestively anal) "star-puckered moral" of the "white, never-to-blossom buds / of the mountain laurel."[30] Merrill's example suggests further, then, that loss, death, and reincarnation, her own and those of her queer friends, are at the heart of Sedgwick's project of turning kimono swatches into new collages and weavings.

Is the Selvedge Straight? Queer or (Down) Low Theories of Weaving

In this final section, I shift registers from the formal and material qualities of Sedgwick's weavings, and their poetic and conceptual underpinnings, to return to her embodied practice as a weaver, reading, with a queer ear, several how-to-weave books she owned as examples of *low* (queer and craft) theory, to employ Jack Halberstam's helpful term; and looking, with a similarly queer eye, at the evocative surviving photograph of Sedgwick at the loom.[31] In so doing, I was inspired by a conversation I had with fellow art historian Carol Mavor's late husband, who remembered the erotic relish with which she and Sedgwick spoke, during their time at adjacent North Carolina academic institutions in the late 1990s, about Sedgwick's sudden passion for the loom.

Before turning to those how-to-weave texts, though, it is worth noting that although it is the only textile practice we have a photograph of Sedgwick undertaking, unlike her subsequent practices of *suminagashi* and *shibori* that I go on to examine, she does not discuss weaving in "Making Things, Practicing Emptiness," the late essay in which she reflects on her own textile artistry.[32] She did, however, briefly discuss weaving in her poem "The Navajo Rug" (ca. 1994), which compared the deliriously unwell Gary Fisher to an "eye-dazzler" of a weaving "left to ruin / on a loom / the weaver was forced to abandon," remaining there in the "unfielded, blinding / patches of what's been himself," and commenting, "If you knew him, you can see it all."

Both poem and abandoned Navajo rug contain what Sedgwick characterized as the "dry, thrown storm" of Fisher's "ravishing sentence"; a sentence thrown like a weft shuttle across the warp. In the poem, as in many of her weavings, there are also patches, as if Fisher is as much patchwork as warp and weft. Her comparison of Fisher to a weaving simultaneously emphasizes the *textural* qualities of his idiom and the Fisher-like, queer resonances of her *textile* practice, which might prove surprising to the medium's more normative, mainstream commentators and practitioners.[33]

That is because, as we have begun to see, Anni Albers's *On Weaving* (1965) represents the still-paradigmatic account of the medium. Albers's late-life residence in New Haven coincided with Sedgwick's time at Yale, and my readings of Sedgwick's weavings in conceptual, systemic, *cybernetic* terms follow, in some ways, the modernist, media-specific account Albers promoted. This emphasized weaving's "structural patterns" and argued that the "fundamental form" operated on the "principle of opposites," with the "interlacing of two distinct groups of threads at right angles," the warp and the weft.[34]

As a result of her structuralist commitments, Albers's ideal weaving was an "even, uniform surface, with warp and weft appearing in equal measure and producing the same effect on the front and the back." This "principle of opposites" was further emphasized by "stripes in either warp or filling" or by "checked effects." The discipline of binary-oppositional features, Albers believed, represented a "helpful corrective" to the moral and aesthetic "temptation to mere decoration"—that dangerous, feminine alternative to, or substrate of, Clement Greenberg–ian modernism. For Albers, remaining faithful to the "weaverly components" further acted as a check against "trespassing into another art form." Indeed, for Albers, "playful invention" had to be "coupled with the inherent discipline" of a medium-specific craft; otherwise, it represented an intermedial "bid for attention, rather than a convincing innovation." "Limitlessness," she cautioned, led to "nothing but formlessness, a melting into nowhere," and it was only the "conscientious designer" who sought to forgo her identity and find a form "as anonymous as possible—that is, a form unburdened by dominantly individual traits of the planner" who would succeed.[35]

Albers's modernist emphasis on striped and checkerboard structure was hugely influential, causing late twentieth-century weaving textbook authors Ann Sutton and Diane Sheehan to suggest that "all weavers must have a natural affinity for logic, order, tradition and restraint." Following Albers's death in 1994, however, and around the time Sedgwick took up weaving, many commentators, including Sheehan and Sutton, encouraged their how-to readers to abandon their modernist medium-specific preconceptions. Indeed, according to Sutton and Sheehan, "breaking the cycle of assumptions about the loom and the inherent nature of cloth" required a "healthy skepticism" and an "irreverent attitude towards the 'rules' of weaving" as well as a "fresh, unfettered vision" enabling practitioners to "see old problems and processes in new ways."[36]

In addition, if Sutton and Sheehan compared weaving to writing, because of the way most weavers started at the top and worked their way to the bottom; and if they acknowledged that the "weave draft on point paper" was the "language most often used to record and plan weaves," they argued that "other languages must be used to describe other facets." Indeed, a deep understanding of weaving required broadening "weave vocabulary" into a range of different idioms, they suggested, "facilitated by using as many different graphic languages as possible"; an encouragement toward the *graphic*, in the sense of the sexually explicit, that practitioners and theorists of queer craft, such as Sedgwick, might have pursued with reckless abandon.[37]

After all, there are *queerly* resonant phrases even in Albers, who described the "thrust" of weft "across the opened warp." Similarly masculinist and power laden is her description of the "pounding of the weft," while readers of Sedgwick's "A Poem Is Being Written" essay might pick up further S/M possibilities when Albers described the necessity to "beat the weft into place." There are also S/M dungeon-like resonances when Albers reminds her readers that the heddle rods on their looms were known as "shafts or harnesses." Equally queerly promising are Albers's descriptions of the "interpenetration" of warp and weft and the "exchange of top and bottom layers," as well as her invocation of an "attitude of attentive passiveness."[38] Such foundational queer resonances multiply manifold when we turn to the texts Sedgwick employed to teach herself weaving.[39]

In addition, in looking again at the photograph of Sedgwick at the loom (see figure 2.2), viewers might be mindful of quite how absorbed, alive, energized, and embodied she seems. She sits head down in the familiar, absorptive iconography of reading, meditation, and shame, the famous foot fetishist seated barefoot, left foot forward, pressing down the treadle, right foot retracted and resting; ankles, knees, and hips differently, rhythmically activated.[40] Her left hand, meanwhile, gently lifts the tense weft, her right about to throw the shuttle across, energizing her fingertips, wrists, and elbows. In addition, for a writer always alive to anal possibility, she sits, spine straight, on a stool; the photograph is characterized by both a stilled, concentrated focus and an equally intense, blurred motion in her right hand and profiled head. Indeed, the photograph anticipates, in some ways, Sedgwick's later description, to which we shall return, of seated buddha statues, in the way it, too, emanates a "silence" and sense of "seated presence" that was "so powerful" viewers can "almost feel the column of [her] spine" and "nerve centers rising up between [her] knees."[41]

Sedgwick's mid-1990s weavings represent an idiosyncratic, intermedial, postmodern form of the practice, combining cybernetic high theory with persistent queer affect, both joyful and melancholic, as well as sadomasochistic energy, in an idiom exploring Silvan Tomkins, the interface between analog and digital systems, and the difficult-to-conceptualize space between 2 and infinity, as well as further memorializing the AIDS-related mortal metamorphoses of James Merrill and Gary Fisher and coming to terms with Sedgwick's own, increasing metastatic unraveling.

When compared to her earlier patchworks, Sedgwick's weavings suggest an artist increasingly coming into her own expert, idiomatic realm. And, having taken two weeks of intensive classes at the Penland School of Craft with acclaimed Australian fiber artist Liz Williamson, Sedgwick purchased a floor loom and contemplated abandoning the academy and becoming a professional weaver.[42] Sadly, the pressure on her increasingly dissolving spine proved too serious a risk, and she had to abandon, prematurely, her weaving practice, returning to develop her less pressurizing, earlier patchwork aesthetic, as we shall see.

Apart from when she sported them as scarves in the *New York Times*, however, Sedgwick's weavings remained a comparatively private, unexhibited practice. The remaining three chapters of the book explore her exhibited work, commencing with her comparatively modest first public show, *Floating Columns*.

3

FLOATING COLUMNS

(1999–2000)

The Floating World of Sedgwick's Fused Silk Works

The first public exhibition of Eve Kosofsky Sedgwick's collages, *Floating Columns*, took place at the Rhode Island School of Design in 1999, followed by a better-documented showing at Cedar Creek Gallery in Durham, North Carolina, during the spring of 2000. The show's subtitle, *Works in Silk, Paper, and Soie Mariée* (marriage silk), anticipated the idiom of her final exhibition: *Works in Fiber, Paper, and Proust*, as we shall see. At Cedar Creek, the show was co-sponsored by the Duke English Department, where Sedgwick was then teaching. Her pieces were part of a group show.

The exhibition featured ten Sedgwick textiles, arranged at eye height in an undulating pattern, along a white wall, behind a row of ceramics, lamps, and sculptures fashioned by other artists, whose work was arranged to harmonize

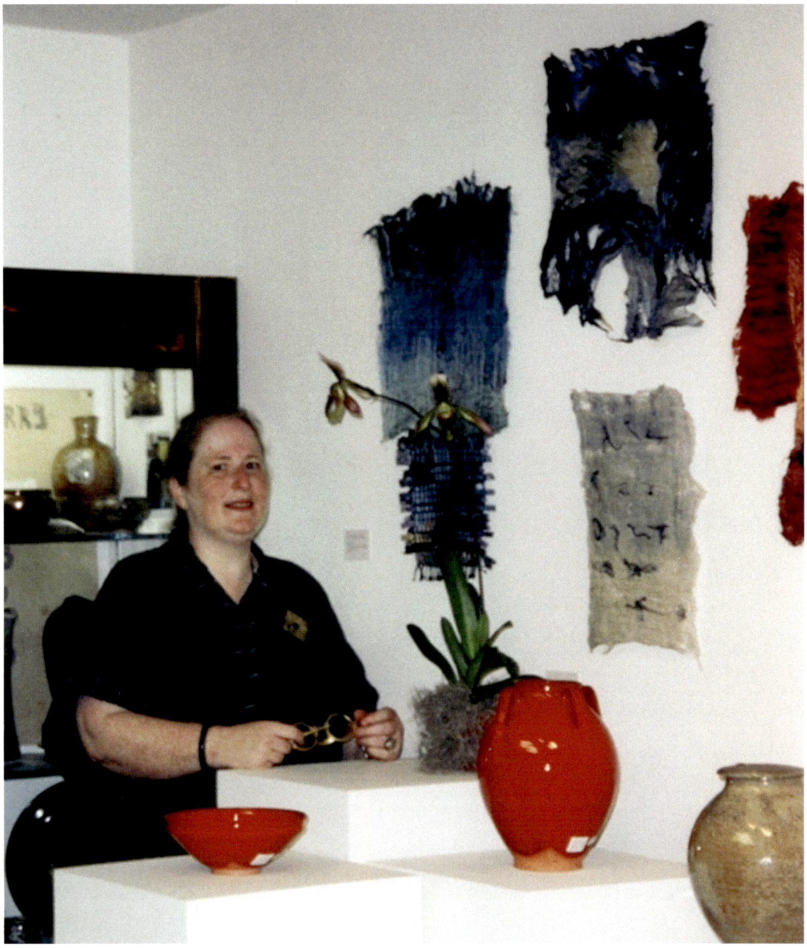

Figure 3.1. Eve Kosofsky Sedgwick at the *Floating Columns* exhibition, 1999. Photograph: H. A. Sedgwick. Collection of H. A. Sedgwick. © H. A. Sedgwick

with Sedgwick's palette. In addition, Sedgwick's work incorporating photographs of Buddhist sculptures was juxtaposed with three real-life examples. Sedgwick was growing increasingly interested in Buddhism in this period, as her 1999 talk "Come as You Are" reveals, now newly available in a 2021 open-access version.[1]

Almost all Sedgwick's collages, and all the patchworks involving text or photographs, were hung singly, pictorially, in a row, except for a pair of more abstract colored textiles hung together in a column, second in the sequence. All the patchworks were multipart, some more emphatically, again juxtaposing

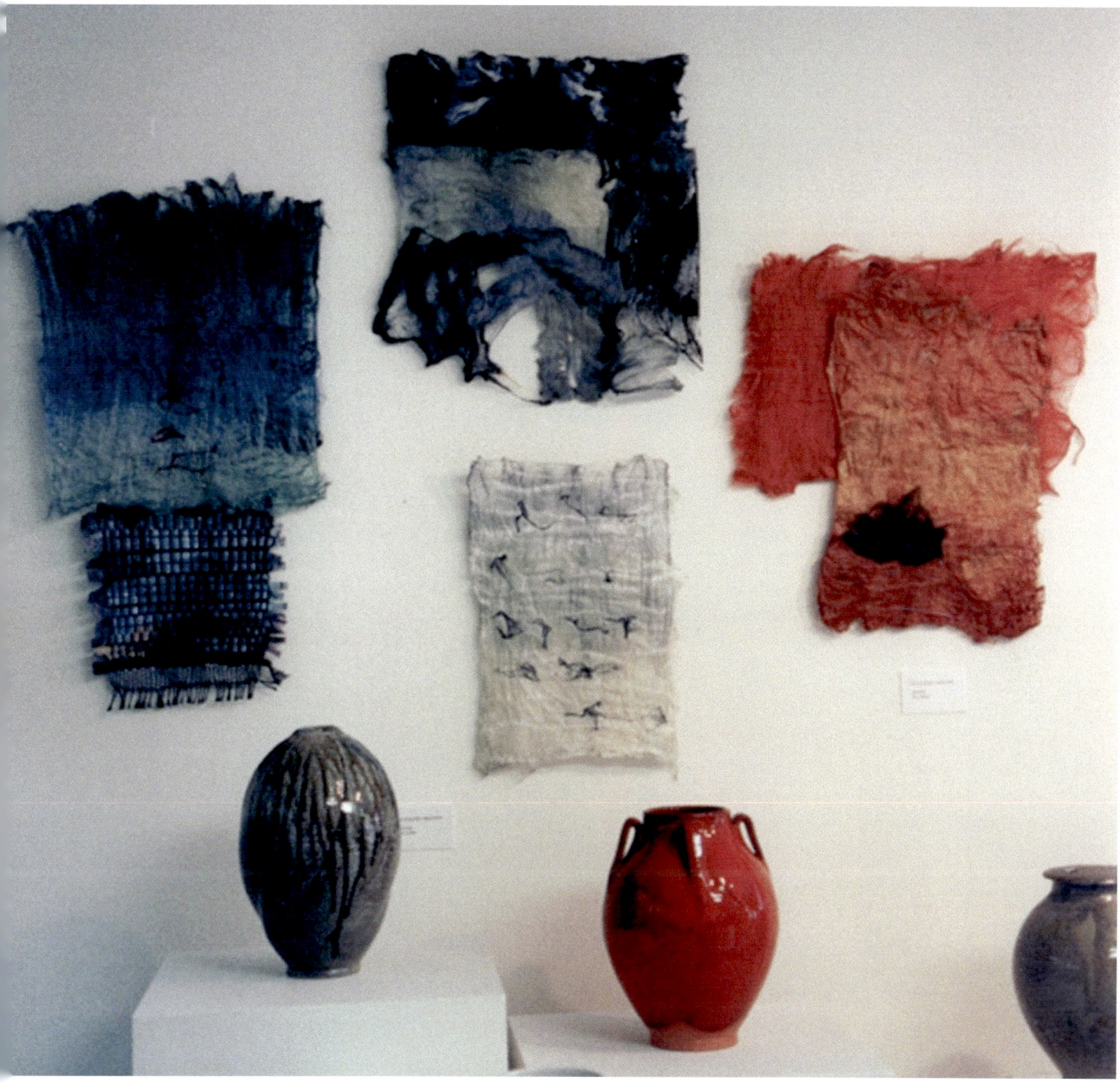

Figure 3.2. Works from the *Floating Columns* exhibition, 1999. Photograph: H. A. Sedgwick. Collection of H. A. Sedgwick. © H. A. Sedgwick

different modular, roughly rectilinear elements; patchwork represented one of Sedgwick's favorite ongoing idioms. Sedgwick's archive includes several surviving pieces, on which I focus, as well as a group of other fused silk patchworks that formed part of her exploration process. Some of the originally exhibited pieces are now absent, likely sold or given to friends.

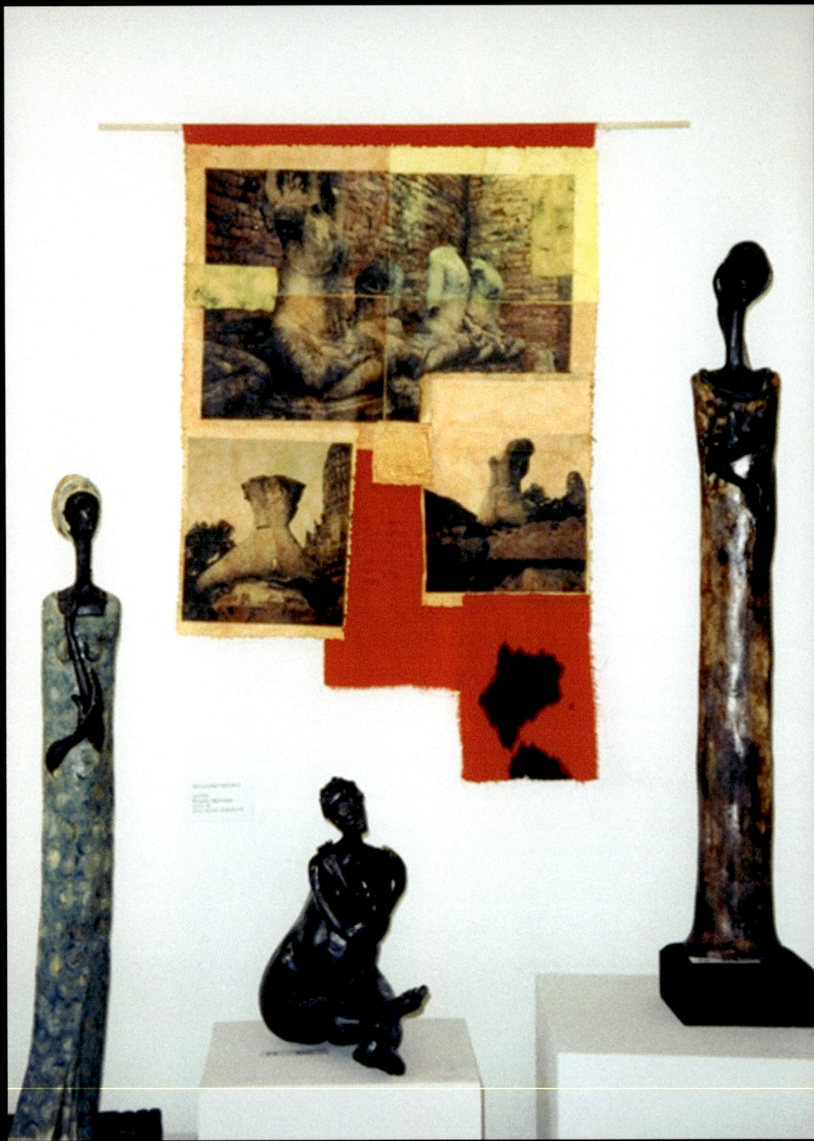

Figure 3.3. Wall hanging from the *Floating Columns* exhibition, 1999. Photograph: H. A. Sedgwick. Collection of H. A. Sedgwick. © H. A. Sedgwick

The exhibition's title, *Floating Columns*, encourages spectators to pay attention to the portrait orientation of most of the rectangular pieces, with their descending modular elements, and to notice the vertical, columnar installation of the two more abstract pieces, hung one above the other.

As such, each patchwork differently evokes Sedgwick's troubled spine. The fusing of different pieces of silk recalls the dissolving together of her vertebrae; the two separate, but vertically juxtaposed pieces suggesting the more fearful idea of vertebrae severed. The solid columnar form of two of the three sculptures juxtaposed with Sedgwick's patchworks also added poignant resonance.

In addition, except for the two largest pieces, hung from a supporting bar, like a Tibetan *thangka*—a traditional Buddhist painting, usually on cotton or silk, depicting a mandala scene, the life of a Buddhist deity, accompanied by many bodhisattvas—most pieces *float* in front of the white walls, to which they are invisibly attached at the top; the light paper and silk ripple away from the wall with a movement of adjacent air, recalling the relatedly free-floating warp threads in Sedgwick's earlier weavings.

The potentially billowy experience anticipates a passage from "Making Things, Practicing Emptiness," the essay in which Sedgwick later reflected on her artistic practice, in which she described a photograph of a Buddhist monk seated on the banks of a river, repeatedly raising and lowering an engraved board onto the surface of the water, "each time 'printing' the river with images of Buddhist deities which are carried away downstream."[2] In addition, Sedgwick's archive characterizes two of her pieces as prayer flags. In "Making Things," she described how every time the wind blew, Buddhist prayer flags "imprinted" the surrounding air with their texts and images. As a result, there was a "promulgation of something—something that simply exists—by no one, to no one," in a kind of "unanswerable impersonality." That was because, once the prayer flags were fashioned and in place, "no one sends the message," and no one necessarily "seems to receive it." Yet something happened, beside and beyond the "splitting 'point' of directional address," in a way that was "somehow efficacious; if only through the prayer flags' promiscuous refusal to generate the rhetorical dyad of subject and object, or agent and acted-upon" as well as the "dualisms of active/passive, subject/object, and speaker/hearer."[3]

A similarly impersonal event might have taken place during *Floating Columns*, especially in those cases, at the start and end of Sedgwick's sequence, where her works contain no figurative images or text. After all, all the exhibited pieces were created by exposing to heat juxtaposed pieces of fiber, paper, and silk, the synergy of chemistry and temperature suggesting again Sedgwick's ambition to generate a "TEXTURE BOOK" with no "FIRST PERSON."[4]

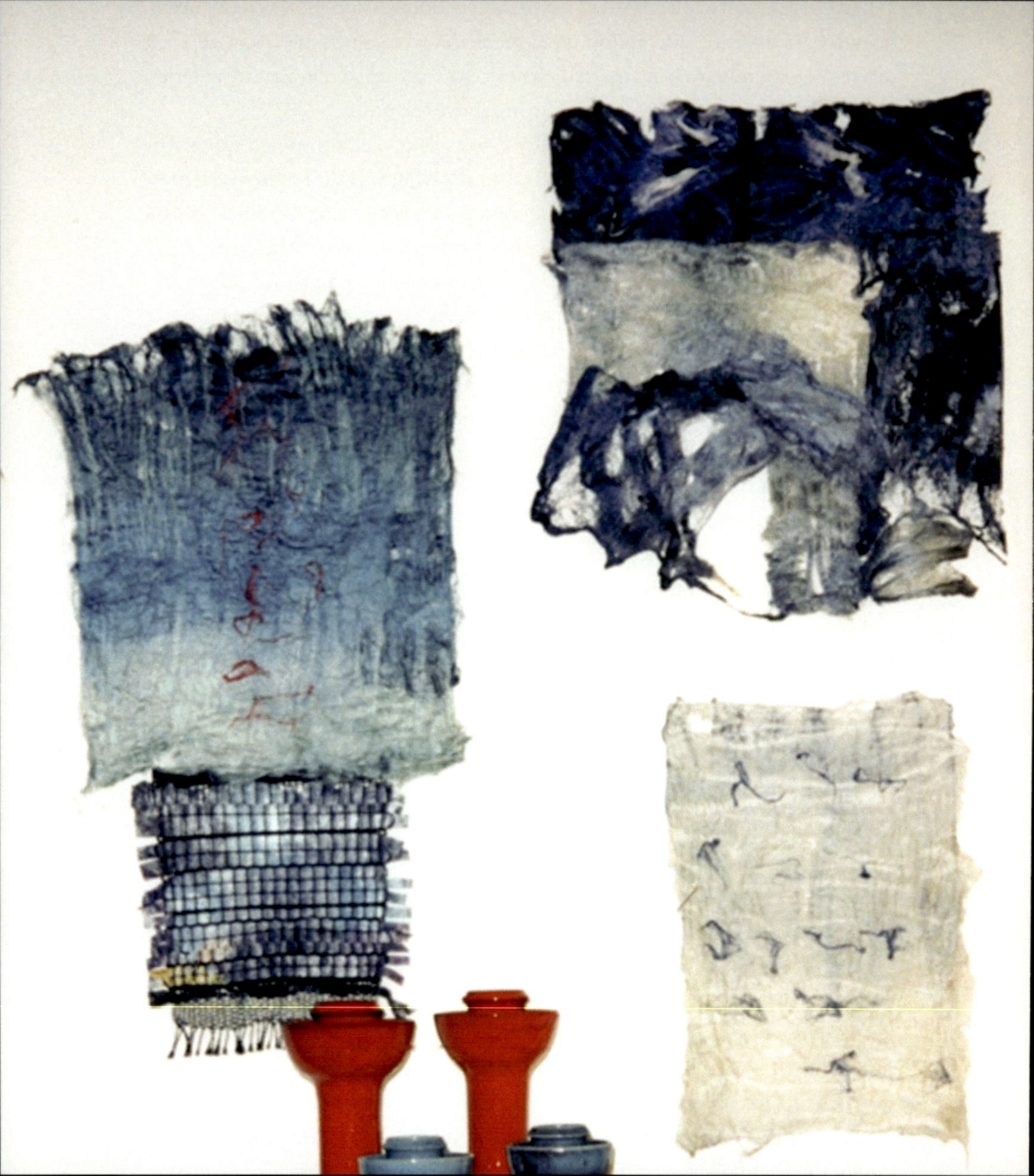

Figure 3.4. Works from the *Floating Columns* exhibition, 1999. Photograph: H. A. Sedgwick. Collection of H. A. Sedgwick. © H. A. Sedgwick

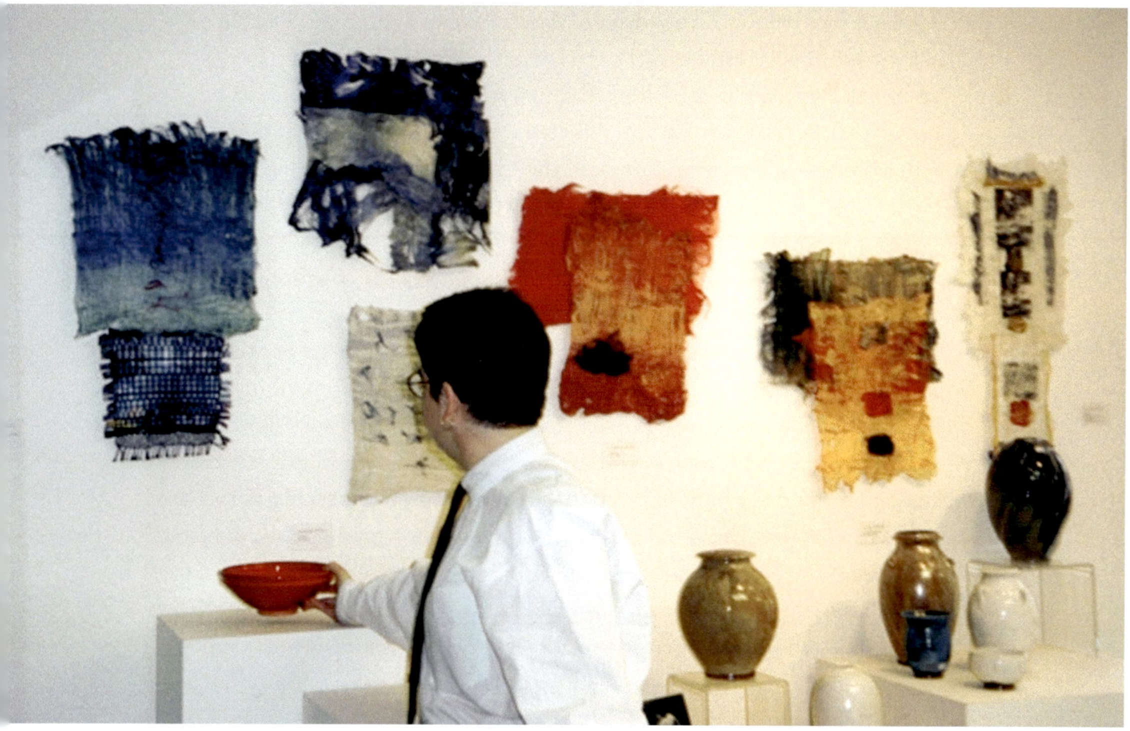

Figure 3.5. Works from the *Floating Columns* exhibition, 1999. Photograph: H. A. Sedgwick. Collection of H. A. Sedgwick. © H. A. Sedgwick

Sedgwick's pieces resemble Buddhist prayer flags in further ways. The rectangular cloth patchworks, full of primary colors, are hung in the traditional left-to-right order of blue (symbolizing the sky and space), white (representing the air and wind), red (alluding to fire), and yellow (evoking the earth). Sedgwick does not include green examples, representing water, usually found between red and yellow in the sequence, perhaps signaling that her elements were out of balance, since, in traditional Tibetan medicine, all five elements were required to maintain harmonious health.[5]

In addition, Sedgwick seemingly combines, in the more abstract fourth and fifth pieces, juxtaposing a descending vertical portrait module in front of a horizontal landscape module, the two kinds of Tibetan prayer flags. These are the horizontal *Lung ta* form, translated as "wind horse," and the vertical *Darchor* form, meaning "flagstaff." Her patchworks recall more strongly the *Lung ta* version since they are hung from their top edges rather than their sides. Notably, the Cedar Creek exhibition opened on March 29, shortly after the Tibetan New Year, the traditional, auspicious time to hang new prayer flags.

Sedgwick's abstract, melted, hotly fashioned, and sensuously fused silk pieces do not just evoke the spirituality of Tibetan textiles. The show's title might also pun on Japan's so-called *ukiyo* culture of the "floating world" between 1600 and 1867; the word *ukiyo*, suggesting the transitory, everyday world, evokes the homophone for Sorrowful World, the existential plane of samsara, from which Buddhists, with the exception of buddhas and bodhisattvas, sought release into nirvana.

The floating world is, perhaps, primarily remembered for its licensed red-light and theater districts and its kimono-wearing geisha, captured in a series of Japanese woodblock prints, popular in late nineteenth-century Europe and America.[6] As such, Sedgwick's exhibition quietly embraces a bodily sensuality within and beyond the bounds of marriage, signaled by the presence of the *soie mariée*. For example, the fused character of Sedgwick's marriage silk hints at the silky, embodied, interpenetrating, relational pleasures of her own marriage and a gay marriage then increasingly sought across the United States, especially given the hot temperature of the majority of the palettes Sedgwick employs beyond the single, more virginal white second piece, marked with indigo calligraphy (the second in the series).[7] In the context of the gay marriage debate, viewers might interpret Sedgwick's fusing of *soie mariée* in another way, as a queer symbolic attack on the institution of heterosexual marriage, heated up beyond its material limits and deformed.

There is also a homophonic pun, in French, as we have seen, on the words for silk, *soie*, and self, *soi*, suggesting, in the relational fusing of silks, the tactile pleasures of a masturbatory self-relation, central to Sedgwick's corpus and Jacques Derrida's closely related "Silkworm" essay, as we have seen. Like Sedgwick's controversial 1991 essay, "Jane Austen and the Masturbating Girl," Derrida's meditation on silkworms told of "agile fingers" and focused on the desire to "lock oneself away with oneself in oneself," where one could perform "gesture[s] towards oneself," following an "unveiling."[8]

Indeed, when it came to the "possibility of auto-affection," Derrida specified several possible relations "*à soi*," including touching one's own "epidermic surface" and penis, as well as its silky secretions, that "very fine," "shiny, gleaming" sperm. Indeed, in the silkworm essay, Derrida was concerned with "*several self-affections*" "*beyond any coupling*" and with "tendencies" with more "passive aims," whether "*labial*," "*salivary*," or "*rectal*." In a Sedgwickian phrase, he described the pleasures of "*fainting to the bottom*" of oneself. And if the essay is concerned with a "form of event without precedent" and keeps "vigil for the coming of the 'without eve,'" it is an essay that seems profoundly *with* Eve in many ways.[9]

In addition, Sedgwick's prominent use of *soie mariée* in her subtitle calls to mind the idea of *soie moiré*, with *moiré* referring to the second-order, floating pattern formed when two sets of parallel lines are inclined at an angle of five degrees to each other, also known by the Sedgwick-resonant phrase the *beat phenomenon*. The word *moiré*, meanwhile, derives etymologically from a traditional silk textile with a rippled or watered, thus "floating," appearance. This was fashioned by laying two textiles on top of each other, the upper translucent, the lower matte, whose warp and weft subsequently generated stretching moiré patterns; a stretching again representing a textile parallel to Sedgwick's erotic pleasure at enjambment's straddling together and pushing apart.

Alternatively, a single piece of fabric could be folded in on itself and compressed, so that the warp and weft fibers were flattened, felted, and fused, generating a related bent, ribbed effect. In the context of Sedgwick's notoriously masturbatory oeuvre, this closing together of individual warp and weft fibers might recall Luce Irigaray's account of what happened when women's two labial lips met, echoed, at a more macro scale, in Sedgwick's layered juxtaposition of fabrics in the patchworks, and, in the first piece, by her now-familiar use of scraps of silks to form weft layers.[10]

But, as with her weavings, Sedgwick's floating columns characteristically refuse the straight rectilinearity of flag, portrait, and landscape formats in favor of ragged edges and queer loose ends. As such, her patchworks might embrace further then-contemporary queer politics, not just because of their references to masturbation and homo marriages within the self-same.[11] After all, the early modern Japanese floating world was, as we have seen, most famous for its theaters and sex workers; a public sex culture to rival modern Manhattan's. Indeed, the summer before *Floating Columns* debuted at Rhode Island, New York City mayor Rudy Giuliani started rezoning the city to end queer public sex. This threatened queer sociability and Manhattan's hard-won safe-sex culture, which took root in the city's bars and bathhouses; this rezoning was critiqued in two key books first published in 1999, the year of the Cedar Creek Show: Samuel Delaney's *Times Square Red, Times Square Blue*; and Michael Warner's *The Trouble with Normal: Sex, Politics, and the Ethics of Queer Life*.[12]

Having laid out the broader contours and contexts of the show, in the second part of the chapter I consider three of Sedgwick's pieces in more detail:

those involving Buddhist texts and images. Viewers might consider each a queer *thangka*: a traditional Buddhist textile painting, as we have seen, depicting a mandala, the life of the Buddha or other Buddhist deities, often organized in framed sections, with some sky in the background. In Sedgwick's case, she employed photographs of one or more Buddhas, in meditative poses, all framed in some way, and some seen against the sky, on a silk or mulberry ground. Again like traditional *thangkas*, Sedgwick's three collages are unsigned, unframed, and portable, a patchwork that could be folded or rolled up when not on display.[13] Indeed, the word *thangka* translates as "the thing that one unrolls" in classical Tibetan; Sedgwick returned to an interest in scrolling forms in one of her later Marcel Proust works, as we shall see.[14]

Traditional *thangkas* were designed to be displayed, for brief periods, on monastery walls, during festivals, or more sustainedly in the private quarters of monks. They were also carried into the houses of devotees near death. While Sedgwick's works were displayed on the gallery wall, they were hung during the Tibetan New Year, as we have seen, and associated with a figure in the bardo of dying, Sedgwick herself; the patchworks were designed to act as meditation aids and sources of focus and energy, for the artist and her spectators. Indeed, devotees thought both monk and lay *thangka* makers, as well as viewers, with Sedgwick combining both roles, gained spiritual insight and merit from their production and contemplation. In addition, Sedgwick's collages employ quotations from a range of twentieth-century Buddhist texts, again alluding to traditional *thangkas*, which included inscriptions on the back, or hidden under the paint on the front, usually the mantra of the deity depicted. As such, Sedgwick's collages represent, perhaps, our first sustained experience of *reparative reading*.

Feeling Dicey, or The Dalai Lama Writes . . .

The sixth piece Sedgwick included in *Floating Columns* centered on a passage by the fourteenth (and current) Dalai Lama, with whom, two years earlier, in May 1997, Sedgwick had spent three days in a Buddhist monastery in upstate New York, where a group pondered together the idea of dependent origination. The quotation (see figure 3.6) was printed, in black text, on a square piece of cream mulberry paper, above a gray-white piece of silk with ragged golden edges, overlain, at its bottom center, with threads of gold and red fiber, the colors worn by Tibetan monks (red threads signaling good luck in Tibetan Buddhist culture and the ties that connect all living things).

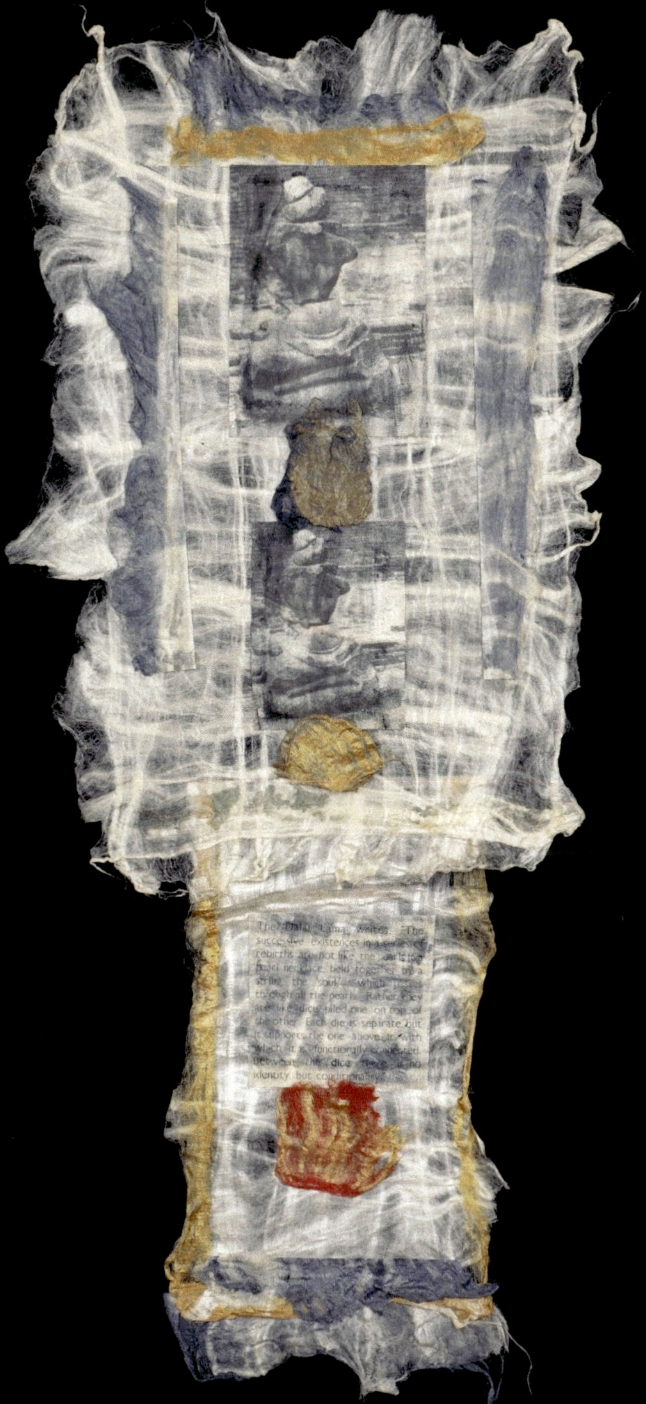

Figure 3.6. Eve Kosofsky Sedgwick, *Prayer Flag*, 1999. Photograph: Kevin Ryan. Collection of H. A. Sedgwick.

The text reads:

> The Dalai Lama writes, "The
> successive existences in a series of
> rebirths are not like the pearls in a
> pearl necklace, held together by a
> string, the 'soul,' which passes
> through all the pearls. Rather they
> are like dice piled one on top of
> the other. Each die is separate, but
> it supports the one above it, with
> which it is functionally connected.
> Between the dice there is no
> identity, but conditionality."

Sedgwick's quotation originally derived from H. W. Schumann's *The Historical Buddha* (1989), but she probably encountered it through Sogyal Rinpoche's then recently published and extraordinarily popular *The Tibetan Book of Living and Dying* (1998).[15] Sedgwick reincarnates the formerly right-justified prose as an enjambed eleven-line poem, our first example of her sustained pattern of transformative quoting techniques within her textiles. Her line breaks are rationalized not by any metric consistency but through the more characteristic rationale of rough rhyme. Like the successive lives described by the Dalai Lama, the rhyme scheme works incrementally but unpredictably, with sonic resemblance predominating over, and alternating with, direct repetition. "Passes" appears just once, with no subsequent afterlife; and "but" comes close to "connected," two lines later, but could not be called a rhyme.

Unlike the predictable rhyme scheme of a sonnet, or a pearl necklace, where, ideally, each pearl is identical to the last or is alternated with other pearls of contrasting scales or colors, Sedgwick's forms evoke something chancier about living and dying.[16] Elements are piled rather than lined up. Each patch is separate but connected to the next, supporting it, but no two elements are identical, and the fusing of the silk strands, in the overall substrate, is less systemic, creating a layered, worn, wispy, webby effect. In some ways, Sedgwick orders her elements like stacked dice, alternating abstract patches of gold and red fiber with indigo image and text, with the indigo color providing vertical framing elements in the top module and a horizontal bar along the base of the piece, in an overall gestalt alternation of word/image/frame and more decorative ground.

Sedgwick locates the Dalai Lama's text on a centered square patch of paper in the bottom portrait module. Immediately below it is a similarly centered but smaller square patch of wispy red and gold threads, the gold echoing in the ragged edges of the lower module, as well as in two similar patches punctuating her two photographs in the upper module, and in a frame-like bar close to the top of the piece. Sedgwick's images, meanwhile, comprise two identical photographs of decapitated eighteenth-century stucco statues of meditating Buddhas, seated on a lotus, "mutilated by trophy hunters," which she took while visiting a medieval temple complex in Ayutthaya, Thailand, in 1999.[17]

In "Making Things, Practicing Emptiness," Sedgwick described the surviving remains of these statues as embodying a "fully absorbing, rock-steady and inextricable full-lotus leg twist, even in the most mutilated examples," with their arms and heads lopped off. She also thought, as we have already seen, the statues emanated a "silence" and "sense of . . . seated presence" that was "so powerful" you can "almost feel the column of their spines and nerve centers rising up between their knees, even in the literal absence of most of their bodies"; a resonant image for the spinally challenged artist. Indeed, Sedgwick knew of few more palpable images of "how it can be that—in the words of the Heart Sutra—form does not differ from emptiness nor emptiness from form," in that the statues gave a "sense of how dynamic and living a thing emptiness is in Buddhist thought—the attributes that make the Dalai Lama compare emptiness to the space inside a bell."[18]

According to Buddhist art historian Dorothy H. Fickle, such statues were originally "gilded or decorated with flowers, scarves, or squares of gold leaf" and were usually viewed reverently from below, by devotees who bowed and laid gifts before them. In Sedgwick's more austere, monochrome photographs, the statues are unadorned and seen from above, although the patches of gold above and below them on the patchwork recall the devotees' gold leaf or fabric offerings. Made by devoted anonymous craftspeople, the statues in the temple complex were intended to "serve as a reminder" and model of the "Teacher and of his teachings."[19]

But as spectators might have predicted, one of the key attractions of these sculptures, for Sedgwick, was that her "own spine was in bad trouble" at the time she took the photographs, the statues offering a comforting, inspiring sense of the magnetic, powerful, peaceful spiritual and relational possibilities still inherent in a body after it had lost some of its most significant attributes—in Sedgwick's case, her hair during chemotherapy, her right breast, and parts of her spine.[20] Indeed, the mutilated statues recall Sedgwick's preference for Audre Lorde's model for her postmastectomy body, which refused restoring prostheses.[21] And while viewers can imaginatively "visualize the complete iconography" of the statues, within the context of many others within the slow-moving

Buddhist figural sculptural tradition, their unrestored state offers spectators a crucial meditation on that which is "broken off" and "that which remains," to borrow a phrase from Fickle.[22]

Sedgwick's photograph emphasizes the "complete frontal view" and what another Buddhist art historian, Silpa Birasri, calls the "perpendicularity" of the "erected trunk" of the sitting figures, which contrasts "sharply with the horizontal mass of the superposed legs."[23] Birasri's description makes the statues sound like they might form part of an uncharacteristically phallic aesthetic for Sedgwick. And if the emaciated, ascetic images of the Buddha are also "peculiarly thin," the photographs represent sculptures far from Sedgwick's usual *fat* art. However, as Birasri also documents, certain Thai critics felt that the statues looked, if anything, a "little feminine," although that was a "matter of praise rather than anything else." The sculptures were also originally modeled in the unglamorous, but queerly anal material of "husk, cow-dung and special clay."[24]

In addition, Sedgwick juxtaposes with her photographs two (more fibrously ragged and silky soft) columns of indigo fabric on either side, while her decision to directly replicate the same photograph of the Buddhas again emphasizes a certain *homo*, rather than *hetero*, aesthetic, which was characteristic of the Thai sculptural tradition. Indeed, according to Fickle, the precise iconography of statues, such as Sedgwick's, could be "traced back through [their] many generations of antecedents to the historical Buddha," with each new statue existing in relation to its precedent like the Dalai Lama's stacked dice, in a "slow and steady stylistic evolution" to the present; the Buddha was originally depicted "sitting immobile under the Bo-tree in his last mental effort previous to his enlightenment," or as "the enlightened One who, although living in his physical body, belongs to the abstract world of Nirvana."[25]

But there's again something queerly familiar about Sedgwick's Buddha image encountered in the context of *Floating Columns*. Like her oft-returned-to icon of Henry James, sitting "in front of the cool green Pacific," her peaceful, patient Buddha sits "with an inward accumulation of material" of which he "feel[s] the wealth," invoking his "familiar demon of patience, who always comes, doesn't he?" when called, to sit close by and breathe his soft breath, to cool, steady, and inspire him. And under the Buddha's bodhi tree, as by James's ocean, "everything sinks in: nothing is lost; everything abides and fertilizes and renews its golden promise," perhaps making Sedgwick think, "with closed eyes of deep and grateful longing," of when, in the fullness of time, she, too, would be able to sit in the bardo after death, her "long dusty adventure over," and to plunge her arm, "*in*, deep and far, and up to the shoulder—into the heavy bag of remembrance—of suggestion—of imagination—of art—and fish out every little figure and felicity, every little fact and fancy" to her purpose. Those things may all be "packed away now, thicker than [she could] penetrate, deeper than [she could] fathom, and there . . . rest for the present, in their sacred cool darkness," but one day, like the Ayutthaya statues on a festival day, covered in golden robes, they will, once again, "begin to gleam and glitter and take form like the gold and jewels of a mine."[26]

Osho's Meditation, or Losing Your Head, with Andy Warhol

Sedgwick's seventh piece again combines photographs of the Ayutthaya sculptures with a Buddhist text, enjambed to bring out its internal rhymes, as well as right justified and internally spaced, to make it columnar in silhouette; a column apparently floating on its smallest element, the single word *head*.

The text reads:

A good
meditation,
Osho says,
i m a g i n e
yourself as
not having a
head.

Who Sedgwick here quotes is uncertain. She might be referring, in the idiom of a Buddhist lay disciple, to an *oshō* (和尚), in which the Japanese word is not the proper name of a person but a generic noun akin to a teacher or master, referring to the monk in charge of a Buddhist temple, in the Zen and Pure Land traditions. This is a reading supported by an untitled circa 1993 poem in which she employs the phrase "My father, / I mean my Master" in a related pedagogical context.[27] Given her capitalization of Osho, however, she might be quoting the controversial twentieth-century Indian guru Bhagwan Shree Rajneesh, who called himself Osho toward the end of his life, but whose homophobia and repulsive views on HIV/AIDS Sedgwick would have found anathema.

Unlike the Dalai Lama collage, with its self-conscious repetition of the same monochrome photograph of the Thai Buddha statue from the front, organized within an overall vertical, *vertebral*, columnar form, Sedgwick this time employed, adjacently, three different photographs of Ayutthaya statues from the rear, two located on either side of the quotation, toward the bottom of the piece,

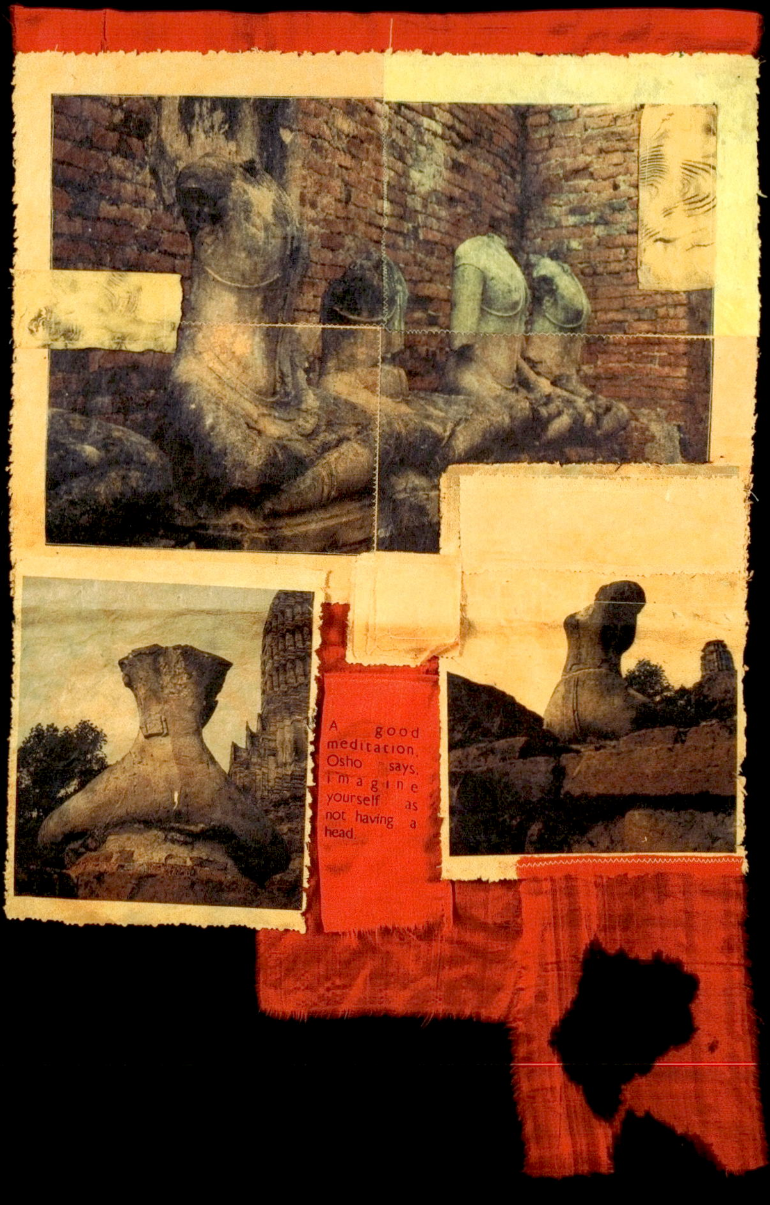

Figure 3.7. Eve Kosofsky Sedgwick, *Prayer Flag*, 1999. Photograph: Kevin Ryan. Collection of H. A. Sedgwick. © H. A. Sedgwick

and five, shot from the lower left side, at the top. These were again printed on ragged mulberry paper and layered on a single piece of ragged Tibetan red silk, with the quotation printed on a smaller micro prayer flag, of the same-colored silk, again stitched only at the top, allowing it to billow out, imprinting the air.

At the bottom right, Sedgwick fishbone-stitched onto the torn-edged, lower-right photograph a further piece of ragged red silk, stained with two patches of black ink, recalling the map of Thailand, or as if she had sloppily left a black pen in contact with the red fabric causing an unwilled, uncontrolled inky bleed across the silk fibers, her mind elsewhere. This aleatory stain contrasts the carefully controlled, machine-printed ink letters of the quotation and the precisely calibrated multicolored inks forming the photographs.

The spilled-ink patches suggest Sedgwick's developing interest in the behavior of fluids, especially in conjunction with the images of the Thai bronzes, whose variegated patinas reveal the effects of weathering; and in relation to the patch to the top right of the upper photomontage, which recalls the surface of a pond into which a stone has been dropped, or the surface of a *suminagashi* ink bath stirred into motion.

Fluid dynamics was a topic Sedgwick discussed in "Making Things, Practicing Emptiness." This documented how *suminagashi* patterns, achieved by floating ink on water, had originated in twelfth-century Japan. Unlike the European marbling earlier gracing the cover of *Epistemology of the Closet*—which was "all about keeping these liquid elements under the artist's control," by making the "water viscous with carrageenan, or by combing through the ink in regular patterns with toothed implements"—*suminagashi*, "playing on the immemorial Taoist and Zen fascination with the potent but unwilled behaviours of water," employed chemicals "not to thicken the water, but . . . to make it even more liquid."[28]

For Sedgwick, *suminagashi* represented the "most meditative of arts," using "successive drops of ink to make a lot of concentric circles, anywhere from four or five to hundreds of them, and then you sit back and watch as the complex drama of competing surface tension keeps the water surface breathing, shifting, expanding and self-enfolding," only intervening with a "soft breath, or by brushing it lightly with a feather." What resulted, Sedgwick documented, was a "snapshot of a living spatial dynamic," a "veritable badge of chaos" akin to the "infinitely receding, self-similar bifurcations of roots, branches, and capillaries in a tree, or of rivulets in a delta," and to the ragged fibers of a torn piece of mulberry paper or red silk.[29]

In the center of her patchwork, Sedgwick included a postage stamp–like swatch of cream mulberry paper, bearing neither text nor image but suggesting the emptiness at the heart of this particular form and, in so doing, again alluding to the Heart Sutra, "perhaps the central text of East Asian Buddhism," in Sedgwick's view, and one of her favorites, with its assertion that "Form does not differ from emptiness, emptiness does not differ from form. / Form is emptiness, emptiness is form," with "No appearing, no disappearing. / No taint, no purity."[30]

Indeed, spectators might read the entire collage as a riff on the Sutra, with the bronzed stucco mass of the statues again appearing dignified and present, even as seen from behind, as they gradually disappeared into empty space, their extremities robbed by trophy hunters, their surfaces disfigured by the weather; and with Sedgwick not differentiating between what, in other contexts, might be the taint of the bleeding ink stain, on the bottom right, and the text- and image-formation of the ink in the printed passages.

The most important parts of Sedgwick's collage are, perhaps, the four pieces of mulberry paper toward the top that she machine sewed together before imprinting them with the image of the five Buddha statues; the paper again the byproduct of silkworms' evocative metamorphosis. Her technique here, especially as used to depict the mutilated Buddhas, encourages viewers to think further about the relationship between parts and wholes, with the bodies hung on the gallery wall captured by her camera but quartered by her paper, in anything but a seamless manner, with the triangular herringbone stitches providing the most jagged of edges.

Similarly, when it comes to the stucco statues, Sedgwick further encourages spectators to think about change and continuity, similarity and difference. The patinas of the individual poured bodies of the ceramic Buddhas contrast with one another in their deindividuating, pattern-forming, repetitively serial sequencing, from left to right, and with the differently various modular form of the ceramic bricks behind them, which, in turn, anticipate the four similarly tessellating rectangular pieces of mulberry paper on which Sedgwick printed the photograph of the statues.

Sedgwick probably learned her techniques of serial photography, in the case of the Dalai Lama piece, and of stitched, multipart photographs, in the Osho exhibit, from Andy Warhol, to whom I'll repeatedly return. In the early 1990s, Sedgwick had cotaught a course at Duke on Warhol's life and work with Michael Moon. In the same period, she authored an article, "Queer Performativity: Warhol's Whiteness/Warhol's Shyness," first published in a 1996 collection coedited by several of her and Moon's PhD students, who had taken the course.

As William V. Ganis has documented, serial photography and stitched photomontage were both central to Warhol's late practice. In 1999, the year in which *Floating Columns* was exhibited at Rhode Island, *Andy Warhol Stitched Photographs* debuted at the Paul Kasmin Gallery in New York, where Sedgwick could have seen it.[31] Warhol and Sedgwick had much in common. He had traveled to Thailand in 1956, and his stitched photographs were similarly focused on images of "monumental statuary." Warhol's photographs were also machine stitched, in white thread, as in the Osho case, with Warhol sharing Sedgwick's interest in dangling "loose ends." The pair also shared an in interest in the repetition of, and repetition within, the photographic image, which "renders the subjects decorative and abstracted."[32]

There are also, however, differences between Warhol's secular, debunking practice and Sedgwick's more reverential aesthetics, and between Sedgwick's fat and Warhol's thin art. In Warhol's case, each print was "seen in its entirety," whereas each piece of Sedgwick's mulberry paper is overlapping. If one counts from the base layer of red silk, her montage is at least *seven* layers deep. As such, it evokes thick skin, a fat epidermal aesthetic in contrast to Warhol's svelte frame and transparent whiteness, by Sedgwick's account. In addition, like the decapitated Thai Buddhas, Sedgwick characterized Warhol as a further example of her belief that "the people with the most powerful presences" were the ones who weren't "all there," whose presence was "like the withdrawal of a god."[33]

For both Sedgwick and Warhol, the "haptic 'prick' of the needle" involved in fashioning sewn photographs "function[ed] as the Barthesian *punctum*," with Warhol having undergone abdominal stitching following his shooting by Valerie Solanis, and Sedgwick's torso having been scarred by postmastectomy stitches.[34] Indeed, Sedgwick seems to reference her surgery further by the apparent absence of breasts and nipples on the difficult-to-gender statues and through the scar-like curved line underlining the statues' right breast area, running from the sternum to the lymph nodes under the armpit; the site of further exploratory surgery, in Sedgwick's case, to ascertain whether her cancer had metastasized.

Like Warhol, Sedgwick's Osho montage plays with both modernist medium specificity and postmodern intermediality. Her collage combines mulberry paper and silk, two differently textured and structured products of the silkworm. It offsets a comparative smoothness of material surface with raggedness of edge, and adhesion by invisible bonding, in the case of the photographs on the mulberry paper, with binding by stitching, in the case of the individual components of the composite photograph. The shadowy buckling of Warhol's sewn photographs also finds its correlative in Sedgwick's free-floating flag-like elements, and his *paragone* between sculpture and sewn photography matched by her comparison of the volumetric three-dimensionality of sculpture, within the photographs, and the layered, planar, epidermal *two-and-a-half-dimensionality* of her patchwork.

Finally, Sedgwick's sewn photographs, like Warhol's, similarly index "two distinctly different machines," the camera and the sewing machine, with Sedgwick juxtaposing their forms of repetitive, mechanical reproduction with the more chance-inflected, handcrafted elements of her montage, such as the surface of the water in the *suminagashi* swatches, and the impossible-to-replicate, individually ragged edges of her torn fibers.[35] As such, the exhibit further explores a *cybernetic* conceptual dimension that we have already encountered in her weaving, heterogeneously mixing, and constantly volleying between, "digitally structured [and] analogically structured representational mechanisms."[36]

Sitting, Centered

Sedgwick's final *thangka* contains four lines of unattributed uppercase text, perhaps in her own voice, in another column-like off-center block, toward the right:

> SITTING, CENTRED,
> PAYING ATTENTION AND
> TO FEEL IT: LITERALLY,
> SPINE DISINTEGRATING.

Sedgwick repeatedly capitalized the texts she quoted in her textiles, her uppercase font recalling the notes attributed to Shannon Van Wey, in *Dialogue*, especially in the first three lines, where it is easy to imagine the therapist's listening mien being described:

> Grave,
> never offering back the face of my emotion,
> only, the face of you listening,
> it sinking in,
> the violet in your thick cheeks.[37]

James Merrill's capital-letter-employing," disembodied spirit guide Ephraim, in *The Changing Light at Sandover* (1984), also comes to mind, the poem's séance-cusp of life and death appropriate to Sedgwick's spinal bardo.

Sedgwick prints her text on a swatch of ragged, fraying woven orange cloth. Either the dye on this swatch has differentially faded, due to its having been bleached in the light, or the dye in the bath failed to reach the right side, at the point of dipping, such that the color dissolves spectrally into, or chromatically

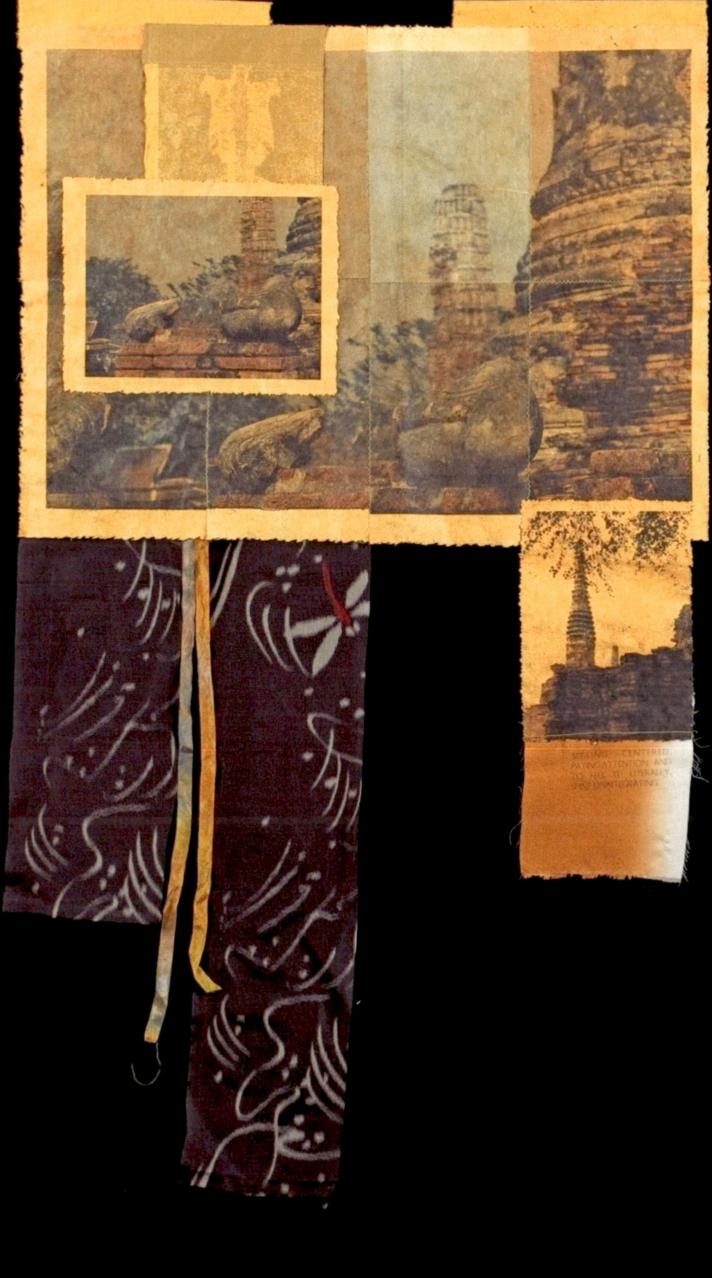

Figure 3.8. Eve Kosofsky Sedgwick, *Prayer Flag*, 1999. Photograph: Kevin Ryan. Collection of H. A. Sedgwick. © H. A. Sedgwick

radiates out from, a column of brilliant deathly white on the right; a polychrome, posthumous bardo to which we shall return.

Sedgwick patchworks her text together with various elements. Immediately above the quotation is a ragged mulberry paper photograph, in colonial picturesque mode, of a weathered brickwork Ayutthaya stupa, shot through the ink-spatter-like leaves of a tree, framed against the sky.[38] The stupa's ceramic courses again recall vertebrae, dissolving toward the top, but their longevity and ability to survive the ravages of the Burmese invasion and destruction of the site perhaps gave Sedgwick hope of her ongoing duration.

The mulberry paper on which the image is printed and the silk on which the text could be found were both fashioned, as we have seen, by *invertebrate*, backbone-free mulberry worms, perhaps reminding Sedgwick of the fiber-art creativity she might still manage as her spine dissolved. Indeed, if she had to renounce weaving because of the pressure on her spine, this did not stop her from fashioning *Floating Columns*. Sedgwick *back*stitches together the two swatches, the photograph and text combining to form a column of their own.

Immediately above this *unbacked*, ragged and frayed, stitched-together and comparatively resilient column of text and stupa, again light enough to flag in the breeze, is another, this time *backed*, eight-piece, white-herringbone-stitched composite photograph of the abandoned and plundered Ayutthaya Buddhas, to which the swatch containing the text is glued. Sedgwick's herringbone stitches here recall, reparatively, the eons-lasting fossilized spines of postmortem mammals. The composite photographs depict the most ravaged statue so far, comprising only the figure's remaining knees and upper calves, resting on a brick pedestal, set against a ruined landscape with trees and two spinal-column-like stupas framed against the sky.

Unlike the Warholian composite photographs Sedgwick employed in *Osho*, where she printed a single image across a multipart paper substrate, here the image is a more David Hockney–like photomontage, in which different photographs combine to make a single frame; a photomontage visible in the differing exposures across the images, especially the more bleached swatch second from the top right.[39]

The statues represent the "most mutilated example" with which to imagine the "beat-up" Buddha's "fully absorbing, rock-steady and inextricable full-lotus leg twist."[40] Indeed, while the smaller stupas in the background help viewers' attempts to imagine the Buddha's rock-solid backbone, in the absence of his trunk and spinal column, his two knees, separated into two different photographs, are so separate that spectators might read the one on the left as a breast, Sedgwick's separated right breast perhaps, after her mastectomy.

Contained within the photomontage is a closely related image, again backed by, and framed against, a piece of mulberry paper. This comprises a single unmontaged shot, playing off the resonant registers of the intact and the fragmented. Immediately above and behind it is a washed-out print of a bone scan of Sedgwick's trunk, with a prominent spinal column, colored red. In 1987 Warhol had produced, for a special issue of the German art journal *Parkett*, 120 signed, numbered copies of a composite image of four human skeletons, repeated four times in black-and-white prints joined by white thread. These memento mori photographs arrived at the journal's office the day after his death, having been mailed to Germany before he entered the hospital in which he died.[41]

In addition, Sedgwick's body scan recalls the moment in her narrative poem "Trace at 46" where she imagines dyes like the "luminous streak / of radium or barium the body gulps along / some unaccustomed channel" that will show up "on the X-ray."[42] The scan also evokes Sedgwick's reflections on paranoia and reparation, as we have seen, especially the paranoid fantasy/reality of one's transparency to others and the related, diagnostic hermeneutics of depth and detection, within a broader context of the reparative aesthetics of a laboriously, idiomatically pieced-together collage.[43] In addition, like the Venus de Milo, with its arms truncated similarly close to the shoulder, Sedgwick's body scan suggests the beautiful longevity she might have hoped for, through the parallel image of an ancient Greek sculpture extant two thousand years after its creation; a statue of a fragmented woman, like the mutilated Buddhas, implying the paradigmatic, long-durational *beauty* of partial forms. (We shall return to further mutilated classical sculptural forms.)

The final columnar component of the collage is suspended immediately below the photomontage. The lower column is bisected vertically into four elements, each made of kimono scraps. The two thinner, inner columns are more abstract and colorful and echo the leaf-green, brick-pink, and tangerine tonality of the photographs. The two kimono columns on the outside are more pictorial. They depict, in an aerial perspective, against a matte black background, marked with thin, columnar white calligraphic reeds, ribs, and dots of swirling water, a lone white-winged dragonfly, as it moves on a stream, with a red thorax, its color echoing the bone scan, with its similar white rib cage and red spinal column.

Like the Heart Sutra's meditations on the inextricability of form and emptiness, and W. B. Yeats's 1939 poem "Long-Legged Fly," which compares the long-lasting achievements, but brief lives, of Caesar and Michelangelo with the shorter life span but greater evolutionary longevity of the daddy-long-legs as a species, Sedgwick's final *thangka* invites us to fix our eyes "on nothing" as well as to contrast the different life spans, vulnerabilities, and metamorphoses of a dragonfly, a diseased human spine, and the "topless towers" of the Ayutthaya stupas in their "lonely place[s]."[44]

In so doing, the collage reminds us that if nothing lasts for long, nothing is entirely lost. Cities get abandoned to tourists and mice, Buddhas and stupas get vandalized, and bodies are transformed by tumors. But, like dragonflies, which represent the final, short-lived incarnations in a quite various tripartite life cycle, of egg, nymph, and fly, new, longer-lasting varieties of beauty and spiritual, aesthetic, and cultural opportunity emerge. Like Yeats's "long-legged fly upon the stream," Sedgwick's mind, at earlier moments concerned with masturbating "girls at puberty," here "move[d] upon silence."[45]

Metamorphic insect life also ongoingly preoccupied Marcel Proust's narrator, as we shall see, who compared his changing characteristics, and those of his family and friends, to a "metamorphosis more appropriate to an insect."[46] Indeed, in a passage suggesting the body's vulnerability to internal problems and anticipating the Dalai Lama on reincarnation as a series of dice, Proust declared that he had always considered every person he knew to be

> a sort of multiple organism or polyp, not only at a given moment of time—so that when a speck of dust passes it, the eye, an associated but independent organ, blinks without having received an order from the mind, and the intestine, like an embedded parasite, can fall victim to an infection without the mind knowing anything about it—but also, similarly, where the personality is concerned and its duration through life, I had thought of this as a sequence of juxtaposed but distinct "I"s which would die one after the other or even come to light alternately, like those which at Combray took one another's place within me when evening approached.

In addition, Proust pondered which "cells of . . . an individual" might prove "more durable than the individual himself."[47] Sedgwick would return to these images and ideas, as we shall see, in the case of her *Polyp*, in *Works in Fiber, Paper, and Proust*. But that is to get ahead of ourselves. First, we must conclude this chapter and then spend more time *In the Bardo*, the subject of Sedgwick's second public exhibition.

Following the disappointment of having to prematurely give up weaving, and ongoingly interested in the *cybernetic* interlacing of the digital and analog, camera and eye, sewing machine and sewing hand, Sedgwick returned to her earlier epidermal, *two-and-a-half-dimensional* patchwork practice, involving cast-off kimono swatches and mulberry paper, with new sophistication and passion. Thinking ongoingly about the miraculously *metamorphic* life cycles of silkworms and long-legged flies, increasingly conceptually engaged with Buddhism, and returning to its often difficult-to-gender Southeast Asian sculptural iconography, Sedgwick began to employ Buddhist quotations reparatively, as food for thought, rather than critically, and to engage with more figurative forms of queer iconography, especially those in which parts were missing, dissolving, or fusing, the relationship between parts and wholes complex, unfurling, and in which form and emptiness were fluxing, interpenetrating, rather than oppositional. In addition, Sedgwick continued to find inspiring a group of gay artists she profoundly admired: James Merrill, Andy Warhol, and David Hockney, among them, with whose help and in whose virtual company she was learning to *craft*, with increasing skill, resilience, pleasure, and interest, her life in the unpredictably elastic bardo between her metastatic diagnosis and eventual death.

4

IN THE BARDO (1999–2000), OR EPISTEMOLOGY OF A DIFFERENT CLOSET

"The Warm Decembers," or In the Bardo with Anthony Trollope and Henry Martin

Why is Eve Kosofsky Sedgwick's circa 1978–87 narrative poem "The Warm Decembers" so called? Is there more to be said about the poem's relation to Sidney Poitier's 1973 film, *A Warm December?* The film focuses on the triangular relationship between the widowed Matt Younger (Poitier); his daughter, Stephanie (Yvette Curtis); and Katherine (Esther Anderson), whom Younger falls in love with and who turns out to have sickle cell anemia. The warm December of the title alludes to the brief period the three share before Katherine's untimely death.

Sedgwick's poem, meanwhile, similarly focuses on the late life of Victorian novelist Anthony Trollope, who is age sixty-five when the poem occurs, with two years left to live. In 1880, when most of the plot happens, he is "old for that age," that is, old for the period and prematurely aged, even if he retains a "youthful envy" of Sedgwick's fictional character, the journal editor Cosmo Martin.[1] Readers hear much about Trollope's visibly weak right arm and asthma, a chronic condition I return to.[2] At the poem's first dinner, meanwhile, where everyone resembles a "shape from the studio or . . . cemetery," Trollope can barely stay awake, dropping off "like an infant." Later, writing to his real-life friend, the American journalist, lecturer, and actress Kate Field, he describes how

> the hour
> grows late, the old fowls gape into the farmyard,
> while yet the fabric of the light is durable—it seems.[3]

Within what Poitier's film and the poem would characterize as a warm December, Trollope is *in the bardo* of dying, the fabric of his life durable but beginning to split at the seams.

The Tibetan word *bardo* refers to a range of transitional states—between sleeping and waking, being diagnosed with an illness and dying, dying and returning to samsara, or dying and escaping to nirvana. The term derived from *The Tibetan Book of the Dead*, first translated into English in 1927 by W. Y. Evans-Wentz, in imitation of the popular *Egyptian Book of the Dead*; though it is part of a larger cycle of teachings associated with the Buddhist master Padmasambhava (or as Sedgwick playfully called him, *Pandasambhava*). At a less distant historical remove, the phrase *in the bardo* had been popularized in the United States by two then-recent best-selling translations: Sogyal Rinpoche's *The Tibetan Book of Living and Dying* (1992) and Robert A. F. Thurman's *The Tibetan Book of the Dead: Liberation Through Understanding the In Between* (1994).[4]

But Sedgwick's interest in the bardo had long preceded her encounter with Rinpoche's and Thurman's editions of the *Tibetan Book*. Chapter 5 of "The Warm Decembers" ponders the posthumous life of another fictional character, Henry Martin. Sedgwick's interest in Martin's bardo was partly inspired by her lifelong admiration for Merrill's long séance poem, *The Changing Light at Sandover*, and "Book of Ephraim" (1976) in particular, published shortly before she began work on "The Warm Decembers." Indeed, before commencing the poem, she had written an essay on Merrill, including "The Book of Ephraim," which she sent to the poet, who politely acknowledged its receipt.[5]

In Sedgwick's poem, the bardo of the immediate afterlife occurs in a dream in which readers learn that, according to Clare Lucas, Beatrix's mother, her father, Henry Martin, always treated his daughter badly because he desired her sexually; a love that upset his wife because it dislodged her from being the primary object of his affections. Claire informs Beatrix that her father's "dislike" of her continued posthumously; information she conveyed not "with satisfaction" or "maliciously," but because any feeling,

> any vestige of inclination
> in this dead man, especially of a
> feeling so opposite to the grain of nature
> meant that he was not spiritually
> *quite* dead. He was still real.[6]

Indeed, Claire felt at first that Henry's "being dead" was "just an intermission," that he was "waiting for her behind the scenes." But, as time passed, and he did not return, she held on to the idea that his "whiplash of hatred and love" for Beatrix might

> keep him a little
> longer from dispersing in that death-
> that-comes-just-after-death, when the spirit
> so far nearly intact, though fainter and
> subtly off, or subtly tendentious—struggles and gives way,
> losing its resemblance to the lost person
> and even the desire to resemble him,
> and is no longer even the spirit of one person
> but, suggestible and promiscuous, drifts apart,
> worn to the very atoms of the stuff of soul.[7]

Here is a bardo of the immediate afterlife, where individuals die more than once, first physically, before dispersing in that "death- / that-comes-just-after-death." At that point, the spirit, "so far nearly intact," becomes gradually "fainter," as it loses consciousness. The spirit then faints, fades, and dissolves further, becoming increasingly less like itself, "subtly off"-key, or only "subtly tendentious." Finally, it "gives way," as if at a junction to let another person have precedence, "losing its resemblance to the lost person," and, in this queer posthumous scene, "even the desire to resemble him." As a result, Henry's spirit becomes increasingly "suggestible and promiscuous," the diminishing desire to resemble himself coinciding with an increasing wish to resemble others, while his spirit gets variously re-membered in the idioms of the people who recall him.

Before leaving "The Warm Decembers," we must consider one final moment. In chapter 8, Sedgwick quotes Trollope's autobiography, in which he claims he was "flogged oftener than any other human being alive" and that, if it had been "possible to obtain five scourgings in one day" at Winchester, he often "obtained them all."[8] Although, looking back over half a century, he added,

with the doggedness
of the adult he made himself from the child
whipped far beyond the reach
of "perverse" transformation at any psychic
exorbitance, of pleasure to
himself, to his tormentors even

he was not sure whether the boast was true. Tacitly speculating on the origins of Trollope's fantasy tableau—one akin to her own—Sedgwick documented how, "left by his mother in the mother's place / his murderous father's bloated punching bag," Trollope was

even yet, loathly afterbirth, to learn somehow
in his excessive thirties
a possible desire, possible and infectious,
for stories in which bouncy rationalists
are let however briefly or tragically to receive,
to embody with a sibylline humility
and briskness, the afflatus of the Bureau
itself—postal inspector facing down
the postmark forgery! entails unwound!
solicitors who know solicitors
who know the law on heirlooms!—and clerks,
clerks by the score, into whose equivocal sails
may breathe or may not breathe the zephyrs of ambition,
competence, real engagement;
against a background where another
figure is let horrifyingly fail
in the common work of giving face
and shape to some want.

In this narrative "that paralyze[d] with self-reference," Sedgwick, though not "abused," feared a less successful outcome for herself.[9]

Much about these scenes resonates with Sedgwick's second exhibition, entitled *In the Bardo*. The body as a suspended punching bag or piñata. The way her mannequins recall bouncing babies. The fact that, suspended from nearly invisible cords, the figures, like equivocal sails, can again be moved by currents of air

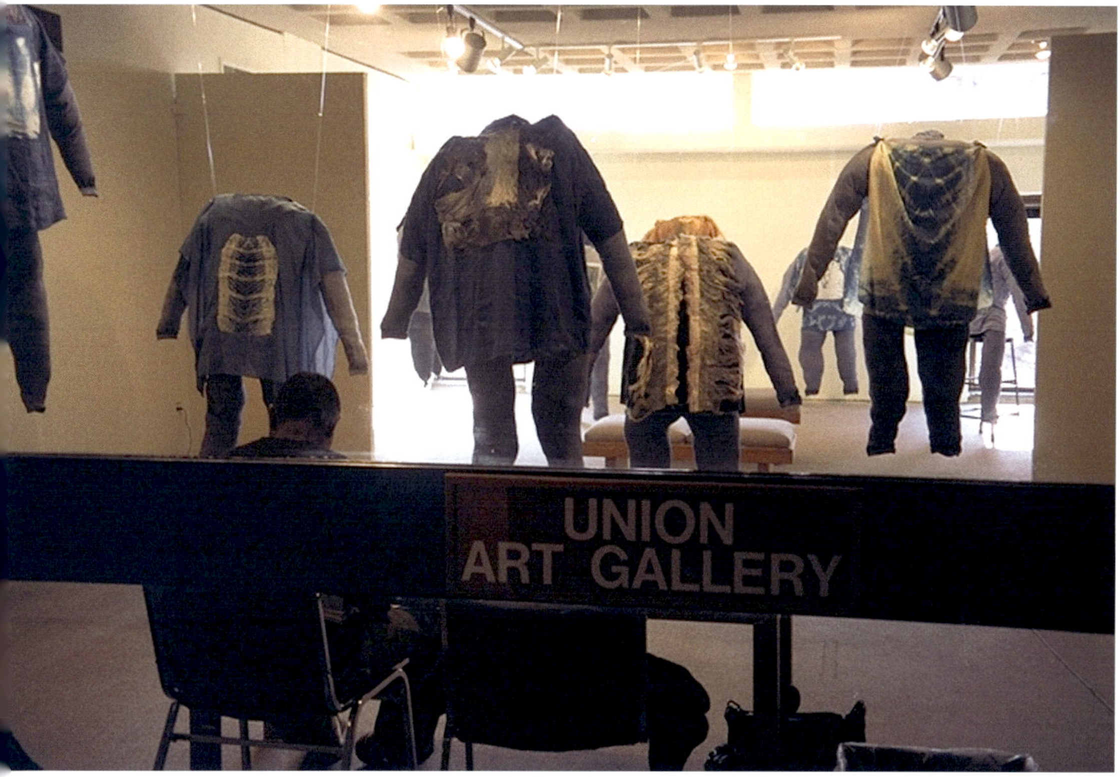

Figure 4.1. Eve Kosofsky Sedgwick, *In the Bardo* exhibition, 1999–2000. Photograph: H. A. Sedgwick. Collection of H. A. Sedgwick. © H. A. Sedgwick

or visitors. The image of a posthumous body as a not-fully-human "loathly afterbirth," a fleshy by-product to be consumed or discarded. But also, an image of a once abused child that will not, ultimately, be defeated as an adult. Instead, in its excessive thirties, or, in Sedgwick's case, mid-forties, the child who was once beaten discovers a queer (and HIV-marked) "possible desire, possible and infectious." In Trollope's case, this was for stories where "bouncy rationalists" receive "briefly or tragically" a lightness and "afflatus." In Sedgwick's, this resulted in a related passion for bouncy, equally light, suspended forms that embodied her own figure. These could be set, like Trollope's characters, in motion by the inspiration of a spectator with real "ambition, / competence," or engagement, as I shall now show. Or be let drop, fading into a "background" where other figures are "let horrifyingly fail / in the common work of giving," if not quite face, since Sedgwick's figures are decapitated, then "shape to some want."[10]

In the Bardo at SUNY and CUNY

In the Bardo opened at SUNY Stonybrook in the fall of 1999 before transferring that winter to the CUNY Graduate Center, where Sedgwick was by then teaching, and where the show was briefly reviewed by her then student, Maggie Nelson.[11] The exhibition featured, as we have begun to see, numerous Sedgwick-scaled soft, stuffed mannequins suspended from the ceiling on wire, recalling the elements in *Floating Columns* that billowed in the breeze, as a sign of their Proustian asthma-like sensitivity to barometric conditions, as well as resembling piñatas that could be knocked off-center by people passing through the installation.

Sedgwick's mannequins did not just register their vulnerability to the outside world of the environment and other people. They suggested their internal precarity. Hung on invisible wire, they recall line-caught fish fatally out of their elements; an iconography central to Sedgwick's favorite bodhisattva, Kuanyin. Shantideva's influential *Guide to the Bodhisattva's Way of Life* (ca. 700) compared the early moments of enlightenment to realizing you were "like a captive fish" in your own karma, in a world in which "nowhere has the killing / of fish and other creatures been eradicated."[12] Martin Palmer and Jay Ramsey's *The Kuan Yin Chronicles: The Myths and Prophecies of the Chinese Goddess of Compassion* (with Man-Ho Kwok; 2009) more optimistically compares fate to a fish who "swims in muddied jade green water / Surrounded on all sides by a trawler net" who "thinks that if [s]he wriggles, [s]he can escape—/ And fate says yes, OK; and equally, no: no way."[13]

Sedgwick's mannequins each lacked heads, hands, and feet, recalling Osho's encouragement to imagine you don't have a head; and evoking an artist who had lost a breast, whose spine was dissolving, and who, in this period, often thought about the Buddhist doctrine of the *aggregates*. This was the idea that the human mind was an assemblage, comprising five aggregates, or *skandas* in Sanskrit (where it translates, roughly, as "heaps" or "piles"): "form, feelings, perceptions, impulses, and consciousness." In addition, Seung Sahn discusses the Eight Consciousnesses: seeing, hearing, smelling, tasting, touching, thinking, the discriminating consciousness, and memory; as well as the Eightfold Path of the right view, livelihood, thought, effort, speech, mindfulness, action, and meditation. And, as Sahn elsewhere notes, "when you wake up in the morning, your body is somewhat different from the body you had the night before," having undergone "extremely subtle changes," and "every seven years you have an entirely new body."[14]

This was a view shared by Thurman, in a text Sedgwick again pondered, which described the body as an "aggregate-conglomerate" imagined simultaneously and sequentially as comprising "many different parts," none of which was identical with "the 'person,'" and some of which were more integral than others. Thurman questions whether the self is "truly the same as or truly different from" a person's hand, foot, breast, head, mind, body, or tumor, as part of a larger conceptual "analysis of unity and multiplicity of parts and wholes" that Sedgwick repeatedly explored across her patchwork, as we have seen. Indeed, Thurman wondered whether a person could be said to be "substantially different" from their "feet and hands," two of the parts missing in Sedgwick's figures. He also notes that when an "ordinary person hurts his hand, he says and thinks 'I am hurt!' Hence there is no substantial difference between the two," but, Thurman simultaneously argues, within the Buddhist logic of noncontradiction, "the hurt hand is not a person."[15]

Taken together, Sedgwick's mannequins make prominent, by their absence, the figures' hands, feet, and heads, making emptiness form and form emptiness in a similar way to the Ayutthaya buddhas. Her textile details also pick out other anatomical elements, including her skull, spinal column, ribs, upper arms, breasts, lungs, heart, navel, and coccyx, as we shall see, as well as various highly irregular, apparently multiplying, cancer-cell-like forms, which proliferate across numerous pieces. Sedgwick fabricated these through the *plangi shibori* technique, in which a piece of fabric was crumpled and tied tightly, leaving a hood of untied fabric at the top, before being dyed, resulting in an off-circular, shell-like shape, hollow in the middle.

Sedgwick's mannequins were dressed in indigo sweatpants and long-sleeved, pale-violet T-shirts, giving the show a characteristic immersive *blueprint* feel, suggesting both a sketch of something coming into being and a record of something lost. The mannequins also wore various other costume items of Sedgwick's making, on the "permeable boundaries" of "craft and art," "woven fiber (cloth) and nonwoven (paper, felt, *soie mariée*)," and "making and unmaking."[16] For example, Sedgwick accessorized one of the mannequins with a couple of the kimono collages we earlier discussed; the first evidence of her evocatively *reincarnating* elements of her earlier work. The fabric swatches are two of the few *surviving* elements from the show in Sedgwick's archive.

Sedgwick's exhibition title derived from the Tibetan word *bardo*, with *bar* translating as "in between" and *do* meaning "suspended" or "thrown." Sedgwick had long been interested in ideas of the "between," as the title of *Between Men* indicates, while spectators were allowed to walk between Sedgwick's hanging, movable figures, as Nelson reveals, throwing them quietly off balance.

In her circa 2003 "Pedagogy of Buddhism" essay, Sedgwick described the impact Rinpoche's translation of *The Tibetan Book of the Dead* had on her, as the first Buddhist text she seriously pondered. In addition, she documented, the

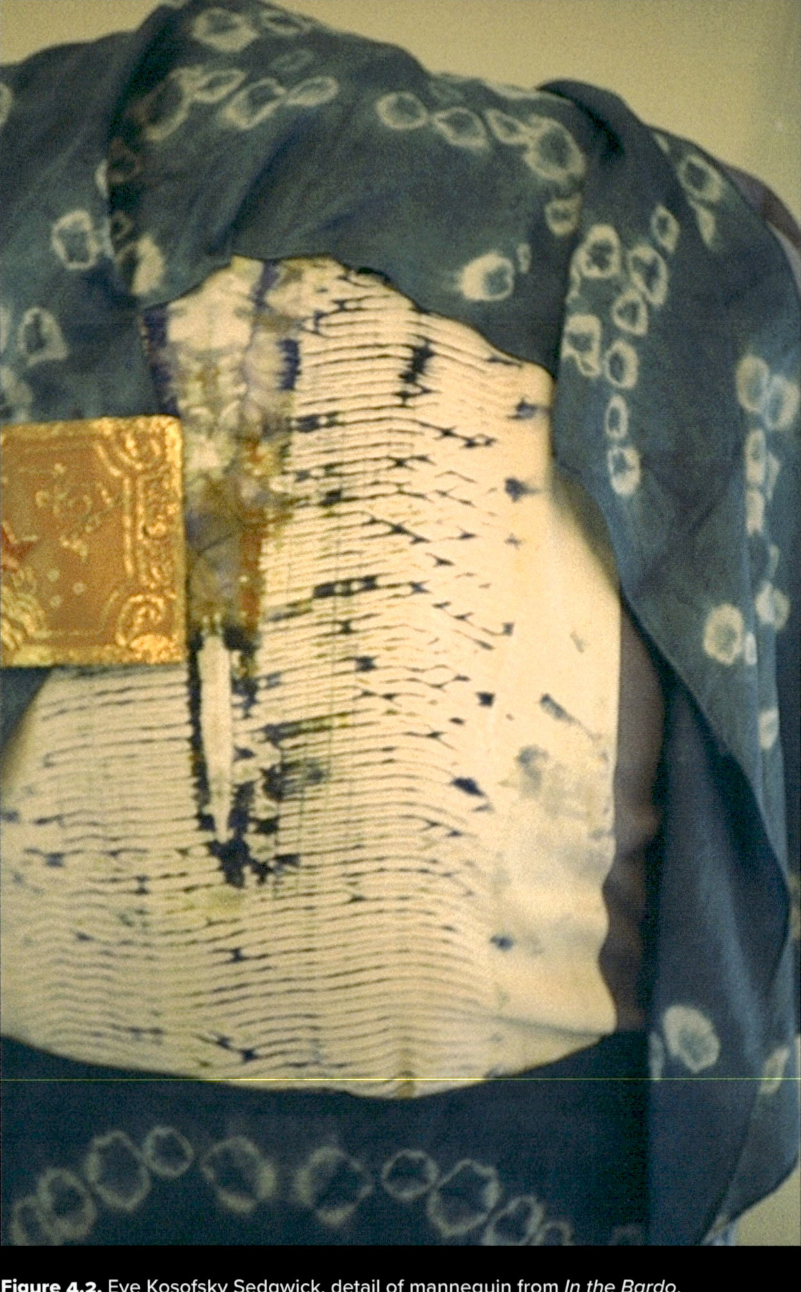

Figure 4.2. Eve Kosofsky Sedgwick, detail of mannequin from *In the Bardo*, 1999–2000. Photograph: H. A. Sedgwick. Collection of H. A. Sedgwick.

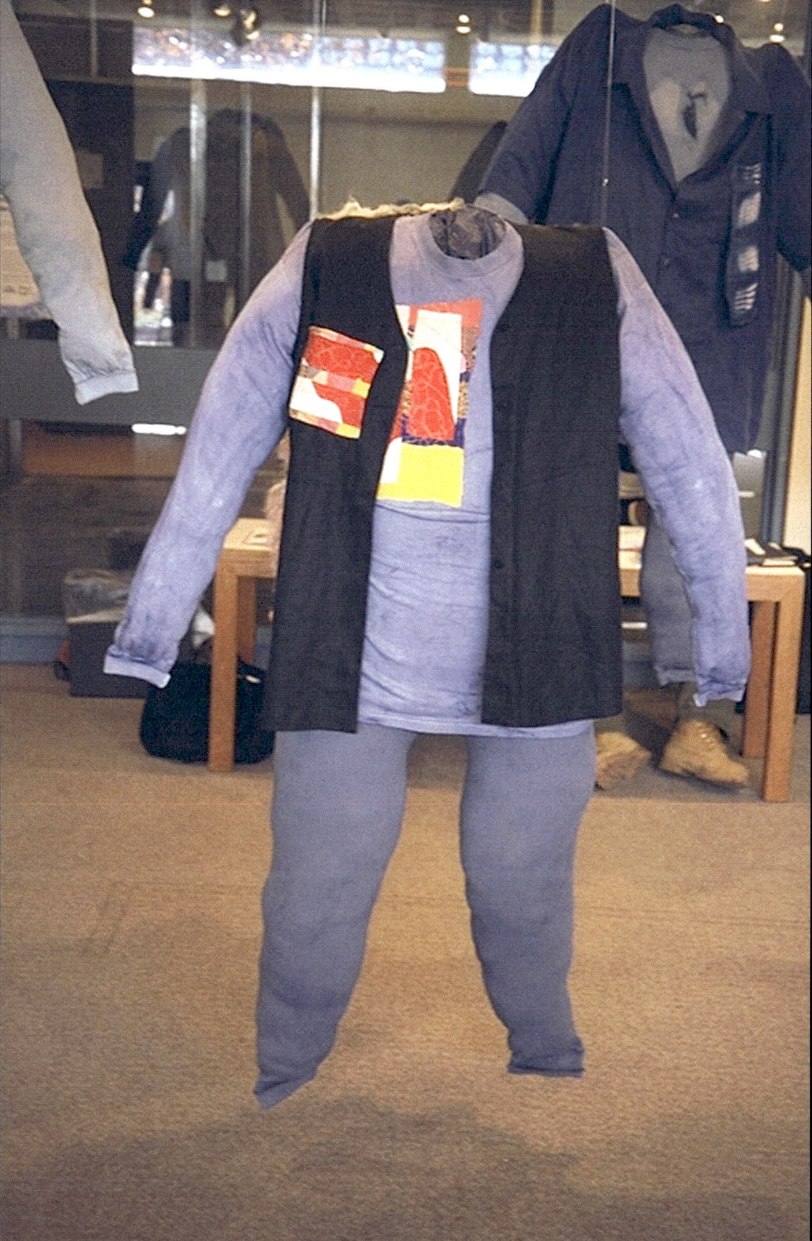

Figure 4.3. Eve Kosofsky Sedgwick, mannequin from *In the Bardo*, 1999–2000. Photograph: H. A. Sedgwick. Collection of H. A. Sedgwick. © H. A. Sedgwick

Tibetan Book was probably the text that most "structure[d her] involvement" with Buddhism.[17]

Constructed as an "extended gloss" on the *Tibetan Book*, Rinpoche's volume offered a "beginner's introduction to Tibetan Buddhism" as well as a self-help "manual for life and death." Sedgwick suggested that the book might prove useful to those suffering from cancer, like herself, or HIV/AIDS, like many of her friends; illnesses that were "gradual and so far incurable," whose subjects were living unpredictably, but ultimately fatally, in "the bardo that extends from diagnosis until death"; a bardo "likely to be experienced differently" because of each individual's relation to the "idea of dying."[18]

As Sedgwick noted, following a rather Zen start, the American account of the bardo, and of the "severe cultural and ontological dislocations of the journey," had grown "exponentially more detailed and expansive" through various anglophone translations.[19] In these, there was an increasing focus on "opening to," "opening around," or "softening around" the experience of the bardo between diagnosis and dying, at least among those living with incurable disease. Sedgwick evoked this opening in the way her soft figures seem to be open to the outside world at their cuffs, ankles, and collars, because of their lack of extremities, although, with Rinpoche's accounts of the phobic treatment and depersonalization of those living with cancer and AIDS in their minds, spectators might read the mannequins' lack of extremities as signs of their "untouchable" status in the surrounding phobic culture.[20]

In addition, Sedgwick suggested, the various Buddhist texts concerned with the bardo of dying emphasized a "non-doing verging on extinction," evoked by her figures floating in space, and the lack of heads—the seat of motivation—as well as hands and feet, where purposes could be put into action. Certainly, her figures have lost their "mobility, speech, sight," a "hand to grasp" and the "feature[s] of a face," to recall a circa 1993 poem by Sedgwick about her mastectomy. As far as viewers can tell, each figure's bowel, the source of so much pleasure for Sedgwick, remained intact.

Given their lack of obvious, visible primary and secondary sexual characteristics, the mannequins may also seem also to be missing a "genital"; although Sedgwick's "thought and hope" might again have been that the mannequins did not need to be "shaped or perceived through the eyes of gender at all—not male, not female, not both male and female, and not neither male nor female."[21]

But if spectators were to gender the figures, the red patch of Tibetan-monk robe silk covering one of their right breasts, juxtaposed with the predominantly red kimono collage marking the same bodily zone on an adjacent figure, suggests that the mannequins have lost a breast. In addition, two other figures have

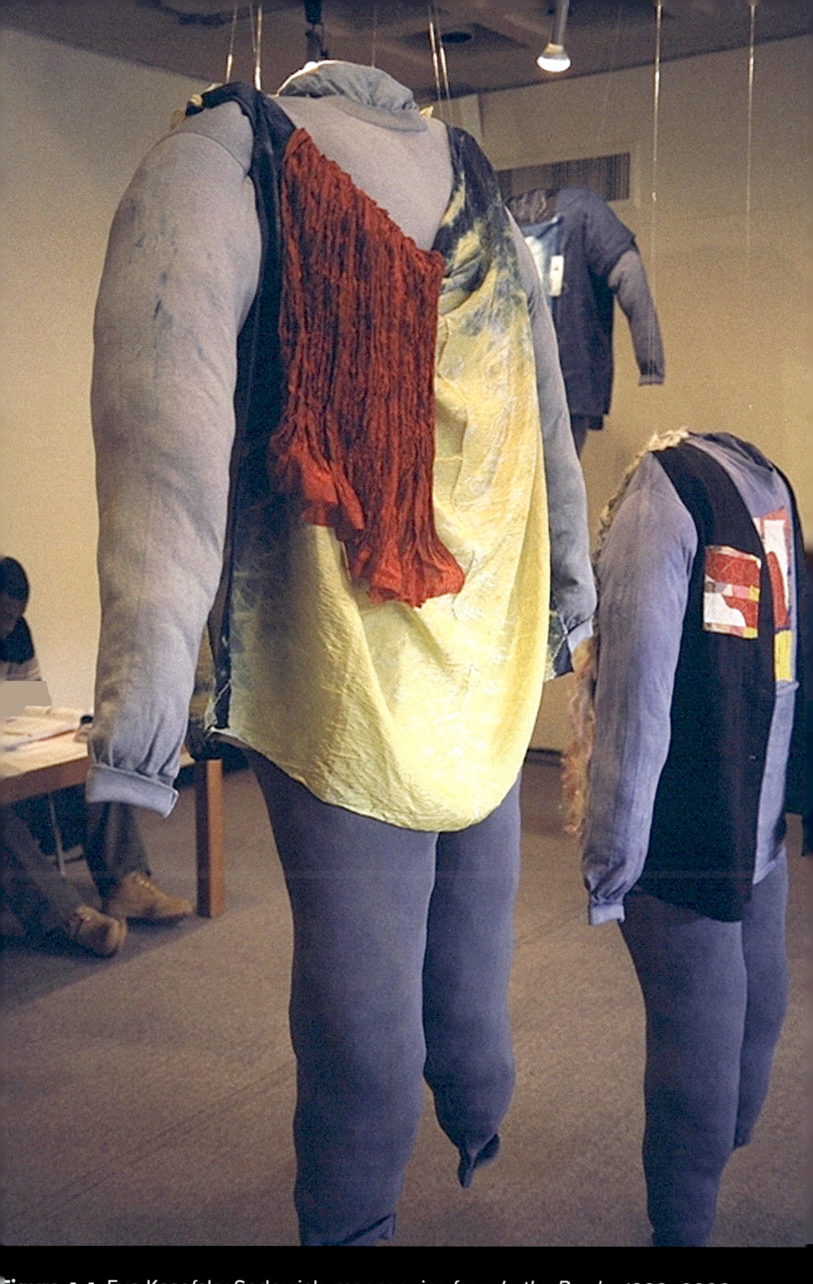

Figure 4.4. Eve Kosofsky Sedgwick, mannequins from *In the Bardo*, 1999–2000. Photograph: H. A. Sedgwick. Collection of H. A. Sedgwick. © H. A. Sedgwick.

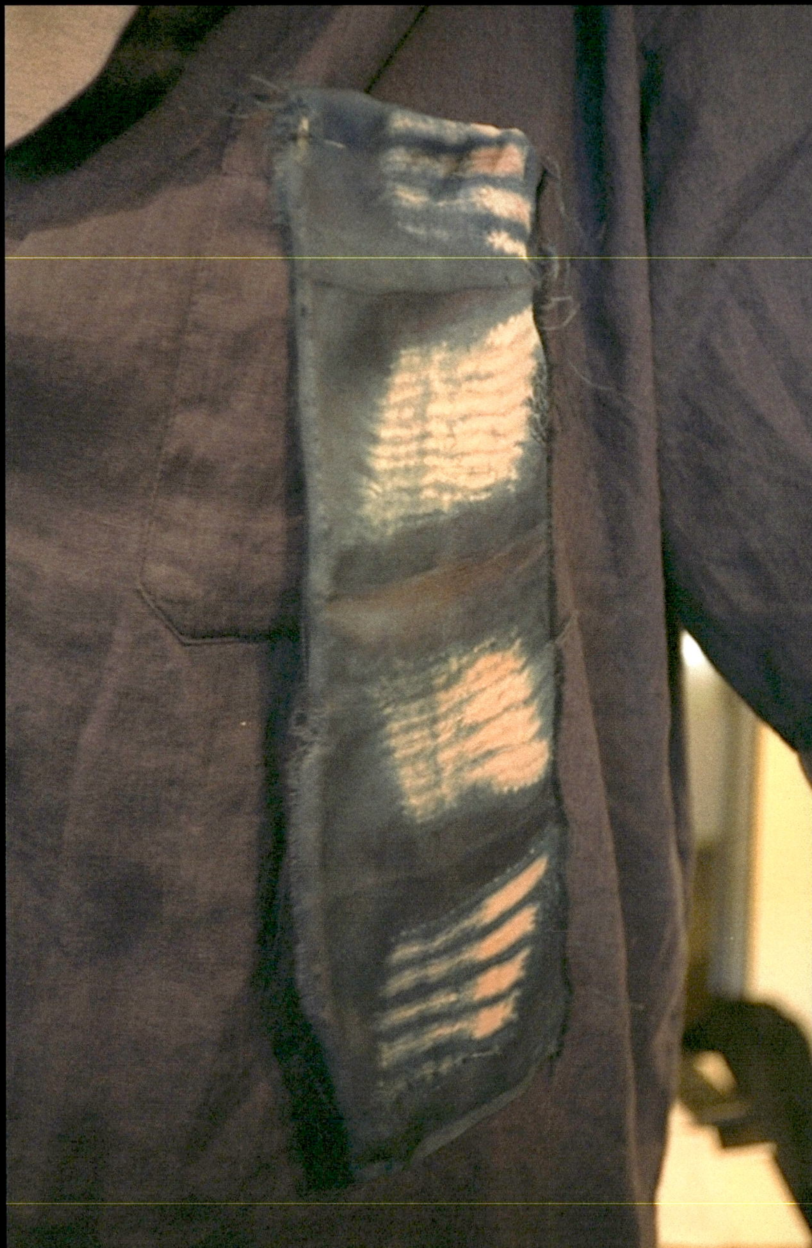

Figure 4.5. Eve Kosofsky Sedgwick, detail of mannequin from *In the Bardo*, 1999–2000. Photograph: H. A. Sedgwick. Collection of H. A. Sedgwick.

square patches on their chests, containing what may be abstracted mammogram images at breast height.[22]

In her roughly contemporaneous "Pedagogy of Buddhism" essay, Sedgwick argued that Buddhist commentators widely discussed the "pedagogy of illness and dying" around the sickbed, deathbed, and elsewhere. This included overlapping opportunities to practice *relationality*, evoked in the exhibition by the numerous closely juxtaposed and differently oriented figures; *emptiness*, signaled by the headless spaces where a consciousness might be; and "being and learning to unbe," alluded to by how Sedgwick's mannequins seem as close to birth as death, given their resemblance to toddlers bobbing up and down in a *trotte bebe*.[23]

According to Sedgwick, from a pedagogical point of view, the bardo teachings were "irrepressibly rich," and the "framework of rebirth" cast the "single human life in the context of a much longer, very complex learning project," spanning potentially millennia, and thousands of reincarnations. In this tradition, each incarnation, and there are numerous versions of Sedgwick in the exhibition, resembled a "vagrant placeholder" more than a "specimen to be immobilized." The exhibited figures' similarity, but not identity, and flexible, suggestible mobility seem evocative in this context.

In the essay, Sedgwick noted how comforting she found thinking about the "companionable space in the imaginable, tutelary difference of a being whom the present I will never know, and who in turn never need wonder about the thread of hope spun somehow into its own, characteristic courage"; a helpful, hopeful thread of connection between lives signaled in the wires connecting Sedgwick's figures to the ceiling within their overall "companionable space."[24] Having explored Sedgwick's first published accounts of the bardo in this section of the chapter, in the next I return to the exhibition in Thurman's virtual company.

A Companionable Space: In the Bardo with Robert Thurman

At the heart of the bardo, as the Dalai Lama noted in his foreword to Thurman's *Tibetan Book*, was "understanding the in-between." As such, the word *bardo* encourages spectators to pay equal attention to the difficult-to-visualize-and-conceptualize spaces *around* Sedgwick's figures as to the mannequins. This may evoke a nothingness that Thurman characterized as "categorically unimaginable" but is a space that Sedgwick's figures seem to be evaporating into, or precipitating from.[25] In addition, Thurman notes that one of the ambitions for the bardo states was to be "*held apart* from suffering; not *held* in anything, but *held out* of binding patterns"; a holding pattern Sedgwick's suspended mannequins embody as they are floated away from the artificial architectural limits of the walls, ground, and ceiling; and a holding they resist, given their dangling, slack arms, without hands.[26]

While Sedgwick's multifigure installation responds to the "multi-life perspective" of Thurman's *Tibetan Book*, and signals the variations within individuality across a lifetime and between lifetimes, their pale indigo and violet outfits express a preoccupation with this life, given what he characterizes as the "soft blue light of the human realms." In addition, Sedgwick's figures allude to what Thurman characterizes as the frequently impersonal "relationality of . . . death," given their facelessness; and evoke, in their suspension between ground and air, what he describes as our "habitual state of deep sleep," our *falling* asleep as a "relaxing into a ground state," as well as the unmindful present tense as a "lost moment of awareness slipping away," if spectators imagine Sedgwick's figures are floating up.[27]

Alternatively, viewers might think about the floating, enlightened mannequins, out of contact with the frictive ground, as embodying an "aloof state of peace, a restful separation from troubles, worries, pains, and entanglements"; a lack of entanglements emphasized by the individual wires holding each figure. But with Thurman in mind, spectators might consider *In the Bardo* as a kind of three-dimensional mandala, especially since he insists that it is "mandatory" to consult works of art containing multiple Buddha deities, whom it is "difficult to visualize" from "verbal, linear descriptions."[28]

As a result, Sedgwick's figures may represent not just her mortal selves, within or between lives, but the numerous powerful "divine Beings" in the Buddhaverse, who "can help us if we are prepared to accept their help" in the bardo of the afterlife. Indeed, Thurman notes, there was a potentially infinite number of beings of all species "dying and traversing the between all the time." If so, then Sedgwick's "between-being[s]" might represent *pretans*, or hungry ghosts, "living beings caught in realms of extreme frustration" given their sizable bodies and inability to feed themselves because of their lack of extremities and a head; an unusually thin art.[29]

Or the exhibition might be closer to the heavenly Pure Lands in which "there is no need to eat or excrete," since such beings have "angelic bodies" and are, like Sedgwick's, "without sexual differentiation." Alternatively, the multiple Sedgwick-scaled figures may represent karmic inertia, the weight of the "preceding" "fleshy body" of her "previous life with its habitual instincts." Her figures' lightness, however, might signal an early postmortem awareness that she is now "free from embodiment" and lacks a "solid body"; the invisible supporting fishing lines are the "cord of compassion" that is only cut if Sedgwick "surrender[s] to distraction."[30]

Then again, Sedgwick's mannequins could be closer to nirvana, given their susceptibility to the currents of air, and if nirvana "literally means 'extinguished,' 'blown out,' or 'gone out'"; especially if Sedgwick's bouncing baby figures have cultivated, as Thurman recommends, "going back into your infant memories of tender cuddling affection and diffusing that toward all beings." After all, if the "mental continuum of a person in the ordinary lifetime is like a huge trunk that cannot be moved by a hundred men; when it is in the between, it is as if floated in water" and, like Sedgwick's figures, "can be brought where you wish in an instant." Indeed, as in the bardo, the mannequins are likely to ghost the viewer's projections and preoccupations. When we encounter such apparitions in the bardo we should not "fear them," "hate them," or "be terrified," Thurman counsels, but instead "recognize them as an image" of "our own awareness."[31]

Sedgwick read widely across Thurman's corpus, and other moments in his writings develop our understanding of the exhibition. Viewers might notice the way her figures resemble butterfly pupae suspended in cocoons, particularly given her predilection for silk work and interest in metamorphic insect life, as we have seen. If so, the exhibition chimes with Thurman's belief that the "transcendent noumenon of Nirvana," once experienced, would reduce the "everyday world to a mere cocoon to be escaped." Indeed, one of the folded *shibori* paper patterns Sedgwick employs recalls the bilateral symmetry of the open wings of a moth, a creature who can both make and devour silk, as we have seen, while another, more ominously, alludes specifically to the death's-head hawk moth.

Alternatively, by thinking about Thurman's comparison of Buddhist enlightenment to Ludwig Wittgenstein's desire that his philosophy would "show the fly the way out of the fly bottle," spectators might embark on a darker reading of Sedgwick's suspended, nearly weightless figures, now recalling the remains of insects, hollowed out by voracious spiders, and hung suspended in their webs, just as her spine was dissolving inside her.[32] This arachnid reading is given credence by Sedgwick's silk work and by the yellow-and-blue *shibori* pattern on one of the mannequin's cloaks, which resembles a web, illuminated in the sunlight against a blue sky.

It is further supported by the differently weblike fused silk waistcoat worn by an adjacent figure, and by the sticky translucent silk cape worn by a further mannequin, with a close relationship to an earlier patchwork we have already encountered from the *Floating Columns* exhibition, another of Sedgwick's formal and material reincarnations.

Sedgwick alludes to her spinal difficulties, meanwhile, in several bilaterally folded indigo-and-blue paper *shibori* pieces, attached to the figures down the axis of where her spinal column was. The interaction between the white and

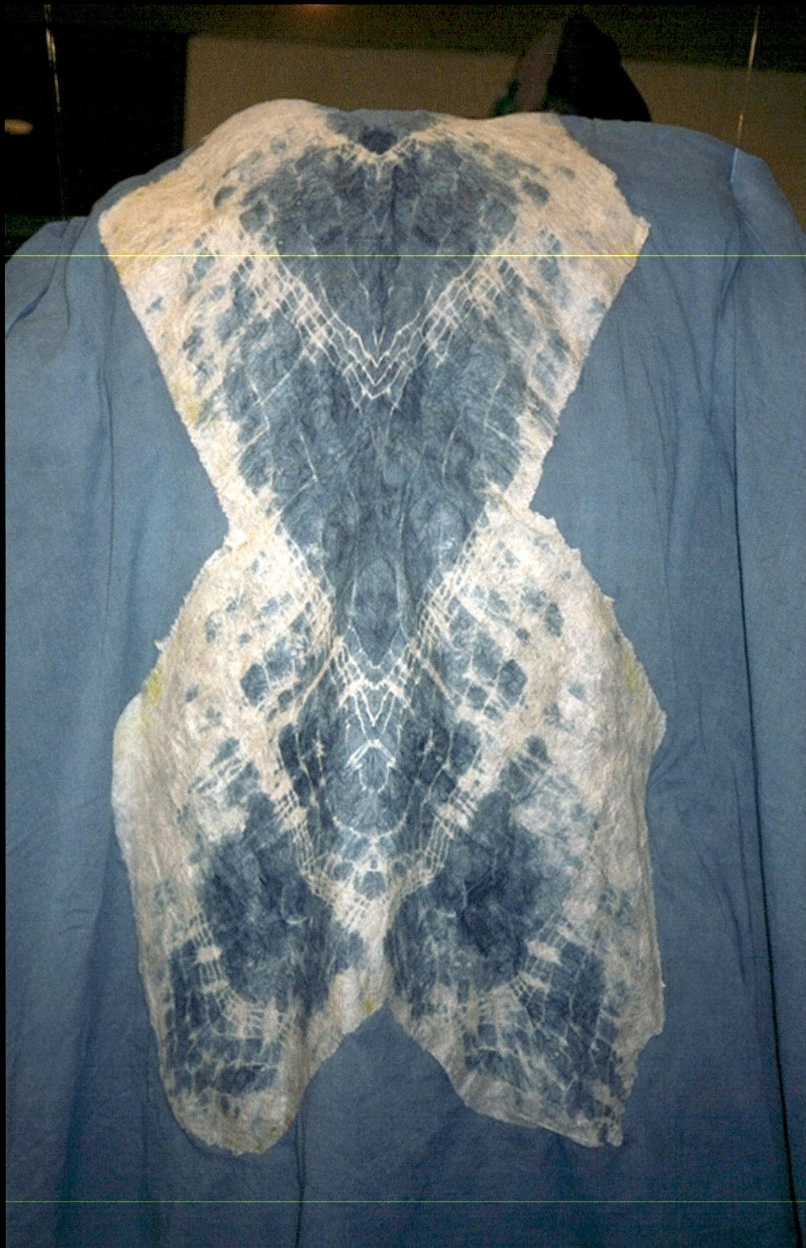

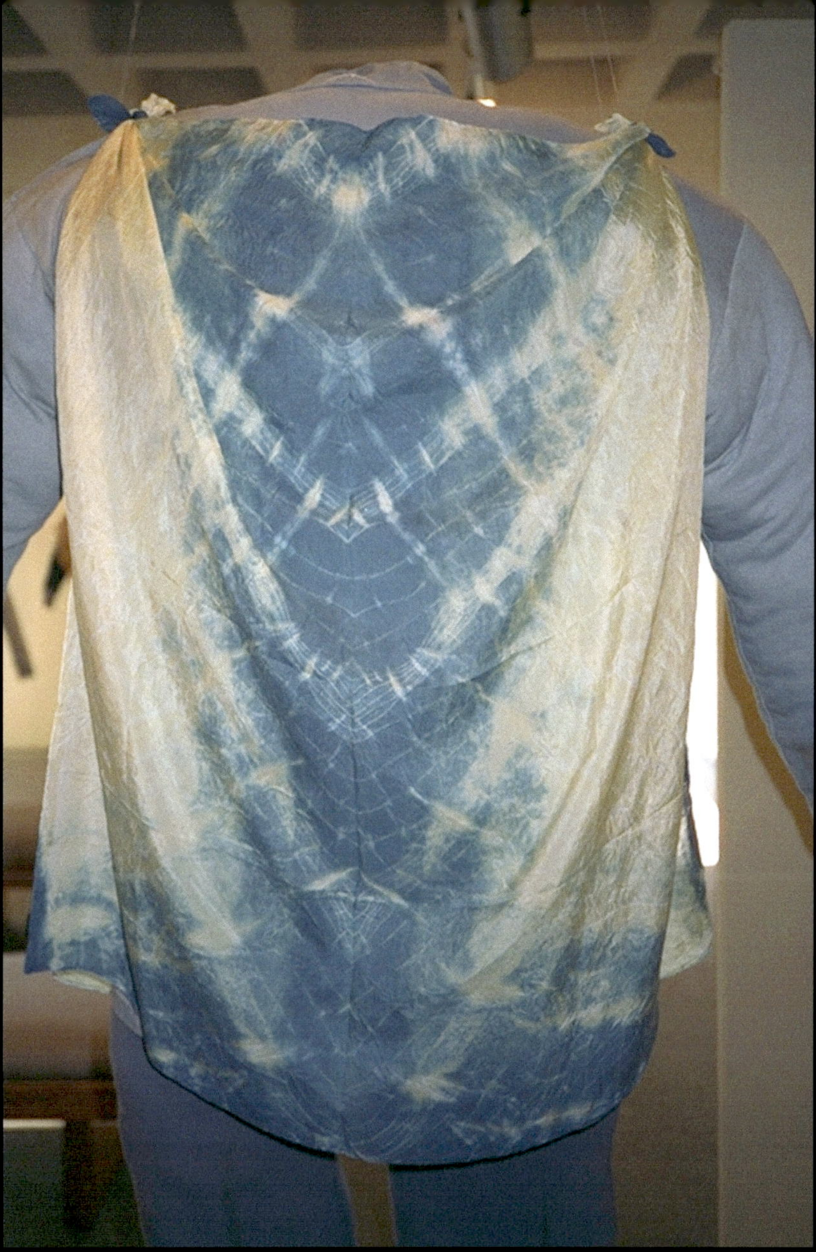

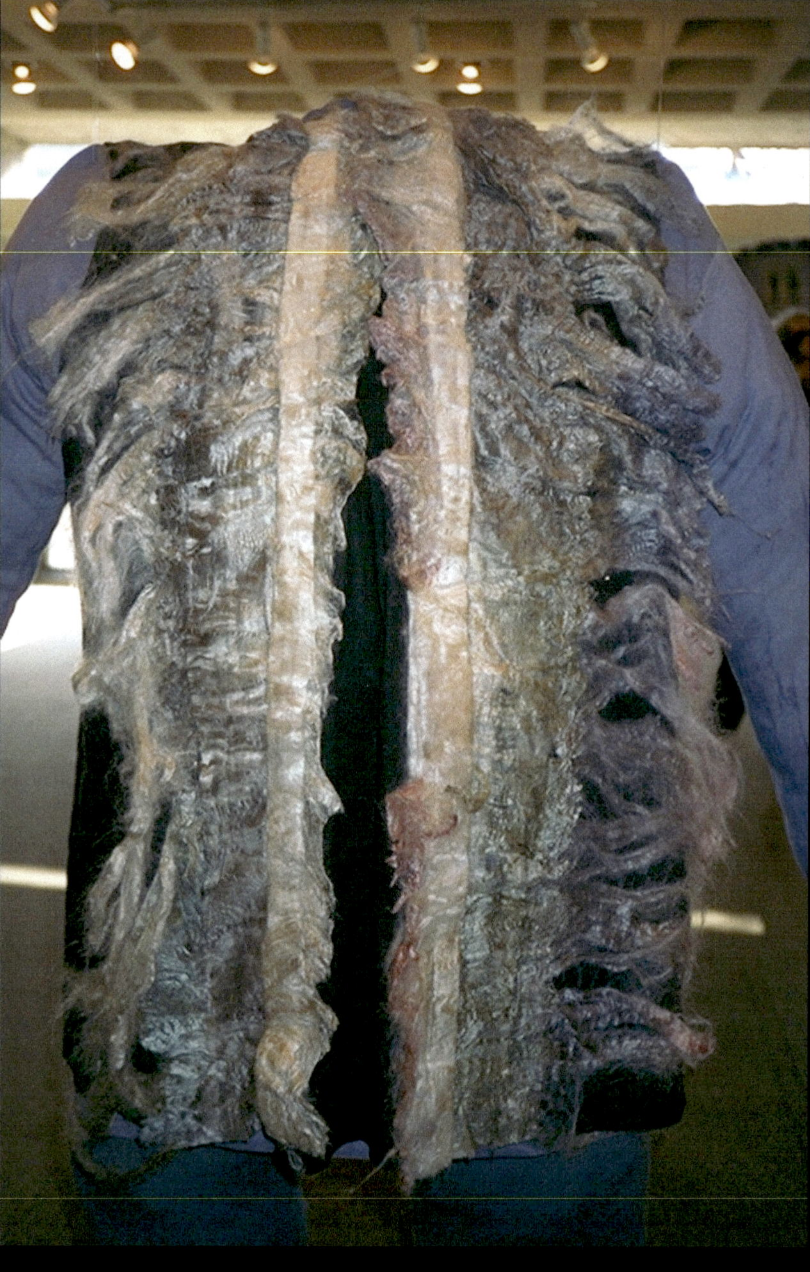

Figures 4.8 and 4.9. Eve Kosofsky Sedgwick, details of mannequins from *In the Bardo*, 1999–2000. Photograph: H. A. Sedgwick. Collection of H. A. Sedgwick.

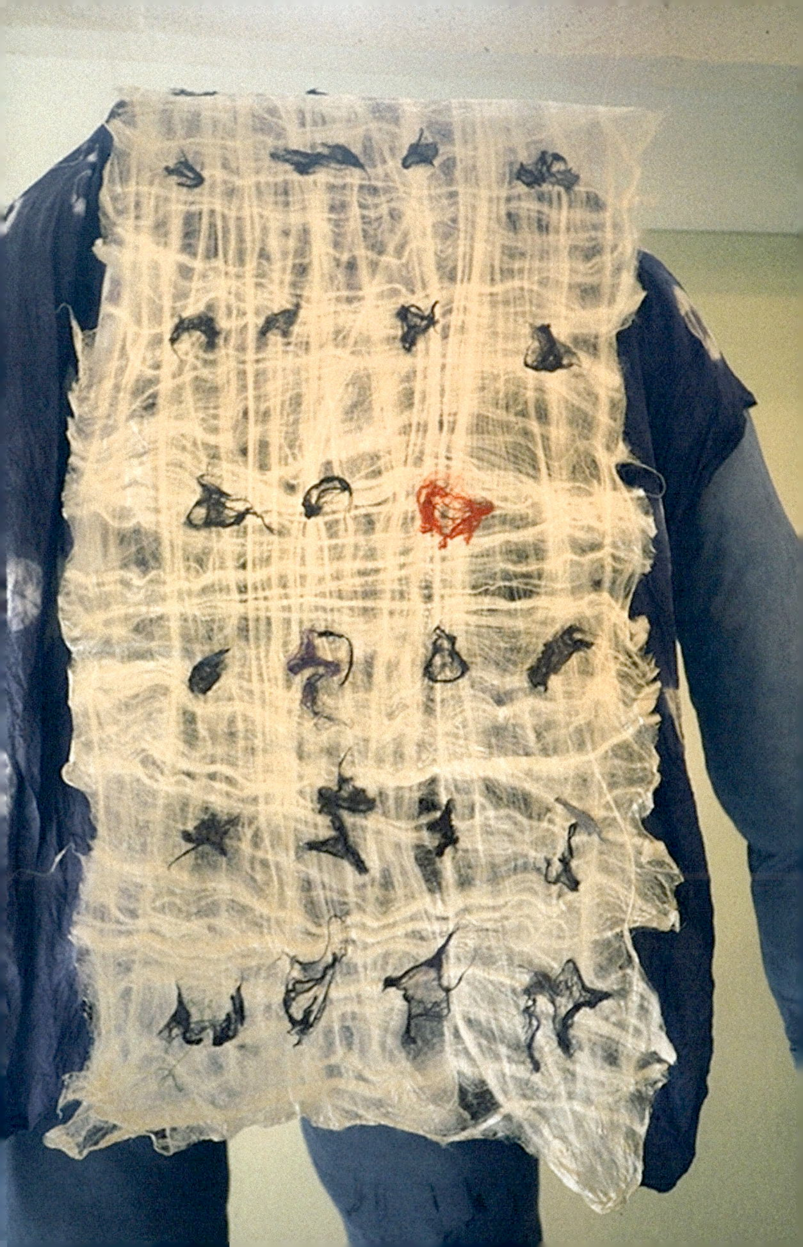

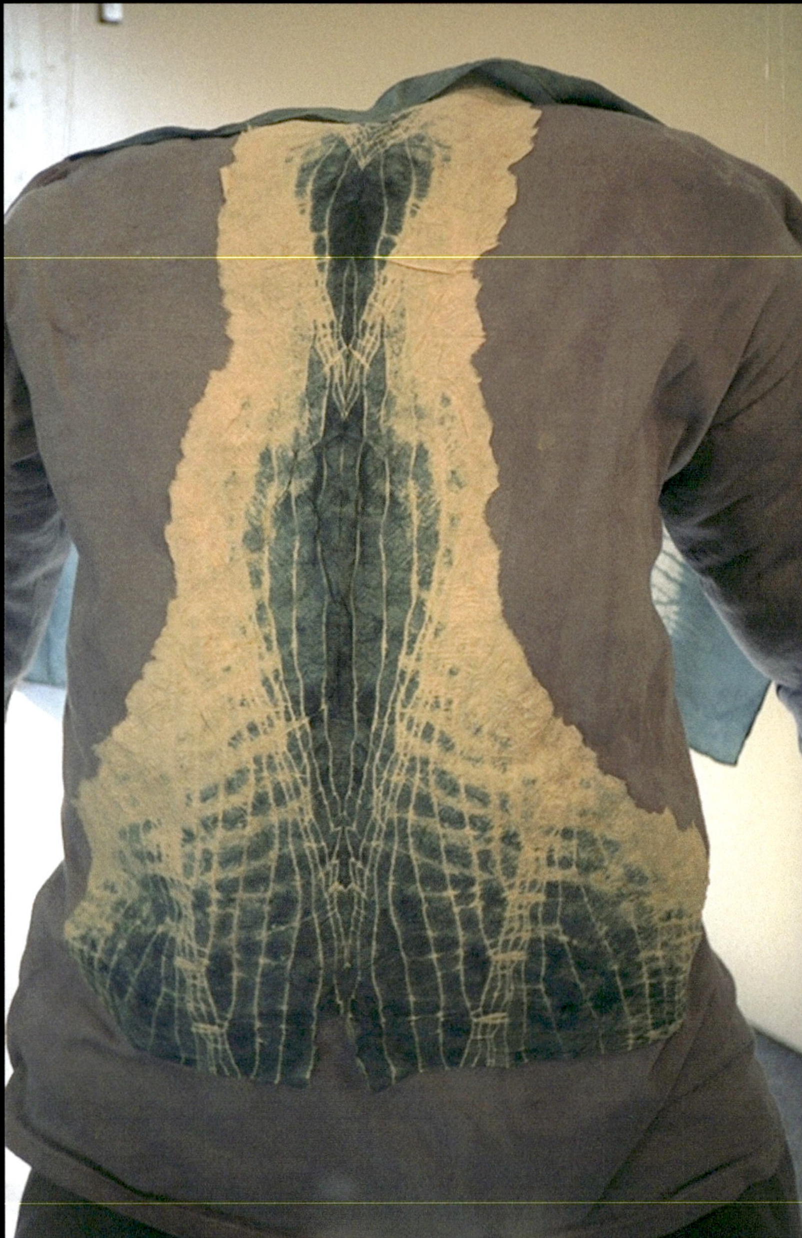

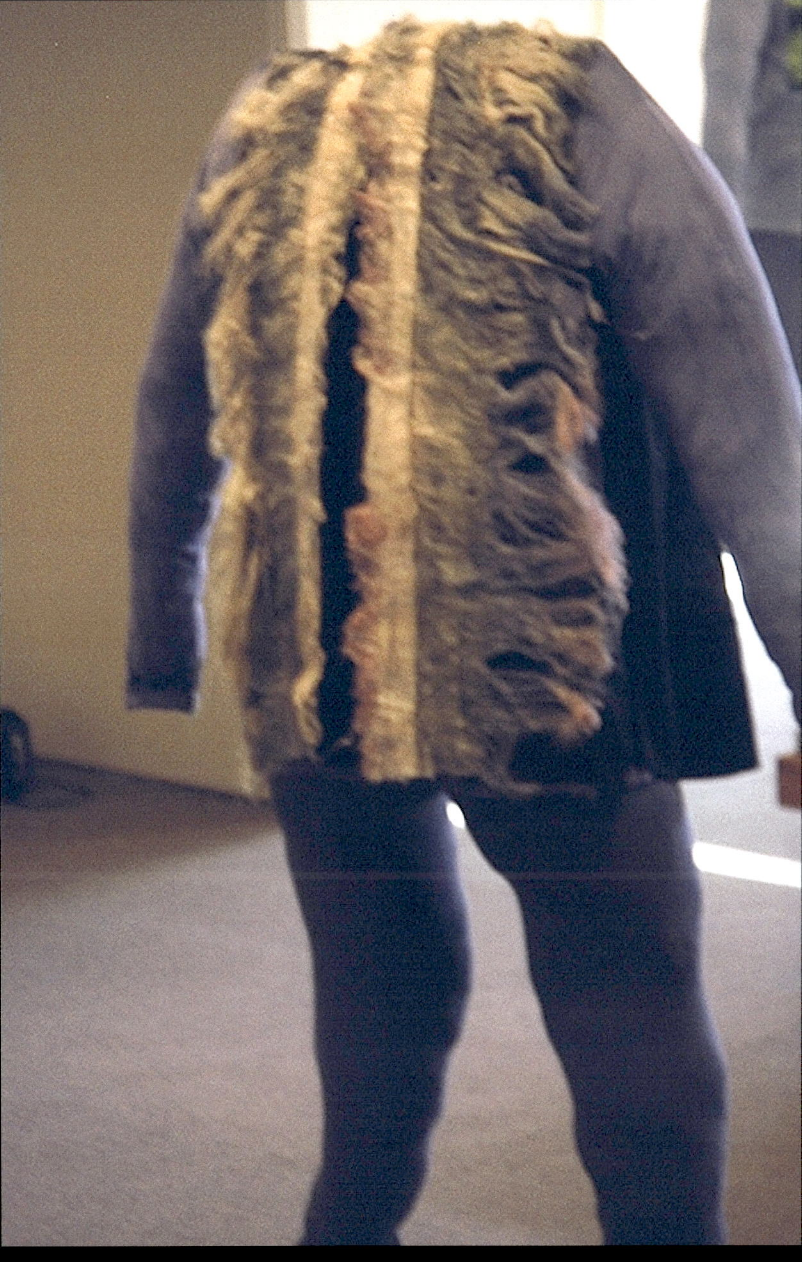

Figure 4.11. Eve Kosofsky Sedgwick, mannequin from *In the Bardo*, 1999–2000. Photograph: H. A. Sedgwick. Collection of H. A. Sedgwick. © H. A. Sedgwick

blue elements, with the white predominating on the outside, suggests the relationship between bone and central nervous system. It also recalls the ideal Buddhist emptiness of a blue sky, and a melting snowy spinal column hollowing out and filling with glacial blue water, an idea suggesting metamorphosis on a geological scale to match the more local metastasis happening in Sedgwick's body. In this piece, the top patch of blue also reads as a love heart, suggesting the extent to which she *lovingly* embraced her unwilled metamorphosis as an aesthetic, relational, cognitive, and spiritual opportunity.

In addition, the back of another figure, wearing a deep-indigo waistcoat, is covered with some more or less translucent colored fused silk, divided down the middle, revealing a void where the spine should be. These elements should come as no surprise since Sedgwick singled out, in her artist's screed, the "vertebral column" as a "central element" of each figure, in response to her "daily experience" of her spine "physically disintegrating, yet still offering a pathway for vital energy and buoyancy," as part of her broader sense of the "need to come to loving terms with what's transitory, mutable, even quite exposed and ruined, while growing better attuned to continuities of energy, idiom, and soul."[33]

Perhaps even more important than Thurman, however, when it came to Sedgwick's understanding of the bardo, was Rinpoche's *Tibetan Book*.[34]

A Second Companionable Space: In the Bardo with Sogyal Rinpoche

According to Rinpoche, life and death represented a series of "constantly changing transitional realities," the bardos, "junctures when the possibility of liberation, or enlightenment," was "heightened." *In the Bardo* resonates with a number of these moments. Rinpoche tells the story of an ambitious father who kept a sack of grain "strung . . . up with a rope from one of the rafters of his house to keep it safe from rats and thieves"; an image resonant in the context of Sedgwick's show. In the story, as the vain father fantasized about his wealthy son becoming as famous as the moon, a rat finds its "way up to the sack of grain and chewed through the rope," and the "bag of grain dropped from the ceiling and killed him, instantly"; suggesting that Sedgwick's show was as a multifigure memento mori expressing the sense that pride might come before a fall.[35]

Alternatively, spectators might think of *In the Bardo* as a ghostly closet containing Sedgwick's former clothes; a reading that gains poignancy in the wake of her death, since Rinpoche reminds us that the Tibetan word for body is *lū*, which means "something you leave behind, like baggage," with the temporary show anticipating Nancy K. Miller's melancholy that all that would ultimately

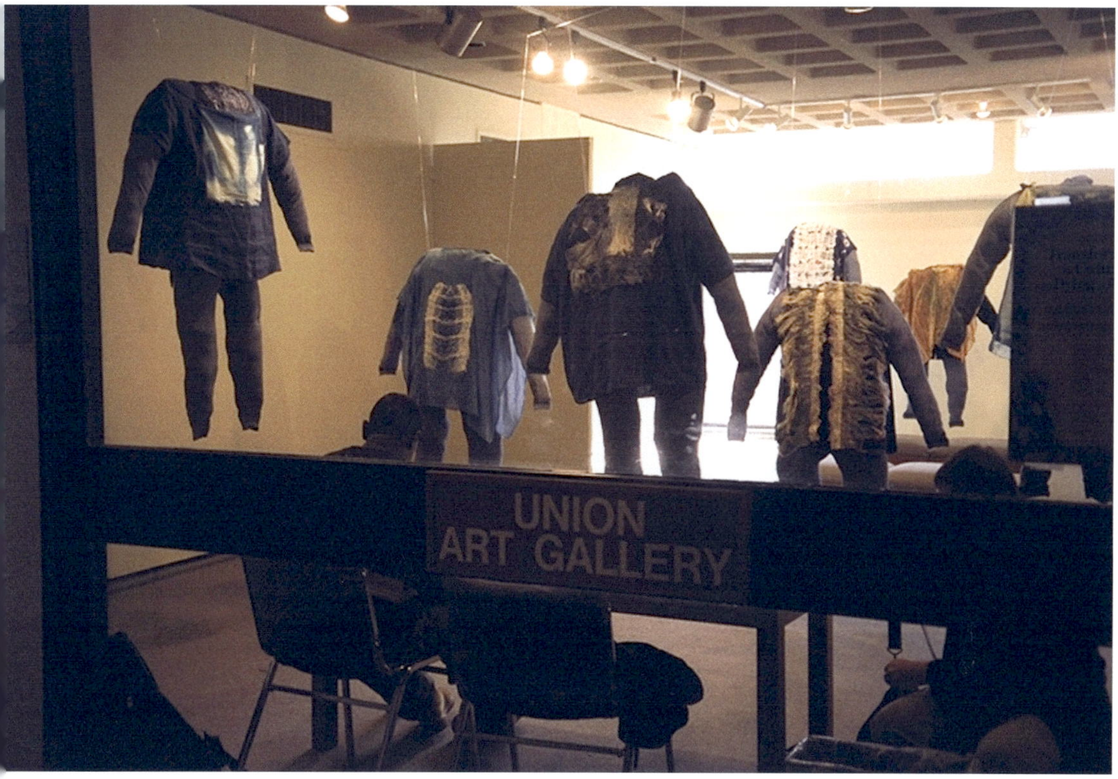

Figure 4.12. Eve Kosofsky Sedgwick, *In the Bardo* exhibition, 1999–2000. Photograph: H. A. Sedgwick. Collection of H. A. Sedgwick. © H. A. Sedgwick

remain of it and of Sedgwick would be textiles her loved ones would have to "sort out, choose, iron, and fold up again."[36] In addition, the way in which the suspended figures seem out of their terrestrial element, especially as lined up for inspection, recalls Rinpoche's image of the moment of death as an "animal lining up for its end in the slaughterhouse."[37]

But how threatening or promising viewers find Sedgwick's figures depends on where spectators stand in relation to the mannequins, and on the angles of view revealed in the surviving installation shots. Depending on the spectator's positioning and the lighting, the figures might appear to be descending, in a line, from the light of heaven, given the top lighting of the SUNY installation, or descending like UN peacekeeping paratroopers into a war zone. As such, they might be coming to the reparative rescue of those in need or moving threateningly toward them like nightmarish headless, wrathful zombies. Either way, questions of life and death are heightened.

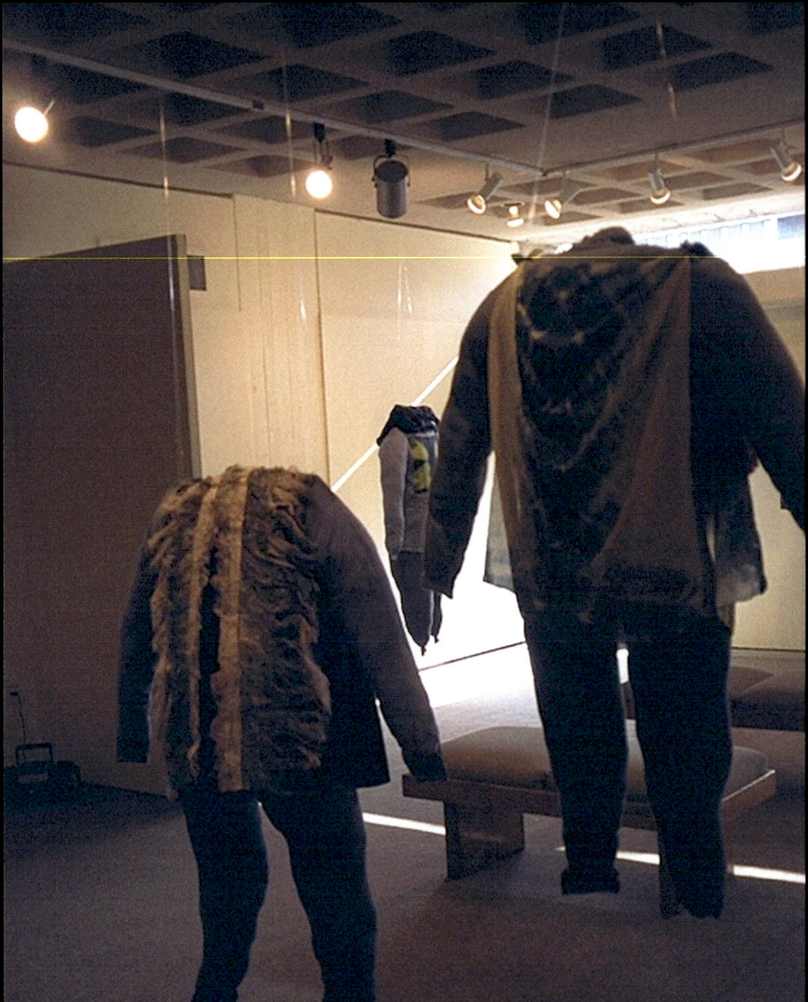

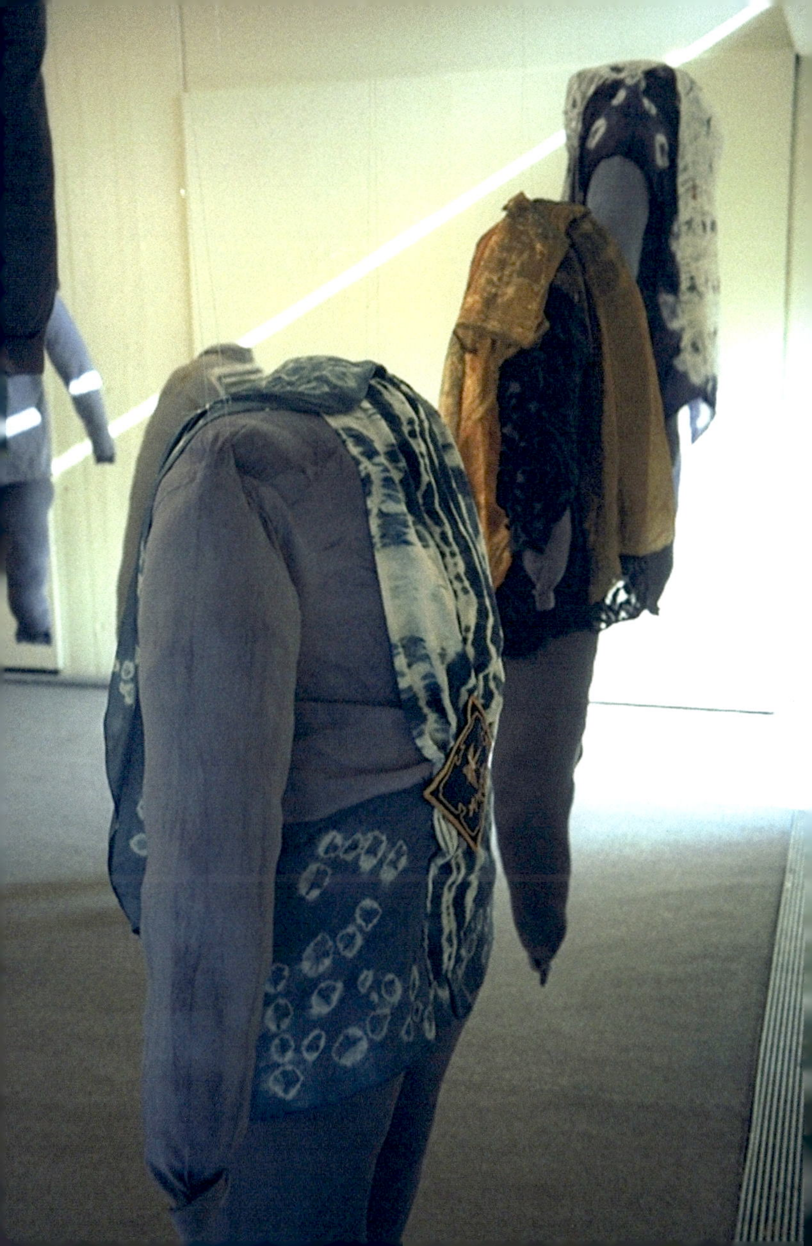

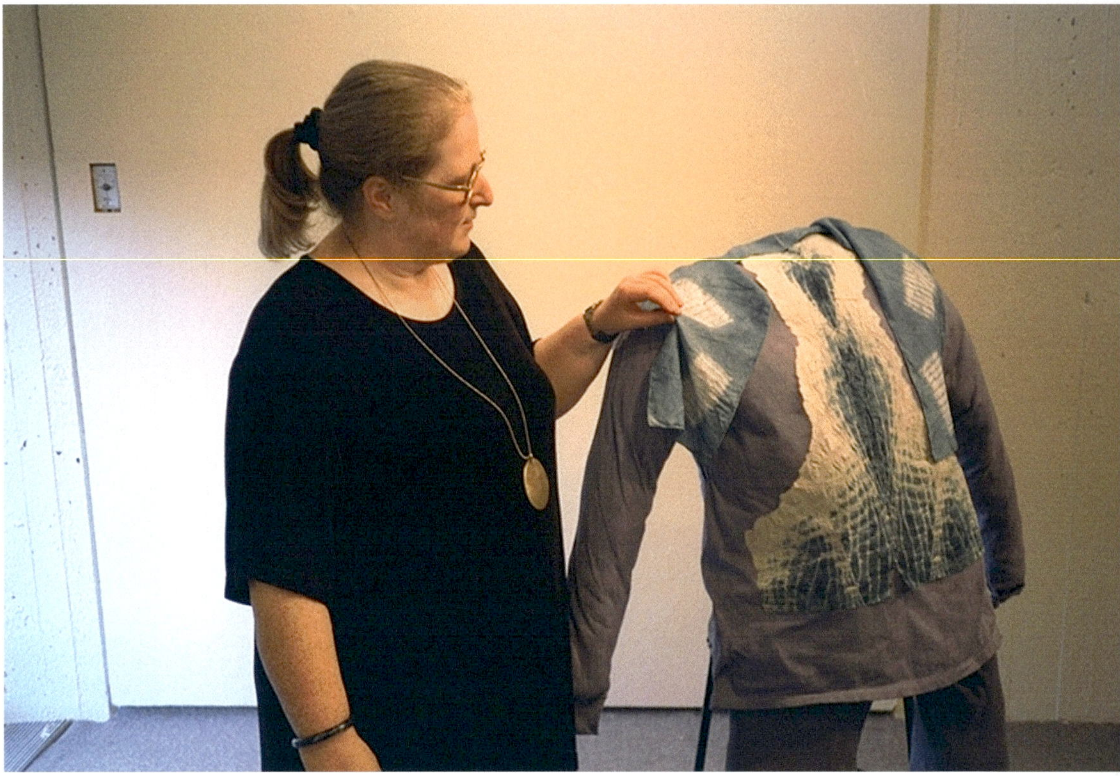

Figure 4.15. Eve Kosofsky Sedgwick at the installation of the *In the Bardo* exhibition, 1999. Photograph: H. A. Sedgwick. Collection of H. A. Sedgwick. © H. A. Sedgwick

If spectators are positioned at the *end* of one of the lines of figures, they might again feel their mortality threatened, as if they were facing a firing squad. If they are positioned between the lines, by contrast, examining closely the figures' costumes, then viewers might feel they were an army inspection officer, looking for irregularities in uniform. In the body scans included on the figures, spectators are also invoked as doctors, examining for problems, recalling the fearful, retrospectively erotic scenes of medical inspection Sedgwick experienced that we have already explored.

Certainly, there is something deathly, as Miller recalled, about the surviving image of the mannequins, ready to be body-bagged up at the end of the show, although, seen with a queer eye, those same bodies suggest a deliciously erotic daisy chain of overlapping figures getting their legs over. Similarly, in a second shot of the figures before their installation, with Sedgwick sewing behind them,

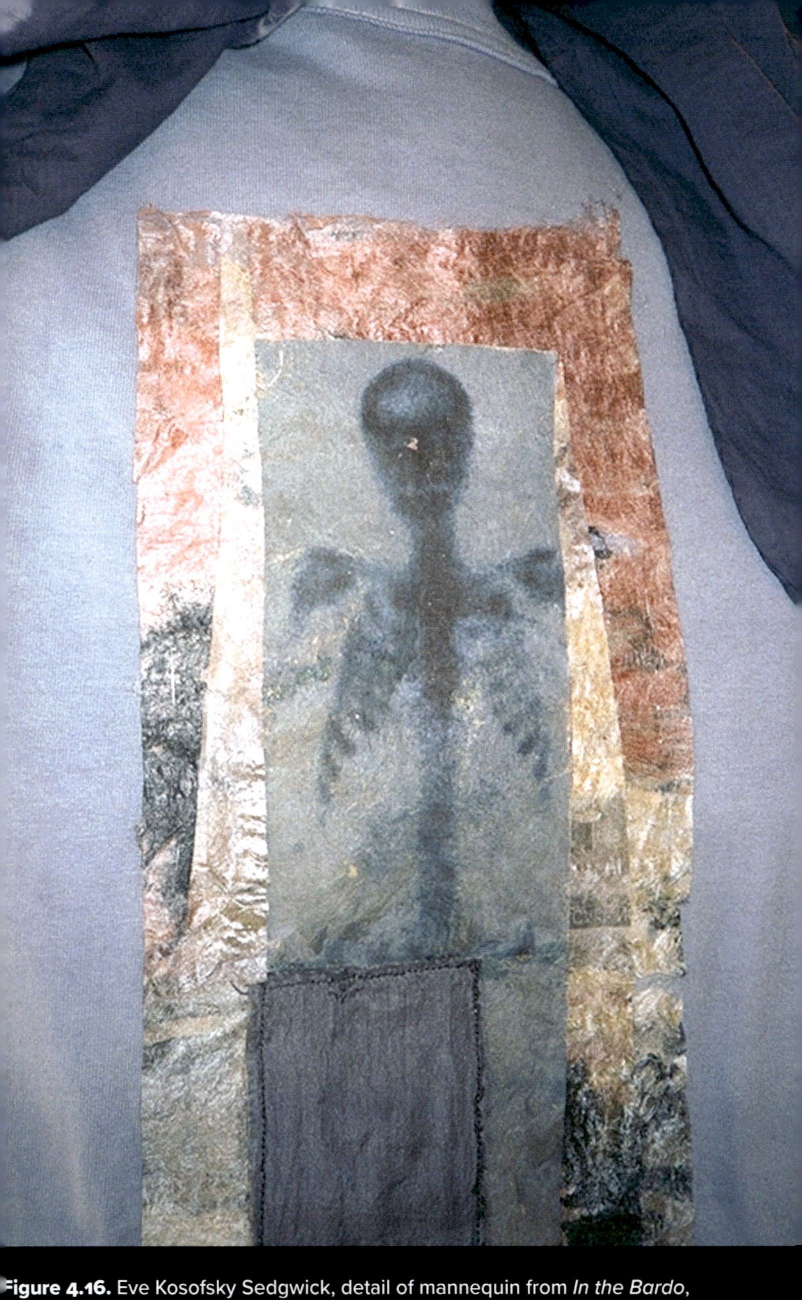

Figure 4.16. Eve Kosofsky Sedgwick, detail of mannequin from *In the Bardo*, 1999–2000 (close-up of body scan placed on numerous layers of fused silk). Photograph: H. A. Sedgwick. Collection of H. A. Sedgwick. © H. A. Sedgwick.

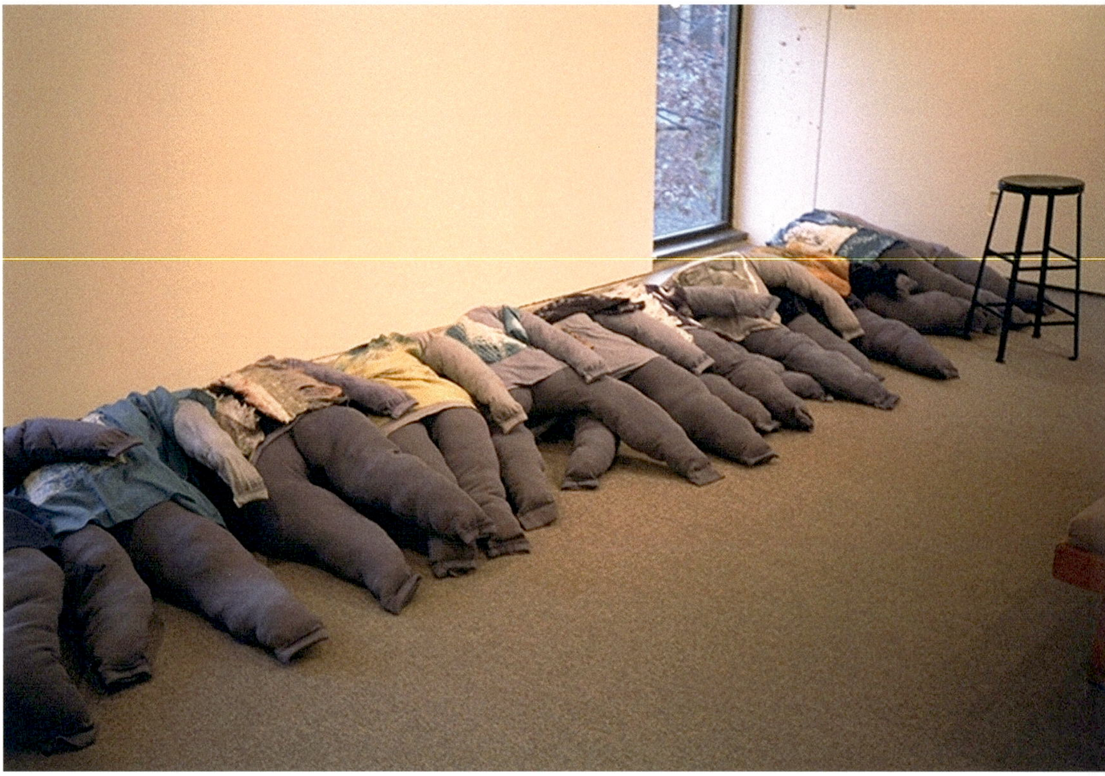

Figures 4.17 and 4.18. Eve Kosofsky Sedgwick, *In the Bardo* (post-installation views), 2000. Photographs: H. A. Sedgwick. Collection of H. A. Sedgwick. © H. A. Sedgwick

like a presiding Fate, the figure in the foreground seems to be going down on the mannequin immediately beneath them.

In the Bardo might also represent images of potential enlightenment. If the figures can easily be swayed, they ultimately come back to balanced rest in the center; an apt image of Buddhism's so-called middle way, whose task is to avoid extremes and "strike a balance." Indeed, according to Rinpoche, the Buddha noted that this "existence of ours is as transient as autumn clouds," like Sedgwick's blue forms suspended in the air, perhaps, and "through weathering changes we can learn how to develop a gentle but unshakeable composure." (Weather is at the center of Sedgwick's last exhibition and late readings of Marcel Proust, as we shall see.)

If the mobile suspended figures might, then, represent the sustained, responsive flexibility required to keep oneself centered in the middle way, their headless forms might signal a more Zen-like notion of satori, or sudden revelation,

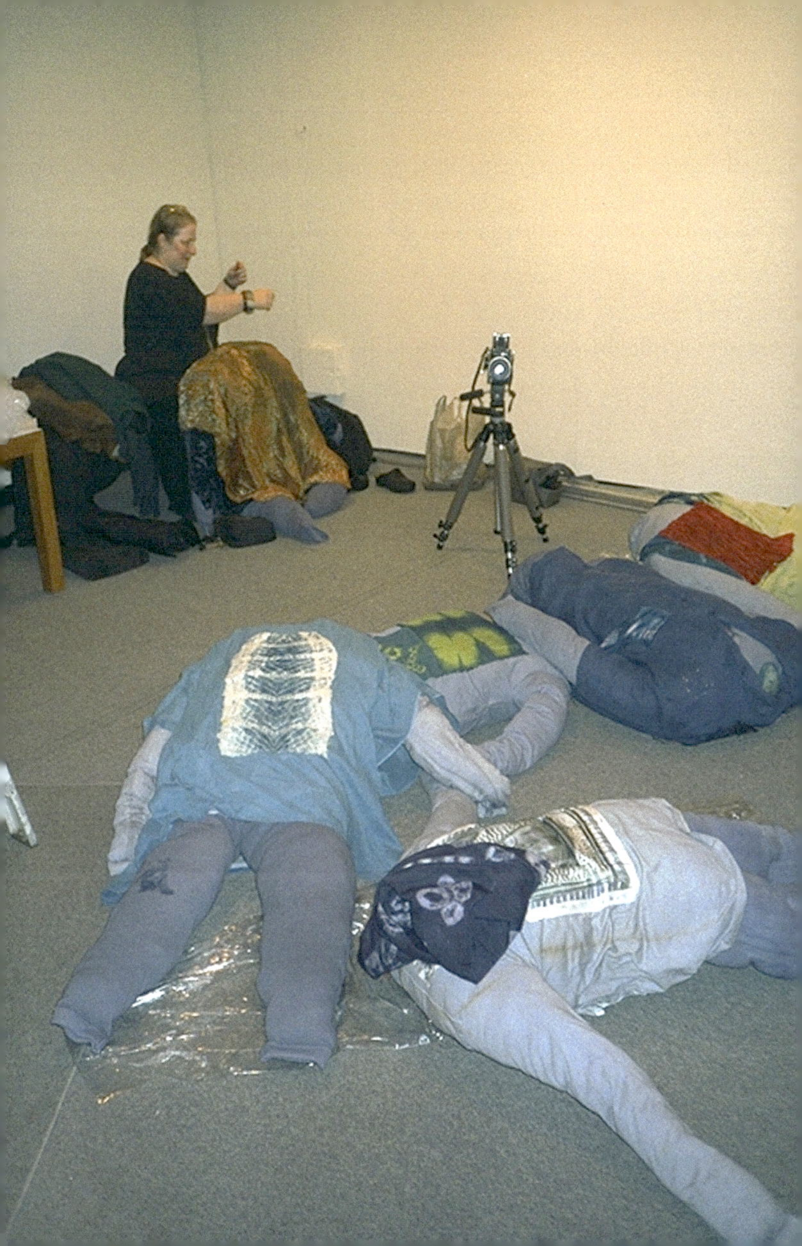

since, as Rinpoche noted, recalling a Zen parable, when the frog from the well saw the ocean, it was such a shock that its head "exploded into pieces." This represented a characteristically silent satori experience, when disciples suddenly found their "mind[s] shattered," such that no words, names, or thoughts remained, "no mind, in fact, at all." In Sedgwick's headless figures, it is as though the mannequins' thoughts are coextensive with their environments, the result of a "gap opened" that "laid bare a sheer, immediate awareness of the present."[38]

Alternatively, *In the Bardo* might represent the ongoing fragility and mindlessness of life. Rinpoche noted that a "tiny crisis pricks the balloon of the strategies we hide behind," suggesting, again, that Sedgwick's figures might be floating down, given their midair position. His metaphors encourage this idea, given his sense of the "power of deflation and doubt" in the journey toward enlightenment and his prediction that, as we die, we will "feel as though we are falling, sinking."[39]

By contrast, Rinpoche compares the moment of enlightenment to a new ability to "see through everything directly, as if you had X-ray eyes," and Sedgwick employs again, on two of the figures, a body scan, from April 27, 1998, of her diseased spine, suggesting the close connection, in her case, between satori and mortality, paranoia and reparation. In the first, Sedgwick's body appears twice, on a ragged piece of cloth, spattered with, and fraying into, gold, characterizing her metastatic changes as both a toxic irradiation and a valuable alchemical transformation.

In the second, Sedgwick juxtaposes the depth-transparency and paranoid reading of her x-rayed body with the surface reading of epidermal layers through the placing of the body scan on numerous strata of fused silk (see figure 4.16).

Sedgwick's mannequins, however, might also represent the moment of precipitating back into karmic life, in a semifamiliar form, rather than escaping samsara into nirvana. Returning to our lives, Rinpoche noted, we are likely to feel "angry, hurt, and frustrated, 'like a fish writhing in hot sand'"; or perhaps, here, given the fishing-wire suspension, like a fish caught again on a line. Certainly, once reborn, we will be buffeted by the breezes that surround the figures, by the "force of conceptual thinking, also known as 'the karmic wind,'" among which the "mental body is unable to remain still, even for an instant."[40]

Rinpoche also brings the uncertain gendering of the figures into last focus when he describes one of his most beloved male teachers, Dudjom Rinpoche, as a person with a "beautiful and gentle face, exquisite hands, and a delicate, almost feminine presence"; apt since Sedgwick's bardo figures represent one of many queer Asian divinities spectators encounter across her oeuvre, as we have begun to see, and as I now go on to explore further.[41]

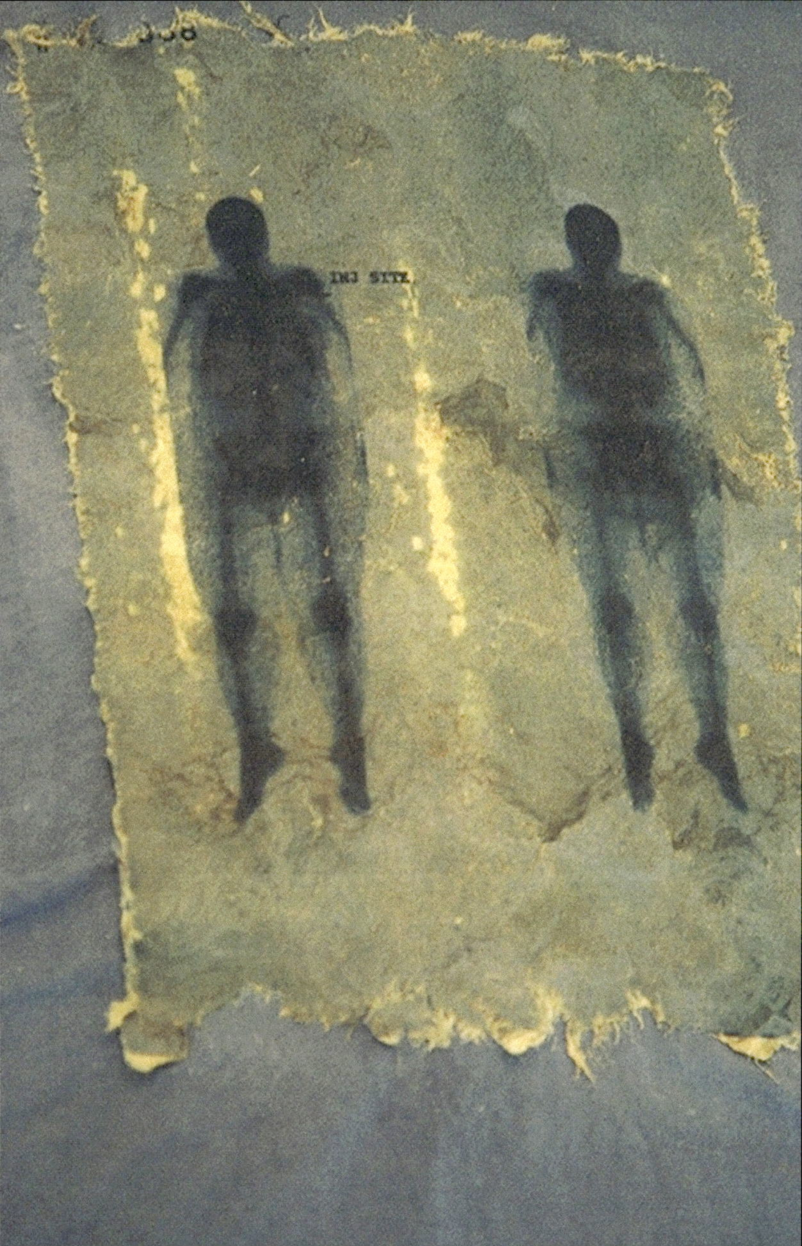

Figure 4.19. Eve Kosofsky Sedgwick, detail of mannequin from *In the Bardo*, 1999–2000. Photograph: H. A. Sedgwick. Collection of H. A. Sedgwick. © H. A. Sedgwick

A Third Companionable Space: In the Bardo with Benedict Anderson

Sedgwick's interest in trans Asian divinities began as early as 1977, with the Javanese *punåkawan* in her narrative poem "Trace at 46," that

> anomalous class, of clownish servants
> all aubergine-shaped, all graceless or incontinent
> in their personal functions, . . .
> a few of whom, dwarfish, unlovely, affected, happen
> at the same time to be immortal.
> In fact, they're gods; more precisely, they
> are the wisest and, in moments of tragedy, the most
> powerful of the gods. One of these is distinguished
> in Javanese by being always addressed
> or referred to in the plural number. Squat and pudgy
> with a woman's distended breasts, an expectant
> gibbous belly and wildly salient ass,
> jewelry, a made-up face, but in male
> clothing if any, his voice tone-deaf and high
> and irresolute and, as no one would have
> predicted, transfixing[.][42]

The *punåkawan* are complex characters, from the wayang tradition of mythology and puppetry, and like Sedgwick's floating figures, "plait . . . / together lines female and male and divine"; a phrase we have encountered before.[43] Sedgwick learned about the *punåkawan* from Benedict Anderson's *Mythology and the Tolerance of the Javanese* (1965); a book she singled out, in *Touching Feeling*, for the help it provided in conceptualizing the difference between analog and digital systems.[44]

That was because Anderson explored and promoted ideas of Javanese syncretism, relativism, and tolerance; concepts suggesting spectators take seriously the *cybernetic* "variety and sharp individuality" of Sedgwick's more-than-two, but less-than-infinitely-variant, mannequins. Indeed, given their suspended status on wire, viewers might interpret *In the Bardo* as her idiomatic take on wayang puppet performance, especially since she owned several Javanese puppets and there is much about the exhibition that resembles her late account of the related Japanese Bunraku puppet theater, discussed in one of her last essays, "The Weather in Proust" (ca. 2004–5).[45]

First, there are the "near-life size puppets," in a "state of illness and exhaustion," suspended on wires that could be manipulated by visitors; wires that

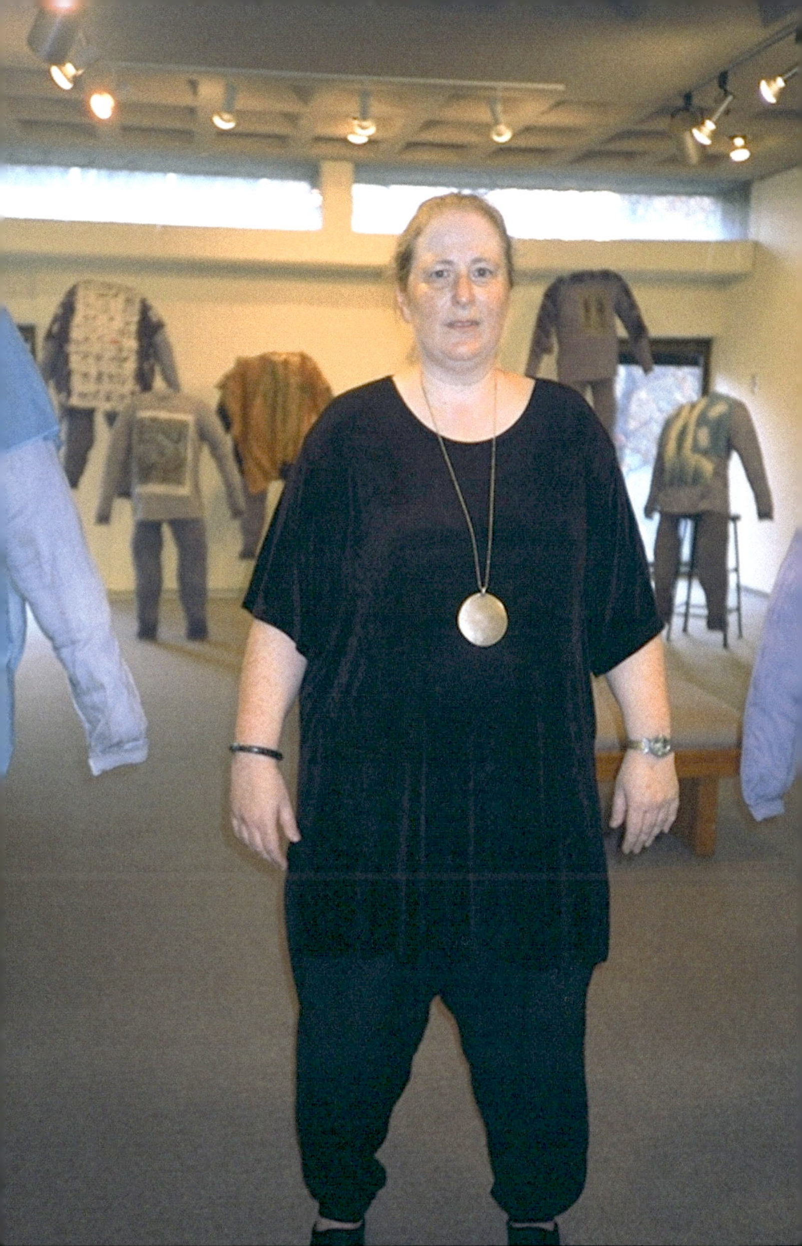

Figure 4.20. Eve Kosofsky Sedgwick at the *In the Bardo* installation, 1999. Photograph: H. A. Sedgwick. Collection of H. A. Sedgwick. © H. A. Sedgwick.

might represent the "tenuous thread" of a dying character's "illusionary life." Second, there are the installation shots in which Sedgwick, like a Bunraku puppeteer, is "dark-clad but quite visible."[46]

Dressed in black, she puts the finishing touches on her show, offering an "almost unbearable immediacy to the sense at once of the puppeteers' complete power over the puppets, and at the same time their radical subordination to them." Like a kind of devoted, tutelary deity "in thrall to" the "insentient bod[ies]" of the "material creatures to which [she] give[s] life," Sedgwick recalls the "image of the medieval 'Death' controlling every movement" of the human puppets.[47]

For Anderson, the anthropological value of working on Javanese culture was the deep "recognition of the logical and social necessity of a moral pluralism"; and, like Sedgwick, he was especially interested in the *punåkawan*, documenting that Semar, the most venerable, was "probably the best loved figure in all *wayang*, a favorite of young and old alike." According to Anderson, Semar was "immensely fat, with heavy breasts and a vast behind"; and although he was "ornamented like a woman, his clothes [were] those of a man, yet his face [was] that of neither man nor woman." The "repository of the highest wisdom," Semar was also characterized by a florid anality and "persistent, uncontrollable farting." In spite of the increasing critiques of the "effeminate" that Anderson detected across and beyond Java, he noted that the *punåkawan*, the "small group of comic grotesque male companions of the chief heroes," remained much loved, such that one of the most distinguished professors at the University of Indonesia owed his following to his "physical resemblance" to Semar and "reputation for a special combination of wisdom and comicality."[48] And it is to Anderson's Sedgwickian combination of the politics of divinity, effeminacy, homoeroticism, and anality that I turn in the final paragraphs of this chapter.

Before finishing with Rinpoche's *Tibetan Book*, however, we need to return to the Dalai Lama's foreword. This compares death to "changing your clothes when they are old and worn out." The metaphor helps explain the alternate epistemology of the closet represented by *In the Bardo*, since it suggests that Sedgwick's return to making clothes, after a period in which she claimed to have given up fashioning textiles for her personal adornment as a "mug's game," was motivated less by a desire to make herself beautiful and more by the Dalai Lama's idea of identity as a temporary, dress-up performativity, with the show representing part of her new textile project paradoxically exploring the "impersonal" and disinterest in presenting a "first-person self to the world."[49]

And yet there is much to be said for thinking about *In the Bardo* as Sedgwick's poignant, powerful staging of her clothes closet; more poignant still now than when I first wrote this chapter during Sedgwick's lifetime, since the exhibition now evokes the wardrobe of my *dead* friend's clothes, but one still powerfully full of her ideas and agency, helping me to, in Rinpoche's words, "endure, accept, and survive" her passing.[50]

The Epistemology of the Fat Woman's Closet, or In the Bardo with Michael Moon and Shannon Van Wey

Walking into *In the Bardo* must have been *dreamy*. More precisely, the installation resembled an "extremely cheerful" dream Sedgwick described in *Tendencies*; the one she had a couple of years before coauthoring her circa 1990 essay on "Divinity" with Michael Moon. In the dream, Sedgwick was "shopping for clothes" at a department store and felt "dubious about whether they would have any clothes . . . big enough" for her. A saleswoman reassured her, adding that "rather than being marked by size numbers, each size-group of clothes was gathered under a graphic symbol." In Sedgwick's case, a "cluster of luscious-looking clothes, hung on a rack between two curtained dressing rooms," was marked by a "pink triangle"; the "penal marker" attached "in the first instance by force to a few [queer] men from the fear that their desire would otherwise remain indistinguishable from the desire of the many [straight] men around them."[51]

With Sedgwick's dream in mind, *In the Bardo* evokes a comparatively unstigmatized department store filled with clothes designed exactly to fit Sedgwick, which might represent a project of *recovery*, in more than one sense. Indeed, most of the clothes were ones she had worn, and all reflected the ways she dressed. Sedgwick would ultimately refashion one of the pieces of *shibori* within the show, as we shall see, to include a line from a circa 1899 death haiku by Japanese poet Roshu:

> Time to go . . .
> they say the journey is a long one:
> change of robes.[52]

This might suggest that *In the Bardo* represents Sedgwick's final, regal journey, except her late poem, "Death," given as part of talks accompanying the exhibition, informed its audience that death was not a "party you dress up for"; "it's strictly come-as-you-are." There was no need for "elevator shoes" or a "girdle to jam your tummy / in," since the point was "not what becomes you, but what's you." Also newly futile were "those silk PJs with feathers" Sedgwick bought "so long before the big affair began," since she had "always slept in the nude." Now she would "sleep in the nude forever."[53]

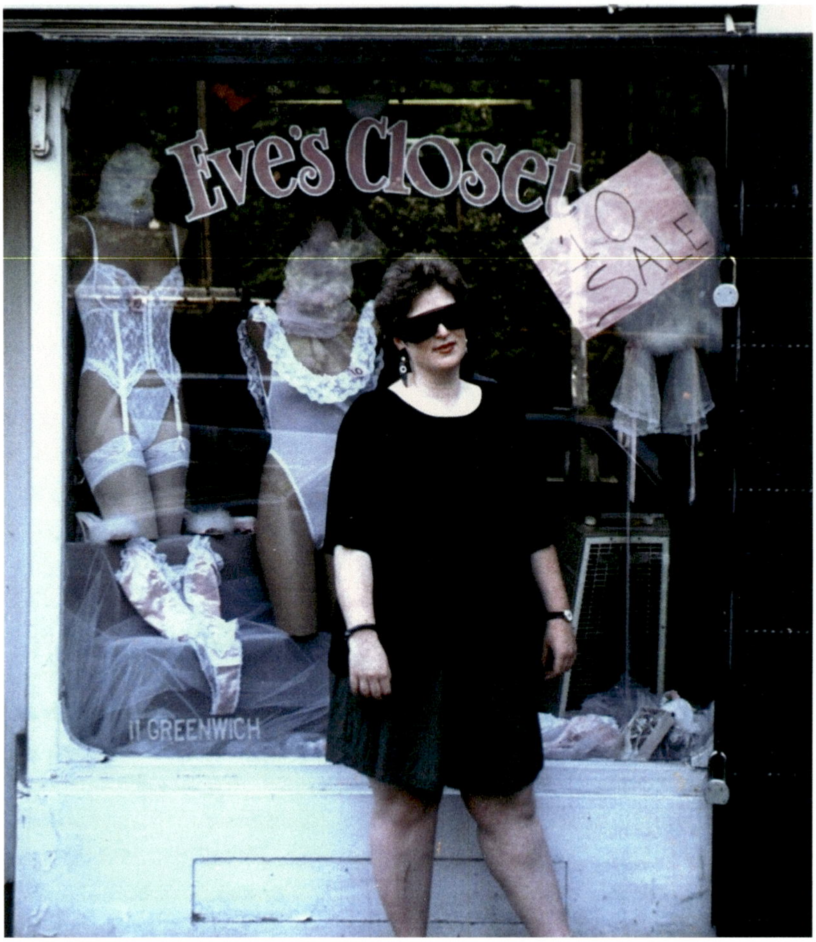

Figure 4.21. Eve Kosofsky Sedgwick, ca. 1989. Photograph: H. A. Sedgwick. Collection of H. A. Sedgwick. © H. A. Sedgwick

If we are to understand *In the Bardo*, then, as a kind of dream department store, it remains unclear quite how unstigmatizing it is. Sedgwick translates Roshu's poem as a "change of clothes" rather than a "change of robes."[54] In doing so, she modestly deemphasizes the status of her textiles from the biblical and Orientalist, religious and regal prestige of *robes*, with their glamour of folded amplitude, in comparison to her more ordinary fat woman's *clothes*, particularly since the exhibition repeats the trope, common in fat-shaming journalism, of the "headless fatty." But that seems an unlikely reading, given Sedgwick's sustained advocacy of fat art, and since her dream department store stages comparatively *thin* viewers as the unhappy shoppers, for whom the clothes are less likely to fit, reversing the scenario where "oversized" women cannot find anything to wear.

Here, viewers need to differentiate between the impacts of clothes that are chafingly small for larger viewers, Sedgwick's dominant experience, and comically oversized clothes into which petite viewers might grow, or in which they might hide. Indeed, "The Warm Decembers" had earlier described Sedgwick and her svelte sister dressed in "identical outfits," whose waistband "chafed" the artist "under the armpits."[55] Sedgwick's late essay "Melanie Klein and the Difference Affect Makes," meanwhile, contained the similarly shaming, irritating memory of going to another department store, as a three-year-old, where she was again offered something too small. This time, she had to make do with her sister's "8 inch or so plastic doll," when she wanted something both "bigger" and "baby- or toddler-shaped, and new," rather than the "smaller and grown-up scale" of the secondhand one she'd been given, which she subsequently lost, having precious little "small-muscle co-ordination." What Sedgwick remembered most about this story, however, was her resultant "descent into the awful whirlpool of tantrum mode" and the aftermath of feeling "abject, flattened by the ordeal" of her rage, "trailing through the innards of the department store in a state of apparent social death"; a visceral whirlpool possible for viewers to generate by spinning the suspended figures, in an exhibition where death could not have been more present.[56]

In recalling the story, Sedgwick emphasized how the "right scale" for one body may be the "wrong scale" for another, and particularly for a person who "needed something chunkier," with "decent-scale, plastic, resiliently articulated parts" that she "could manipulate freely and safely (safely for *it* as well as me)." Indeed, the character of being "pretty chunky" seemed to be the condition for her "loving or identifying with," and not just "abandoning," something. Ideally, the scale and consistency of the object would be such that you could "do a lot of different things" with it and "be in many relations" to it, so that it could "push back against you and where the individual moving parts aren't too complex or delicate for active daily use."[57]

The passage illuminates well the scene of viewing *In the Bardo* for spectators of different scales and brings into sharper focus the kinds of bodies Sedgwick chose for the show. In the context of such dreamy and nightmarish department stores, readers might notice that while I've been repeatedly referring to Sedgwick's *mannequins*, they are the opposite in many ways. Where mannequins are toned, these are fat. Where mannequins are hard, these are soft. Where mannequins are heavy, these are light. Where mannequins are anchored to the ground, these are suspended from the ceiling. And where mannequins have "decent-scale, plastic, resiliently articulated parts," these do not. If anything, many key parts seem to have been lopped or tapered off. These bodies may be large enough for Sedgwick to love and identify with, and, as this chapter hopefully shows, spectators can make and do a lot of different things with them, be in many different relations to them. But the figures are more fragile than mannequins, and easier to knock the stuffing out of, as Miller's poignant memories emphasize.

In this context of fat and thin, hard and soft bodies, spectators might also want to think further about the use Sedgwick makes of two pieces of Milagro relief sculpture in the exhibition. Both depict a human torso, cropped below the head and below the hips. The first, again like the Venus de Milo, lacks arms and is probably female given the presence of a left breast above her rounded navel. Her right breast, like Sedgwick's, is missing. The second is cropped at the top of the neck, halfway down the upper arms, and just above the buttocks. At first glance, this appears to depict a back, given the wavy spinelike line that bisects the torso's center, with what appear to be three ribs on either side, and a right shoulder blade above. Just below the "spine," however, is what appears to be a belly button, suggesting this represents the front of a female torso, after top surgery (see figures 4.22 and 4.23).

If both reliefs register the scarring effect of Sedgwick's mastectomy, and the second her spinal difficulties, she transformed the Milagros from a hard metallic object into a swatch of soft printed fabric, characteristically splintered, in the first case, into four pieces she stitched together, and onto which she printed the images, suggesting further evidence of bodily stitching, patching, and scarring. In Lacanian terms, what was formerly an impenetrable metallic, supposedly miraculous, armored body became a vulnerable *corps morcelé*.[58]

By contrast, the capes worn by several of the floating figures, seen from the back, encourage viewers to expect supernaturally buff bodies straight out of a Superman comic, perhaps recalling the inspiring calendar Sedgwick made of herself in athletic tai chi poses after her diagnosis with breast cancer (see figure 4.7). In addition, especially as seated on a chair, during the installation of the exhibition, one of Sedgwick's figures recalls another of the most famous works of fragmented, but *surviving*, antique sculpture: the Belvedere Torso.[59]

The softness of Sedgwick's "Milagro" panels is emphasized by the puffiness of the stuffed figures they adorn, which are not resolute enough to push back against you when you push against them. In enacting this sumo struggle, they recall a reparative scene, in *Dialogue*, where Sedgwick and her therapist literally push against each other, discovering they were about the same height and "pretty evenly matched." This enables her to feel immediately better, "restored

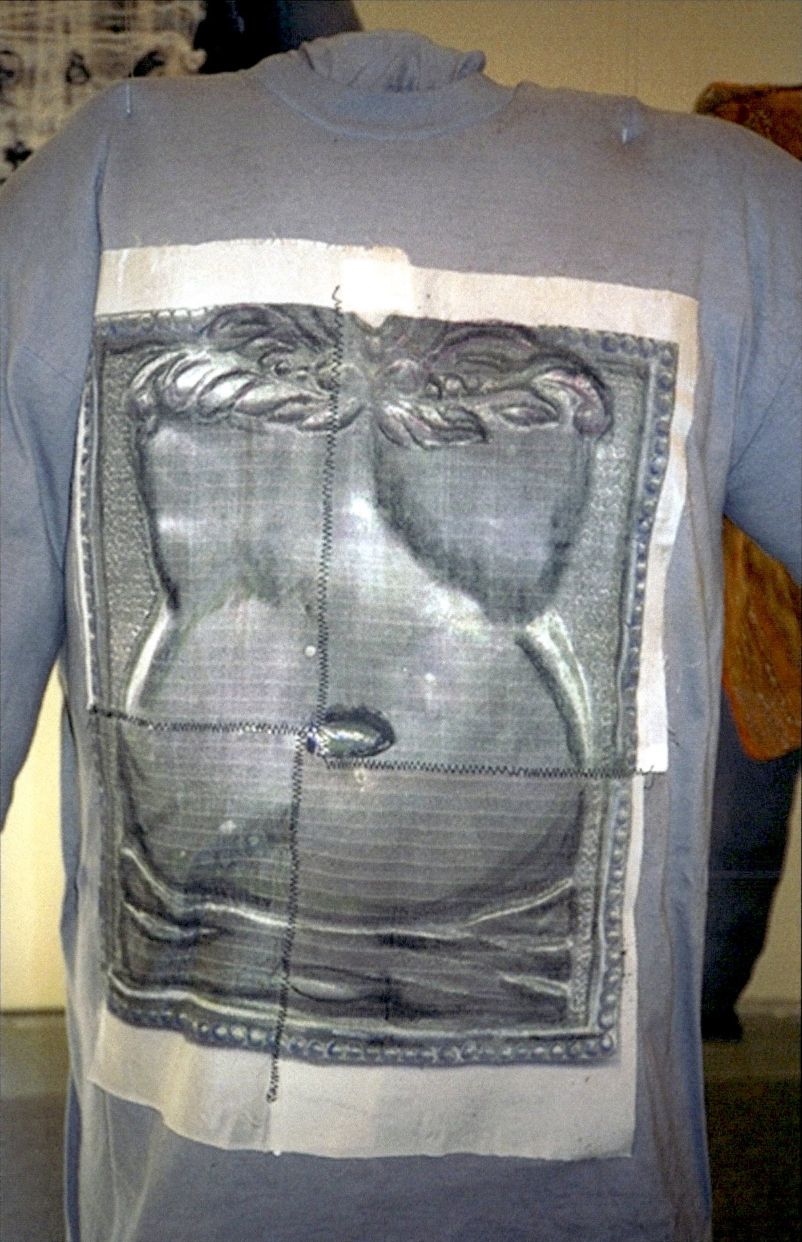

Figure 4.22. Eve Kosofsky Sedgwick, detail of mannequin from *In the Bardo* (front), 1999–2000. Photograph: H. A. Sedgwick. Collection of H. A. Sedgwick.

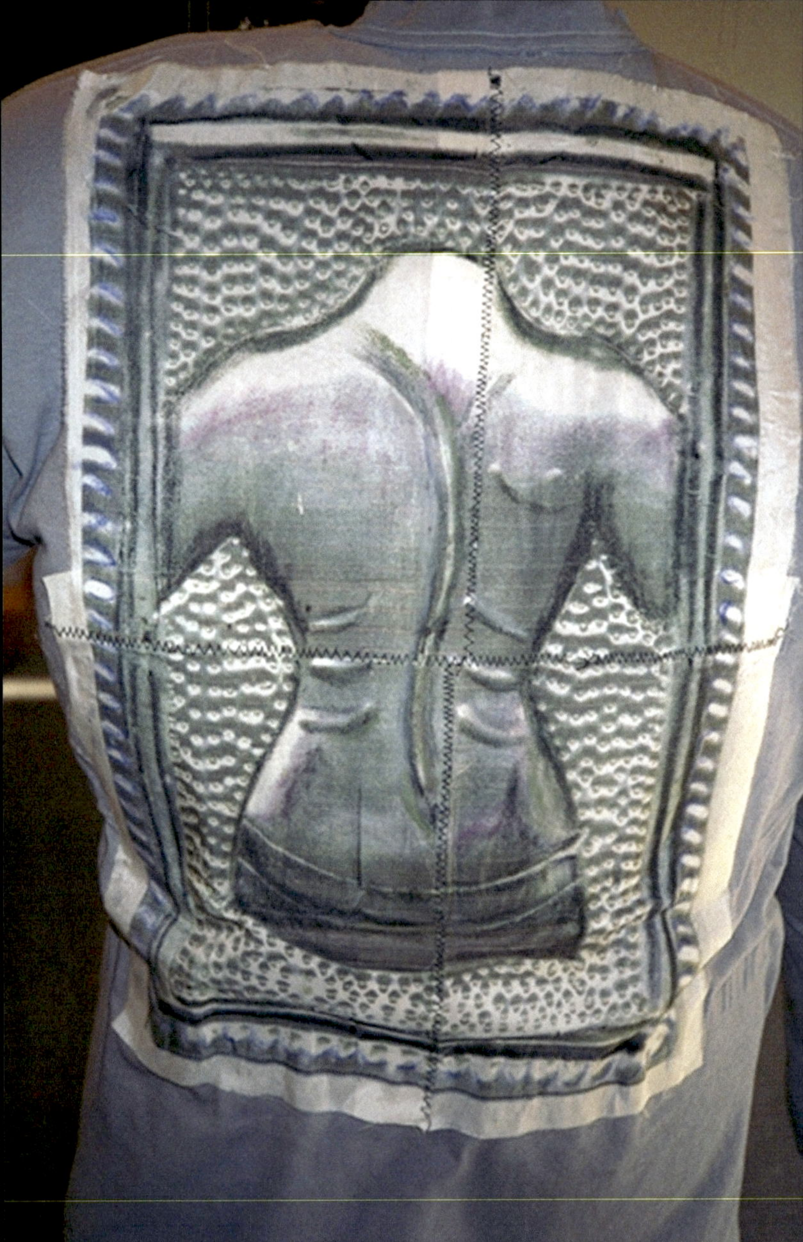

Figure 4.23. Eve Kosofsky Sedgwick, detail of mannequin from *In the Bardo* (back), 1999–2000. Photograph: H. A. Sedgwick. Collection of H. A. Sedgwick.

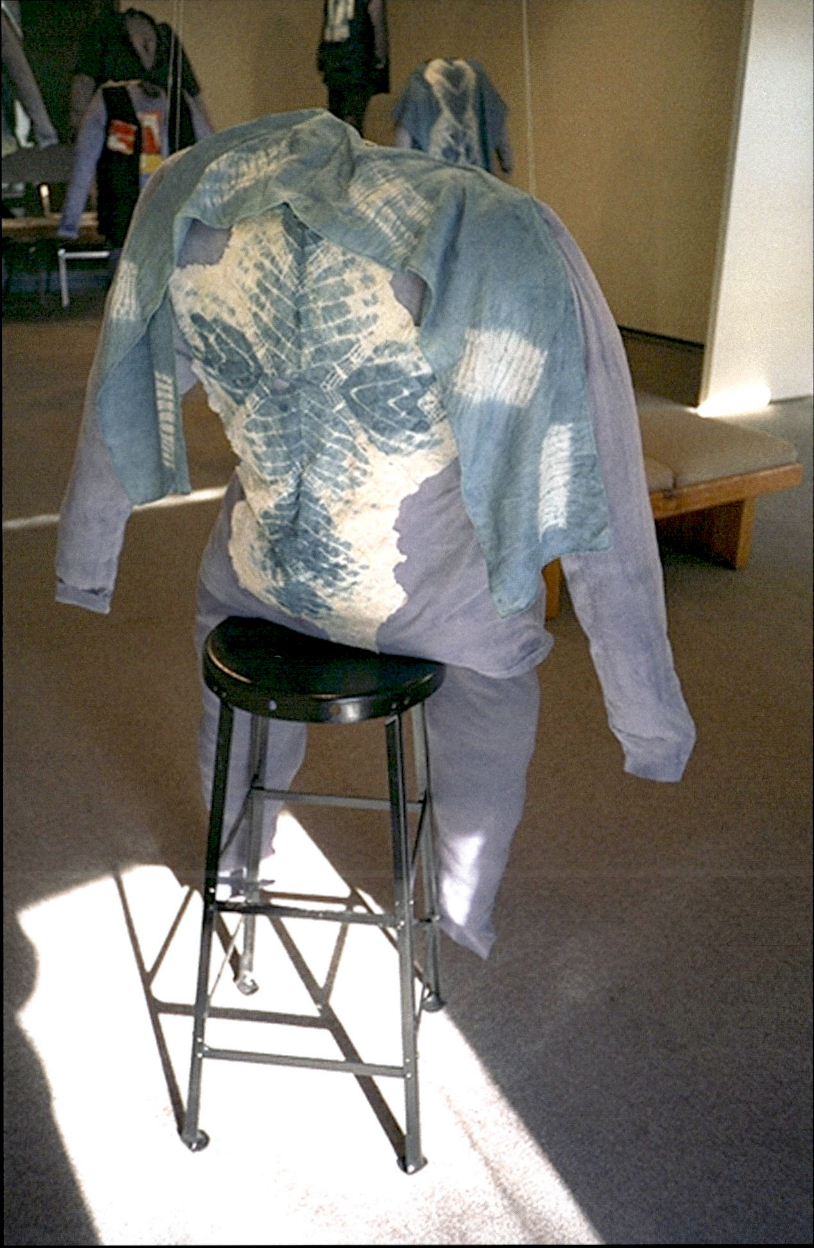

Figure 4.24. Eve Kosofsky Sedgwick, mannequin from *In the Bardo* (back), 1999–2000. Photograph: H. A. Sedgwick. Collection of H. A. Sedgwick. © H. A. Sedgwick

to an adult size—in relation" to the "spectral figure" of her "fear and rage," and "embodied in quite / a new way; dimensional, / powerful. // *Not scared*."[60] The scene might explain further why Sedgwick's *In the Bardo* figures resemble multiple punching bags or piñatas, suggesting she needed to imagine her body and its tumors as a pushover, or something she could push out of the way, even as the figures register her metastatic body as something repeatedly punched by pathology.

Finally, that Sedgwick describes the various suspended figures as *floating* begs the key question of what medium they are floating in or on. Air seems to be the obvious answer, given the absence of water and the figures' presence midair, with the installation anticipating her developing interest in "atmospheric pressure." For example, Sedgwick's posthumous final book, *The Weather in Proust* (2011), described how the "measure of barometric pressure" required a "dynamic interpretive context," involving a "full sense of how changes in the weight of a given column of air . . . will affect both the vertical movement of heat and thus the air's temperature and ability to hold moisture, and also the horizontal travel of air masses that circulate 'fronts' of pressure difference, and thus major weather systems, across the earth's surface." As such, "attending to air pressure to any extent at all seems to presume an expert sensitivity—however amateur—to the entire working" of the "heat/water/steam machine we call *weather*," with a myriad of Proustian adjectives available to describe the "air as a site of alchemical state change."[61]

Sedgwick's interest in barometries is especially resonant in this context, not merely as a thick description of the Buddhist *emptiness* surrounding the figures, but because, "invisible for all its pervasiveness," and while "easy for most people most of the time to take for granted," Proust's narrator is chronically asthmatic and prone to "attacks of breathlessness" that "respond to atmospheric pressure"; asthmatic crises that, like Sedgwick's cancer, feel and are life threatening, in addition to providing the opportunity for aesthetic delight, response, and creativity.

In the Bardo represented, in many ways, a gear change for Sedgwick's creativity as well as a return to some earlier-explored themes and media. The exhibition was her first solo show and contained many more exhibits, and individual, internal components, than *Floating Columns*, adding layer on layer of complex part-whole and whole-whole interactivities, where "empty" missing parts were often as present and important as their formally extant equivalences.

While not abandoning her earlier interest in the intricate layering of patchwork and fused fibers, *In the Bardo* represented a step up from the predominantly *two-and-a-half-dimensional*, fractal and epidermal character of her earlier collages and weavings to a more fully three-dimensional figuration, evoking numerous art historical and anthropological forms, including puppets, punching bags, and piñatas; mannequins, milagros, and dolls; fragmentary classical European and modernist soft sculptures; and bodies armored and broken; as well as metamorphic insects, such as butterflies and moths, and the prey of arachnids.

In the show, Sedgwick also returned to and developed her earlier work, incorporating some of her earliest collages as well as reengaging with the project of self-adornment that her weavings had, in part, represented, thereby resisting an overall teleological artistic development in favor of an ongoing, increasingly capacious fanning of different artistic and relational possibilities, some dreamy, some nightmarish, some paranoid, more reparative, whose variety and kaleidoscopic transformations this chapter has sought to capture in its unusually multi-hypothetical form of argumentation.

As she developed the epistemology of this new closet, the closet of the bardo, Sedgwick also continued to draw on the inspiration of her therapist, Shannon Van Wey, and her extended circle of gay male peers and predecessors, as well as a new circle of Buddhist thinkers, alongside some Southeast Asian anthropologists from her undergraduate days.

Sedgwick would reincarnate further many of these queer and Buddhist reparative ideas, iconographies, and materialities, in her penultimate exhibition, *Bodhisattva Fractal World*. Responding to the exhibits' more discrete, although still overlapping character, the genre of the book changes in some ways at this point, coming to resemble an exhibition catalog after the fact or, perhaps, *avant la lettre*, if future exhibitions occur, and, in so doing, responding to and honoring, as well as exploring, a more patchwork character of its own.

5

BODHISATTVA FRACTAL WORLD

(2002)

Eve Kosofsky Sedgwick's second solo exhibition, *Bodhisattva Fractal World*, opened at Johns Hopkins University in 2002. According to her artist's screed, the exhibition explored the "contemplative space" generated by "thousand-year-old sculptural images" of Kuanyin, the Chinese Buddhist bodhisattva of compassion, from the late Tang and Sung periods, whom we have already briefly encountered. The Sanskrit word *bodhisattva*, the "one whose essence is enlightenment," derives from *bodhi*, signifying perfect knowledge, and *sattvam*, essence or being. Again according to Sedgwick, Kuanyin had a "complex ontological standing" as a "future or past Buddha" who "vowed to forego Nirvana until all other beings [had] become enlightened."[1]

Sedgwick, as we have seen, was particularly interested in Kuanyin's iconographic transition, documenting that the bodhisattva had been portrayed as a man up to about the eighth century and as a woman from around the twelfth, while the most "magnetic" intervening bodhisattvas, like the Javanese *punåkawan* we encountered in the previous chapter, were "harder to classify in terms of gender." Sedgwick's "thought and hope," as we have again seen, was that "even in the expression of a strong sensuality," many of these "regal and loved divinities" may not have been "shaped or perceived through the ideas of gender at all." In popular Chinese devotion, Sedgwick also documented, and "not only among Buddhists," that Kuanyin was imagined to be "occupied daily in protecting beings and dispensing good things," making the bodhisattva a good *reparative* icon.[2]

If Kuanyin might be interesting to queer and trans theorists for *their* multiple, shifting gender identities, one of the reasons the bodhisattva became popular in China was because of the way he/she/they responded to "currents in Taoist thought and iconography"; a responsiveness Sedgwick shared.[3] Chapter 6 of "The Warm Decembers" ends:

> I Ching says about *The Warm Decembers*, "Peace.
> The mean decline, the great and good approach.
> Good fortune and success."[4]

In addition, Sedgwick's screed suggested, *Bodhisattva Fractal World* explored the Japanese *wabi-sabi* aesthetic that "similarly resonated with the Tao." According to Leonard Koren, *wabi-sabi*, the idea that humbly imperfect forms represent an aesthetic and ontological ideal, occupies "roughly the same position in the Japanese pantheon of aesthetic values as do the Greek ideals of beauty and perfection in the West"; although Sedgwick was again not averse to Greco-Roman sculptural ideals in the exhibition, as we shall see, being preoccupied with moments of Eurasian aesthetic hybridity, in the form of some of the Gandharan Kuanyins she worked with, whose classical Greek bodies and drapery forms postdated Alexander the Great's arrival in South Asia in 327 BCE.[5]

Also central to the exhibition were two textile techniques we have already encountered: the "near-aleatory effects of *suminagashi*," or marbling on water; and the "fractal dimension-bending of *shibori*," or "bound resist dyeing." For Sedgwick, these two techniques, "like the subtly unfolding haiku of Zen monks nearing the end of their lives" that she was simultaneously working with, suggested connections between contemporary understandings of chaos and complexity and a group of ancient East Asian embodiments of wisdom and compassion.[6]

Chaos and complexity increasingly interested Sedgwick. During her time at CUNY, she cotaught, with Josh Wilner, a course entitled "Zero, Infinity, Chaos, Sublimity" that examined how science and literature dealt with representational limits. This explored chaos and number theory; investigated the "interrelationship between chaotic behavior and systematic organization"; and focused on work within mathematics and the physical sciences, including "iterability, recursive systems, scaling, period doubling, interference and incommensurability," that could be "related more or less directly to concerns" preoccupying literary scholars.[7]

Two mathematical thinkers were of particular note: F. David Peat and David Bohm. In her posthumous last monograph, *The Weather in Proust*, Sedgwick quoted Peat's thoughts on the dimensionality of string, where he wonders: "What is the dimension of a ball of string? Seen from a great distance, it appears as a dot, a zero-dimensional figure. As we approach, we realize that this dot is a three-dimensional sphere. Closer still, we notice that the ball is composed of a single thread—a twisted line, a one-dimensional figure. Look even closer and the thread becomes a long cylinder, a three-dimensional figure. Under a magnifying glass the cylinder is seen to be made up of individual fibers, tiny twisting lines. So what is the dimensionality of string?"[8] If Peat's thoughts on string encourage spectators to think about Sedgwick's use of individual fibers in the exhibition, Bohm's ideas about the "dimensional play of folding and unfolding" lay the ground for viewers' thoughts about *shibori*. According to Sedgwick, she found Bohm "quite an involving figure," and she drew particular attention to his notions of *implicate*, enfolding, and *explicate*, unfolding, processes.[9] Indeed, her sense of the "fractal dimension-bending of *shibori*" derived in part from the Bohmian way in which patterns that were visible in the final elastic, crinkly, *two-and-a-half-dimensional* textiles represented a complex memory of their earlier tied, three-dimensional, bound form.[10]

Sedgwick's *shibori* aesthetic was, however, different from then-popular conceptions of fractals. These were celebrated, in the words of Kenneth Falconer, for their "unending intricacy" and "ever-repeating form," the same pattern repeating at multiple scales, all the way down. While spectators might have expected Sedgwick to have warmed to the "*self-similar*" character of fractals, as part of her broader redemption of a *homo* aesthetic, her passion derived, more queerly, from Benoit Mandelbrot's founding idea of fractals as "highly irregular objects" that "should be regarded as commonplace, rather than exceptional," unlike classical geometric forms that emphasized "smooth or regular objects such as circles, cubes or cones." These were *straight* geometric forms that Sedgwick's textiles again resisted in the name of irregular, queer variants. In addition, given the iconography of *fracture* that runs through the show, as we shall see, Sedgwick was perhaps thinking about the Latin etymology of the word *fractal*, *fractus*, meaning "broken," as well as the idea of *fractions*, such as her *two-and-a-half-dimensional* forms. By contrast, she resisted the idea of fractals as endlessly detailed "at increasingly fine scales," because of her passion for the fuzzy, blurry, and sloppy, classic *wabi-sabi* idioms.[11]

Given the iconography of extended fingers and arms that recurs through the show, as we shall again see, Sedgwick seemed more interested in what Falconer called the appearance of "'fractal fingers' or 'dendrites'"; and (given her interest in *suminagashi*), in "hydrological data," especially the "balance between the pressure and surface tensions" of different liquids in contact. Also potentially relevant, although absent from Sedgwick's screed, was the potentially *reparative* fact that scientists had developed "fractal methods for the early detection and classification of cancer tumors," including "mammography for the diagnosis of breast cancer."[12]

Having laid out the conceptual and material groundwork for the exhibition, in the remainder of this chapter I adopt a more patchwork methodology, as I look in sequence and detail at its individual exhibits.

Bodhisattva Fractal World, or I Think to Myself, What a *Wabi-Sabi* World!

Sedgwick's title piece for the exhibition was a roughly rectangular patchwork, pinned to the wall in landscape orientation, featuring text stamped onto three pieces of ragged rust-orange-and-white (or faded-bloodred-and-white) *shibori* silk, with one word per swatch (see figure 5.1). Sedgwick glued these patches on a ground of blue, gray, and white *suminagashi* silk. She laid out the text in her favorite, haiku-like, three-line verse form, the seven-syllable phrase recalling the meter of a haiku's middle line; apt since death haiku written by Japanese monks represented one of the key sources of the exhibition, as we shall see. Her brief poetic lines are first left justified, then right justified, and finally off-center, as they zigzag down, suggesting a polar opposition between right and left and a resolving, mediating, off-center Buddhist middle way. Sedgwick joins the swatches containing the first two words, forming a descending step. The word *WORLD* is belated, fractured from the rest as if by a missing third line; a characteristic use of empty space she frequently employed in her 1990s lyrics.

Sedgwick sloppily rubber-stamped her uppercase text, the uneven ink apparent in the thinness of the *D* of "BODHISATTVA" and the first *A* of "FRACTAL." Her uneven horizontal lineation suggests that the text is floating and sinking, resisting *straight*forward printing conventions. In addition, Sedgwick suggests that she is still learning how to print or write and the viewer how to recognize letters; an experience, perhaps, akin to seeing the world anew through the

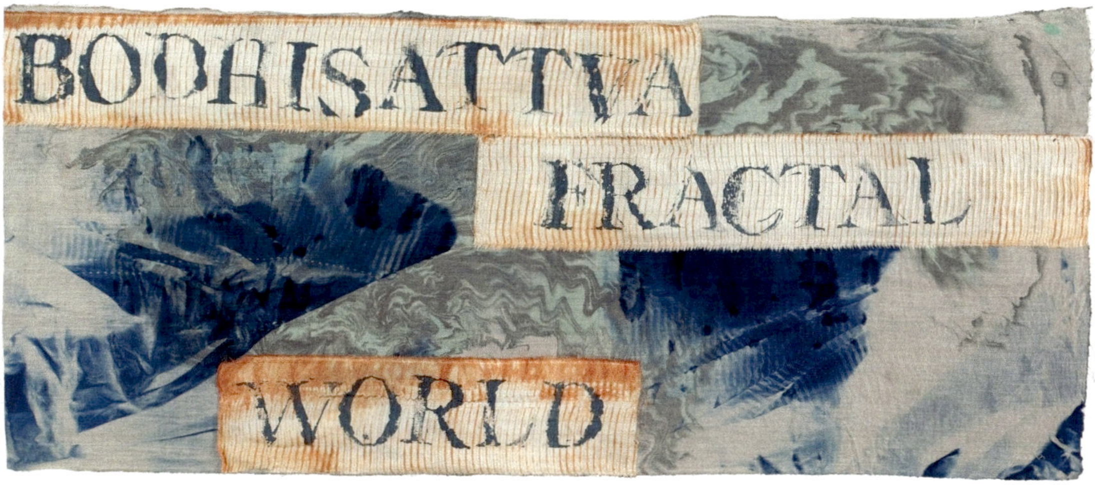

Figure 5.1. Eve Kosofsky Sedgwick, *Bodhisattva Fractal World*, 2002. Photograph: Kevin Ryan. Collection of H. A. Sedgwick. © H. A. Sedgwick

mortal eyes of life-threatening illness, through a body defamiliarized by surgery; or to rebeginning the world in a new incarnation.

The title piece establishes the exhibition's *wabi-sabi* aesthetic. According to Koren, *wabi-sabi* represented a beauty of things unconventional and imperfect, like the ink of Sedgwick's lettering; impermanent and irregular, like the fraying shapes of her swatches; unpretentious and incomplete, with no period ending her sentence; earthy and murky, in the ocher palette of the text patches; modest, fragile, and humble, in the exhibit's small scale; in need of repair or in self-conscious disrepair, as in the hint of bodily injury in the bloody, bandage-like swatches; as well as fashioned by natural processes or out of natural materials, as in the *suminagashi* technique.

Wabi-sabi was also a characteristically *thin* art, since *sabi* originally meant "lean," "withered," or "chill," while *wabi* referred to the "misery of living alone in nature, away from society, and suggested a dispirited, cheerless, emotional state." However, following the positive examples of hermits and ascetics, *wabi-sabi* came to be considered an "opportunity for spiritual richness"; with the aesthetic combining a devotion to the inward, subjective, and philosophical with an attention to the outward, objective, and experiential. If *wabi-sabi* was, traditionally, a thin art, it was not meant to cross over into "ostentatious austerity," so Sedgwick's two-ply collage is probably thin enough for an artist characteristically attuned to the fat over the flat. Spectators might also think about *wabi-sabi*, in Sedgwick's terms, as a *queer*, rather than *straight*, art since Koren noted that the aesthetic was emblematized less by the "rectilinear, precise, contained," closet-like "box as metaphor," and more by the circular "bowl," inclined to be "open at [the] top" to the world. These are characteristics viewers might note in the exhibit's roughly rectangular form; the way Sedgwick's sentence resists rectilinearity; and the way her fabrics' frayed edges suggest their openness, resulting in increasingly "delicate traces" and "faint evidence, at the borders of nothingness," as the woven silk again dissolves, at its edges, into a queer, increasingly open mesh, and then, at the edges of the individual threads, into the plaits of fibers making them up, in "Peatian" fashion.[13]

For Koren, *wabi-sabi* was best emblematized by the "minimalism" of ninth- and tenth-century Chinese poetry and monochromatic ink painting, the period of South and East Asian sculptural history that preoccupied Sedgwick, although her poetic examples often derive from later periods. In addition, Koren suggested that forms of "crude, anonymous, indigenous Japanese and Korean folk-craft" well emblematized the *wabi-sabi* anti-ideal. Sedgwick never directly signed her textiles, although, given my love of her first person, I have found it more difficult than Koren suggests is appropriate to generate readings that don't depend on "knowledge of the creator's background or personality."[14]

If *wabi-sabi* forms often incline toward a "spectrum of greys," "indigo," "brown and blacks," Sedgwick floated gray ink on her watery ground to generate her *suminagashi*, printed her text through dipping stamps into brown inks, and stained the surface of her largest swatch with two patches of indigo. In addition, Koren claims that *wabi-sabi* forms often possess a "vague, blurry, or attenuated quality—as things do as they approach nothingness (or come out of it)." Sedgwick's fonts resist the model of permanent print legibility; the font's expected "hard edges take on a soft pale glow," and their "once-substantial materiality" appears "almost sponge-like" as it absorbs the surrounding colors or is dissolved into them. Koren's work also reveals that Sedgwick was not the only person to have connected *wabi-sabi* with fractals. He documented that in *The Fractal Geometry of Nature* (1982), Mandelbrot elucidated a geometry that could be used to "mathematically describe irregular shapes and textures," such as the "grainy, tangled, wispy, wrinkled and the like"; textures Sedgwick's textiles achieved by virtue of their fraying edges, *shibori* technique, and fat, fractal wrinkles that often survived being laid flat and ironed, or the pulls of gravity when displayed on the wall.[15]

If Sedgwick's account of *shibori* was, in some ways, fractal, she first learned the technique from Yoshiko Iwamoto Wada, Mary Kellogg Rice, and Jane Barton's 1983 book, *Shibori: The Inventive Art of Japanese Shaped Resist Dyeing*. This revealed that the root verb, *shiboru*, meant to wring, squeeze, or press. In the context of fabrics, this referred to the tying and binding of the cloth in three dimensions, by folding and crumpling, stitching and plaiting, plucking and twisting, and binding and knotting, before dyeing it, so when the cloth was later unbound and laid flat, "soft- or blurry-edged" resist patterns emerged, whose motif was the polar opposite of their previous state. Or, if one wanted a "sharper-edged resist," as Sedgwick sometimes did for text, then a "stencil, paste, and wax" could be employed to form the letters, although an element of the unexpected was "always present." That the dyer was working in "concert with the materials, not in an effort to overcome them," represented a resonant notion for a "dy[e]ing" artist approaching the end of her life.[16]

As we saw in our discussions of *In the Bardo*, Sedgwick was particularly fond of a signature *shibori* motif, the *meyui*, or "tiny squared rings," formed by generating a "central unit of concentric rings" in the three-dimensional fabric (see figure 4.2); *meyui* that I previously read as evoking proliferative cancer cells and that spectators might consider in terms of what Wada refers to as "open-wound binding," especially given the bloody, gauzy character of Sedgwick's exhibit.[17]

In addition, the exhibit represented Sedgwick further exploring another central *shibori* genre: the temple banner, as well as referencing Buddhist priestly garments often made of patchwork, "a symbol of poverty long after poverty itself had been abandoned." These were often fashioned in silk, Sedgwick's favorite material, which "retains the sheen of a pearl," a pearlescence present in her lustrous silver gray, and indicating a key idea central to her late aesthetic: the beauty generated by bodily discomfort, by the sand in the oyster.[18]

Finally, viewers might consider the way Sedgwick's *shibori* technique recalls her earlier S/M interest in clamping and binding bodies. Her 1974 poems "The Palimpsest" and "Lost Letter" describe "marks of claws" and other "uneven horizontal stripes in red," such as those produced in "a whipping," on a human "trunk that's bent and tied / over [an] abdomen-high table, waiting for stripes."[19] These anticipate the bloody, claw-mark-like parallel stripes running vertically down Sedgwick's text swatches, congealing around the word *WORLD*. Spectators might additionally think about the menstrual and wounded evocations of what Wada characterizes as the "bleeding of dyes" in *shibori*; bloodstained swatches Sedgwick frequently employs.[20]

Reality Is Cloudlike, or Floating Clouds and Warholian Flowers

A little butterfly that had gone to sleep at the foot of the window seemed to be appending with its wings at the corner of this "Harmony in Grey and Pink" in the Whistlerian manner, the favourite signature of the Chelsea master.

—Marcel Proust, *In Search of Lost Time*, vol. 2

Sedgwick's second exhibit pondered an eighteenth-century Japanese death poem by Shagai:

> Reality is flowerlike:
> cold clouds sinking through
> the dusk.[21]

The haiku compares reality to a flower and cold clouds, with considerable explanatory work done and elided by the colon. This establishes a three-way relation, not quite an equivalence among reality, a singular flower, and multiple clouds, since reality is, from the outset, *metamorphic*; first flowerlike, then like clouds. On first reading, the relationship between those two is sequential, although, once readers have the poem in mind, the relations become less temporally syntactic. In the first case, the flowerlike reality might be short-lived but, like a gestalt, quickly grasped. In the second, reality is more embodied, durational, has a temperature: It takes time for cold clouds to sink into the dusk.

In contextualizing and capitalizing Shagai's haiku, Sedgwick again organizes it diagonally, emphasizing the loose *K* rhyme between "LIKE," "SINK," and "DUSK."

> REALITY IS FLOWERLIKE;
>   COLD CLOUDS SINKING
>   THROUGH
> THE DUSK

The grammatically contained first line harmonizes with its simple present tense, supporting the perception that there is something straightforwardly declarative and static about flowerlike reality. Sedgwick, however, changes the punctuation, concluding with a semicolon rather than a colon, transforming the relationship between the first and second parts of Shagai's poem, making them more sequential and less causal or parallel. Her setting of the more metamorphic cloudlike reality sinks toward the ground, buffeted one way, then another, by winds at different barometric heights. She elides Shagai's final period, to suggest his death in medias res, unable to finish his sentence.

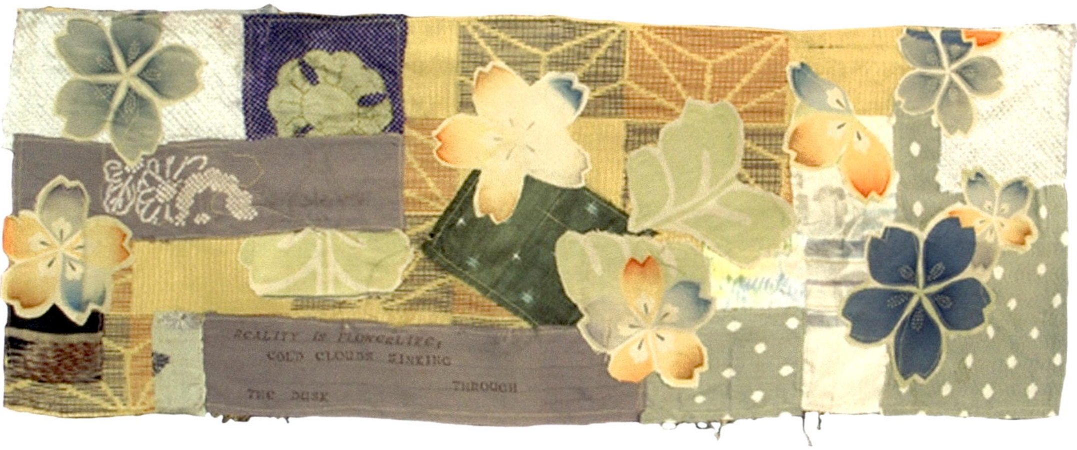

Figure 5.2. Eve Kosofsky Sedgwick, *Reality Is Flowerlike*, 2002. Photograph: Kevin Ryan. Collection of H. A. Sedgwick.

Above the text, Sedgwick distributes nine more or less intact blue- and rainbow-colored five-petaled flowers, in a beautiful, serpentine line, interspersed with three light-green leaves and a similarly colored flower toward the top left. She sets these against an unlucky thirteen swatches of differently patterned kimono and ikat silk. Twelve derive from *shibori* kimonos, the remaining, largest single swatch bearing witness to a related tie-dye process in which individual fibers, rather than the fabric, were tie-dyed, before being woven.[22] In the patchwork, Sedgwick hemmed some of her swatches in some places and snail-trail embroidered others, as in her earlier kimono collages. These snail trails emphasize further that reality is flowerlike. She seems to have glued together the remainder of the patches, letting their edges fray.

If viewers imagine looking down at the hanging from above, Sedgwick's desktop working orientation, the flowers appear to float on the surface of some murky water. If spectators encounter the piece hung vertically, as in the exhibition, the flowers appear to be billowing in a similar breeze to that affecting the text below and clouds above. The flowers are themselves cloudlike and allude to the water cycle. They rise, rainbow colored, from the left and evaporate to become blue, like the sky, and then condense and sink down again toward the middle, taking on the rainbow palette of the dawn or dusk, before evaporating up again, blue toward the top right. At the point of the fifth flower from the left, viewers are offered a fork in their path, an existential choice. Spectators can follow the rising diagonal floral path up to the right, or drop down to the blue flower below, perhaps encouraged by the snow that appears to be falling on the right side of the collage, only to rise again into the rainbow flower above it to the right, then continue up to the top right. (Settling snow is a repeated leitmotif in the exhibition, as we shall see.)

In addition to this word-image parallel, Sedgwick plays the game of finding images in the clouds, such that viewers recognize that they are flowerlike, and vice versa; recalling her dislike, in "The Warm Decembers," of "inexpressive, over-precise clouds / that could not change in shape."[23] Toward the top right, my attention also volleys between my perception of a green leaf and rainbow-colored half-flower, and my re-cognition of them as green birds, moths, or butterflies chasing each other toward the blue flower at top right.

If reality is flowerlike and cloudlike, Sedgwick invites spectators to think further about the radical metamorphosis between these and other perceptions. Viewers might again think of the transformations undergone by silkworms to become moths, given the butterflies here, and the way this silk hanging risked ending up as other moths' food. This is a view encouraged by the horizontal purple swatch toward the top left with its arched, caterpillar-like body approaching floral forms, perhaps to eat. As such, reality here is metamorphic, Taoist, and Buddhist, if viewers recall that, in certain forms of Buddhist pedagogy, "solidity is an illusion of the senses" and that seeing and understanding are processes that can take seconds, to differentiate within a gestalt, or lifetimes, given the life cycle of a silkworm.[24]

Sedgwick's inspiration for the panel partly derived from Kumiko Sudo's *East Quilts West* (1995), which was in her library. Like Sedgwick's collage, Sudo's monograph represented a "cross-cultural quilting" primer, teaching students how to combine "traditional American quilt construction methods of piecing, layering, and applique, with the traditional Japanese stitching technique of *sashiko*," with Sedgwick's *sashiko* method, originally used to repair and strengthen fabrics, resonant in the context of her feelings about needles, since the word translated as "little stabs."[25]

According to Sudo, in Japan, patchwork, like Sedgwick's, was partly an attempt to prolong the life of an old fabric, a poignant project in the context of Shagai's death poem and Sedgwick's late-life bardo. Patchwork was also a "spiritual exercise" in Japanese Buddhist culture, since, according to overlapping Shinto traditions, "all things, including cloth," had "a spirit." In addition, as Sudo notes, "quilted armor" was employed as "protection against arrows and swords" and quilted clothing "against the cold." This suggests that Sedgwick's collage registers and resists her repeated experience of "little stabs" and that the patchwork, thematizing cold clouds, also sought to quilt her from temperature extremes.[26]

On page 114 of *East Quilts West*, readers find themselves particularly close to Sedgwick as they discover the flower template she employed. On page 26, meanwhile, "Sakura, or Cherry Blossom" shows an effect of variously patchworked kimono silks, complete with floating flowers akin to Sedgwick's. The cherry blossom represented the Japanese national flower and was often compared to samurai spirits, who, like bodhisattvas, lingered in "this life when needed . . . , like cherry blossoms which never die on the branches but fall off in the blowing wind." This was an idea celebrated in an early April festival, so poignantly just after the death of Shagai, whose life was cut short.[27]

Two other passages from *East Quilts West* resonate. The first is Sudo's account of "Cho No Mai, or The Dance of the Butterfly," which featured a "dancer with a costume covered with a large butterfly design gracefully flitting from one flower to another in springtime." The second was "Kasumi, or A Hazy Sky," in which readers learn that the "greenish shapes on the top and bottom of [the] design" were traditional Japanese motifs called *kasumi*, employed to "symbolize a hazy sky or mist," while the "many-patterned clouds reflect the morning sunlight" and "circular bluish prints suggest fog in the morning"; ideas that all echo in Sedgwick's collage.[28]

Sedgwick's patchwork may have further Taoist resonances. In *The Way of Zen* (1957), a text Sedgwick taught in the course Asian Encounters, Alan Watts compared the Tao to "a cloud in the sky," evoking Sedgwick's hanging seen pictorially, while, seen on the desk horizontally, the collage evokes his Taoist reminder that a "river is always changing, from moment to moment." To get a better sense of Tao, Watts recommended looking at "rain or snow," the latter present in the two silver-blue swatches Sedgwick employed at the bottom right. The progress of her clouds from left to right, meanwhile, recalls Watts's assertion that life was like a "floating cloud that appears" and death a "floating cloud that disappears." Sedgwick's most abbreviated flower in the top right, looking like the contour of a pair of breasts seen from above, similarly recalls Watts's statement that the body might "appear and disappear like a cloud in the sky."[29]

Much is also to be learned from a third volume in Sedgwick's library: Isimura Hayao and Maruyama Nobuhiko's *Robes of Elegance: Japanese Kimonos of the 16th–20th Centuries* (1988). This revealed that Sedgwick's Rorschach-like collage again had a partly Japanese genealogy, in that kimono designs frequently contained "riddles and clues" requiring viewers to decode a "hidden meaning." Cloud shapes, "flying clouds blown by the wind," and "cloud motifs with fluttering butterflies" were all popular, while an indigo background, such as Sedgwick employed in three cloud-flowers, symbolized an "evening scene"; the evening of Shagai's and her own bardo.[30]

Like Sudo, Sedgwick was interested in the hybrid intersections of East and West, her collage recalling Andy Warhol as well as Taoism and Buddhism. We have already encountered Warhol's influence on Sedgwick's stitched photographic collages. Here, his *Flowers* are relevant.[31] To date, scholars have understood these to be "minor work, marking the end of his genuine production," if not exemplary of "meaningless image content" or akin to "strictly decorative, 'upper class wallpaper,'" with all its "feminine and queer associations." For Elissa Auther, Warhol's flowers are significant for just that reason, since they "activate the decorative as the queer."[32] But in the context of Sedgwick's and Shagai's work, Warhol's queerness is perhaps secondary to the *Flowers*' "funeral tone," especially since Sedgwick replaces Warhol's square format with a more coffin-like horizontal rectangle.[33]

Finally, and as the epigraph to this section suggests, Sedgwick's harmony in purple, gold, and blue has numerous Proustian (as well as Whistlerian) resonances. One of the things she liked most about Marcel Proust was his metamorphic sense of reality, with the narrator insisting that "recognitions" expressed an "important part of life."[34] With Sedgwick's patchwork in mind, viewers might think about the narrator's famous passion for Japanese paper flowers that "open[ed] their petals in a bowl of pure water."[35] The narrator also suggested that "the appearance of people, like that of the sea," was dependent on the clouds, which were often "themselves barely visible" but could change the "color of everything by their concentration," "mobility," "dissemination," and "flight."[36] Indeed, Sedgwick's collage emblematizes well her later artist's screed for *Works in Fiber, Paper, and Proust*, which described a sustained Proustian mysticism that did not "rely on the esoteric or occult, but on simple material metamorphoses as they are emulsified with meaning and language."[37]

Limpid Three Bodhisattvas: Theatricality and Absorption, or Blue Is the Warmest Color

In the exhibition, Sedgwick's favorite bodhisattva, Kuanyin, first appeared in the form of a quilted triptych, seated in the pose of *royal ease*. Titled *Limpid Three Bodhisattvas* (see figure 5.3), Sedgwick cyanotyped her three Kuanyins across more than twenty swatches of ragged, fraying, mostly square swatches of indigo- and denim-blue cotton. In the two identical, diminutive, flanking examples, Kuanyin sits, looking down in meditative introspection, her left leg pendant, left arm hanging down, and her bent right wrist resting on her raised right knee. The larger, central figure sits in half lotus, her weight resting on her

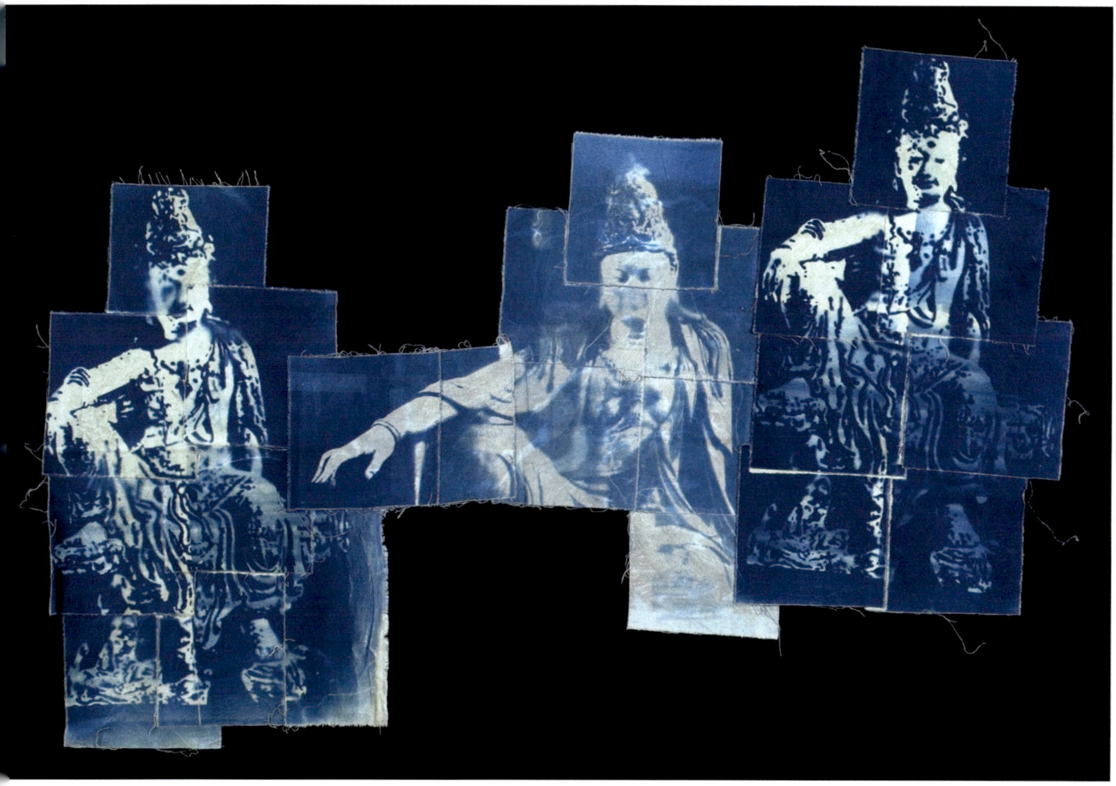

Figure 5.3. Eve Kosofsky Sedgwick, *Limpid Three Bodhisattvas*, 2002. Photograph: Kevin Ryan. Collection of H. A. Sedgwick. © H. A. Sedgwick

left palm, her right elbow resting on her right knee. Her right forearm, hand, and fingers extend elegantly into space, in a favorite Sedgwick iconography.

The bodhisattvas' downcast faces recall Silvan Tomkins's "attitude of shame" and reading, which we have already encountered, with its lowered eyelids, eyes, head, and "force field-creating power," generating the "kind of skin that sheer textual attention can weave around a reading body" to the extent that a "noisy bus station or airplane can be excluded from consciousness, an ongoing scene refused, a dull classroom monologue ignored." But, Sedgwick and Adam Frank insisted, this did not equate with a "pernicious idea of reading as escape." The posture registered "extroversion . . . as much as introversion," was as public as private, since all a reader had to do to transform their "inner life" experience into an audible performance was to begin reading aloud, and "even this may not be necessary." Sedgwick and Frank also suggested that there was "something about sustained and intense engagement" that "simply *is* theatrical," since the "additional skin shimmering[,] as if shrink-wrapped around a body-and-book[,] . . . sharply and sheerly delineates the conjunction or composition, making figural not escape or detachment but attention, interest."[38]

While Sedgwick had long been interested in art historian Michael Fried's theorizations of theatricality and absorption, much about the *Limpid Bodhisattvas* speaks to the Tomkins passage.[39] Sedgwick makes literal, material, the "force field-creating power," the "additional skin shimmering[,] as if shrink-wrapped around" Kuanyin's meditative body in the form of the fabric swatches that contain and extend beyond it, whose silhouette represents a kind of geometric equivalent to her body's curvaceous outline. Sedgwick also suggests the bodhisattva's powerful force field in the apparently electrified loose threads extending beyond the woven swatches' edges, speaking further to the "sheer textual attention" *woven* around the reading body, although here the skin of Kuanyin's attitude is less sheer than matte, more likely cotton than silk. Viewers might also think about the relationship of Kuanyin's skin and textiles: because of the sensation of the two against one another and because the fabrics Sedgwick prints these details on represent a second "kind of skin" invoking the spectator's tactile imagination.

If Sedgwick closely frames the bodhisattva's image, suggesting the power of meditation, like reading, to exclude the world, she refuses the idea of introspection as quietist by not cropping her images sharply around the bodhisattva's contours, but at a remove, in squares suggesting a real, latitudinal, longitudinal world. The figure's royal ease also balances a meditative introspection, in the downcast face, raised right knee, and left leg in half lotus in the central Kuanyin, with a compassionate concern for the world through the pendant left leg, in the framing examples, and with the central bodhisattva offering a hand to hold. In addition, Kuanyin is neither self-absorbed nor ashamed. She is a bodhisattva famed for her skillful relationality, having successfully evacuated her karmic personality in the service of others.

The cyanotype is also, importantly, a *patchwork*. Sedgwick could have selected a cotton swatch large enough to contain the bodhisattvas' whole forms or the entire triptych. Instead, her multipart collage again emphasizes the Buddhist doctrine of the aggregates, with the central bodhisattva missing the swatch representing her crotch as well as her right and left lower calf and foot. This speaks to a body, like Sedgwick's, missing some crucial elements—a breast, increasingly an erotic life—but still able to function as integral. More positively, Kuanyin's missing crotch might speak to Sedgwick's hope that her bodhisattvas need not be perceived through the eyes of gender.

The collage's overall castellated upper silhouette resembles the Buddhist stupas Sedgwick encountered in Thailand, as we have seen, while her trinity of bodhisattvas signals Kuanyin's miraculous ability to appear in multiple locations simultaneously, given the repetition of the two flanking figures, and in different avatars through time, thanks to the variant central version.

Sedgwick's cyanotype also recalls the Victorian photographic practice of Anna Atkins. While unmentioned in "Making Things, Practicing Emptiness," Atkins, among the "great domestic photographers of the nineteenth century," was surely on Sedgwick's mind, since it was Atkins, not Clementina Hawarden or Julia Margaret Cameron, who was famous for her cyanotypes.[40] The juxtaposition of Sedgwick's indigo-and-white palette with Atkins's interest in marine biology suggests her bodhisattvas are sinking to the bottom of the ocean. In so doing, they recall Ariel's song from William Shakespeare's *The Tempest* (1610–11), especially as mediated through Henry James:[41]

> Full fathom five thy father lies;
> Of his bones are coral made;
> Those are pearls that were his eyes:
> Nothing of him that doth fade,
> But doth suffer a sea-change
> Into something rich and strange.[42]

Here, fathoms deep, Kuanyin seems to sit, her bones transformed to bleached coral, especially in the case of the central bodhisattva, given the dendrite-like structure of her extended fingers. Kuanyin also undergoes a further sea change between the first and second panels, then back again to the iconography of the first. In addition, the bodhisattva has metamorphosed from the rich polychrome of the original three-dimensional statue, as it was first captured in a two-dimensional color photograph, before being bleached black and white in Sedgwick's monochrome acetate version, and blue-printed in the final blue-and-white version.

Kuanyin's pearly eyes further recall the pearlescent gray of the title piece, a palette signaling the beauty born of dis-ease, the sand in the oyster shell, the polyp-tumor in the body of an artist suffering from metastatic cancer. Pushing against Ariel's song in a more Taoist direction, Kuanyin also seems to be in the process of fading across time, with the central bodhisattva representing a muted, less indigo-saturated version of the flanking figures.

Finally, Sedgwick's blue is again Derek Jarman's. I return to the British filmmaker here because he shot a version of *The Tempest* in 1979, involving blue-tinted film, and because his more famous 1993 film, *Blue*, his last, represented a meditation on a different kind of sea change, that of a body increasingly blinded by CMV (cytomegalovirus). The film also meditated on the half-life of queer textiles, such as Sedgwick's, themselves vulnerable to insect infestation, with Jarman's bitter assertion during the film that "we have to live with AIDS while they spread the quilt for the moths of Ithaca across the wine dark sea." Like Sedgwick, Jarman seems to have hated the quilt. Living with her own challenging disease, Sedgwick had begun, like Jarman and many of the African American vocalists she admired, "singing the blues."[43]

Bodhisattva Fractured World

Bodhisattva Fractal World featured four images deriving from conservation X-rays of a sculpted bodhisattva's arm, originating in a 1985 monograph, *Guanyin: A Masterpiece Revealed*, concerned with the restoration of a twelfth-century Chinese wooden statue seated in royal ease. The catalog featured nearly ninety images of Kuanyin in various stages of repair, but it was figure 13 that most caught Sedgwick's attention. This featured an X-ray of Kuanyin's right hand.[44] *Bodhisattva Fractal World* contained two landscape-oriented hangings inspired by the X-ray, the first featuring a single image, the second a group of three; pieces suggesting we hear the near homophone of *Bodhisattva Fractal World* as *Bodhisattva Fractured World*.

In the first exhibit, Sedgwick took the original black-and-white X-ray and cyanotyped it in indigo and white across four pieces of overlapping, roughly square, unhemmed cotton swatches. Because many of the patches fray into longer, distinct threads floating out to the left, the patchwork anticipates another hanging in the exhibition, employing an eighteenth-century Japanese death poem by Choko:

> This final scene I'll not see
> to the end—my dream
> is fraying.[45]

Sedgwick's metamorphic, abstract resurrected X-ray emphasizes what is hidden inside the statue, queerly reversing the polarity of inside and out, performing a kind of coming out. Her patchwork respects the integrity of the bodhisattva's extended arm but crops two panels of dead space below her wrist and hand. Sedgwick's printing of the original image across four panels, however, paradoxically fractures Kuanyin's arm further. The white right edges of the first two panels from the left and the fraying edge of the cotton weave throughout both interrupt the otherwise continuous ink printing the bodhisattva's arm (see figure 5.4).

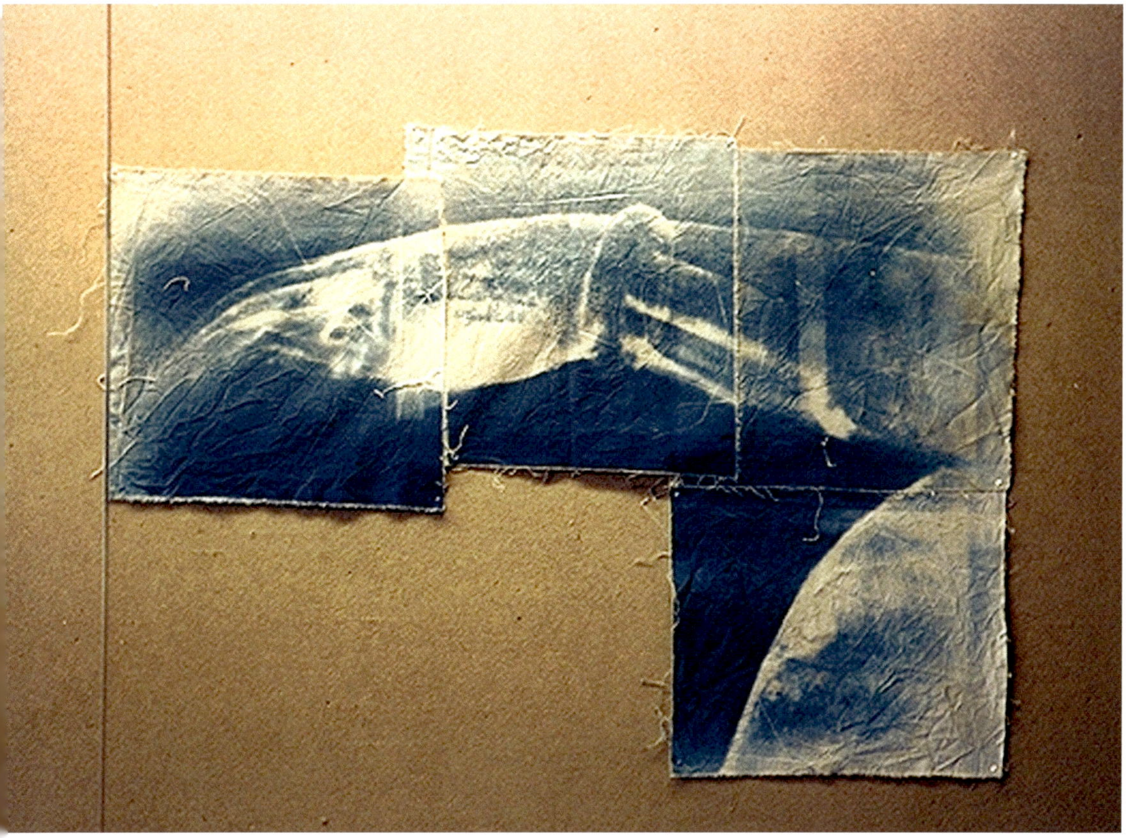

Figure 5.4. Eve Kosofsky Sedgwick, untitled collage, 2002. Photograph: H. A. Sedgwick. Collection of H. A. Sedgwick. © H. A. Sedgwick

While employing roughly square swatches, Sedgwick characteristically resists the straightforward rectilinearity of the original photograph in the name of something *scrappier*, more layered. The patch on the left is out of line with the upper edges of the two swatches to the right, and the right contour of the collage slants diagonally from the top right, while the lower edge of the second piece from the right descends in a diagonal from the top left.

Sedgwick complements her *scrappy*, stepped cropping with characteristically *sloppy* printing, blurrier than her source. Her technical process again alludes to Atkins. Because of their blue-and-white patterns, Atkins's plants seem to be floating on the surface of water or sinking into it. As a result of the resemblance, Sedgwick's hanging again recalls *The Tempest* and evokes Taoist transformation. If *Guanyin: A Masterpiece Revealed* emphasized the possibility of restoration, of returning the belatedly monochrome statue to its original polychrome, as in Ariel's song there is a more deathly knell to Sedgwick's hanging, given her autobiographical context, and since this is a fraying final scene in which the rectilinear structure of the weave, like the skeletal and tissue structure of Sedgwick's body, is breaking down, separating into its constituent elements. The collage's contour threads, like tumors, act in an increasingly autonomous, free-floating manner, extending into the surrounding space, like the hair of a person sinking into water. Sedgwick's indigo-blue cyanotype ink further emphasizes this sense of sinking and drowning, suggesting that water has steeped deep into the bodhisattva's white skeleton. White, meanwhile, was the color of mourning across much of Asia and a color Sedgwick associated with the glasses of her friend Michael Lynch, who died from AIDS.[46]

As in much of Sedgwick's textile work, however, especially that inspired by Proust, Kuanyin's apparent death is the prelude to a marvelous transformation. In Ariel's song, the father's bones become coral; a life-form with roots, like one of Atkins's plants; and with rock-hard surfaces made up of thousands of living polyps. Polyps are invertebrates, with a saclike body and mouth encircled by stinging tentacles, which absorb calcium carbonate from the surrounding sea to build a hard limestone skeleton, which, in turn, protects the polyp's delicate body; an animal that was to preoccupy Sedgwick in her Proust works, as we shall see. And so, if her source image records multiple historical scenes of sculptural fracture and their repair, Sedgwick's hollowing collage suggests that her osteoporosis, resulting from the early menopause induced by her cancer treatment, might be ultimately reversible. In addition to evoking a polyp, Kuanyin's sea change is into something resembling a shrimp, swimming in left profile, its antennae extending into the water. As a result, there is a transformation from a humanlike figure, with its still-vulnerable, but patched-up, fractured interior skeleton, prosthetically supported by dowels and nails, into a creature with a crunchy exoskeleton to protect its soft core.[47]

Sedgwick continued to work with the conservation X-ray in a second collage. This featured three landscape-oriented cyanotypes, again printed on overlapping pieces of quilted cotton, layered across the three patchworks (see figure 5.5). Sedgwick again prints her second hanging across an unlucky thirteen, mostly square, pieces of fabric. There are again two key exceptions: a smaller, rectangular swatch toward the top left, presumably providing additional strength to support the suspended weight of the pieces below; and the piece at the right side of the second line, its upper-right corner diagonally cropped. Because none of the edges are hemmed, many of the swatches are characteristically disintegrating.

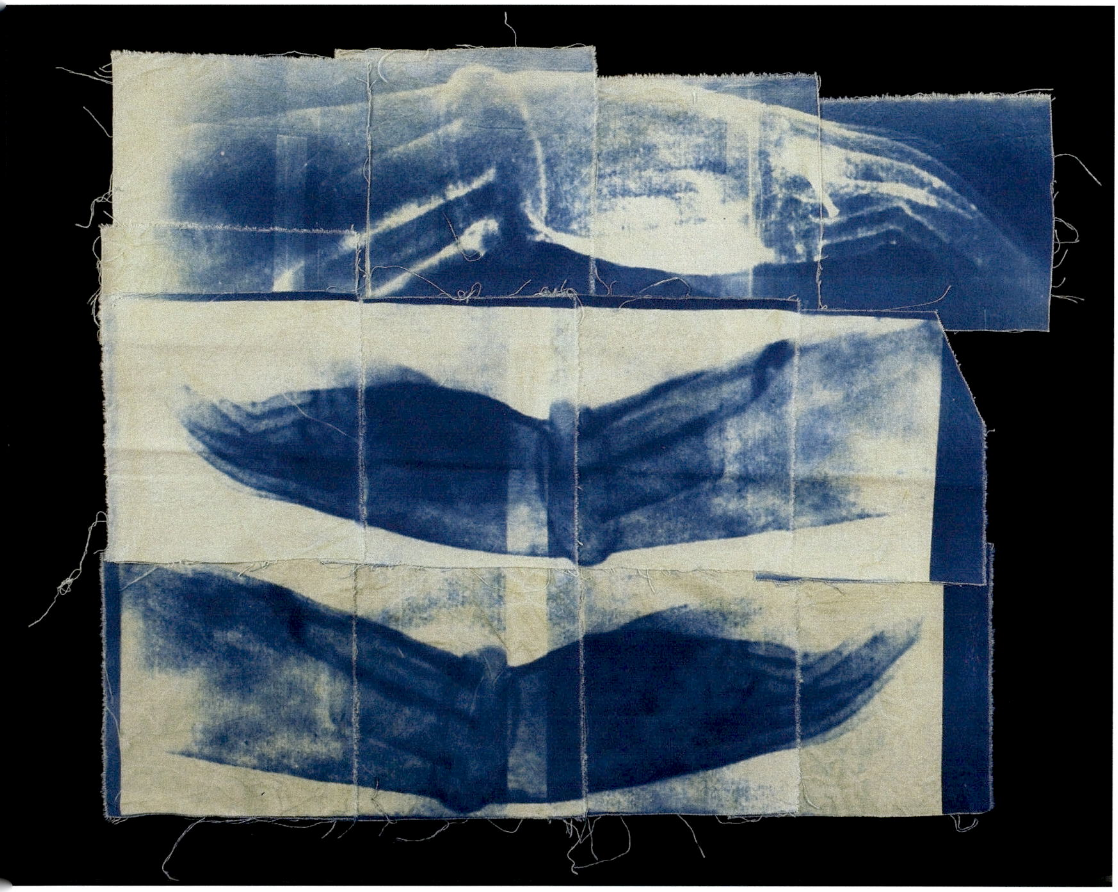

Figure 5.5. Eve Kosofsky Sedgwick, untitled collage, 2002. Photograph: Kevin Ryan. Collection of H. A. Sedgwick. © H. A. Sedgwick

The top patchwork returns to the source image but crops it more emphatically, cutting out the bodhisattva's right knee in favor of a more concentrated focus on her right arm. In addition, Sedgwick employed her transparency in reverse, flipping it over horizontally so that the wrist extends to the right rather than the left. In the pair of images below it, she has turned her source acetate over vertically, so the wrist again extends to the left, upside down, in the second patchwork down. These are disorienting, transforming reorientations that make it difficult to recognize the source, changing the feeling of weight, directionality, and polarity. Where, in the top image, the bodhisattva's wrist appears white against blue, in the second and third rows Sedgwick employed a *negative* of the original, so the exposed area of the arm has gone blue, while the shaded area around it remains white. In this new, contrasting context, viewers might ponder the concepts of positive and negative in the context of the AIDS crisis and think about the polarizing, transformative effects of HIV on the body, as it transitioned from negative to positive.[48]

Spectators might additionally think about the layout of the patchwork as akin to poetry, with Sedgwick's favorite three-line form containing four beats per row, especially since there is a kind of inverted visual rhyme between the descending extremity of the image at the end of the first line, of a white arm against a blue ground, and the ascending image, at the end of the third line, of a blue arm against a white ground, as if reaching up to meet it. This is the *aba* rhyme scheme James Merrill employed for his haiku in "Prose of Departure," his meditation on friends dying of AIDS, one of the sources of Sedgwick's own autobiography, further supporting the potential relevance of the AIDS crisis.[49]

The less rectilinear second hanging feels more damaged than the first. Sedgwick incorporates a clear series of descending stepped crops at the top right, the first cutting into the upper edge of the bodhisattva's arm. Sedgwick also chops out an inverted right-angle triangle at the top right corner of the second line. The sense of drowning is further emphasized, in the second exhibit, by the way Sedgwick's cyanotype ink initially surrounds and is beginning to soak into the white, bony skeletal structure of the bodhisattva's arm, in the first line, before almost entirely saturating it by the second and third lines. That sense of sinking further emerges across the three lines, with the bodhisattva's arm raised up, as if out of the water, in line 1, but dropping down with the weight of the elbow in lines 2 and 3. This is a body, perhaps like Sedgwick's, increasingly more cut into, amputated, disorienting, and disoriented in form, and saturated with feeling blue.

I Have Always Known, or Epistemology of the Path

Sedgwick's fourth exhibit was a ragged, roughly square collage of *shibori* silk, comprising at least twelve ribbons of rectangular, horizontal swatches glued together (figure 5.6). Sedgwick hung the piece pictorially, recalling the Japanese word *kakekotoba*, translated as "hanging word," a term used to convey double meanings. She pinned the collage to the wall without a frame to emphasize its fraying edges, evoking an entomological specimen, again resonant given its silk ground. On the hanging, she printed in uppercase letters a famous death poem by ninth-century aristocratic Japanese *waka* poet Ariwara no Narihira, as translated in Kenneth Rexroth's *One Hundred Poems from the Japanese* (1964). This was a verse, exceptionally, not found in Yoel Hoffmann's *Japanese Death Poems*, Sedgwick's usual haiku source in the exhibition. Narihira's poem

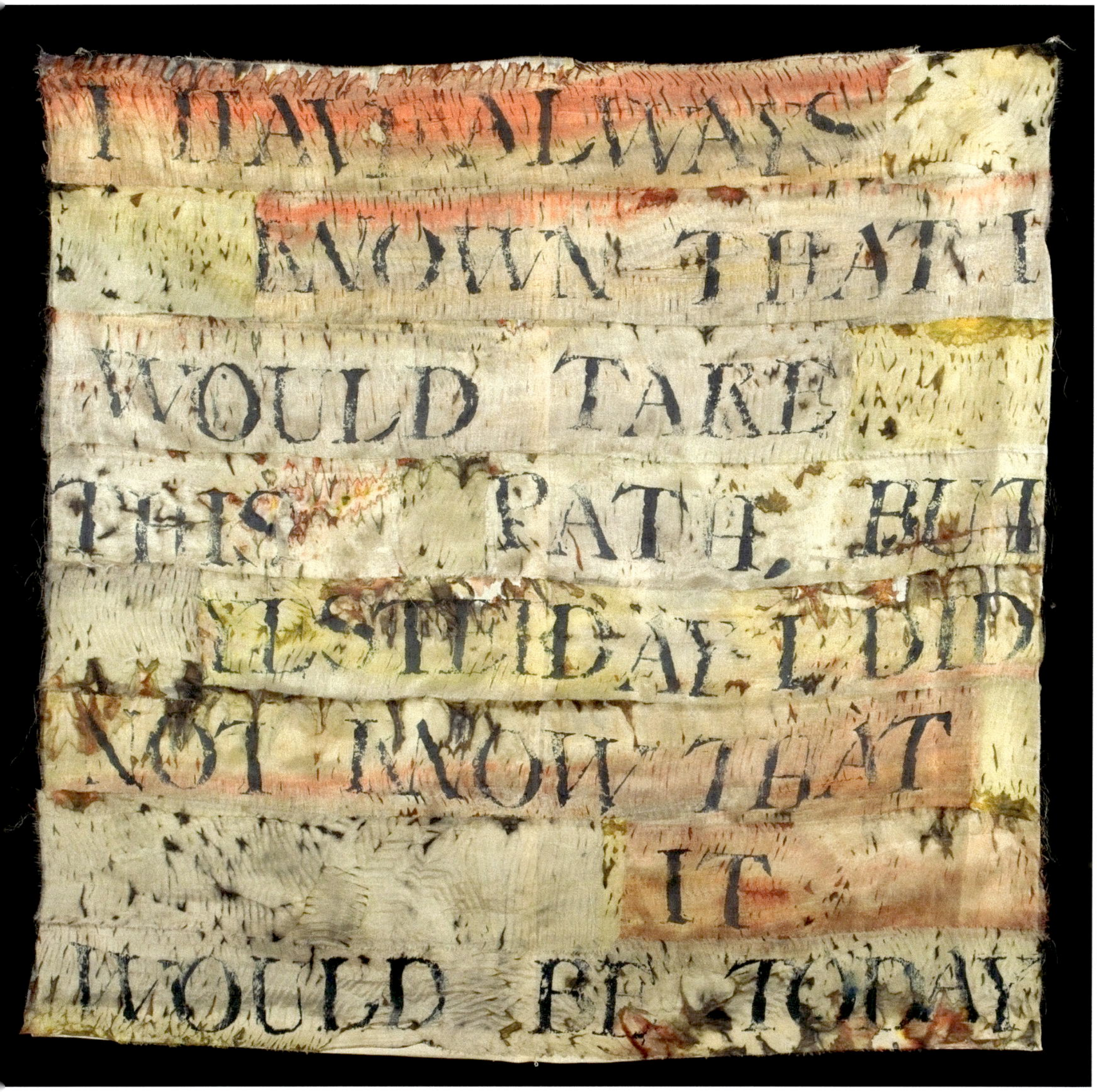

Figure 5.6. Eve Kosofsky Sedgwick, untitled collage, 2002. Photograph: Kevin Ryan. Collection of H. A. Sedgwick. © H. A. Sedgwick

derived from a corpus of eighty-seven surviving, more or less securely attributed verses, frequently employing the 31 syllable (5–7-5–7-7) *uta* form more familiar to European readers from its shortened haiku (5–7-5) variant. The poem represented the final verse from Narihira's haibun, *The Tales of Ise*, its combined prose-verse form having possibly inspired Sedgwick's autobiography.[50]

Sedgwick employed a standard translation of Narihira's poem:

I HAVE ALWAYS
KNOWN THAT I
WOULD TAKE
THIS PATH, BUT
YESTERDAY I
DID NOT KNOW THAT
IT WOULD BE TODAY.

Unlike Narihira's calligraphic original, Sedgwick rubber-stamped uppercase letters on her hanging, making it more like the typeface version of later, printed translations. Like many of Narihira's poems, within *The Tales of Ise*, however, her verse is composed on a silk ground. For example, Narihira describes how, like for "a silkworm, yes," it was "better far to have been born / in spite of its short-lived life."[51]

Narihira's novella is composed of episodic narrative prose interspersed with lyrics, whose poetic and relational effects, as H. Jay Harris notes, rise "as much from the spaces between the short sentences as from the sentences themselves," spaces Sedgwick's hanging chromatically emphasizes.[52] The lines Sedgwick employs occur in the final "Dan" (section) of the *Tales*, which begins by telling of how "long ago a man fell gravely ill."[53] Narihira describes how the man "knew in his heart that he was to die":

In this end—this road
deathward all men must travel:
This I always knew
but yesterday or today . . .
no! never had I thought it.[54]

In relation to the poem, Harris comments that Narihira, aware that he will die, is neither ready nor willing to do so "today" but, out of this dilemma, provides an "elegant end to his symbolic life" within the tales.[55] Sedgwick's take on the poem is more sanguine, in a variety of senses:

I HAVE ALWAYS
    KNOWN THAT I
  WOULD TAKE
THIS   PATH, BUT
    YESTERDAY I DID
  NOT KNOW THAT
                IT
WOULD BE TODAY

Sedgwick takes as read Narihira's biographical context, the bardo of grave illness that she also was inhabiting. She also omits his sense that "he knew in his heart that he was to die." That may be because she was then still wrangling with what her 1997 essay "Reality and Realization" described as "that most ordinary and yet oddly privileged encounter, the *tête-à-tête* with mortality": in her case learning a cancer she thought was in remission had become incurable. Such an encounter, she acknowledged, did "involve a privilege, though not an absolute one, with respect to reality": It "concentrate[d] the mind wonderfully" and made "inescapably vivid in repeated mental shuttle passes the considerable distance between *knowing* that one will die and *realizing* it"; "repeated shuttle passes" evoked in the horizontal *shibori* wefts making up her Narihira hanging.[56]

Rather than Narihira's masculinist generalization that "deathward all men travel," "Reality and Realization" ponders a range of the "very exigent uses" different people had "for the idea of dying—whether shaped by depression, hysteria, hypochondria," or "existential heroics," uses coupled with the "seemingly absolute inaccessibility of our own death to our living consciousness." As such, Sedgwick notes, death offers the "most heightened example of reality, where reality is taken to indicate precisely a gap between knowing something on the one hand, and on the other understanding it as real."[57]

In her closely related "Pedagogy of Buddhism" essay, Sedgwick had been left wondering, "Do I really, *really* realize, even now, that I'm mortal?" This was a "constricting, obsessional" question with a "first-person singular" that seemed more like "a specimen to be immobilized," as the hanging had been pinned to the wall, "rather than a vagrant place-holder," as the ink forming the text only partially printed the letters, and faded over time.[58] These combined forms suggest both the poignant mortality of the text's printer and the uncertain epistemology underlying the hanging's "I have always known"; what Sedgwick characterized as the "shrunken impoverishment of any Western psychology of knowledge and realization," "compared with its density and richness in Buddhist thought."[59]

Sedgwick makes this shrunken impoverishment literal, in the hanging, by the way the ink fails to reach to the edges of the stenciled letters. In addition, the spaces at the beginnings and ends of many lines represent a visualization of what "Reality and Realization" called the "stuttering, exclusive perseveration of epistemological propositions," particularly given the twice-repeated "KNOW." After all, the confident, apparently obvious present perfect tense of "I HAVE ALWAYS KNOWN" is later interrupted by a "BUT," reading, thereafter, as "a stubborn hysterical defense" against really knowing mortality, or what Sedgwick characterized as a "true recognition of materiality." This is a textile materiality that, in the hanging, poignantly frays at the edges as well as fades across its exposed surfaces. That temporalized textile materiality seems closer to the challenging epistemology of mortality than at least the first half of Narihira's quoted sentence, which, again in words borrowed from the essay, "can't stop claiming mastery as the flat, propositional object of a single verb, shivering in its threadbare near-transparency: the almost fatally thin 'to know.'"[60]

Indeed, the hanging alludes to the ontology of the second part of Sedgwick's description in various ways. The *shibori* fabric, being first bound and then unbound, is springy and elastic, fat in contrast to the flatness of paper. As a result, and thanks to the pinning at only the corners, the hanging is again barometrically sensitive, so that it might be seen to be "shivering." As viewers also see at the top of the hanging, the ragged, fraying fabric is "threadbare," "almost fatally thin," indeed nearly transparent at the top left. Sedgwick's lineation also plays an effective part. Traditionally, the poem is translated into English in a four-line form:

> I have always known
> That at last I would
> Take this road, but yesterday
> I did not know that it would be today.

Sedgwick respects the central punctuation, marking, with a comma, the pause between the two parts of the sentence, but her shouty capitalization again recalls her conceptualization of Western epistemology as a "stubborn hysterical defense," while her omission of the final period does not provide the traditional translation's comforting closure, where the speaker finishes his sentence before he dies. In the hanging, by contrast, just as it takes a long time for the speaker to "KNOW," given the mind-blanking gap at the start of the enjambed second line, death arrives before Sedgwick's speaker can place their final punctuation mark.

In addition, Sedgwick at least doubles the length of time, through her eight-line version, and the many spaces within it, that it takes the poet to have the idea, to suggest a slowness of catching on. Her rhyme scheme also evokes a constant, anxious, or defensive circling back to earlier moments in the verse. "TODAY" poignantly recalls the earlier, soon-to-be-lost "I" and the living poet's mistaken sense of their own permanence in "ALWAYS." The "IT" of the speaker's final moments circles back to both "THAT" and the now denying and resistant "BUT."

Sedgwick's metrics also make for maximum poignancy with the diminishing number of syllables across the first four lines, down from four to three to two, suggesting that time is running out, before the "BUT" launches the second half

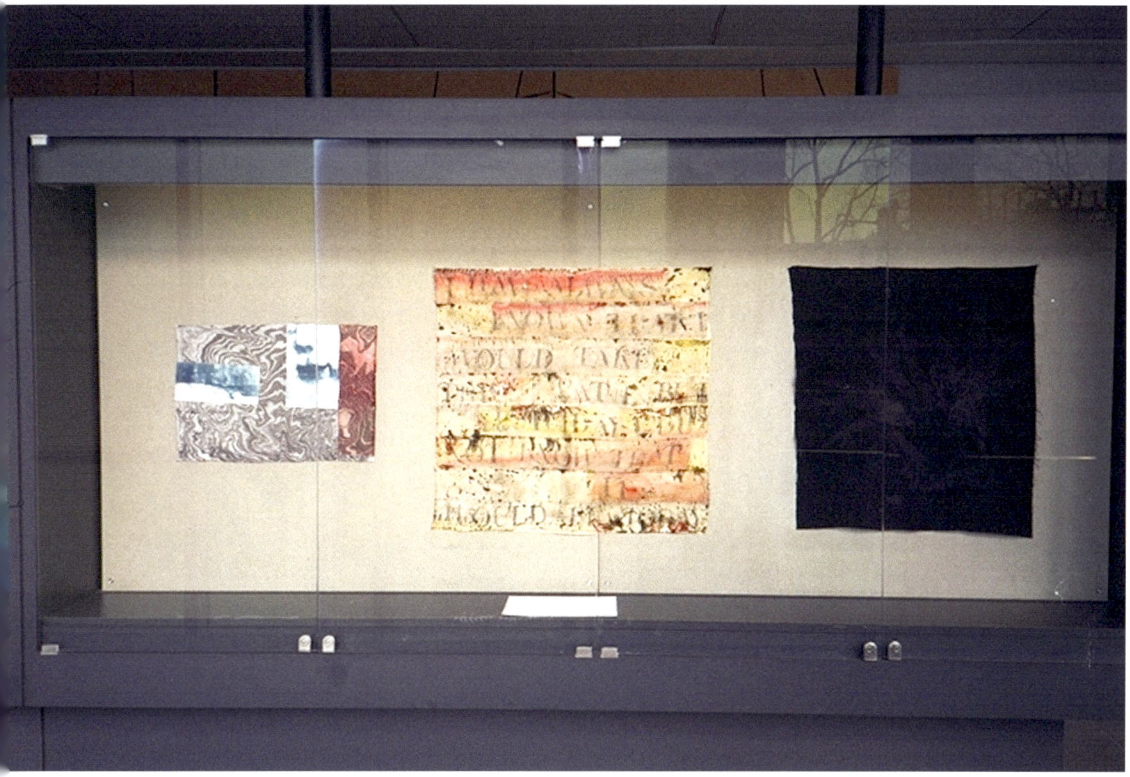

Figure 5.7. Eve Kosofsky Sedgwick, *Bodhisattva Fractal World* (installation view), 2002. Photograph: H. A. Sedgwick. Collection of H. A. Sedgwick. © H. A. Sedgwick

of the sentence, a pattern then recurring in the latter half of the poem, which diminishes from five to three to the single syllable of the now impersonal and isolated "IT," where formerly there was an "ID," and before that an "I."

The word "YESTERDAY" is, perhaps, the hardest word to read, given its failed printing, pointing to the impossibility of going backward. This sense of a movement into black nothingness must have been particularly emphasized in the layout of the exhibition, where viewers shuffled from the smiling face of Kuanyin to Narihira's poem to what, in the photograph, appears to be an inky black square depicting nothing, while outside, reflected in the glass, are the bare branches of winter trees.

Sedgwick's *shibori* method, meanwhile, suggests that something that had been wound up tightly has found release as it is laid out flat, perhaps like the speaker. Finally, the collage's palette again evokes the mortal body, with its urine-yellow recalling incontinence pads, its sanguine pink staining the epistemological parts of the sentence "I HAVE ALWAYS / KNOWN" and "I DID NOT KNOW THAT IT," the body's materiality emphasizing the inevitability of mortality.

In such a chromatic context, the poem becomes another of Sedgwick's "Bathroom Songs," suggesting a poet who, amid the "clinging scenes" of epistemological "karma," could "tinkle in the loo," but who found "Letting go of Number Two," of a more substantial part of herself, a "wee bit more forbidding." The ink on the untitled hanging is fast fading, so let us, now that she has "gone, gone, forever gone," respond, as Sedgwick's parents do in the poem: "What a masterpiece, Evita!"[61]

Bodhisattva with Multiple Arms, or A Little Spied-On Scene

Sedgwick's fifth exhibit witnessed the reappearance of the central *Limpid Bodhisattva*. The large fabric square, with characteristically fraying edges, doubled the figure across the exhibition, just as Kuanyin's earlier flanking images were paired. If the repetition suggested the bodhisattva's ability to appear both in two locations at once and in different forms over time, the form of Sedgwick's Kuanyin here drew on a broad South Asian iconography of multiarmed divinities signaling their superhuman status and ability to act on multiple fronts simultaneously. This was a "grotesque," "monstrous," *queer* iconography of Kuanyin that proved difficult for eighteenth- and nineteenth-century art historians, devoted to Greco-Roman classicism, to come to terms with.[62] Sedgwick was less abashed, recalling the work of another late nineteenth-century photographer, Eadweard Muybridge, famous for his time-lapse sequences of creatures in motion; an invocation suggesting that her viewers could slow down time and freeze-frame Kuanyin's elegant movements to see different frames in sequence.

Sedgwick's archives enable us to reverse engineer her icon to ascertain the many incarnations of Kuanyin that occurred within her process. Sedgwick began with a color photograph of a polychrome sculpture. She scanned the image into her computer and generated a monochrome version. She produced a negative, so that black patches became white and vice versa. She printed that negative onto acetate, using this as a cyanotype resist, with the image reversing in polarity again, so that the former black areas came out white and white areas blue-black. This reversing polarity might again have responded to the "nodal point" of summer 1996, in the development of AIDS treatments, when, "for many, HIV could plausibly be treated as a chronic disease."[63]

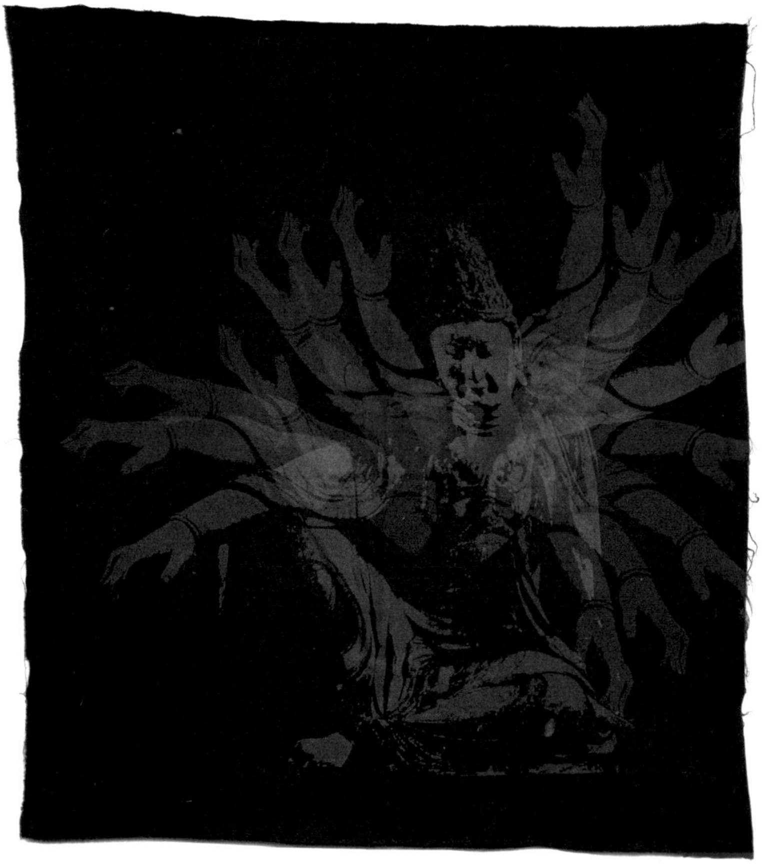

Figure 5.8. Eve Kosofsky Sedgwick, untitled cyanotype, 2002. Photograph: H. A. Sedgwick. Collection of H. A. Sedgwick. © H. A. Sedgwick

Sedgwick did not generate only one acetate. She layered twelve or more before exposing her fabric to the light. The additional acetates were smaller crops of the bodhisattva's right forearms, akin to those employed in her fracture pieces. These were posed in *apana mudra* with the two outer fingers raised, signaling the air and earth, and two inner fingers lowered, evoking fire and water, a balance of the elements imagined to be efficacious in eliminating toxins in the body, to prevent disease; a reparative aesthetic resonant to an artist living with advanced cancer.

Moving clockwise, the unstoppable, beautifully unfolding hands of time represent a poignant metaphor. The first two additional arms were direct repetitions, each moved 10 degrees closer to the perpendicular. After this, Sedgwick flipped her acetate images over *vertically*, through 180 degrees, for the remaining four arms on the viewer's left, since Kuanyin's palm, after this point, no longer faces down but up (see figure 5.9). Following this, Sedgwick flipped her acetates *horizontally* through 180 degrees, for the remaining mudras, on our right, to represent Kuanyin's left arm.

Sedgwick's positioning of the overall icon represents characteristically sloppy crafting, with the bodhisattva's hands repeatedly cut off; a further meditation on the *aggregates*, pondering how crucial Kuanyin's extremities were to her sense of identity and iconographic legibility. On the right, meanwhile, Kuanyin's fingers dissolve suddenly into threads of cotton at the ragged edges, as if her body extends more impersonally, dendritically, and texturally beyond the swatch. This recalls the Buddhist idea of the red threads extending out from birth, connecting the baby to everyone who will be important to it across its lifetime, and evokes Kuanyin's simultaneously impersonal and personal relationality. In so doing, the icon recalls again the closing pages of Sedgwick's autobiography: that "inexhaustibly pleasing," similarly "time-lapse graphic" that sees her therapist "occupy the place where [Sedgwick] was, encountering [her] ghost without recognition, unmaking [her] mistake" while she is simultaneously "turning back, seeing it," "lov[ing] that his care for [her] was not care for [*her*]."[64]

Much about the scene resonates here. The time-lapse graphic obviously; Kuanyin's ghostly, only just visible appearance; the inhuman impersonality of thread the bodhisattva's touch dissolves into; the way the fraying threads unmake, by disappearing, Sedgwick's "mistake" in printing the icon too large for the swatch, with Kuanyin and Shannon Van Wey both, by comparison, more "alert to [their] surroundings." Further recalling Van Wey's "calm buoyancy," Kuanyin again seems to be floating on the water's indigo surface, if imagined from above, doing a kind of butterfly backstroke. "Bobbing up gently" is how Sedgwick describes her therapist.[65] In addition, while she does not specify the weather in *Dialogue*'s final scene, she twice describes the "gray building" where Van Wey practices, alongside the bank "mulched with its slippery pine needles." These suggest it is autumn. Similarly, in one of the icon's installation shots, viewers can see a distant gray roofline, and the silhouettes of leafless trees, reflected in the vitrine, which becomes a mirror thanks to the icon's dark-indigo backing.

The final scene of *Dialogue* became a key "object of reflection" for Sedgwick, as we have seen; something she could "turn inward toward"; a "condensation of sweetness" she could suck on; a clitoral "enigmatic pebble" she could "secretly finger." Whenever she felt "frustration or fear," it would "make [her] smile." Like a slightly baffled Sedgwick, who nevertheless "doesn't resist" the scene's

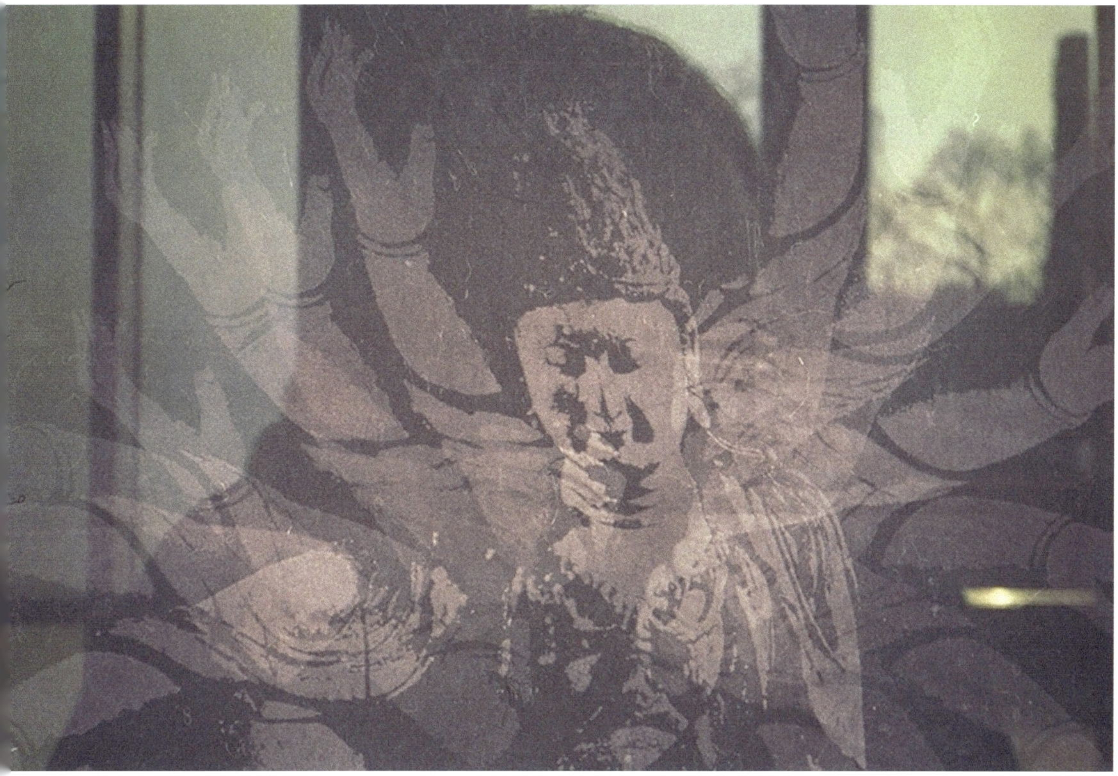

Figure 5.9. Eve Kosofsky Sedgwick, untitled cyanotype (detail), 2002. Photograph: H. A. Sedgwick. Collection of H. A. Sedgwick. © H. A. Sedgwick

invocation, the icon's viewers "can't quite figure out" her hanging because her acetate didn't quite "resist" enough, producing a turbulent indigo opacity. But, again like Van Wey, Kuanyin is engaged in a sequence of "immediate, involuntary substitution[s]," given the sheer number of her arms "doing reparative work," all seen through a reflecting glass, which reveals the icon, viewer, and spectator's backdrop.[66] As Sedgwick put it in her 1973 poem, "An Essay on the Picture Plane," whose scene was, similarly, "a street at 8 or 9 / in cold weather":

> The place is marked where things will disappear
> and what is there is salvaged from the horizon.
>
> The vertical plane makes the absence present
> to you, who are absent both from the horizon
> and from the fabric itself before you
> which is too articulate. Be thankful

for the absence is at least here, because it is stretched,
stretching clear to the edges, and immobile.
Be grateful too when sometimes it resolves
as a woven thing with just a woven depth.[67]

Or, as she put it in *Dialogue*, twenty-six years later:

This little spied-on
scene: how does it endow [us]
with hidden treasure?[68]

I Shift My Pillow Closer to the Moon, or Moon at the Window

Sedgwick's sixth exhibit contained a nineteenth-century Japanese death poem, by Saiba, which reads:

I shift my pillow
closer to the
full moon.

According to Hoffmann, Saiba died on the day of the autumn full moon, and the poet referred to "the act of moving his bed closer to the window through which the moon [was] shining."[69] On her collage, Sedgwick radically realigned Saiba's lineation (see figure 5.10). Following modernist typographic conventions, she employed two different fonts at different scales: a large-scale upper case for the first "I SHIFT," and a smaller, fancier capital case for "MY PILLOW CLOSER TO THE FULL MOON." She printed the entire text on a panel ten degrees left of the perpendicular. She also printed the first two letters perpendicular to the rest, running up vertically from the bottom, setting the last seven words on descending, increasingly tabbed rising curved lines, from the top left to bottom right, except for "TO THE FULL," which she tabbed back left. After a final spurt of energy, up toward the moon, the poem sinks to the ground. To emphasize the deathliness of Saiba's haiku, and its communication across the life-death divide, Sedgwick's horizontal moon-crescents of texts, pointing up, invert the design of Merrill's Ouija board, with its crescent of letters pointing down, a séance scenario recalled by her Ephraim-like capitalization.[70]

Thanks to Sedgwick's typography, Saiba's poem is initially difficult to comprehend, since viewers must recognize that the second letter they encounter, the *S*, is not a capital, like the first-person singular *I* that begins the verse, and

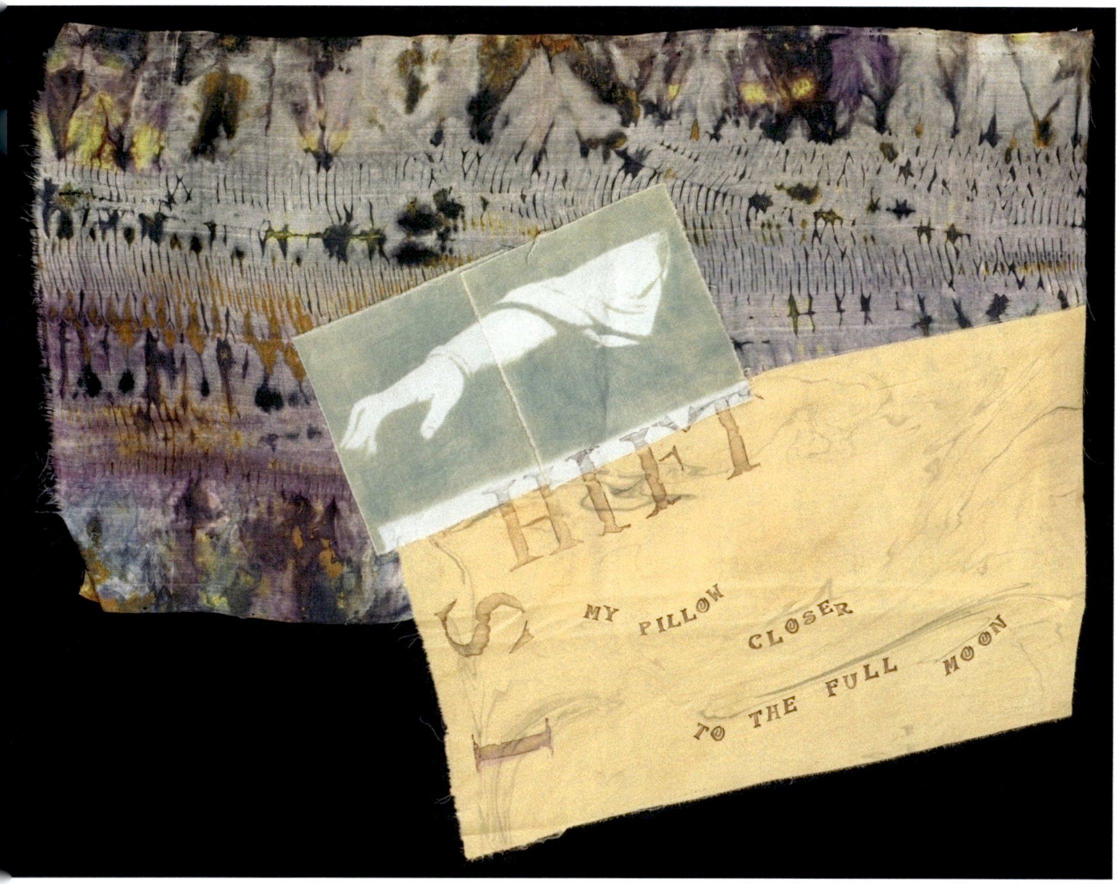

Figure 5.10. Eve Kosofsky Sedgwick, untitled collage, 2002. Photograph: H. A. Sedgwick. Collection of H. A. Sedgwick. © H. A. Sedgwick

does not form the word "IS." Instead, the *S* represents the commencement of an enjambed second word "S / HIFT." As a result, before readers get to the first verb, Sedgwick has disoriented them; a disorientation appropriate to the final moments of a poet's life. She has also emphasized a shifting first and third person—the "I"s of the line—"I am," and "[s/he] IS," her own and Saiba's respective personae. The "IS" further evokes the poem's poignant present tense, emphasized by the even capitalization, admittedly at two scales, and Sedgwick's characteristic decision to crop the final period; a grammatical ploy following the original Japanese. Further disorienting the formalist, Sedgwick makes it difficult to say how many lines she transforms Saiba's haiku into. Her layout might be an example of her favorite three-line haiku form, although all her lines lack the requisite syllabic pattern:

I SHIFT
MY PILLOW CLOSER
TO THE FULL MOON

But viewers might read it as a seven-line verse:

I S
HIFT
MY
PILLOW
CLOSER
TO THE FULL
MOON

Unusually, her lineation does not emphasize Saiba's internal rhymes. She might have arranged the lines, as below, to parallel "I" and "my," as well as "pillow," "closer," and "to the":

I
shift my
pillow
closer
to the
full moon

Or she might have emphasized the echo of *pill* and *full*; or of *ow* and *clo*, as in the variants here:

I shift my pill
-ow closer to the full
moon

or

I shift my pillow
clo-
ser to the full moon

As a result of her chosen form, Sedgwick's setting does not circle back on itself aurally, hesitantly turning back in time at the end of the poet's life. Instead, the present tense, without emphasized rhymes, moves irreversibly forward to the moment of death. Her recasting suggests that the precise form of the last moments of life is hard to pin down into a conventional structure, as her first-person "I" moves from a shouty, rectilinear capitalization in the first two words, perhaps signaling a *straight* death, where the "I" must turn a corner to complete its verb, into a more curvilinear, melodic, floaty, dancy descent toward the ground. That, or Sedgwick's rising curvy lines, whose ends circle up, emblematize the poet's antigravitational orientation toward the moon, whose chromatic glow Sedgwick nicely captures in the bottom-right swatch; a lunar preoccupation she inherited from her NASA-photographer father.[71]

Sedgwick sets Saiba's text across three of the four swatches of sloppily cut fabric. The upper patch is a large piece of roughly rectangular, abstract *shibori* silk pinned in a corpse-like, horizontal landscape orientation, its purple-and-gold palette echoing the text's purple ink and golden ground, reversing the chromatic polarity of gold in purple, on the *shibori*, to purple on gold, for the text, and suggesting the polarizing difference between life and death.

Sedgwick stamps most of the poem across a similarly fraying, roughly rectangular scrap of intermittently purple-marbled peach silk. As a result, Saiba's referentially complex purple prose perhaps dissolves, at his life's end, into simpler and more abstract, semiotically less dense or even empty, colorful mark-making that does not indicate an obvious first person. Sedgwick sloppily prints the top of the letters forming the partial word "HIFT" so they overlap two pieces of ragged white-and-green cotton that are attached to the silk but not glued to the hems. These fraying pieces, like the poet at the end of his life, can float up freely, toward the moon.

Sedgwick printed across the upper-middle two patches Kuanyin's extended right arm. Decontextualized from its body, as in the fracture pieces, the limb appears ghostly, floating, like a Victorian spirit photograph, perhaps reaching for the poet at a similar cusp of life and death. A second photograph from the installation, meanwhile, suggests how idiomatic Sedgwick's palette was. There, she sports a loose green-and-white blouse, a similar color to the patches of silk on which Kuanyin's arm appears, while the artist's flushed skin and strawberry blond hair are echoed in the *shibori* palette at the top of the hanging. The words may be, in some senses, Saiba's, but their setting is characteristically Sedgwick's.

Kuanyin's extended arm also recalls Michelangelo's *Creation of Adam*, on the Sistine Chapel ceiling, further emphasizing a moment of contact between the mortal and divine, at the point of Saida's death, as well as the tactile appeal of the different fabrics Sedgwick employs. The cool, soft silk and the warmer, rougher cotton evoke the pillow and bedding the poet pulls closer to the window, to die witnessing the moonlight. The moon was a symbol of transience,

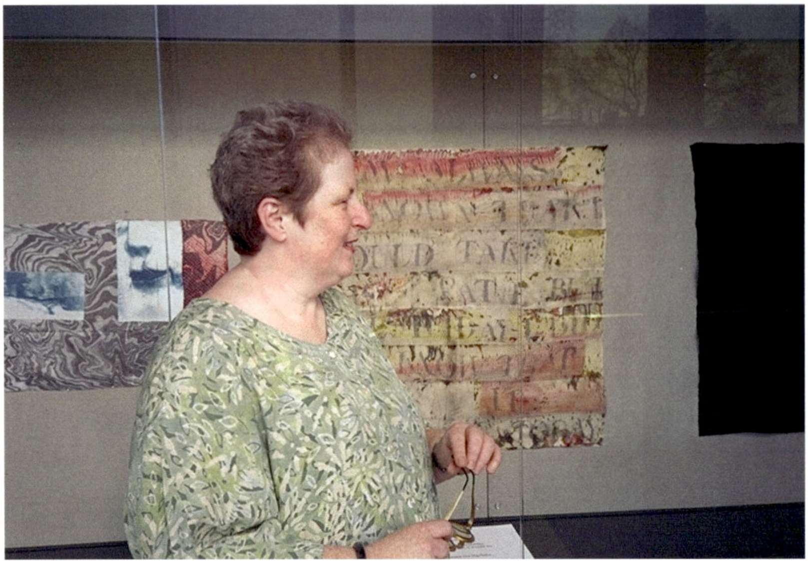

Figure 5.11. Eve Kosofsky Sedgwick at the installation of *Bodhisattva Fractal World*, 2002. Photograph: H. A. Sedgwick. Collection of H. A. Sedgwick. © H. A. Sedgwick

in Buddhist philosophy, as it waxed and waned; of enlightenment, as it waxed; and of constancy, as the satellite remained when much else was lost, as in Ryokan's famous nineteenth-century haiku:

> The thief left it behind:
> the moon
> at my window.[72]

Now I Understand, or Episstemology of the Renga

In Sedgwick's seventh exhibit, she employed Ryuho's seventeenth-century death poem:

> Now I understand how
> the third verse of moon and flowers
> is interwoven.[73]

Commenting on the verse, Hoffmann documents that Ryuho referenced the Japanese *renga* tradition—literally translated from the Japanese as "linked poetry"—where multiple poets took turns to write a poem with elaborate rules governing where seasonal images should crop up and how often certain words,

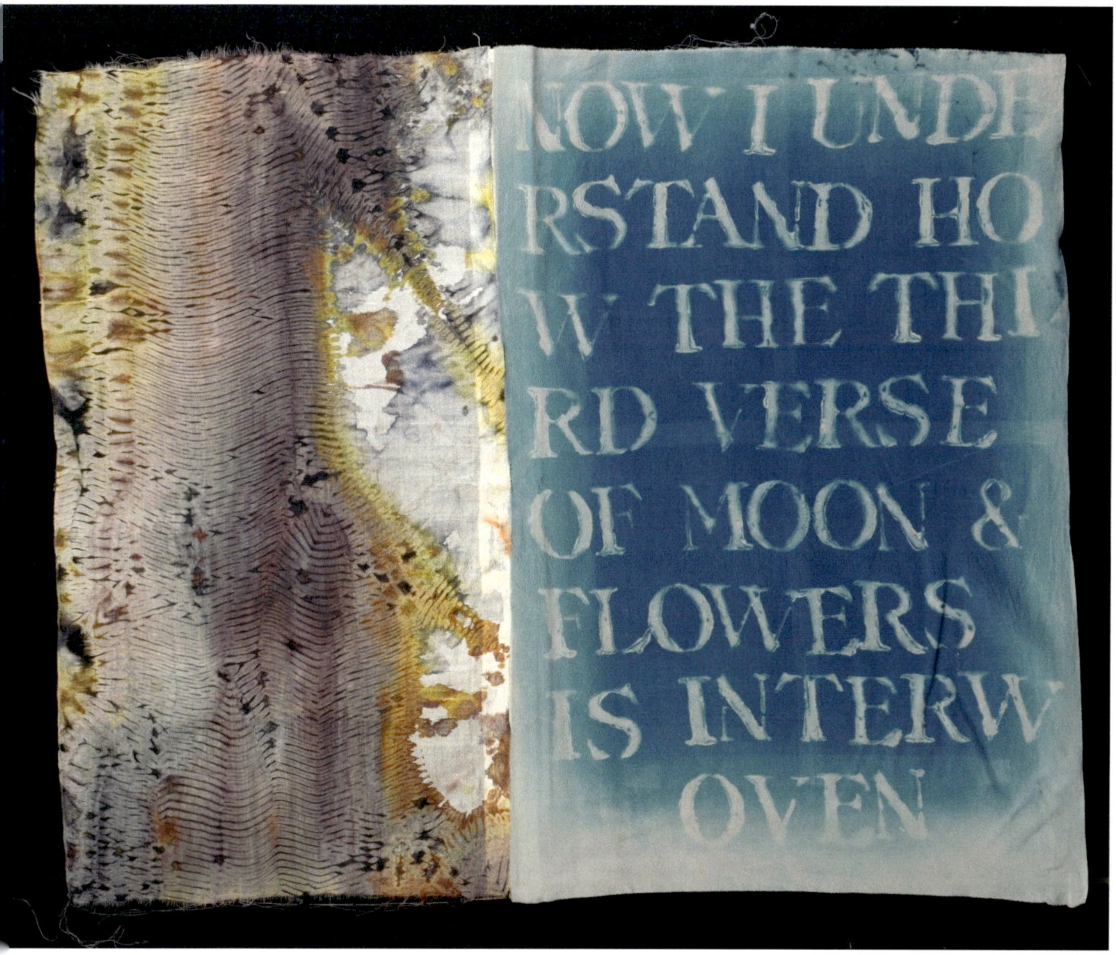

Figure 5.12. Eve Kosofsky Sedgwick, untitled collage, 2002. Photograph: Kevin Ryan. Collection of H. A. Sedgwick. © H. A. Sedgwick

such as *flower* or *moon*, appeared. In addition, Hoffmann notes, a *renga*'s third verse had to be "somewhat detached from the images of the first and second." Thus, in his death poem, Ryuho "seems to be alluding to the detachment of the third verse from the preceding ones," implying that if the art of earlier verses could be learned from a master, it was only in later life that poets could teach themselves the "art of detachment and ultimate departure."[74]

Sedgwick cyanotyped Ryuho's verse onto the right panel of a diptych (figure 5.12). To its left, she attached a piece of *shibori* silk, in a characteristic palette dominated by a pinky blood red and urine gold, signaling, in an abstract but corporeal idiom, a body in trouble or evacuating itself, a first person at the edge of its decomposition. She bound the diptych's two parts at the back along a resonant, stable central spinal column of denser cotton providing strength and contrasting strongly with the off-center, apparently dissolving and bleeding column of color on the *shibori* swatch, perhaps more akin to her own spine.

Sedgwick characteristically capitalized Ryuho's text and omitted the closing period, to suggest again an important life sentence interrupted by sudden death, in this case at the moment of satori enlightenment. Her letters are snow white, an image of frozen water that forms a leitmotif across the subsequent pieces of the exhibition:

NOW I UNDE
RSTAND HO
W THE THI
RD VERSE
OF MOON &
FLOWERS
IS INTERW
  OVEN

Sedgwick transformed Ryuho's haiku into a headline-capitalized, eight-line verse of her own, whose syllables again prove difficult to count because of the way she broke up four of the key words—"UNDE/RSTAND," "HO/W," "THI/RD," and "INTERW/OVEN"—each disassembled without her more usual hyphenation at such moments; another image, perhaps, of dispersing bodily aggregates. Sedgwick centers the text as a kind of further floating (spinal) column on the right panel. The column seems to be floating because viewers might read the ice-white text as resting on the surface of blue water, if imagined from above, and because the weight of the column is carried on its shortest, four-letter, line.

Again characteristically, Sedgwick's lineation emphasizes Ryuho's internal rhymes. The rhyme scheme provides a kind of sonic equivalent to the interweaving Ryuho describes, given its *abacdcad* form, with two groups of three-line rhymes—*aba*, *cdc*—before something appropriately different happens in the final, third couplet—*ad*—which weaves together rhymes from the previous triplets. Of the again unlucky thirteen words that constitute the sentence, Sedgwick presents nine intact: "NOW I," "THE," "VERSE / OF MOON & / FLOWERS," and the immediately adjacent "IS." She enjambs the remaining four, making them difficult to read: "UNDE/RSTAND HO/W," "THI/RD," and "INTERW/OVEN." As a result, there are two moments of comparative clarity in the poem. The first line begins in a confident simple present tense, "NOW I," with sense being subsequently scrambled during the period of supposed understanding, until the fourth, fifth, sixth, and seventh lines, where that satori-like clarity of achieved understanding, of the third "VERSE / OF MOON & / FLOWERS," is supported by an unprecedented run of six words presented in their entirety; a further interweaving of sense and nonsense to support the overall theme. Poignantly, Ryuho's understanding is itself fading, around the borders and base of the cyanotype where the fabric has lost its color through bleaching, or, more likely, because of Sedgwick's sloppy craft process.

By contrast, the *shibori* sheet on the left remains vibrantly colored, with all its leaky, not necessarily live-bodily, materiality, suggesting fabrics used by morticians as well as incontinence and sanitary pads. Sedgwick's setting makes Ryuho's another thalassic song in her oeuvre, one recalling Bashō's account of the bodily indignity of urination in *The Narrow Road to the Deep North*. This described how

Bitten by flies and lice,
I slept in a bed,
A horse urinating all the time
Close to my pillow.[75]

Finally, viewers might think about the *shibori* panel as an abstract expression of the *woven* poetic theme on the right, given the warp-like verticality of the central column, and the weft-like horizontal lines found throughout that bloody pink patch, its presence the result of how the fabric had been tie-dyed; a dy(e) ing followed by a laying out flat that resonates powerfully with Ryuho's death poem.

Tender Winds Above the Snow Melt Many Kinds of Suffering, or Fishing in a Bodhisattva's Bowels

Sedgwick's eighth collage (figure 5.13) employed a poem by Kyutaro, who died in late winter 1928:

Tender winds above the snow
melt many kinds
of suffering.[76]

With its focus on snow, the poem is seasonally appropriate to the period of Kyutaro's death, but snow was, as Hoffmann notes, an overdetermined trope for the poet, following an incident when, as a thirteen-year-old messenger, his employers scolded him for playing in the snow on Emperor's Day; his behavior taken as an affront to the nation. Kyutaro wrote a poem about the incident, the death poem recalling the mixed blessings of the earlier scene:

In heavy snow
I clean forgot
To raise the nation's flag.[77]

In later life, Kyutaro became a radical anarchist, firing a gun at a government official. He was sentenced to life imprisonment in 1923 and committed suicide five years later, leaving the later poem as a farewell note.[78]

Sedgwick characteristically capitalized Kyutaro's poem, which she stamped, unevenly, letter by letter, in purple ink, so that while she respects the lineation of the English translation, her inconsistent indenting makes the lines resist the rectilinearity of conventional book printing, as if gently disturbed by a tender wind; perhaps also signaling Kyutaro's rebellious refusal to keep *in line*.

Sedgwick inserts the poem inside a patchwork composed of ten swatches of glued fabric. Eight are roughly square and reveal the now-familiar Kuanyin. The remaining two are roughly rectangular and feature an abstract *suminagashi* pattern, where the gray-and-snow-white ink has been floated on the surface of water and coaxed into ripples by the breath, the poem's tender's wind, perhaps, before the fabric received its imprint. The swatch in the middle of Kuanyin features an additional stamped image of three koi carp, part of an extensive range Sedgwick employed in her conceptually ambitious, but self-consciously lo-fi, craft; here suggesting a parallel with the stamped text, as if each letter were akin to a fish, and vice versa.[79]

Sedgwick joins, with gold glue, the patches of mostly cotton *pata*, a traditional material in Buddhist devotional art. Her gold adhesion again recalls Japanese *kintsugi* ceramics, in which broken, but precious, pieces of pottery were glued back together with gold lacquer, their vulnerable, restored state adding to their value: the first sign of this piece's interest in *reparation* and recalling a Sedgwick whose body had lost a breast and been sutured back together.

The layers of fabric rise from the bottom left to the carp closest to our vantage point. The koi are not depicted face on, like Kuanyin, but from above; a cubist or Taoist effect of multiple, flexible, perceptual/conceptual perspectives. As in many of Sedgwick's projects, there is a key *exception* to this mostly uniform layering up to the trunk of the bodhisattva: The square *at* the bottom right represents the highest patch.

This experience of layering undulation, of above and below, resonates with the poem's theme, with its winds *above* snow; the waveforms of the *suminagashi*;

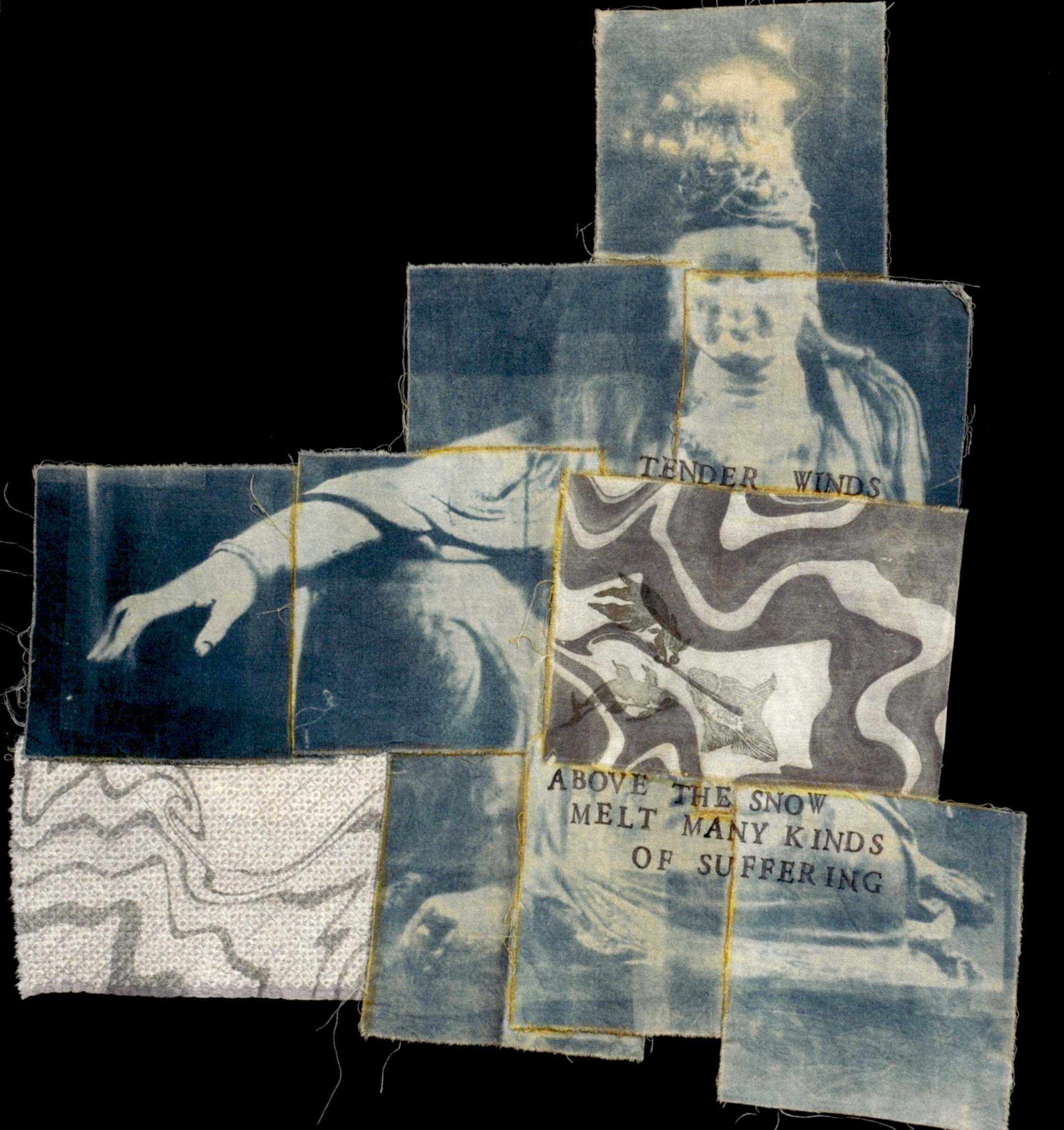

Figure 5.13. Eve Kosofsky Sedgwick, untitled collage, 2002. Photograph: Kevin Ryan. Collection of H. A. Sedgwick. © H. A. Sedgwick

and the carp's related aqueous environment. The blue-printed bodhisattva also seems again to be quietly fading away and sinking into the ocean, as in Ariel's song; a healing aqueous transformation signaled in Kyutaro's poem, where tender winds *melt* many kinds of suffering. The koi interrupt Sedgwick's setting of the poem, which is metamorphosed from a three-line haiku into a four-line verse:

TENDER WINDS

ABOVE THE SNOW
MELT MANY KINDS
OF SUFFERING

In Sedgwick's uppercase setting, characteristically without a final period, perhaps recalling her early treatment-induced menopause, the sentence stops prematurely to signal the poet's life cut short by his imprisonment and suicide. Sedgwick separates the first line from the remaining three. The opening line shares with the tender winds that it describes its position above a patch with a drifting snow-white pattern and a denser verbal layer below. Sedgwick achieves this denseness in the remaining lines by the rhymes that occur between "WINDS" and "KINDS," with the "IN" appearing acoustically a third time in "SUFFERING." She also achieves the increasingly condensed density by the way in which, unlike the waltzy, mobile, three-syllable first line, with its internal rhymes of "TEN" and "IN," circling back on themselves, the remaining three lines have a more regularized, alternate-emphasis, four-syllable beat. Indeed, only the *oh* of "SNOW" fails to find a rhyme, further suggesting a form cut short, without sonic resolution, leaving hovering a plaintive exclamatory "O!"

Like the poem, the pyramidal form of the patchwork comprises ten swatches across four lines, with the first line containing a single swatch, the second a pair, the third three, and the lowest four. The masonry-course patches look unsteady. This derives from the missing right side of the otherwise pyramidal collage and the way the lowest panels do not rest evenly on the ground. Indeed, the collage suggests an ultimate subsidence to the left.[80]

Sedgwick's needless and needle-less patchwork technique is interrupted twice: by the presence of two *non*-blue-printed swatches and by the textural differential between the nine cotton *patas* she employs for Kuanyin's body and the carp, and the piece of kimono silk she utilizes at bottom left. The bodhisattva's body is made up of nine glued swatches, which characteristically fray at the edges, as if the electrical energy of Kuanyin's body has created a static charge that extends out into the photograph's black background, but suggesting her vulnerability at her extremities, as these same cotton threads could unravel the panel's tight weave.

Sedgwick's characteristic insistence on printing Kuanyin's body across the complex aggregate of patchwork pieces, and the decision to crop out her abdomen, suggest that she was again thinking about what it meant to be living with a breast cancer that had metastasized to her spine. The interruptive carp panel represents an empty space where key parts of Sedgwick's torso—integral vertebrae, a missing breast—once were. Spectators might also read the three koi as akin to tumors, foreign bodies clustering together, plotting. But the gold *kintsugi* glue Sedgwick again employs emphasizes that illness and injury add value to a ceramic or human body rather than subtract from it.

The patchwork also characteristically evokes Sedgwick's queerness. Spectators might think about the hanging—a poignant phrase if Kyutaro hung himself in his cell—in the context of Sedgwick's wider interest in *fisting* and other anal pleasures. Again relevant here is the "fascinating passage" in James's *Notebooks* in which he offered a "rich . . . , pregnant address" to his "male muse"—a pregnant address resonant here in the context of Kuanyin's gravid torso:

> I sit here, after long weeks, at any rate, in front of my arrears, with an inward accumulation of material of which I feel the wealth, and as to which I can only invoke my familiar demon of patience, who always comes, doesn't he? when I call. He is here with me in front of this cool green Pacific—he sits close and I feel his breath, which cools and steadies and inspires, on my cheek. Everything sinks in: nothing is lost. Everything abides and fertilizes and renews its golden promise, making me think with closed eyes of deep and grateful longing when, in the full summer days of L[amb] H[ouse], my long dusty adventure over, I shall be able to [plunge] my hand, my arm, *in*, deep and far, and up to the shoulder—into the heavy bag of remembrance—of suggestion—of imagination—of art—and fish out every little figure and felicity, every little fact and fancy that can be to my purpose. These things are all packed away, now, thicker than I can penetrate, deeper than I can fathom, and there let them rest for the present, in their sacred cool darkness, till I shall let in upon them the mild still light of dear old L[amb] H[ouse]—in which they will begin to gleam and glitter and take form like the gold and jewels of a mine.[81]

Much about this passage resonates with Sedgwick's icon. Kuanyin's right arm is extended, if not quite to the shoulder, then to the elbow. Her fingers are not clenched into a fist but extend, equally suggestively. Like James, the bodhisattva sits in a meditative position; stable, peaceful, and comfortable enough to last for weeks. An "inward accumulation of material," of cotton within cotton, within silk, is also present, whose "wealth" is signaled by the "glitter and gleam" of the gold glue and expensive luster of the cocoon. Everything here is rising up, as we have seen, rather than sinking down into the bodhisattva's bowels, where the carp swim in the *suminagashi* folds of Kuanyin's intestines, a place where viewers can "fish out every little figure," "felicity," "fact and fancy" they desire. In addition, spectators might recall the "sacred cool darkness" of Lamb House manifesting in the variously blue shadows surrounding the divinity.

Alternatively, beholders might think about Kuanyin's bodily cavity as representing the bladder, rather than bowels, given its aqueous nature and Sedgwick's thalassic idiom, signaled by the carp's presence within the wave-born *suminagashi* pattern. If the potential pleasures of urination suggest a minimally gender-inflected urethral eroticism, in which possessing a bladder and urethra trumps the sexual and gendered significance of the penis or vagina, it is clear from the patchwork, as well as Sedgwick's oeuvre more generally, that those pleasures were meditational and self-relational; more masturbatory than socially sadomasochistic. Unlike the paradigmatic infant in Melanie Klein's account, who pisses on the bodies and ideas of others, Sedgwick's bodhisattva enjoys the internal pleasures of her waterworks, the filling up and emptying out of her inner space.[82]

Sedgwick's use of gold glue, meanwhile, again encourages viewers to think about the aesthetic possibilities when a golden liquid, like urine, comes into contact with silk and cotton, the most common materials of quotidian underwear and expensive lingerie; and when a combination of ink, oil, and water comes into contact with fabric, given her *suminagashi* technique and blue printing, recalling the importance of urine in the fabrication of both Indian yellow and indigo.[83]

From a trans perspective, as I have already briefly suggested, Kuanyin is, perhaps, most obviously interesting as a divinity who began life as a male Indian figure who transformed into more feminine forms, then into a Chinese woman. In the context of Buddhist pedagogy, ontology, theology, and belief in successive reincarnations and multiple simultaneous avatars, Kuanyin's gender might, however, matter less than we expect. How bodhisattvas skillfully manifest depends on their supplicants' expectations and needs.

That Kuanyin carries, safely within her torso, three live, undigested carp also resonates in the context of Buddhist iconography, since Kuanyin is a bodhisattva of compassion associated with fisherfolk.[84] She taught her devotees that they were caught, like fish, in the nets of their own karma. She saved the carp son of the great Water Dragon king, who, caught in a net and taken to market, was bought by the bodhisattva and released back into the sea.[85] She refused all animal-flesh offerings and singled out the killing of fish as abhorrent, instead offering up her own body as flesh for feeding. Pilgrims visiting monasteries devoted to Kuanyin, therefore, often find fishponds there. In addition, in Shantideva's influential *The Bodhisattva's Way of Life*, Kuanyin asks where fish and other creatures can be taken so that they cannot be killed.[86]

Sedgwick's answer seems to be deep inside, not in the form of digested food, but in the cooperative, trans-species space of a safe, womb-like haven, and it seems important from a queer, as well as vegan theoretical, perspective that Kuanyin is not here accompanied by a child, as she is in many depictions, but instead shelters a fish.[87] After all, one of the reasons the bodhisattva is so popular across Buddhist Asia is because she is believed to help those hoping to conceive children.[88] Sedgwick, however, was nonreproductive, and in containing three fish rather than a fetus, her image suggests a queer form of nonreproduction, one promising a coy/koi, metamorphic queer future where there are fewer people and more animals, underscoring the important role vegetarianism plays in devotion to the bodhisattva, however many silkworms were destroyed to make the silk panel immediately adjacent to her.[89]

In a similarly queer way, and this time unlike the austere Shantideva, Sedgwick's icon challenges the idea of the body as an undesirable sack of shit, with the bowels the least palatable part. Instead, like James, Sedgwick understands the products of the bladder and bowels as desirably charged, internal commodities to be hoarded at some moments and released pleasurably into the world at others.

The *Bodhisattva's Way of Life* also offers us a final, now-familiar way to view Sedgwick's patchwork. There, Kuanyin claimed that people were "neither the marrow nor the sweat," "neither the lymph nor the intestines," and neither the "rectum," "excrement," or "urine," as part of the Buddhist doctrine of the aggregates; an aggregation here emphasized in Sedgwick's patchwork procedure.[90] To make the point, in the story of the Princess Mia Shan, Kuanyin cuts off her own arms and eyes to cure her father; a miraculous ascetic devotion that leads to her accruing more positive karma, which Sedgwick registers in the abbreviation of Kuanyin just below her left shoulder.[91]

From this perspective, it is, perhaps, especially important to end this section by elucidating Sedgwick's carp as a symbol of abundance and fertility in India, Avalokiteshvara's home, and of good fortune in China, home of Kuanyin, as well as of transformation, since koi are believed to gain the power to become dragons by swimming upstream in the Yangtze River.[92] As a result, the presence of the carp represents part of Sedgwick's wider determination to think about her cancer as an *opportunity* to understand herself and the world differently while not idealizing that experience. Indeed, Sedgwick's ambivalence is precisely emphasized by the carp iconography, since the Kuanyin legends tell of a demonic gold carp, who listened to the bodhisattva's daily sermons and then set out to harm her devotees, until Kuanyin captured it and imprisoned it within a bamboo basket.[93] Good and bad, Sedgwick understood, were inseparable at every level.[94]

Today, Then, Is the Day, or Melting Ice Caps: The Weather in Fusen

Kyutaro's preoccupation with wintry weather recurred in a second large indigo-and-white hanging by Sedgwick (figure 5.14). Comprising a single swatch, the piece contained a pattern of some sixty, now-familiar, cancer cell–evoking, shell-shaped, ice-crystal *plangi* tesserae, alongside Fusen's death poem:

> Today, then, is the day
> the melting snowman
> is a real man.[95]

Fusen died in the depth of winter, on December 29, 1777. The image of a man melting like a snowman is, therefore, appropriately seasonal and transient. In addition, as Hoffmann documents, snow sculptures were often fashioned in Japan of the Indian monk Darum, or Bodhidharma, who wandered to China in 520 CE and founded Zen Buddhism; a figure, like Avalokiteshvara, who migrated from South to East Asia.[96]

In the hanging, Sedgwick sloppily hand-printed the poem, in white paint on an indigo ground. She reverses the polarity of the classic black-on-white, text-ground relation, with her snow-white quotation descending like snowflakes, if read vertically, or floating on an aqueous indigo, into which it is sinking and melting, or from which it is crystallizing, if imagined from above.

Sedgwick does not reprint Hoffmann's translation verbatim. She emphasizes the sense of a poem cut short by capitalizing the text, to suggest a present tense in which no character is more important, and eliding the final period, even as she respects the two mid-sentence commas. In addition, she transforms Fusen's lineation, so that the poem reads:

> TODAY,
>   THEN,
> IS THE DAY
>   THE
> MELTING

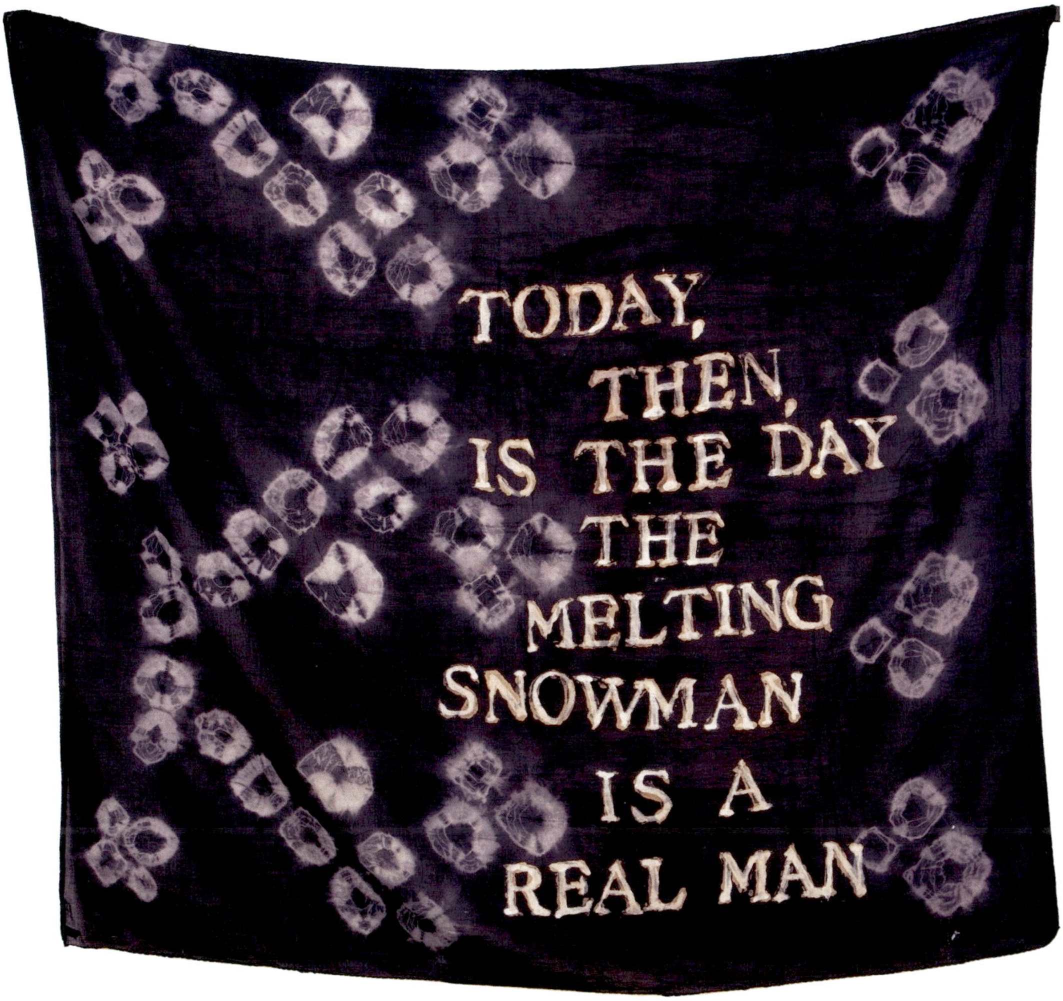

Figure 5.14. Eve Kosofsky Sedgwick, untitled hanging, 2002. Photograph: H. A. Sedgwick. Collection of H. A. Sedgwick. © H. A. Sedgwick

SNOWMAN
IS A
REAL MAN

The text appears roughly centered around the vertical spine of the three "THE"s, emphasizing the definite article and representative character of the scene. This is not any day, but *the* day, and *the* melting snowman is an everyman, transformed into *a* suddenly distinct and individual man at the end of the verse and his life. That said, the poem initially drifts to the right, as if buffeted by tender winds at different altitudes, with only three words beginning at the left margin. Sedgwick tabs two words one space to the right ("MELTING" and "REAL"), and three words two tabs ("THEN," "THE," and the second "IS").

Sedgwick offsets the whole poem from the center of the fabric, giving a further sense of the verse slipping downstream, as the spectator reads left to right. The sense that the text is in motion is increased by its waltzy rhythm, with its sequential groups of three syllables: "TODAY, THEN," "IS THE DAY," "THE MELTING," "SNOWMAN IS," "A REAL MAN," which, thanks to Sedgwick's lineation, pulls and slows up against an increasingly insistent, and consistent, iambic pentameter in the last four lines, as things draw to a close, as if a heartbeat or inhalation/exhalation are newly apparent at the end of the poet's life.

Compared to Hoffmann's lineation, Sedgwick's poem is slower and more spacious thanks to her shorter lines. Her indented lines further suggest something is missing at each end, having melted away; a visual image of a man melting at his extremities, perhaps, suggested by the poem's faintly anthropomorphic, again wobbly column-like form, in the context of a long architectural history in which white marble columns, caryatids, and (snow) men were closely related. If read as architectural courses, with each word approximating a member, it looks as if the words "TODAY" and "SNOWMAN" are most likely to give. "TODAY" sinks diagonally toward the left, unsupported, while "SNOWMAN" is similarly out on a limb but this time descends to the right, suggesting it might fracture, painfully, at around the *ow*—the sound of pain—causing the verbal edifice to topple.

Sedgwick's *abaacdad* rhyme scheme is similarly destabilizing. She emphasizes the repetition of certain words and parts of words through her lineation—"TODAY" and "THE DAY"; "SNOWMAN" and "REAL MAN." When the sound returns, it recalls its previous incarnation but is quietly transformed into something else. Similarly, the initial *aba* pattern sets up the expectation for an alternating rhyme scheme, again like the rhythm of an in/out breath, the expansion and contraction of the heart. But the repetition of the *a* rhyme twice in a row at line 4 is interruptive, as if two in-breaths occurred without exhalation, and with "MELTING," the new *c* rhyme, failing to find a resolution, unless in the *n* sound of "MAN," again suggesting a form (of life) cut short or transformed.

At a more micro level still, Sedgwick further emphasizes the sense of melting into the ground through her method of printing individual letters. If they examine the letters closely, spectators can see that she did not print each letter of the word "REAL" cleanly, clearly, and once and for all, but overlaid each letter twice on the creased fabric, first in a fatter, sloppy fawn brown, the paint seeming to have *bled* beyond the frame of the font, then with a highlighting, thinner white paint. This offers more clarity than the fawn version, but the overlap, especially of white on sludgy brown on an indigo ground, suggests the melting of these ice capitals down to slush before dissolving into a watery substrate that is anything but "ground."

At the micro scale, it is also clear that the fabric is a weave, with warp and weft forming little squares between them, which appear as diamonds because Sedgwick prints the text across a swatch oriented on the bias. Recalling the fractals she referenced in the exhibition's title, whose patterns repeat at different scales, these structural, geometric diamonds are echoed, at a larger scale, in the decorative crystalline *plangi* forms she tie-dyed onto the fabric. As well as melting or forming ice or snow crystals, these recall diamonds set on a ring and suggest a different posthumous transformation from the poem's melting snowman. They suggest a burial in the ground, after which a former carboniferous form got compressed, at high pressure, over millennia, to compose a diamond.

They don't look much like it, if you Google it, but for a long time these cells were how I imagined multiplying cancer cells, and the overall lesson of the piece seems to be: A snowman can become a real man, and vice versa; water can become ice and snow, and vice versa; bodies can become earth or water or precious stones; cells can become tumors, and tumors can proliferate or remain indolent. One thing is certain: Change is everywhere, and while some is reversible, and much of it magical, some of it is also tragic, neither desirable nor consciously willed.[97]

While Sweeping the Yard, or I May Be Some Time

Snow was a popular subject for Japanese death poetry, as we have seen, and Kyutaro had been so preoccupied with the weather, as a young man, that he forgot to raise the nation's flag. An even more forgetful snow scene was the subject of our next hanging (figure 5.15). This was an off-white flag-like piece of silk suggesting surrender. The swatch featured a late, haiku-like text, by Bashō, roughly printed in teal and umber ink:

While sweeping the yard
it forgets about the snow
—a broom.

(It is haiku-*like* because of the correct meter of its first two lines but not its final one.) Sedgwick's setting characteristically capitalizes Bashō's translated text and revises his lineation:

WHILE SWEEPING THE YARD
IT FORGETS ABOUT THE
SNOW—
A BROOM

Because of its uppercase font, use of dashes, well-spaced text against a white ground, and inspiration from Bashō, the piece bears a close relationship to Sedgwick's autobiography, in which she adopted the poet's *haibun*, part-haiku, part-prose, form. Bashō evidently felt a particular fondness for the verse Sedgwick selected since he exceptionally provided, to accompany its original calligraphy, a painting of fellow poet Han Shan.[98] In reproducing the poem, Sedgwick both honors her source and stamps her mark by employing an English translation, capitalizing Bashō's lettering, and employing a stenciled font rather than approximating his calligraphy. Her "flag" is also landscape rather than portrait oriented, and more austere and spacious, without the drawing.

In quietly transforming the poem, as well as working on an appropriately snowy-white silk, Sedgwick engages with Bashō in a kind of belated *renga*. This was the practice in which groups of poets assembled at verse-writing parties to write anthologies, as we have seen, with what Makoto Ueda calls "bothersome rules of linkage." Engaging in respectful competition, the poets prompted one another in sequence with their verses, seeking to riff off, outdo, and critique each other, as the party progressed. As a result, Bashō's *haibun* volumes were filled with his own poetry and the poems of his prestigious peers and forebears.[99]

Again perhaps inspiring Sedgwick, Bashō repeatedly alludes to his practice of writing on silk and hanging poetry on a wall. In *The Narrow Road to the Deep North*, he recalled that "towards the end of the day," he "stopped at a small tea house, where a young woman named Butterfly" handed him a "small piece of white silk" and asked him to "write a poem choosing her name as the subject." He also documented hanging a "linked verse of eight pieces" on a wooden pillar on the threshold of his home. Indeed, *The Narrow Road* reveals that Bashō, like Sedgwick, was interested in silk and snow, the latter as part of a broader *hie* aesthetic, concerned with "cold, icy beauty," in Ueda's phrase, that we have frequently encountered.[100]

Following Ueda's lead, Sedgwick's hanging provides minimal punctuation. Ueda noted that since haiku poems presented an "observation or sentiment in all its immediacy, before it [was] intellectually conceptualized," he translated

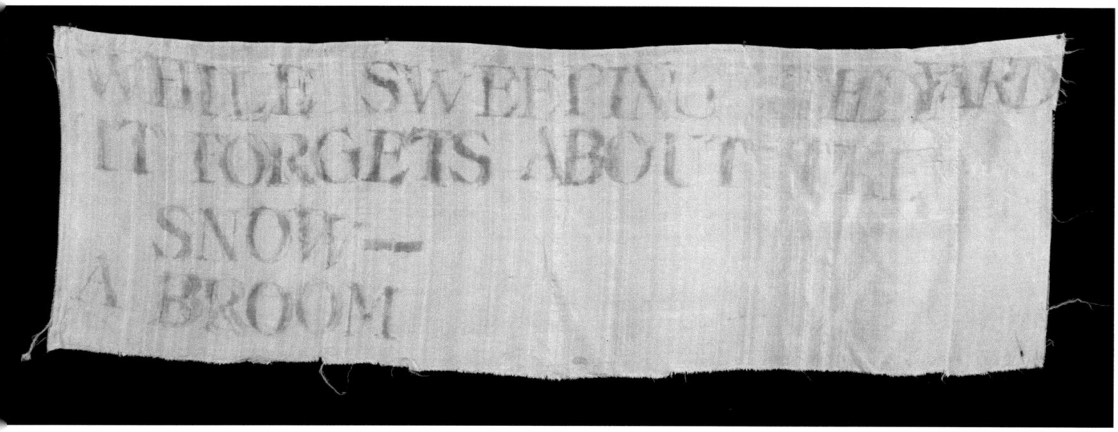

Figure 5.15. Eve Kosofsky Sedgwick, untitled hanging, 2002. Photograph: Kevin Ryan. Collection of H. A. Sedgwick. © H. A. Sedgwick

Bashō employing neither a capitalized first letter nor final punctuation point.[101] Making a different decision, but with a related effect, Sedgwick capitalizes the entirety of her text, and the only punctuation marks she provides are a pair of dashes, à la Emily Dickinson, at the end of the third line.[102]

Both the spare verse form and the way Sedgwick varies the forms of her hyphens—the first lighter than the second, both at different angles to the horizontal—seem to me Dickinsonian. I also allude to Dickinson because, in her short essay "Interlude, Pedagogic" (ca. 2003), Sedgwick recalled a "ravishing Dickinsonian winter afternoon" when a group of her peers gathered to "silently 'witness' the civil disobedience of a dozen union employees." Suddenly, a "beautiful, thick, silent and silencing snow began to fall," and her heart "almost burst with exaltation at the spare and indicative Americanness of the scene, like reading Thoreau but also like a movie." She documented the "silence, immobility," and "secularized religiosity of [her] own function of 'witnessing' the scene" in which the "profuse, gratuitous, equalizing, theatrically transformative" snow seemed "to guarantee the totality and symbolic evenness of this pure, signifying space."[103]

While apparently surrendering, rather than resisting, Sedgwick's hanging recalls the scene in several ways. The "contingency of the snow, in that slow unfolding of the afternoon," is echoed by the apparently random, uneven distribution of the text as it unfolds across a foldable white fabric. The text is "projected heart-stoppingly" onto a not-quite-cinematically-scaled "screen." The earlier scene's sense of mortal threat is signified in the disappearance, into forgetfulness and the white ground of the snow, of the broom, Bashō, Sedgwick, and her ink. At Amherst, Sedgwick had begun to worry whether the traffic would or could "stop for these anomalous figures in the road." And just as she pondered whether "nerves" were "fraying" that afternoon, so the edges of her unhemmed silk unravel. Similarly, "questions of standing devolved into dangerous questions of footing" in both snowy scenes, with Bashō seeking to make a footpath by brushing away the snow, but a snow gaining the upper hand, if the disappearance of Sedgwick's first "THE" is anything to go by, made more emphatic by the way she again lines it up with the second, slightly more legible example. Indeed, the letters all slip and slide from the straightforwardly, securely footed vertical and horizontal.[104]

But a melt and ruination may already be underway, given the slushy three-color tonality of the overall exhibit. If the silk ground suggests a thick white curtain of descending snow, if read pictorially, or cold blanket of snow on the ground, if examined horizontally, the letters are again a muddy confusion of earthy umber overlaid on a watery teal blue, confusing rather than clarifying the font, as if suggesting snow blindness. As a result, it is as if the earth, frozen white, and water, flowing blue, are increasingly covered in muddy brown traces.

If the poem is partly about the making of white form, as snow is brushed from one place to another, the subject of the poem—the person brushing or the broom employed—arrives late in the verse, at the start of the fourth line. They are also increasingly self-forgetful, and if a person, then one already an "IT" in line 2. There is also an increasing disappearance of definite articles, with both the *the*'s nearly gone, leaving only an *a*, with the legible remains of the poem reading "WHILE SWEEPING / IT FORGETS ABOUT / SNOW—/ A BROOM." In addition, there's something deathly about the ash-white as well as snow-white color of Sedgwick's hanging. White is also the color of Buddhist mourning, and, in this whiteout, there may be no bloody bandages, but there's also no bodhisattva in sight.

A Change of Clothes for *A Journey of a Million Miles*, or *A Moonlit Flit*

We have already briefly encountered the late nineteenth-century Japanese death poem by Roshu that forms the subject of our next hanging (figure 5.16):

> Time to go . . .
> they say the journey is a long one:
> change of robes.[105]

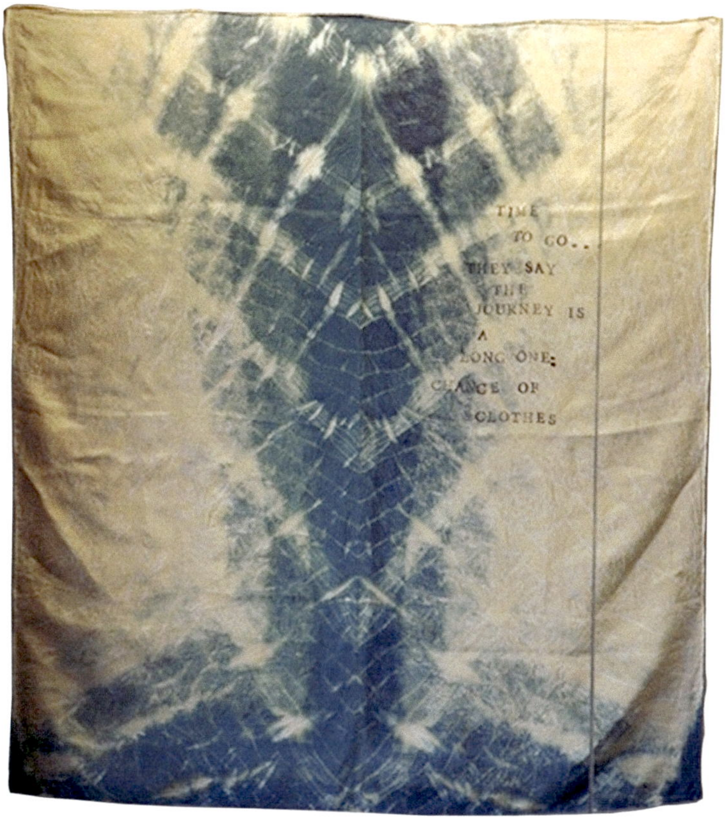

Figure 5.16. Eve Kosofsky Sedgwick, untitled hanging, 2002. Photograph: Kevin Ryan. Collection of H. A. Sedgwick. © H. A. Sedgwick

Or, as Sedgwick capitalized, spatially reorganized, and modestly retranslated it:

TIME
TO GO . . .
THEY SAY
THE
JOURNEY IS
A
LONG ONE:
CHANGE OF
CLOTHES

Sedgwick's floaty, descending version of Roshu's verse transforms and disintegrates its compact, fat three-line haiku into a longer, thinner, more columnar and enjambed, spacious eight-line poem, disaggregating his characteristic 5–7-5 metrics into a still-symmetrical, but more staccato, 1–2-2–1-3–1-2–2-1 form.

According to Hoffman, *koromangae*, or the "change from heavy clothes to light ones," fixes the "approximate date of Roshu's death between spring and summer"; brilliant seasonal weather indicated by Sedgwick's golden-yellow silk. The poem, Hoffmann suggests, also contains a reference to the "white cloth used to wrap the dead in," especially the bodies of Buddhist monks, who "generally put on a white robe near the hour of their death"; a pure white Sedgwick employed in the mournful previous hanging, but here dyes gold, making it more robe-like.[106]

Sedgwick's use of silk nods to the lightweight clothes worn after *koromangae*, and to her late poem "Death," which described, as we have again seen, how dying was not "a party you dress up for" but was "strictly come-as-you-are." It was important, she noted, not to "get too / formal," perhaps explaining the creases she left in the underironed fabric. Indeed, this silk is a giving fabric, with folds allowing for bodily expansion, appropriate to a deathly scene where it was not necessary to wear a "girdle to jam your tummy / in." The poem also concludes with a silk-related question: "Why did I buy those silk PJs with feathers / so long before the big affair began?" since she had "always slept in the nude" and now would "sleep in the nude forever." The transformation here of silk into not pajamas but an abstract hanging suggests an artist now less interested in self-adornment than she had been while crafting *In the Bardo*, as she approached the final nudity of her death; the central indigo column again is akin to a spine, penetrated by, and dissolving into, the sublime byzantine gold ground.

The indigo spinal column, surrounded by and emitting a golden shower of light, also recalls a spout of water, thrust up by a fountain, showering down; fountain imagery is central to Sedgwick's unfolding readings of Proust, as we shall see. Indeed, Sedgwick characterized Proust's description of the Guermantes fountain as representing an "emblem for the possibility of non-oppositional relations of many kinds: between pattern and contingency; the eternal and the ephemeral; the universal soul and . . . the individual," a "spring and a fall," "flexibility and economy," "chaos and complexity," as well as "exhaustion and transmutation," and "condensation and cloud formation"; a "stylized, artificial epitome of the unending processes by which water is propelled through its life-giving round of physical metamorphoses," a "water cycle" useful for thinking about the "rebirth cycle."[107]

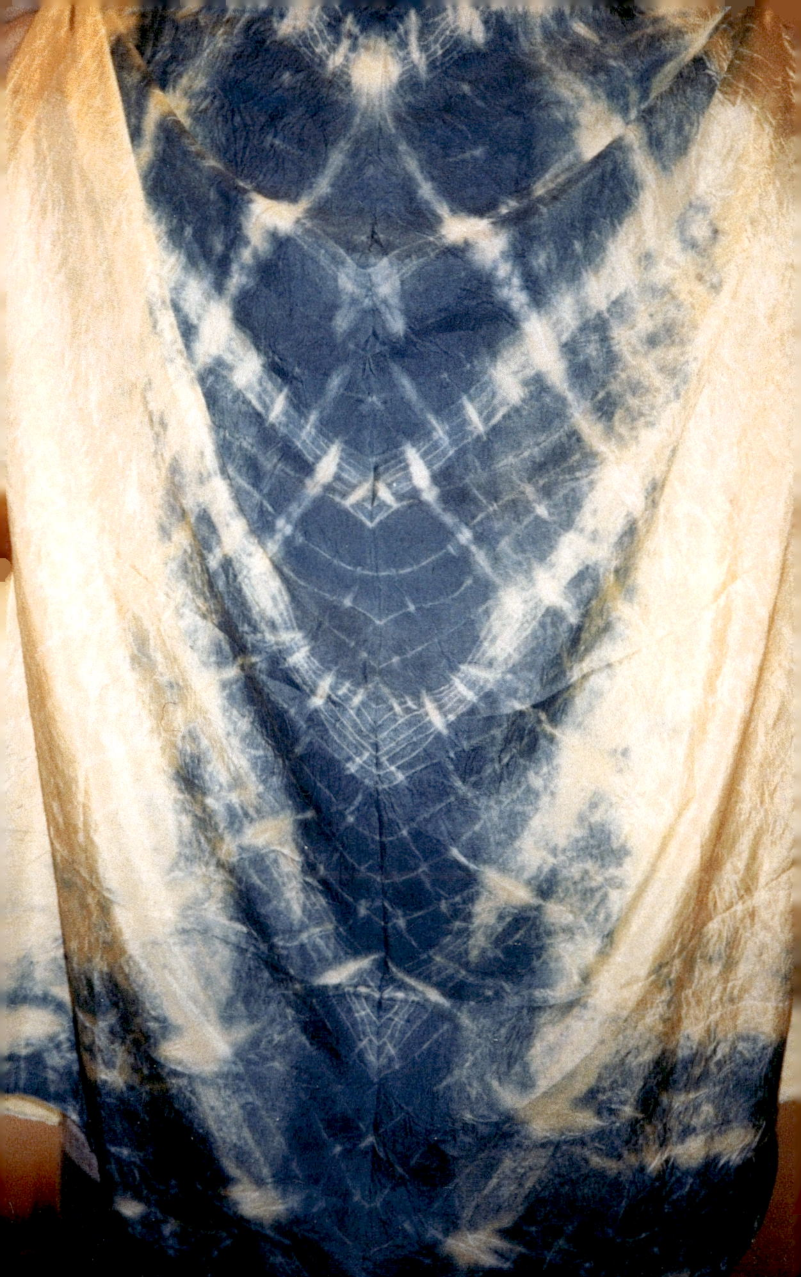

Figure 5.17. Eve Kosofsky Sedgwick, untitled *shibori* hanging, 2002. Photograph: H. A. Sedgwick. Collection of H. A. Sedgwick. © H. A. Sedgwick.

The rebirth cycle was especially appropriate in the case of the hanging since Sedgwick resurrected a fabric she first employed for *In the Bardo*, a piece of *shibori* silk folded double, to produce the vertically symmetrical pattern, and tied before dyeing to generate the weblike lines. In its first incarnation, she suspended the piece like a cape from the shoulders of a mannequin, complete with creases from the tie-dying, and folds according to the pull of gravity (see figure 5.17). In *Bodhisattva Fractal World*, the piece retained its gentle production creases but was ironed flatter and pinned against the wall, making it more pictorial, less sartorial, less affected by currents of air.

Sedgwick exhibited a second, closely related hanging in *Bodhisattva Fractal World*, reversing the chromatic polarity of the first, with its central golden spread against a deep-indigo ground (figure 5.18). In its second incarnation, Sedgwick added a 1730 death poem by Saikaku:

> I borrow moonlight
> for this journey of a
> million miles.[108]

According to Hoffmann, the poem represented a "hyperbolic expression" for the "journey to the yonder world" after death.[109] Replacing Saikaku's silver moonlight, a key image of death haiku, as we have seen, with a rich golden sunset or sunrise, Sedgwick also centered his text, emphasizing the loose rhyme of "THIS" and "MILES":

I

BORROW MOONLIGHT FOR THIS

JOURNEY OF A MILLION MILES

In addition, she placed a new, un-Zen, but Sedgwickian emphasis on the first person singular, with the "I" centered as line 1, another "I" found almost immediately below it in "MOONLIGHT," and another just to the right of that in "MILLION." As a result, it is as if the emphatic first person singular dissolves first into light and then into the massively aggregated phenomenon of "A MILLION MILES." In addition, Sedgwick again bends Saikaku's straight lines into a sagging, fat, smile-like curve; a sense of pleasure emphasized by the triple repetition of words beginning with the letter *m*—"MOONLIGHT," "MILLION," and "MILES," suggesting a contented "MMM."

The golden yellow that Sedgwick employs on both *shibori* hangings evokes two characteristically thalassic scenes from "The Warm Decembers." The first focuses on the urine-gold sheets, hung out to dry in an "attic room," of an

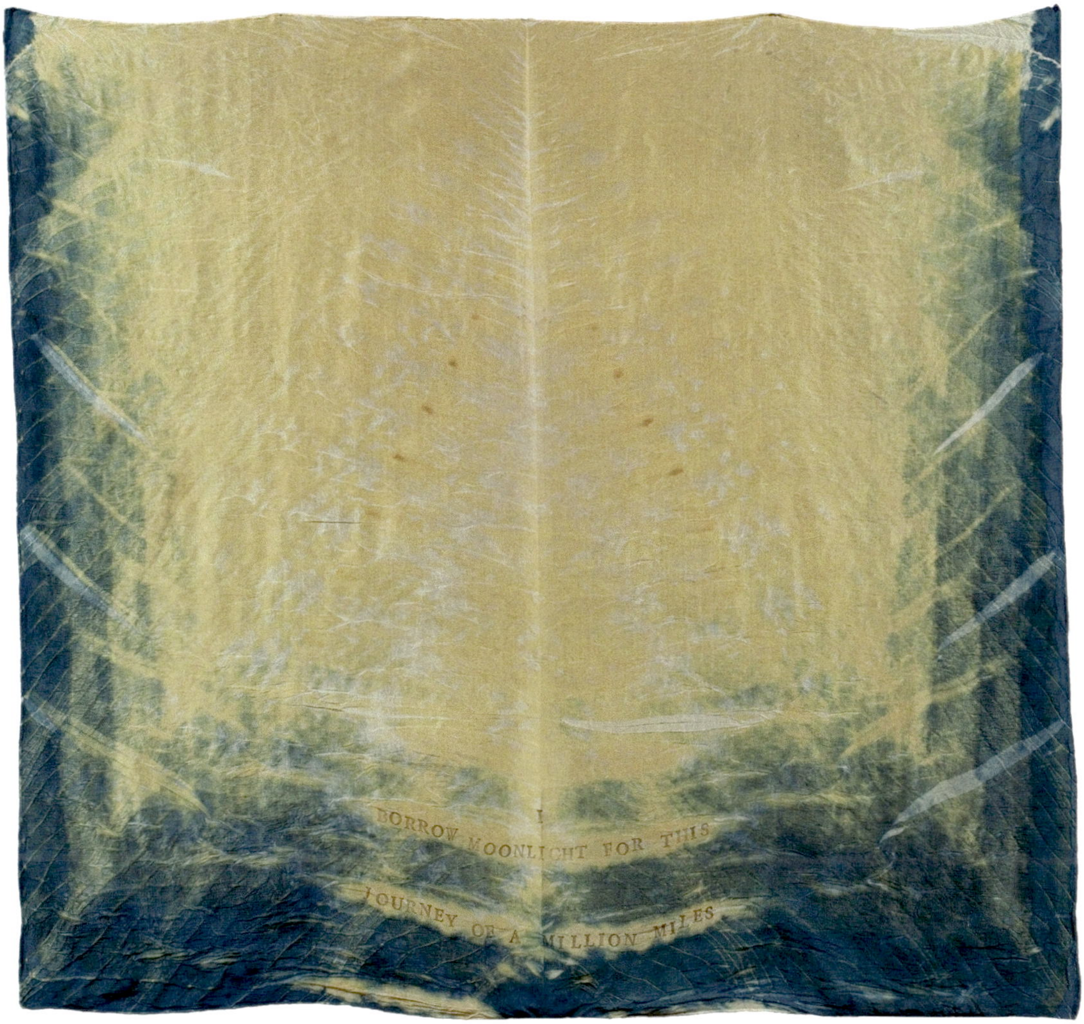

Figure 5.18. Eve Kosofsky Sedgwick, untitled *shibori* hanging, 2002. Photograph: Kevin Ryan. Collection of H. A. Sedgwick. © H. A. Sedgwick

unidentified child who repeatedly wets its bed with violent consequences but who, ultimately, survives and "finds somewhere an art"; a fiber art like this perhaps. In addition, Sedgwick's golden palette and tie-dye technique recall the "sloppy landscape" in which a similarly "gilded, scored" Beatrix, caught short, on a moonlit flit to London, with a painfully "distended bladder," squats down to take a leak: "the moon behind her / inking the sandy road ahead of her," surrounded by "sea" and "fresh water." The vertical, creased wall hanging also remembers the "curtains of water" that Beatrix lifts up to drink from a "mantled pool," while Sedgwick's confusion of land, sea, and sky recalls the way "not only the land / and the water, or the sea water and the fresh water, / but the water and the air, over and over the same places," "condensed" in front of Beatrix.[110]

The contexts of the poem suggest that there is less thalassic pleasure in the exhibited piece of piss, and something more threatening to the body, since Beatrix's "one big urination after dark" causes her to grow ill; a pathology accompanied by "soft ignorant twining nosy pains," a twining signaled in the visible evidence of tie-dyeing across the swatch, its fashioning recalling the way "the rush of liquid" from Beatrix's bladder was increasingly "strangled."[111]

Beatrix ultimately recovers from her urinary tract infection, but Sedgwick's late poem "Bathroom Songs" suggests the increasingly close association, in her mind, between "tinkl[ing] in the loo" and death. As we have seen, the poem compares the imagined, "wee bit more forbidding" scene of Sedgwick's future death to her earlier toilet training, a parallel suggesting that, like toilet training, dying was about "learning, forcibly, to change the process of one's person into a residual product—into something that instead exemplifies the impersonal" in a "taboo form," as Sedgwick phrased it in "Come as You Are." Like Sedgwick's parents, who commend the "masterpiece" she produced down the pan, *I Borrow Moonlight* suggests the floating of the poem and poet toward an all-consuming sunset, even as reading Saikaku's poem, extending down toward us, seems to pull us away from it. But even that text represents the last moment before the speaker is "gone, gone, forever gone," "utterly gone," in Sedgwick's words, into either "enlightenment" or "svaha," whatever that means.[112]

This Final Scene, or How Divine

Another haiku we have briefly encountered forms the subject of Sedgwick's *This Final Scene*, which incorporates lines from Choko's (ca. 1731) death poem (see figure 5.19):

> THIS FINAL SCENE I'LL NOT SEE
> TO THE END—MY DREAM
> IS FRAYING[113]

Choko was forty-six when he died in November 1731; a resonant age for Sedgwick: the age of the eponymous antihero of her narrative poem "Trace at 46" and the age at which she, having discovered her cancer had metastasized,

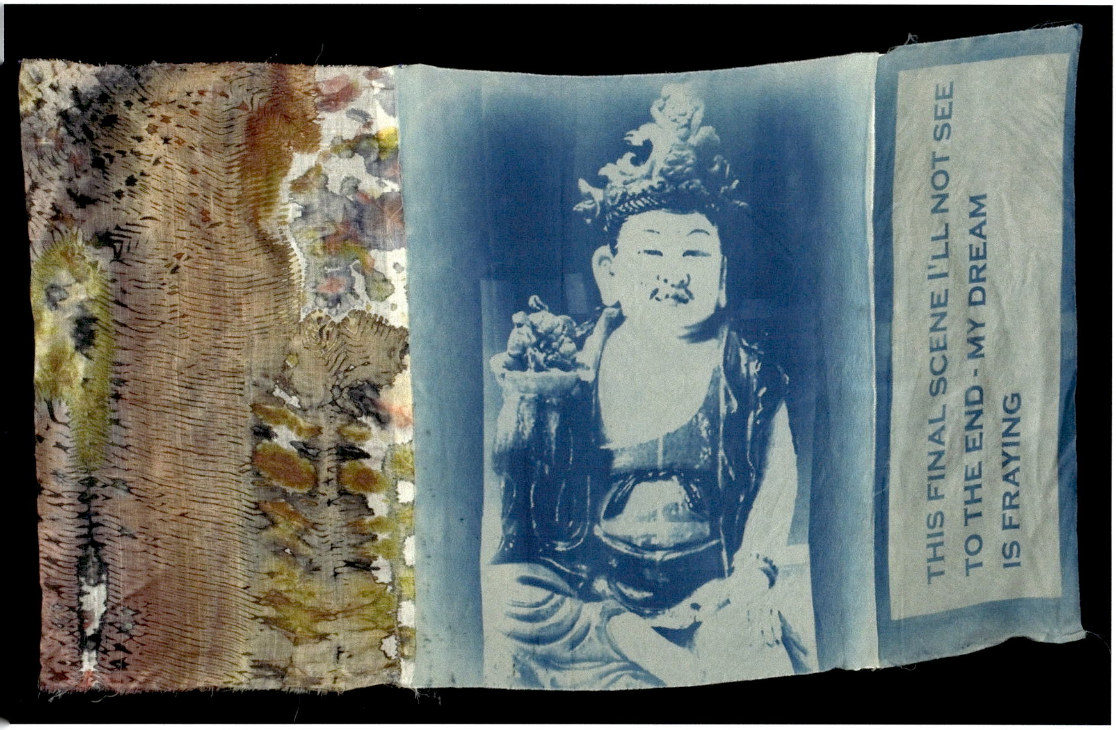

Figure 5.19. Eve Kosofsky Sedgwick, untitled collage, 2002. Photograph: Kevin Ryan. Collection of H. A. Sedgwick. © H. A. Sedgwick

commenced her reparative craft practice. According to Hoffmann, Choko's life also felt prematurely shortened. He died on the second day of winter, missing the final season and completion of his traditionally allotted fifty-year life span.[114]

In translation, Sedgwick's poem retains much of Choko's haiku form: its three-line structure, and the seven-syllable first line followed by a five-syllable second line, which recalls the metrics of a haiku's second and third lines. The dangling last line, however, suggests the poem's fraying to its conclusion, while readers might again feel shortchanged, or brought up short, by a poem two syllables short of the haiku's seventeen.

Sedgwick cyanotypes the poem on the right side of a triptych, a second three-part form, comprising three adjoining pieces of silk, in portrait orientation. The left swatch features another combined *shibori* and *suminagashi* pattern in white, lime green, pink, black, rust, and mustard. The central panel contains a cyanotype of Avalokiteshvara rather than the more usual Kuanyin. To read the poem, meanwhile, spectator must rotate the panel or tilt their heads left, stretching the right side of their necks; a painful neck formed one of Sedgwick's early symptoms, requiring her to wear a brace.[115]

As in Hoffmann, Sedgwick's characteristically capitalized lines are left justified. In the process of making the panel, she did not stencil the letters directly onto her ground. Instead, the surrounding white block must have been a solid dark ground with letters cut out, since they have gone marine blue, having been exposed to the light; a movement into the light resonant in the context of many accounts of the final moments of life. As such, the letters represent an engraving as much as a printing, the negative cutting-away process of a relief rather than a positive stamping down; resonant metaphors of the positive and negative we have repeatedly discussed.

While the rectangular panel in which Sedgwick fashions the text possesses a rough, coffin-like rectilinearity, she again did not iron her hanging flat. As a result, the fabric's surface remained creased and (de)formed into a more unpredictable, curvilinear shape at the edges. In addition, she again cropped the top-left corner of the swatch on the right, in the shape of a right-angle triangle, ensuring that the fraying would be prominent there. Thanks to the needless cut, the fraying panel does not reach its predictable, geometric end.

The text block seems to be floating in that violently abbreviated direction, downstream, from bottom to top, given the way the text pulls the reader's eye from left to right; water that, given the fabric's creases, seems to be rippling. As if resisting that mortal flow, toward the abbreviated, frayed corner where the panel comes to an end, the poem's internal rhymes pull back in the opposite direction, from right to left, given the way in which "SEE" recalls the earlier "SCENE," "I'LL" returns us to "FINAL," and "DREAM" takes us sonorously back to "END."

At this late stage, life no longer seems real. The poet will miss a performative, theatrical final *scene*. A *dream*, rather than reality, is being cut short, presumably to allow for an initially disorienting new awakening. This is a coming-to that, in Proust, often returns the narrator to something more real. For example, on certain days, he describes how "the weather was of the sort which, by modifying, by *awakening* one's sensibility, brings one back into relationship with the real."[116] Such an awakening might require a *wake*, though, in the sense of a funeral.

At the opposite end of the triptych is a piece of abstractly expressive silk. The *suminagashi* sections are toward the top right, with their blotchy colored inks floating on an off-white ground. Sedgwick made the bulk of the panel, however, using *shibori*, given the characteristic horizontal parallel lines. As such, the swatch suggests two possible orientations toward death: a going with the flow, in the *suminagashi* sections, and a constrained, tight resistance in the *shibori* parts. The rusty palette evokes a different kind of fraying: the rusting action of moisture on metal, producing a surface of increasingly disconnected parts that can be sloughed off, resonant again of the Buddhist aggregates and Sedgwick's metastatic, postmastectomy body, with missing, formerly integral, parts and tumors working against the whole. The panel also characteristically recalls the bloody residues left on a bandage or sanitary napkin, which we have repeatedly encountered.

The central panel features an image of a bodhisattva Sedgwick employed nowhere else, which I have been unable to source. Because of its pencil mustache, it seems to represent, if not the masculine Avalokiteshvara, then, given the shape of its eyes, an early Kuanyin before her full transition; an identity further suggested by the Chinese-ceramic, blue-and-white tonality of the image. Sedgwick must have again digitally scanned the photograph and printed it on a transparency, so that the black ink of the bodhisattva's body acted as a resist to the light dyeing its clothes and surrounding space blue; a resist-dye process related to, but different from, that of the *shibori* panel on the left. As such, Kuanyin's body, in order to manifest in the cyanotype, had to resist the light with all its might and saturated inky power, to continue shining luminously blue-white. The bodhisattva was not ready to be enlightened, to die into nirvana, wanting to remain in samsara, our world of the blues.

The just visibly enthroned bodhisattva, with "his" elaborate crown and patterned gown, is seated in half lotus. But, as my scare-quoted pronoun suggests, and perhaps because of the "mock-sleazy" John Waters–like pencil mustache, Avalokiteshvara remains difficult to gender.[117] That is because the bodhisattva's primary sexual characteristics are masked by the figure's half-lotus pose and the drapery that covers what might have been a diacritically revealing left nipple. Avalokiteshvara's right nipple is also solarized out, recalling the youthful Sedgwick overexposed on the front cover of *Fat Art, Thin Art*, whose left nipple is similarly absent. The bodhisattva's double chin, meanwhile, suggests a fat art akin to the creases of fabric in the right panel, its large ears signifying the figure's longevity; a durability that resists the brevity of life suggested by Choko's text.

Especially in the watery cyanotype blue, the overall "dwarfish," "aubergine-shaped" figure, with its "affected" appearance, recalls the Javanese *punåkawan*.[118] If so, then Sedgwick was meditating again on a wise, powerful, queer little god. "Squat and pudgy," like Avalokiteshvara, the "transfigured" *punåkawan* similarly was "distinguished / in Javanese by being always addressed / or referred to in the plural number"; a "they," in contemporary nonbinary parlance, revealing a "plaiting / together of lines female and male / and divine"; or, perhaps, male, female, and the John Waters–associated performer Divine given the bodhisattva's high, shaped eyebrows, one of the drag performer's trademarks. Indeed, Sedgwick's bodhisattva resembles a fantasy love child of Divine and Waters, incorporating their combined features.

Avalokiteshvara lacks the *punåkawan*'s "distended breasts" and "expectant gibbous belly," and spectators can't see the bodhisattva's "wildly salient ass." Present is Avalokiteshvara's elaborate jewelry, made-up face, and "male clothing if any," given the just-visible right nipple. The resemblance to Waters, a person with an appropriately aqueous name, also encourages viewers to predict a "high / and irresolute voice," a "waddling, thoughtful step," and, if the statue were iron, a "soft torso / heavy and magnetic with intentness, with joy." Spectators would also expect that, as a bodhisattva, Avalokiteshvara's life is "always in the present tense" and, given the bodhisattva's epicanthic eyes, taking place "between Chinese-high horizons."[119] In addition, Avalokiteshvara here seems to be sinking down into, rather than drowning in, the cyanotype liquid, while its Divine predecessor *punåkawan* were famous for having bowels that were "loose and hot," such that the "loins of the little god" regularly generated a "thin puddle spreading" away from their body. The *punåkawans*' lives were also characterized by a kind of "'pure' narration, all flow, every obstruction washed / away or worn through."[120]

Taken together, then, as a triptych braiding a swatch, on the left, featuring two Japanese textile processes, *shibori* and *suminagashi*; an Indo-Chinese divinity in the middle recalling a Javanese god; and lines of Anglo-Japanese on the right, the hanging suggests a narrative sequence in which abstract bloody and cloacal bodily matter coalesces, briefly, and comparatively faintly, into a continuously trans-figured and trans-national body. In its final scene, this utters a dramatic monologue in which speech is interrupted and remains unresolved and incomplete, as it fades into a coffin-shaped white ground, which decomposes around the swatch's edges into the surrounding empty air, with the poet dying and the bodhisattva choosing to return to life.

Smile, or Twins

On Sedgwick's desktop computer, I found several images of Kuanyin I sourced to books she owned on Chinese Buddhist bronzes. A key exception was a crowned bodhisattva, with eyes closed, gently smiling (see figure 5.20). Photographed in situ either by Sedgwick herself or by her husband, Hal, during their time at the Dazu temple cave complex in China, dating from the ninth to the thirteenth centuries, and combining Buddhist, Taoist, and Confucian iconographies, the face of the dove-gray-and-white bodhisattva is carved from

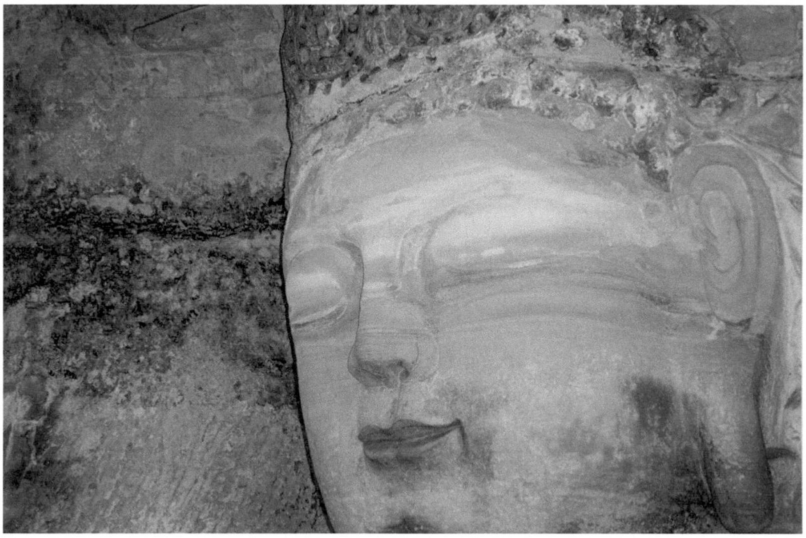

Figure 5.20. Rock-cut Chinese Buddhist divinity at Dazu, ca. ninth to thirteenth century. Collection of H. A. Sedgwick. © H. A. Sedgwick

a horizontally striated pink-and-gray rock face.[121] The left side of her face is joined to the rock behind it, blending into it, while the silhouette of her right cheek is more demarcated, by an emphatic contour line and greater color contrast. The bodhisattva's crown makes use of a blue-gray vein in the stone while her face capitalizes on patches of darker gray providing the shadow inside and around her nostrils, picking out her smiling lips and the cleft within her chin, and indicating shadow beneath and within her ears, around her eyes, and below her left cheekbones; as well as suggesting birthmarks or other blemishes on the lower-right side of her face.

Within the bodhisattva's face, the veining of the marble descends, in approximately horizontal bands, from a cloudy gray at the top, through a striated white and gray, to a fawn brown and patches of charcoal gray at the bottom. As such, the divinity's face resembles a twilit cloudscape, with dark clouds encroaching from the bottom right. The colorful patches and striation suggest both the emotional weather *within* the bodhisattva's mind and the actual meteorology *surrounding* it, to which she has become attuned; her mind not quite the ideal cloudless sky of Buddhist meditation, but a more human approximation. With eyes peacefully closed and smiling mouth communicating inner joy, Kuanyin appears to be meditating, or perhaps sleeping, her head rested gently against the pink wall, her skin's cooler tonality suggesting less intense internal weather than the surrounding pink sky; red sky at night anticipating a good following day; red sky in the morning, heavier weather to come.

Described in these ways, the image suggests Sedgwick's growing preoccupation with meteorology, in Proust and elsewhere. Looking carefully at the carving, viewers might recall Proust's narrator's sense that "on certain days" the weather could be "of the sort which, by modifying, by awakening one's sensibility," brought one "back into relationship with the real."[122] This is a real life "not as it appears to us, that is to say permanent, but as it really is: an atmosphere so swiftly changing."[123] Indeed, the statue may not have "kept a weather eye open," as its eyes are closed, but now that the "weather has changed," the smiling bodhisattva, like the narrator, is "filled . . . with joy"; or, to cite the most frequently cited account of Proustian weather for Sedgwick, "atmospheric changes, provoking other changes in the inner [person], awaken forgotten selves, counteract the torpor of habit," and "restore their old force to certain memories."[124]

Whoever took the photograph, Sedgwick was evidently enamored with it, making three works transforming it, two of which appeared in *Bodhisattva Fractal World*; the third remains in her archive. In all three, she fashioned a cyanotype, transforming the photograph from a polychrome original into a blue-and-white monochrome fabric print.

The perhaps experimental piece in Sedgwick's archive is the simplest of the three. This focuses on the bodhisattva's face, cropping much of the wall behind it, transforming the original rectangular landscape image into a square. Much of the focused contour of the earlier image is lost in the sloppier cyanotype printing, along with nearly all the color variety. As a result, the right side of the bodhisattva's face becomes more abstract and difficult to differentiate from its ground and to recognize as a face.

Sedgwick makes that process of facial recognition additionally difficult by inserting an interruptive portrait-oriented swatch of brightly colored, abstractly patterned yellow-and-pink *shibori* across its left eye as if a kind of eye patch that blinds the bodhisattva and similarly challenges the viewer's perceptual capacities (see figure 5.21). As a blinded, and partially blinding, blue fabric screen, the piece again recalls Jarman's *Blue*, but Sedgwick and the viewer's blindness are not as complete as the filmmaker's. The bodhisattva has lost only her left eye, and might open her resting right eye, but recognition remains challenging for the spectator, as Sedgwick has transformed the precise detail and contour in the photograph into a blurry, watery tone. Compensating, however, the partially sighted Kuanyin's hearing, perhaps, is becoming more acute, as signaled by the prominent left ear. In addition, the cotton Sedgwick employs for the bodhisattva, and the silk

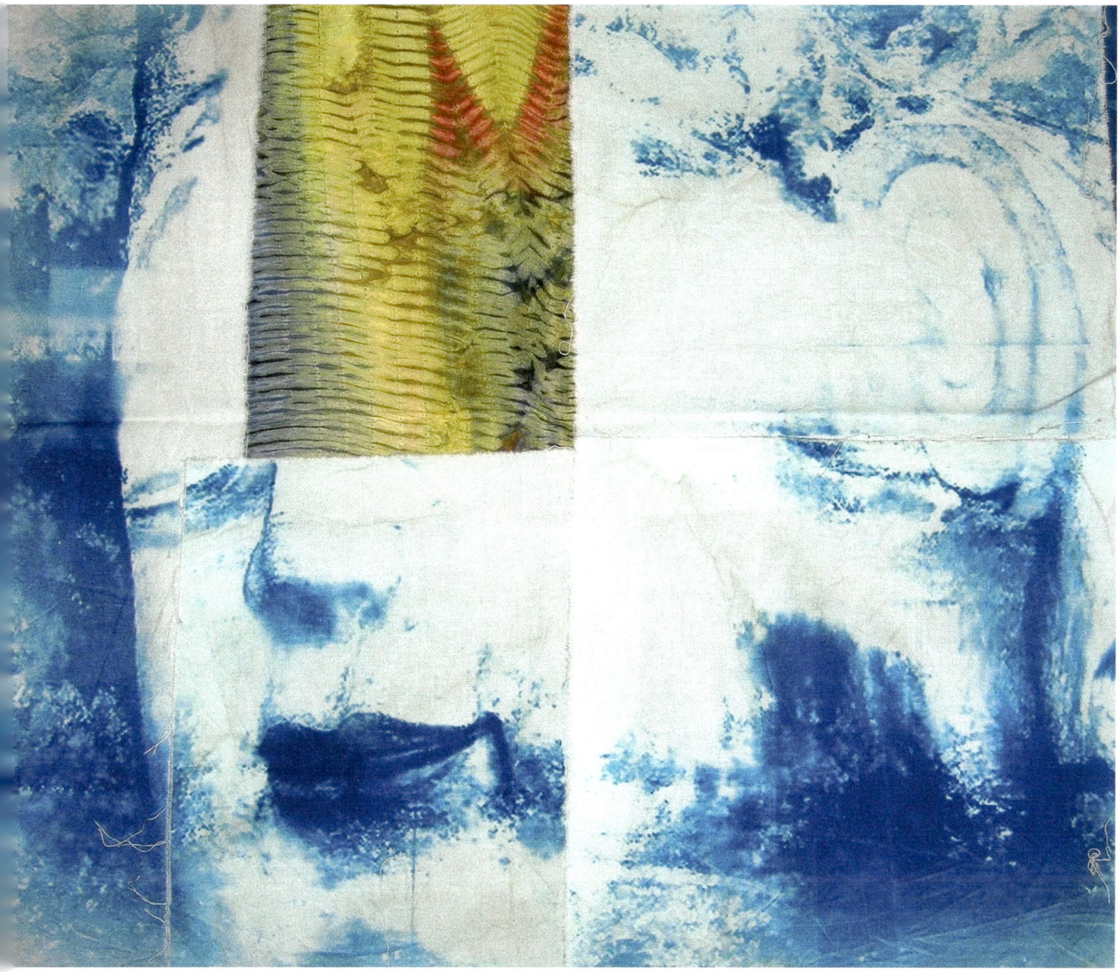

Figure 5.21. Eve Kosofsky Sedgwick, untitled collage, 2002. Photograph: Jason Edwards

for the swatch, suggests an increased tactility, of feeling the different textures and temperatures of the fabrics, strongest at their intersection.

Sedgwick further emphasized this sense of interruptive, incoherent aggregates in the first exhibited version (figure 5.21). This comprised a patchwork of four elements. Sedgwick juxtaposes two cyanotype patches depicting Kuanyin's smiling face, on the right, and the join between her head and her crown, on the left, with a pinky gray-and-white *suminagashi* ground that recalls the color and inky-wash veining and blotch pattern of the bodhisattva's face in the original photograph (see figure 5.20). The marbling also recalls the cover of *Epistemology*,

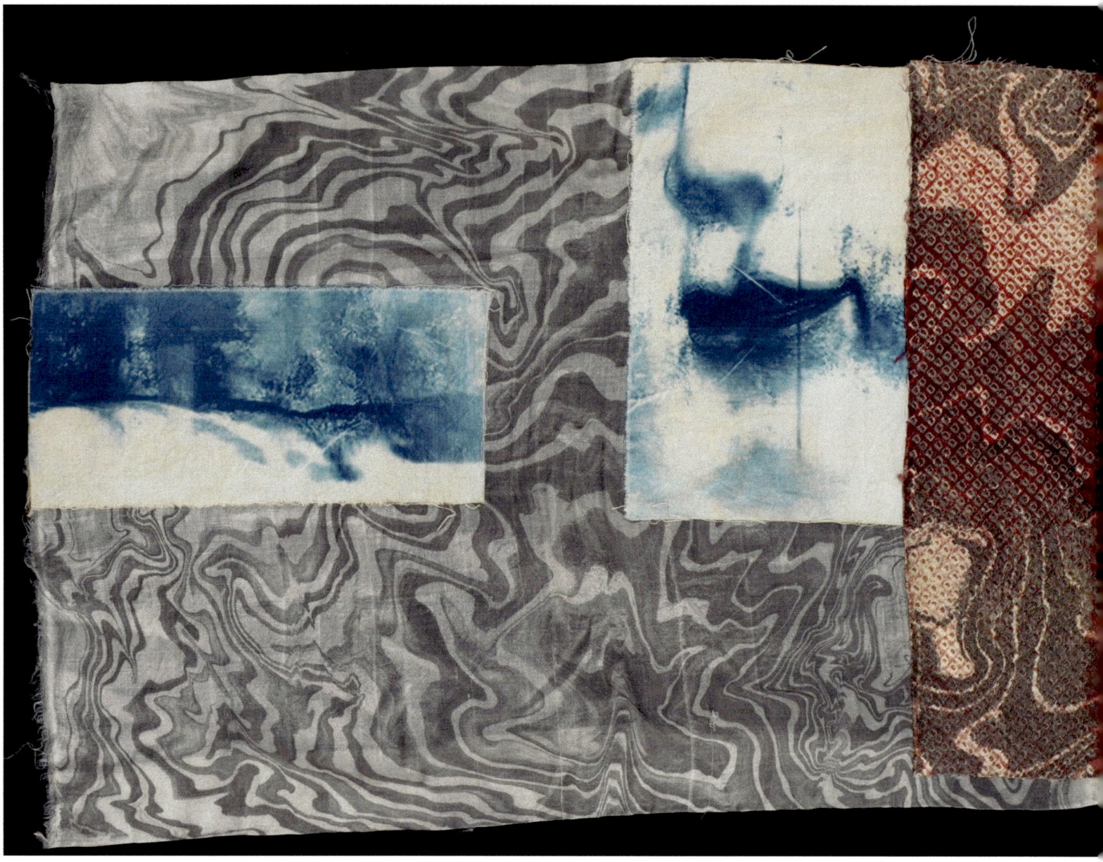

Figure 5.22. Eve Kosofsky Sedgwick, untitled collage, 2002. Photograph: H. A. Sedgwick. Collection of H. A. Sedgwick. © H. A. Sedgwick

suggesting the cave as a kind of closet, out of which the bodhisattva might step, transformed, to return to samsara or to move into the light of nirvana.

The final part of the patchwork is a swatch of again *suminagashi* fabric, located on the right, in portrait orientation, its pattern originally produced through the *shibori* technique, its tiny diamonds the result of fabric tied into numerous little teats. The bloody pink of this marbled section, as well as its smudgy veining, again recalls the pink and gray marble behind the bodhisattva's head in the original photograph (see figure 5.20).

Taken as a whole, the exhibit alludes to the original photograph through its rectangular landscape orientation, pink-gray palette, marbling, and figuration. It suggests an intimate formal and ontological relationship between the minute behaviors of water, oil, and ink in *suminagashi*; the creases and patterns in fabrics documenting the folding and unfolding of *shibori*; the aggregation and disaggregation of the body; the moment-by-moment atmospheric and meteorological transitions of the weather; the epochal geological formation of limestones; and the shifting play of affect within and across the body. This is a Taoist world in which everything is in motion, forming and deforming, at a range of scales and across radically incommensurate time periods. Indeed, Sedgwick emphasizes the meeting of weather and geology in the abstract left patch depicting the join of the crown and the bodhisattva's head, which resembles hills, worn smooth by an earlier process of glaciation and the present impact of rainy weather above.

If imagined from above, the patchwork bodhisattva seems again to be floating, horizontally, on its back, on the currents of the *suminagashi* water, oil, and ink below; or, if viewed face on, sinking down into it. Sedgwick emphasizes this sense of an encounter with water by the way she attaches the two patches at a gently buffeted diagonal rather than perpendicular to the edge of the collage. Rather than drowning, though, the bodhisattva seems to be descending, with gravity, in both senses; floating happily downward toward and into the ground, with quiet purpose, perhaps from another, heavenly realm, smiling as she goes.

The smile again, perhaps, recalls passages in Proust and suggests a different sense of aggregates than the parts of an individual Buddhist body; this time an idea of bodies as aggregates of a larger social whole. Readers might recall the narrator's description of how there "hovered" over Albertine's lips—and *hovering* is the word for Sedgwick's bodhisattva—a "smile that did not strictly belong to them," a smile that he had already "seen on the faces of certain people when they said to Bergotte, with a knowing air: 'I've bought your book, it's not bad,' one of those collective, universal smiles which, when they feel the need of them—as one makes use of railways and removal vans—individuals borrow, except a few who are extremely refined, like Swann or M. de Charlus, on whose lips I never saw the smile appear."[125] Readers might also remember a second passage Sedgwick repeatedly employed across her final show: "For beauty is a series of hypotheses." Proust's narrator wondered of what beauty was composed and asked whether it was "anything more than the complementary part . . . added to a fragmentary and fugitive stranger by our imagination, overstimulated by regret." Had he been free to get down from his carriage and speak to the girl he was pursuing from afar, the narrator might have been "disillusioned by some blemish on her skin which from the carriage [he] had not distinguished";[126] blemishes apparent on the veined marble skin of Sedgwick's bodhisattva. Sedgwick, however, was less deterred than fascinated by affecting, and affect-full, blemishes, asking, in "The Warm Decembers," "How many men were there who, dreaming of the scar, / thought it was the cheek they were in love with."[127]

If Proust's narrator gives up his attempt to "penetrate into" the girl's life, "for beauty is a series of hypotheses which ugliness cuts short when it bars the way that we could already see opening into the unknown," Sedgwick's image is more preoccupied with "a smile," which, she seems to hope, might furnish her with an "expected key or clue with which to read the expression on her face, to interpret her bearing." And if the statue risks becoming "commonplace," at least to Proust's narrator, because of its blemish, Sedgwick is precisely able to perceive the divinity *in* her disguising human blemish.[128] If so, then the exhibit again echoes the end of Sedgwick's autobiography, wherein she practices a meditation in which you try to recognize that every person you encounter "has been, in some earlier life, your mother" or, "more likely, in many lives," and, "as you gaze you can see what kind of mother they were to you; you can see as well, slowly, what kind of a child you were to them." Over and over

> you're like Aeneas
> encountering a stranger,
> Venus, and guessing
>
> just from the rosy
> glow of their neck and their feet,
> and their stately step,
>
> though too late, "Surely,
> stranger, you are a goddess.
> Surely, my mother."[129]

Sedgwick was "pretty good at this meditation" and could find "in almost every face" she encountered "the place of a smile or an intelligence—a shared one," "the sense of [a] possible, beautiful care" and "compassion."[130]

Much about the hanging recalls the passage, especially the "rosy glow" of the rock around the bodhisattva's face, as if a baby with its head resting against an endometrial wall; a wall thickening with nourishing blood vessels in the collage's right swatch. The collage was, then, another image that represented a sustained "object of reflection" for Sedgwick, one she could "turn toward" that would "make [her] smile" just as it contained a smile; a "condensation of sweetness," an appropriately stony "enigmatic pebble" to be pocketed, carried, and secretly, reassuringly, pondered and "finger[ed]."[131]

The final piece in Sedgwick's mini-trilogy continued her maternal meditation, doubling the bodhisattva companionably into the form of twins (figure 5.23).

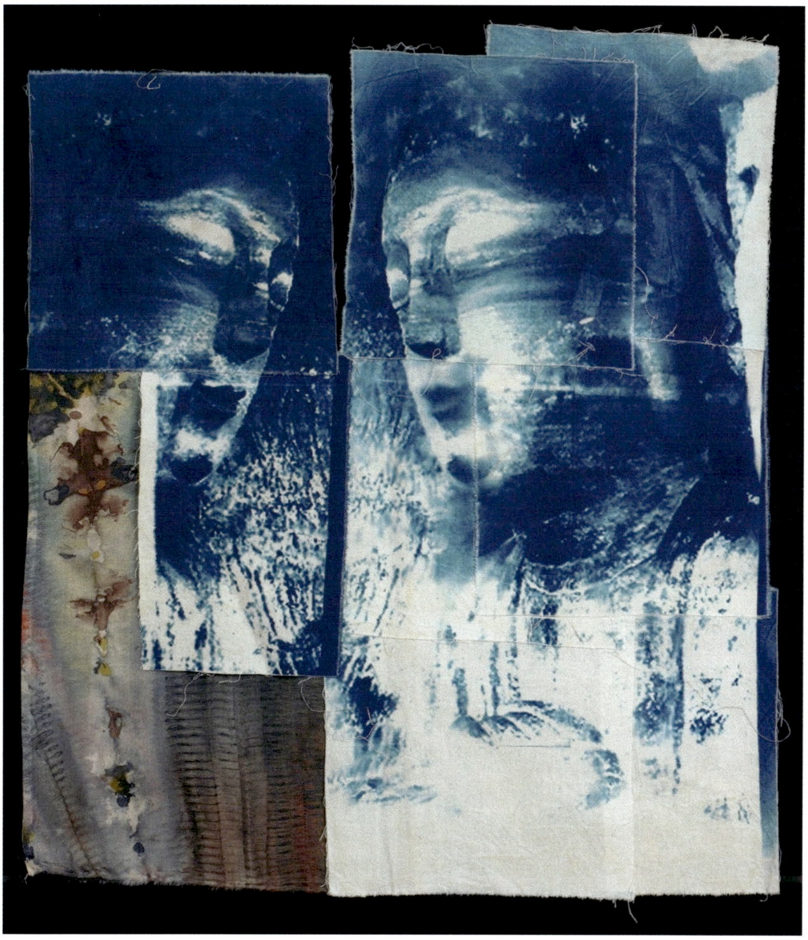

Figure 5.23. Eve Kosofsky Sedgwick, untitled collage, 2002. Photograph: H. A. Sedgwick. Collection of H. A. Sedgwick. © H. A. Sedgwick

The patchwork comprises nine swatches: a single piece of *shibori* silk, bottom left, joined together with eight pieces of cyanotype depicting Kuanyin, this time in two near-identical forms, one the mirror image of the other, the second again fashioned by flipping the transparency of the original photograph vertically. The *shibori* swatch's left-hand location, pink-and-black palette, and horizontal striation all recall the marble wall to the left of the bodhisattva in Sedgwick's source image; a background location she additionally signals by placing the cyanotype patches on top of the *shibori*.

Sedgwick again crops the bodhisattvas into fragments and breaks them up into their aggregates by printing them *across* multiple smaller patches of overlaid fabric. Sedgwick also suggests the bodhisattvas' overlapping interrelation, rather than individuality, by their closely related appearances, as fraternal/sororal, if not identical, twins, and joint immersion in the aqueous indigo of the maternal waters of a womb, again complete with a fleshy, pink, veined endometrial wall at bottom left.

In depicting twins in utero, Sedgwick meditates again on the overlapping relationship between the same and the different, the *homo* and the hetero, with a mirroring aesthetic emphasizing rhyming sameness. The patchwork also extends, in an ancient Buddhist Asian direction, the opening gambit of *Epistemology of the Closet* with its famous assertion that "many of the major nodes of thought and knowledge in twentieth-century Western culture as a whole are structured—indeed, fractured—by a chronic, now endemic crisis of homo/heterosexual definition, indicatively male, dating from the end of the nineteenth century."[132]

In addition, the patchwork speaks to one of the central gambits of "The Warm Decembers." This was Sedgwick's desire to find "new ways" of "experimenting with, and honoring," the queer forms of "intense creativity" of "passionate readers" (and here viewers), who were interested in instances of "ontological thresholds and of the perverse, desiring energies that alone can move across them" when there was a gap between "a person alive and dead; a person and a photograph; a sister and a sister; a present and a past; a person child and adult; people with the same name; a happening and a dream of it; a writer (or a model) and a character; an I and a she or he." And, I might add, a color photograph and a cyanotype; a cyanotype flipped left and right; printed on two or six swatches; and a bodhisattva imagined to be a singular or plural entity; able to appear simultaneously and sequentially at different times and places and in variant ontological forms and who sought to "make the difference between I and she or he no *more* weighty than these other differentials."[133]

Queer spectators might also think of recent conceptualizations of "liking" and "likeness" suggested by one of Sedgwick's friends and most brilliant students, Jonathan Flatley, with whom she worked on Warhol. In Flatley's terms, the collage might encourage spectators, reparatively, in the direction of a "tendency toward liking" things rather than toward critique and "scholarly scepticism." This would form part of a broader "pedagogical effort to help us expand our own capacities for liking" and to generate a "condition of possibility for affective affiliation." For Flatley, likeness is "distinct both conceptually and experientially from sameness," on the grounds that "to be similar to something is precisely to not be the same as it," but, instead, to be "neither incommensurate nor identical—related, but distinct"; "similarity" representing a "third term aside the same-different binary."[134] In Warhol's work, this found its best form, Flatley argues, in "mechanical forms of reproduction such as stencils and stamps," as well as "stickers" and "photo-based silkscreens," all media Sedgwick employed.[135]

Proust also again seems to hover in the twin bodhisattvas' vicinity. For instance, looking at the ongoingly metamorphic exhibit, viewers might recall Proust's narrator noticing that when he thought of the Balbec girls, they were the "mountainous blue undulations of the sea," and it was the sea he really "hoped to find," if he went to some town where they had gone, since "the most exclusive love for a person is always a love for something else."[136] In addition, with the submerged, fluid-saturated, womb-like character of the patchwork in mind, spectators might remember Proust's narrator noticing that the girls' "characteristics did not belong only to [them]. They were those of their parents," since "the individual is steeped in something more general than himself."[137] The narrator also recalled that if he possessed memories of Albertine, it was "a series of [her], separate from one another, incomplete, a collection of profiles or snapshots"; best emblematized by that most "strange development" of "inversion."[138] Finally, Sedgwick's deliberately sloppy technique recalls the narrator's reflection on the way in which Time could "introduce bold contrasts in two successive aspects of a single person," such that they resembled, across successive encounters, "rather bad portraits of themselves hanging side by side in an exhibition."[139]

Another 256k Shades of Gray, or *For Beauty Is a Series of Adjectives*

Several works Sedgwick displayed in *Bodhisattva Fractal World* functioned, as we have begun to see, as transitional objects segueing into *The Weather in Proust*. Our final three objects continue this trend, explicitly focusing on passages from *In Search of Lost Time* rather than Japanese death poems. In its later exhibition context, Sedgwick titled the exhibit *Hypotheses II*.

On a horizontal silk hanging, Sedgwick meditated on a phrase from *Within a Budding Grove* (volume 2 of *In Search of Last Time*) we have just encountered: "For beauty is a series of hypotheses" (see figure 5.24). She painted the letters, in white block capitals, through a stencil on the surface of a gray-and-white *suminagashi* ground, its underlying patterns flowing through and beneath Proust's phrase. In addition, Sedgwick reinforced the central, spinal moiré "BO" section with a piece of *shibori* patterned in a series of tessellating diamonds.

The exhibit recalled Michel Foucault's similarly monochrome panel on the NAMES quilt, which Sedgwick photographed on her visit to Washington in

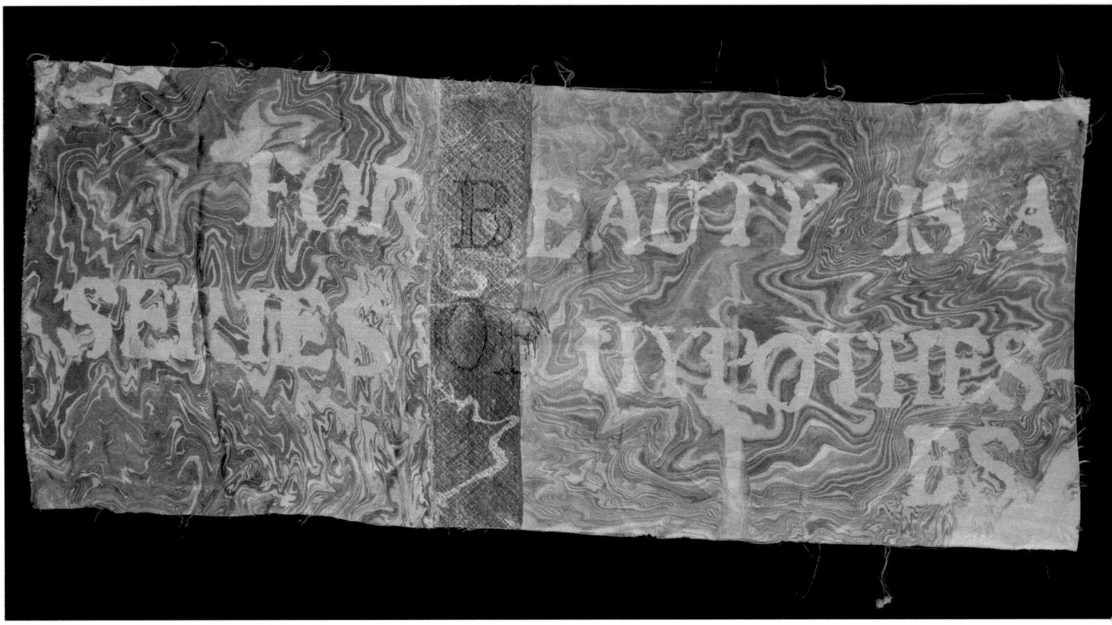

Figure 5.24. Eve Kosofsky Sedgwick, untitled collage, 2002. Photograph: Kevin Ryan. Collection of H. A. Sedgwick. © H. A. Sedgwick

October 1987 and discussed in *Tendencies*, as we have seen. This included sentences from volume 1 of the *History of Sexuality*: "Where there is power, there is resistance," "a plurality of resistances . . . spread over time and space." "It is doubtless the strategic codification of these resistances that makes a revolution."[140] Sedgwick recalled and articulated Foucault's ideas of plural, powerful, strategic resistances spread over time and space through her two fiber art techniques, since *shibori* was all about resistances to dyeing that took time and unfolded over space while *suminagashi* was the product of a plurality of aqueous forces interacting with one another. Sedgwick also characteristically capitalized and recast Proust's phrase to make a haiku-like and -lite poem:

> FOR BEAUTY IS A
> SERIES OF HYPOTHES-
> ES

Like a haiku, the first line contains five syllables, but Sedgwick cuts short the second, which could have made up the requisite seven, by hyphenating the word "HYPOTHES- / ES," amputating the final syllable, generating a rhyme between the second and third lines, and recalling the earlier "IS" of line 1. Sedgwick locates the final syllable as a trailing, right-justified line, where the partial word functions as an abbreviated form of her initials "*E[K]S*," and so, perhaps, as a rare, encoded signature.

Presumably, Sedgwick could have chosen a smaller font to ensure her second line fitted within her ground. Her awkward hyphenation effect must be deliberate, resonating with the (cut) second half of Proust's sentence: "which ugliness cuts short when it bars the way that we could already see opening into the unknown." If Sedgwick's abbreviating is "ugly," in terms of its sloppy crafting, the unpredictably needless cut might be in the service of something beautiful, since it was unknowable in advance and requires a series of hypothetical explanations. Just as good and bad are inseparable at every level, Sedgwick suggests, so are beauty and ugliness.

Further sloppy crafting is apparent in the pattern-interrupting vertical line of bleach that runs down from the *T* of "BEAUTY" through the *P* of "HYPOTHES-"; a nod, perhaps, to Julia Margaret Cameron's "excitingly amateurish surface textures," which we know Sedgwick admired.[141] Given the continuity of the *suminagashi* pattern, as we have seen, Sedgwick seems to have monochrome marbled the silk and then, perhaps, painted it with bleach, given the flatness of the letters, through a stencil; white paint would have had a more three-dimensional presence. The bleach must then have eaten through the marbling below; a technique less akin to printing, with its black ink pressed on white paper, and more like etching, and thus, in a resonant metaphor for an artist concerned with fat and thin art, *eating* into the surface of a plate; a metaphor she employed repeatedly in "The Warm Decembers."

Reversing the polarity of black ink on a white ground, except for the central panel, with its black-outlined gray ink against a non-binary-contrasting gray ground, Sedgwick makes Proust's sentence further difficult to read by the way the bleached letters bleed at their edges, decomposing their forms, just as the hanging frays at its unhemmed extremities. The letters also undulate, horizontally and vertically, across the fabric, *ice caps* again melting into the similarly monochrome *suminagashi* ground; ice caps that represented more than a pun given Sedgwick's interest in the water cycle.

Sedgwick's use of a monochrome palette suggests she had reconceived the subtle effects of black and white. In her circa 1997 essay "Paranoid and Reparative Reading," she had praised the rich possibilities of Tomkins's seven-affect system, comparing it to the "analog models of the color wheel." She contrasted this with a digital scanner or copier that could "reproduce any work of art in

256,000 shades of grey." However "infinitesimally subtle its discriminations," Sedgwick argued, there were "crucial knowledges it simply cannot transmit unless it is equipped to deal with the coarsely reductive possibility that red is different from yellow is different again from blue." But, in this exhibit, there is "no reason to believe" that the analog spectrum of black, white, and gray need constrain our "understanding of difference, contingency, performative force, or the possibility of change." Indeed, it perhaps offers "crucial" access to "certain important ranges of difference," the microdifferences *within* the apparent binaries of black and white, water and ice, especially since an effect of printing the *B* of "BEAUTY" in a different color from the rest of the word was to emphasize "EAU" as the start of a possible new word, *EAU* the French for "water."[142]

For Beauty Is a Series of Hypotheses, or More Paranoia and Reparation

Sedgwick returned to Proust's phrase "for beauty is a series of hypotheses," this time giving the sentence in its entirety, in a second hanging displayed pictorially in *Bodhisattva Fractal World* and horizontally in *Works in Fiber, Paper, and Proust* (figure 5.25). The exhibit comprises six overlapping rectilinear pieces of hard-wearing but fraying denim-colored cotton, in three courses, across whose surface Sedgwick reproduced a now-familiar image of Kuanyin, having flipped her earlier acetate 180 degrees vertically.

Around the bodhisattva, Sedgwick printed Proust's sentence, unevenly, in white fabric paint, either through a stencil or, given the blotchiness of the lettering, via rubber stamps. The effect is unlike reading Proust in the original: The sentence is in English, decontextualized from the plot, and recontextualized in relation to Kuanyin. In addition, whereas readers mostly receive Proust through the medium of right-justified, consistently printed black ink against a white or cream paper ground, Sedgwick reverses the polarity, highlighting the narrator's words in white against blue. She also sloppily varies the distance between letters and words, and distributes both unevenly across only roughly horizontal lines, with the effect that they look like snowflakes falling on, around, and behind Kuanyin or like stones sinking to the bottom of the ocean, accompanying the goddess as she calmly descends, her bones again becoming coral, her eyes pearls, as she and Proust's words undergo a characteristic sea change into something rich and strange.

Sedgwick does not respect the autonomy or anatomy of Proust's words, emphasizing parts of his speech, as if the viewer is a novice reader, spelling out

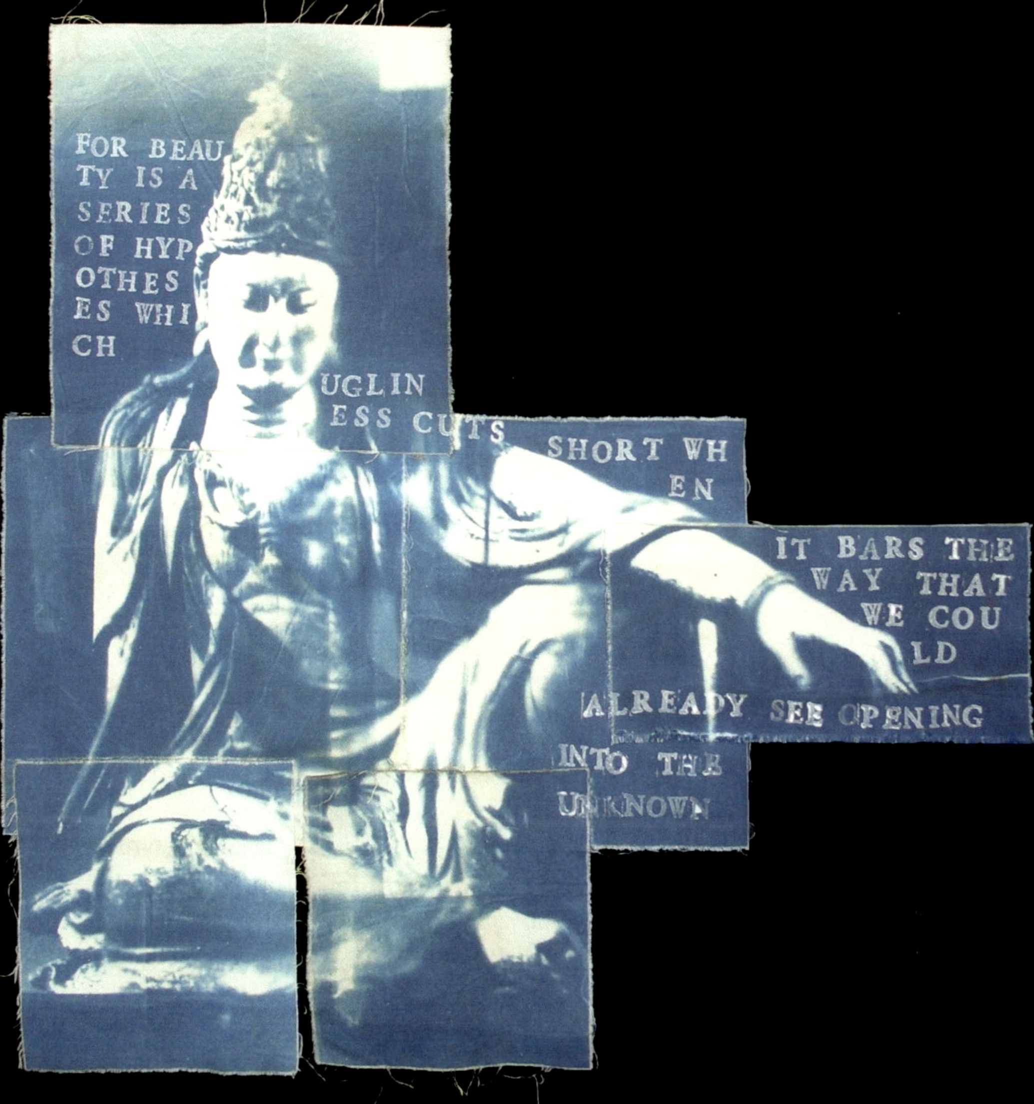

Figure 5.25. Eve Kosofsky Sedgwick, untitled collage, 2002. Photograph: Kevin Ryan. Collection of H. A. Sedgwick. © H. A. Sedgwick

and recognizing some words, from their previous experience, but not knowing enough to recognize the outlines and meanings of others:

FOR BEAU
TY IS A
SERIES
OF HYP
OTHES
ES WHI
CH

UGLIN
ESS CUTS
SHORT WH
EN
IT BARS THE
WAY THAT
WE COU
LD

ALREADY SEE OPENING
INTO THE
UNKNOWN

Reconceived as a kind of negative concrete poem, with only three of the seventeen lines not resolving in some form of rhyme, the lines do not so much form a pictorial image as articulate the space around one. In breaking down Proust's sentence into smaller, often nonsensical, and difficult-to-recognize and -pronounce parts, Sedgwick shapes the text so that while the original had a *straight* left and right margin, here it begins left justified but is increasingly *queerly* stretched at its ragged right margin; a stretch emphasized by the way it encloses and receives, like a fisted rectum, Kuanyin's left arm.

Proust's text and Kuanyin's body seem mutually accommodating. The bodhisattva listens hard, with closed, concentrated eyes, to the partial word "WHI," which rises to enter better her right ear. Viewers might also think about the text as a thought bubble in her mind before emerging, as a speech bubble, from her mouth at the point of the partial word "UGLIN." "BEAU," meanwhile, resonates with the *"beau"dhisattva*'s difficult-to-gender appearance. Sedgwick's initials, *ES*, also appear frequently: subtly within "SERI*ES*," more emphatically in "*ES* WHI," and again quietly within "*ES*S CUTS," suggesting that she, too, takes ownership of Proust's phrase, breaking it down and reforming it into a new whole, according to her own idiom.[143] Sedgwick's stamping becomes increasingly uneven and invisible toward the end of the sentence, perhaps an effect of impatiently not returning enough to the paint toward the end of the project; perhaps her paint ran out. More likely, the letters deliberately cease to be legible at the "unknown" end of the sentence.

Loosed from the context of the novel, the sentence comes out, like late Sedgwick, in favor of the present tense; of reparative, surprising beauty; and of an unargumentative, hypothetical world in which one does not know what one wants, thinks, or feels, or might find beautiful in advance. In the context of the narrative, as we have seen, it means differently, in the mouth of a lusty, relationally unskilled, type-bound, perfection-seeking narrator:

> Had I been free to get down from the carriage and to speak to the girl whom we were passing, I might perhaps have been disillusioned by some blemish on her skin which from the carriage I had not distinguished. (Whereupon any attempt to penetrate into her life would have seemed suddenly impossible. For beauty is a series of hypotheses which ugliness cuts short when it bars the way that we could already see opening into the unknown. Perhaps a single word which she might have uttered, or a smile, would have furnished me with an unexpected key or clue with which to read the expression on her face, to interpret her bearing, which would at once have become commonplace).[144]

The passage makes clear how much Sedgwick's collage revised it. She focuses on a bracketed aside of the narrator's, not a main part of his argument or story. Kuanyin has just the kind of mysterious smile the narrator finds irresistible; on a face that is divine enough that there is no danger that her bearing would become commonplace. However, if the narrator's love object is a fantasy of a beautiful European girl, Sedgwick's is a difficult-to-gender Asian figure. If the desiring narrator is restlessly sitting in a carriage, Kuanyin seems undistracted by her sexuality and stably seated while the world passes by her and the words fall around her ears. If the narrator's fantasy girl is unlikely to have unblemished skin, Kuanyin has an obvious (re)birth mark on her left cheek. Sedgwick's text is equally blotchy, suggesting her identification with the disappointing, objectified girl, rather than the narrator. And if he wants to "penetrate" into the girl's life, and while Kuanyin's body is open enough to smell her, the bodhisattva seems receptive to spiritual and pedagogical interrelation rather than sexual penetration.[145]

Indeed, much about the patchwork emphasizes that Sedgwick was working in a *reparative*, rather than paranoid-critical, mode. For example, given the way she lays Proust's sentence across six fraying patches of overlapping fabric, with a visible gap between the bottom two, the collage again recalls a reparative practice that was "additive and accretive," that wanted to "assemble and confer plenitude on an object" that would "have resources to offer" to an "inchoate self" and that revealed an "'over'-attachment to fragmentary" forms. The "irrepressible fascination with ventriloquistic experiment" is also central, given that the narrator's voice is imagined by Proust, quoted by Sedgwick, channeled through Kuanyin, and read/seen by the viewer/spectator. Sedgwick's collage also embodies the reparative's "disorienting juxtapositions of present with past": Sedgwick's early twenty-first century laid over Proust's modernist past mapped onto the ancient temporality of Kuanyin's meditation, experienced by viewers in their continuous present tense. Finally, the collage is reparative in its juxtaposition of "popular with high culture," given the way it embroiders the hem of a globally populist Buddhist divinity with *In Search of Lost Time*, perhaps the high-water mark of European queer literary culture. Indeed, Sedgwick notes that, "like Proust," reparative readers "help" themselves "again and again," "extracting sustenance from the objects of a culture—even of a culture whose avowed desire has often been not to sustain them"—or from a sentence that, in its original context, may have rubbed Sedgwick's (paranoid) feminist hackles the wrong way.[146]

A Final Work, Quickened Also by Genius, or *As in Classical Landscapes*

Our final montage (figure 5.26) similarly juxtaposed two passages from the first and second volumes of *In Search of Lost Time* with three overlapping cyanotypes of Kuanyin printed onto a patchwork of seventeen overlapping pieces of fraying, quilted cotton, laid out in three lines. All three iterations of the bodhisattva are scarred by a hole in their foreheads where a stolen jewel formerly marked the *ajna*, or sixth, brow chakra. The location of the jewel in the middle of the forehead, rather than between the bodhisattva's eyes, signals the Hindu genealogy of the iconography and marks the main meridian line bisecting the right and left sides of the body.

The crowned bodhisattva is presumably seated in the lotus position. It is hard to tell because Sedgwick cropped the image around the navel, following a Greco-Roman bust format. Kuanyin sits upright, her arms by her sides, her spine extended through her crown, her chin and eyes tilted down and in, suggesting meditative introspection. The statue was evidently a polychrome example whose earlier coloration partly survived the ravages of time, given the demarcation of its hair, raised into a bun, from its face and crown; the touching,

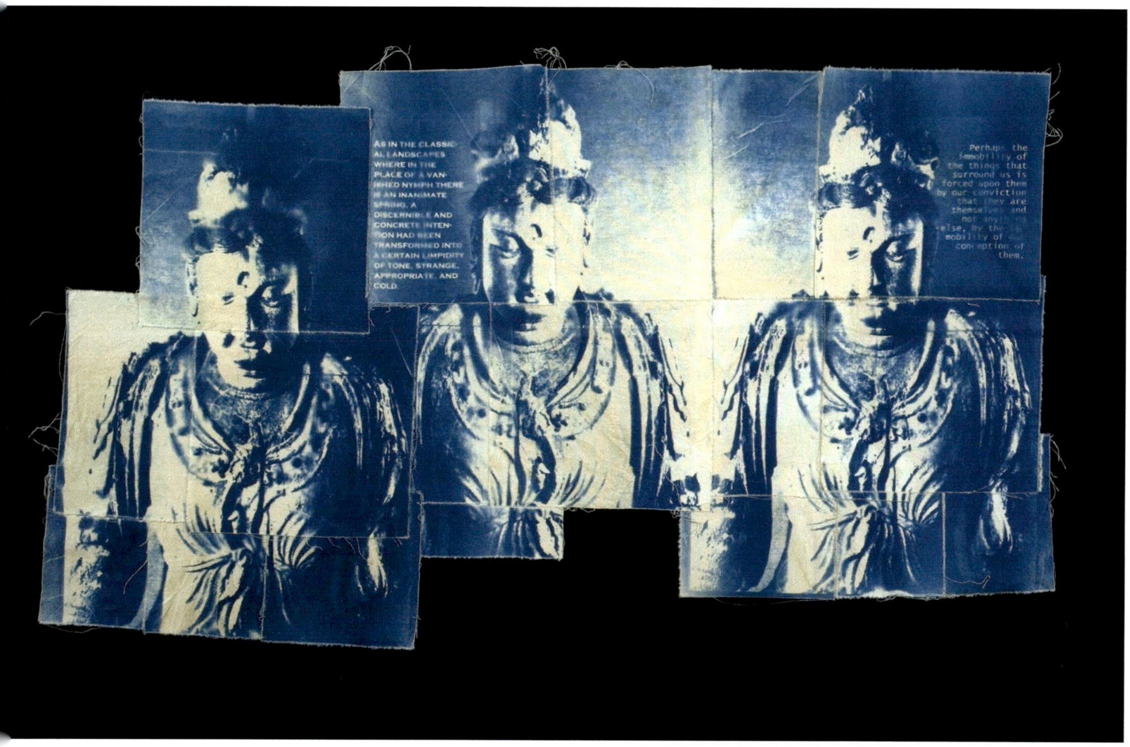

Figure 5.26. Eve Kosofsky Sedgwick, untitled collage, 2002. Photograph: Kevin Ryan. Collection of H. A. Sedgwick. © H. A. Sedgwick

blush- or flush-like strawberry mark, or hemangioma, again on its left cheek; the darker-colored fabric between its necklace and white gown, and the colored bosses on the hem of its cleavage.

The bodhisattva's bust is accentuated by the cluster of drapery produced by a tie just above her waist and below her breasts, suggesting the female Kuanyin, rather than the male Avalokiteshvara, and the statue's Chinese, rather than Indian, origin. The statue's drapery again reveals Greco-Buddhist syncretism of the kind associated with Gandhara, suggesting that this example emerged from a complex confluence of Greco-Roman, Indo-Chinese, and Hindu-Buddhist contexts.

To the left of the central bodhisattva, Sedgwick cyanotyped text from *The Guermantes Way* (volume 3 of *In Search of Lost Time*): "As in the classical landscape where in the place of a vanished nymph there is an inanimate spring, a discernible and concrete intention had been transformed into a certain limpidity of tone, strange, appropriate, and cold."[147] Sedgwick characteristically reformats

Proust's text in an uppercase font, respecting his punctuation but breaking his sentence into smaller, more manageable parts. Rather than reproduce the rectangular text block of the novel's plotted prose, she left-justifies it, giving it the appearance of the fifteen-line lost-sonnet form she repeatedly explored in her early-1990s lyrics. The poem's ragged right edge is again echoed by the fraying swatches it is printed on. Sedgwick's poem reads:

AS IN THE CLASSIC-
AL LANDSCAPES
WHERE IN THE
PLACE OF A VAN-
ISHED NYMPH THERE
IS AN INANIMATE
SPRING, A
DISCERNIBLE AND
CONCRETE INTEN-
TION HAD BEEN
TRANSFORMED INTO
A CERTAIN LIMPIDITY
OF TONE, STRANGE,
APPROPRIATE, AND
COLD.

The lyric has a comparatively short metrical line, and Sedgwick's lineation often, but not always, emphasizes a rhyme, hyphenating and enjambing two words to do so; the remainder of the lines recalling the lyric's prose origin. Sedgwick's hyphenation, in two of three cases, makes thematic sense, with the "VANISHED NYMPH" apparently "VAN-"ishing into thin air at the line's end, while the "CONCRETE INTENTION" that has been "TRANSFORMED INTO A CERTAIN LIMPIDITY OF TONE" finds itself transformed from a single word in Proust's (translated) original into a hyphenated "INTEN- / TION" in Sedgwick's recasting, with its "INTEN-" immediately, strangely, and appropriately dissolved into a certain limpid, cold tone of surrounding blue.

Sedgwick also asks viewers to think about Proust's text in relation to Kuanyin. Thanks to the Gandharan character of the sculpture she chose, spectators find themselves, geographically speaking, at the outer reaches of the "CLASSICAL" world of Alexander the Great. Kuanyin here is a cold, snow-white, substantial, "INANIMATE" sculptural figure, if not quite a "NYMPH," then still at risk of "VANISH[ing]" into the light in which she finds herself cross-lit, which solarizes her face.

In addition, Kuanyin again seems at risk of sinking down and melting into a strange limpid, cold, blue, watery environment, not quite a spring, but more like Ariel's Caribbean. Viewers might also think about the bodhisattva's missing third eye as visualizing the way in which a "DISCERNING AND CONCRETE INTENTION" has been, in this ravaged example, transformed into something "LIMPID," in fact transparent, and quite impersonal. That is because third-eye training, in Taoism and Zen, involves focusing attention on a point between the eyebrows to attune to the surroundings and give a solid foundation for further spiritual praxis, the third eye opening only after that more impersonal foundation has been achieved.

The broader context of *The Guermantes Way* also is relevant. Sedgwick's excerpted sentence occurs as part of the narrator's longer meditation on the skill of the actress Berma in Jean Racine's *Phèdre* (1677).[148] Like Berma, Sedgwick was an artist who, by working with received images of Kuanyin and text by Proust, became "so transparent, so imbued with what [s]he is interpreting, that one no longer sees the performer [her]self"; like Berma, Sedgwick becomes a "window opening upon a great work of art," in fact, onto two. Like Berma, Sedgwick also is speaking "lines of verse," rather than prose, into which, like the image of Kuanyin in the cyanotype, she has "melted" as "into a sort of radiance." Those "line[s] of poetry," conversely, also represent "additional envelopes which, instead of concealing, showed up in greater splendor the soul that had assimilated them to itself and had spread itself through them." So, like Sedgwick's ventriloquism of Proust, Berma's interpretation of Racine was "a second work, quickened also by genius."[149]

The Proustian thought bubble immediately to the right of the right bodhisattva, meanwhile, with its ragged left margin tessellating with the left contour of Kuanyin's silhouette and its right-justified margin lining up with the vertical edge of its cotton substrate, derives from very early in *Swann's Way* (volume 1 of *In Search of Lost Time*): "Perhaps the immobility of the things that surround us is forced upon them by our conviction that they are themselves and not anything else, by the immobility of our conception of them."[150]

Sedgwick again recasts Proust's sentence into a twelve-line lyric with short lines, this time in lower case. Here, there is less rhyme and end-line repetition, with half the lines without rhymes:

Perhaps the
immobility of
the things that
surround us is

forced upon them
by our conviction
that they are
themselves and
not anything
else, by the im-
mobility of our
conception of them.

Sedgwick's imagery again resonates with her quotation. The "immobility of the things that surround us" is emblematized well by the sculpted Kuanyin's static form in space and millennial durability, while the enjambed second "im- / mobility" enacts a conceptual stuttering in its repetition of "im" and "m" and halting inability to move forward within a single line.

But Sedgwick's repetition with a difference also poses a challenge to that "conviction" that things are themselves and "not anything else." Because I was expecting a repetition of the bodhisattva's three forms, it took me a long time, by which I mean years, to recognize that Sedgwick had flipped her middle example over, at the acetate stage, to represent the mirror image of the sculptures surrounding it. As a result, Sedgwick preserves a continuity in the image's iconography, but transforms its material form, in an "ordered procession" that is "apt to grow confused" unless one knows well Sedgwick's techniques.[151] And that is before viewers contemplate the supposed "identity" of a figure who had transitioned from being an Indian man to a Chinese woman and whose subjectivity drew on, and grew within, the overlapping civilizations of ancient India, China, and the outer reaches of the Greco-Roman empire; a classical periphery that would continue to preoccupy Sedgwick's circa 2007 artist's book, *The Last Days of Pompeii*.[152]

Finally, the broader narrative context of *Swann's Way* also resonates with the collage, since Kuanyin's relaxed, downcast eyes and body perhaps "still too heavy with sleep to move," chime with the narrator's famous meditation on the disorienting process of falling asleep and waking up. Just as Sedgwick's bodhisattva seems to have disappeared into an abstract blue ether or water, so the narrator's sleep could be "so heavy as to completely relax [his] consciousness" with the effect that he "lost all sense of the place in which [he] had gone to sleep."

On waking up, the narrator "could not even be sure at first who [he] was," having only "the most rudimentary sense of existence," where, in the collage, it is relatedly difficult to tell the thought from the thinker. After all, whose thoughts are these on the extreme right that "traverse centuries of civilization"?[153]

Kuanyin's, Proust's, his narrator's, Sedgwick's, or ours, as we read them? This layering of subjectivities represented a frequent technique in Sedgwick's narrative poems. Here, she accentuates it through the literal, undulating layering of her seventeen swatches of cotton that she "gradually piec[ed] together," as the narrator "gradually pieces together the original components of [his] ego each time he awakes," with the world increasingly "revolv[ing] around him again" as Proust's text orients itself around Kuanyin's head and toward "the direction of the wall," the "stiffened side" of the fabric.[154]

Sedgwick's collage, then, represents a profound meditation on what Proust's narrator calls the "composite memory," and its artist one of the "faithful guardians of a past" that our minds "should never have forgotten." In first looking at the patchwork, viewers are akin to the narrator waking up. They must establish "the angle at which the daylight came" and the nature of "the passage outside" Kuanyin's head. In addition, given the statue's passing resemblance to Sedgwick, spectators must try to reconstruct what she, "who died years ago," intended "in those far distant days which at this moment I imagined to be in the present without being able to picture them exactly, and which would become plainer in a little while when I was properly awake."[155]

Bodhisattva Fractal World turned from the more emphatic three-dimensional soft sculptural concerns of Sedgwick's previous installation, *In the Bardo*, and from the renewed project of self-decoration that the show represented, to develop on some of the more complex, *two-and-a-half-dimensional*, intermittently and amateurishly embroidered, queerly anti-rectilinear patchwork forms of the earlier *Floating Columns* exhibition, again employing kimono scraps, as well as other pieces of silk and cotton, juxtaposed with Buddhist texts and photographs of Buddhist sculptures.

The overlapping avatars of the Indian Avalokiteshvara and Chinese Kuanyin increasingly came to occupy the ground of the earlier Thai Buddhas and bardo figures, with Japanese death haiku acting as Sedgwick's new reparative mantras. Sedgwick's queer little gods, however, continued to have difficult-to-gender and complexly gendered forms, the earlier *punåkawan* joined by the bodhisattva Avalokiteshvara/Kuanyin, whose transition from an Indian man to a Chinese woman echoed the equally miraculous, metamorphic life cycles of the silkworm and long-legged fly that continued to preoccupy Sedgwick, as thought experiments for her own unwilled bodily changes.

Photography of various kinds remained central to Sedgwick's craft: the earlier vacation snapshots of Thai buddhas and clinical body scans joined by the domestic photography of Atkins's blueprint cyanotypes, Cameron's sloppy surfaces, Muybridge's seriality, more formal conservation and other art historical photographs, and the lunar photographic preoccupations of Sedgwick's own father. *Suminagashi* and *shibori* replaced weaving and fused silks as her preferred textile techniques, while newly emerging preoccupations included the materiality of blood, urine, and other "waste" bodily products; and themes of chance, chaos, and complexity as well as the water and weather systems.

Sedgwick crafted all these diverse elements to be *reparative*, as sources of comfort; forms of cognitive, emotional, and spiritual practice; ways of keeping afloat in an often frighteningly turbulent period of unwilled change; the sheer duration of this chapter a happy product of the unpredicted, but then still unpredictable, length of Sedgwick's hugely creative, late-life, postmetastatic bardo. Slowly but surely floating back up to the surface, alongside the queer canon of Shakespeare, James, Jarman, and Warhol, was *In Search of Lost Time*, the anchor of Sedgwick's final exhibition, *Works in Fiber, Paper, and Proust*.

6

WORKS IN FIBER, PAPER, AND PROUST

(2005)

The Proustian Fabric

In a 2011 review of Eve Kosofsky Sedgwick's posthumous monograph, *The Weather in Proust*, her friend Joseph Litvak recalled the French novelist's "enduring importance" for Sedgwick's oeuvre and her reputation as an "eminent Proust critic." Litvak also documented Sedgwick's early fantasy that *In Search of Lost Time* "remained untranslated" so that she could undertake the job.[1] This final chapter braids together these strands, examining how Sedgwick's reparative craft transformed Marcel Proust.

In Search of Lost Time is profoundly engaged with art and material culture. Across his novels, Proust references more than a hundred artists, with Jan Vermeer's *View of Delft* (ca. 1659–61) the most famous example.[2] In addition, the narrator's future novel was to be intermedial, with "comparisons from the loftiest and . . . most varied of arts."[3]

In her final exhibition, recalling that, in the narrator's words, everyone possessed an idiomatic handwriting, a queer group of "little familiar creatures, at once alive and reclining in a sort of torpor upon the paper," Sedgwick transcribed Proust's sentences in her own hand onto paper and the "different and more flexible form" of fiber to generate a Sedgwickian as well as "Proustian fabric."[4] Through what the narrator calls his "family habit of quotation," she paradoxically explored his sense that, in quoting, "we speak for others, but remain silent for ourselves," and, as a result, escape that "human plagiarism" most difficult to avoid: "self-plagiarism."[5] In so doing, Sedgwick did not select Proust's best-known passages nor "illustrate" *In Search of Lost Time*. She rejected the narrator's caution that, in fiction contemporary to him, there was a "tendency to mix up the genres" and to forget that the novelist's business was to "weave a plot and edify his readers."[6] Instead, she characteristically transformed Proust's plotted prose into her characteristically, queerly enjambed, rhyming lyric poetry, adding what he called a new "element of ordered complexity" and beauty, since, "on hearing a rhyme, that is to say something that is at once similar to and different from the preceding rhyme, which is prompted by it, but introduces the variety of a new idea, one is conscious of two systems overlapping each other, one intellectual, the other prosodic."[7] And, in Sedgwick's case, one Proustian, the other Kosofskian.

Taken as a whole, Sedgwick's final exhibition develops Proust's frequent meditations on the materiality of the book. "People in society," the narrator noted, were too apt to think of novels as a "sort of cube one side of which has been removed, so that the author can 'put in' the people he meets."[8] Resisting that idea, and with a sustained practice of book art already under her belt, Sedgwick recontextualized Proust in several ways.[9] One of her most important interventions was the addition of "colour [and . . .] material" to his monochromatic "virgin page," but there were a "wealth of [other] background" elements.[10]

In translating Proust into her own idiom, Sedgwick made concrete the narrator's observation that his ideas "sh[o]ne on countless people, colour[ing] their thoughts in an auroral light," and sense that his words were "transformed" and "coloured forever" by his suffering over Albertine.[11] In the exhibition, these "changes of colouring," as well as various other "endless small changes," add important "changes of perspective," requiring a host of micro reorientations of focal length and angle of view, compared to the comparatively stable perpendicular or parallel relationship between a reader and page.[12]

In the exhibition, Sedgwick also shared Proust's sustained interest in the close relationship of texts and textiles. His *Days of Reading* associated the "fatal words" "close your book" with the "table-cloth" laid for lunch, and he contextualized other reading scenes with "crochet-work stoles" and the "scattering of Marceline quilts, flowered counterparts, embroidered bedspreads, and batiste pillow-slips."[13] As a result, the narrator of *In Search of Lost Time* wondered whether to "execute the successive parts of [his] work in a succession of different materials," as Sedgwick was to do, in several fat "thicknesses" of fabric.[14]

Like Sedgwick, Proust also found silk poignantly evocative because of its intimations of mortality and resurrection. The narrator finds a musical phrase by Vinteuil to be "as light and soft as silken scarves," perhaps of the kind Sedgwick fashioned for herself; and he characterizes "tenuous and clinging" white silk veils as of a "living substance" woven by a "suffering" silkworm, which drew around itself its "frail and shrinking cocoon." In addition, Sedgwick shared her love of kimonos with Proust's Odette and Albertine, who received their intimates wearing "Japanese kimonos," which haunt the narrator after their deaths.[15] In addition, Proust and Sedgwick were both interested in weaving and patchwork. The narrator noted how life was "perpetually weaving fresh threads which link one individual and one event to another," while patchwork recurs throughout *In Search of Lost Time*, with the narrator composing his novel from a "number of fragments."[16]

The most famous Proustian swatch was the "tiny patch of yellow wall" witnessed by Bergotte, in the moments before his death, within Vermeer's *View of Delft*. The passage remains worth quoting in this context because of its suggestive parallels with Sedgwick, who, in a similar late-life bardo, turned colorful patchwork artist, and whose work, as we have seen, was similarly preoccupied by butterflies:

> His dizziness increased; he fixed his gaze, like a child upon a yellow butterfly that it wants to catch, on the precious little patch of wall. "That's how I ought to have written," he said. "My last books are too dry, I ought to have gone over them with a few layers of color, made my language precious in itself, like this little patch of yellow wall." Meanwhile he was not unconscious of the gravity of his condition. In a celestial pair of scales there appeared to him, weighing down one of the pans, his own life, while the other contained the little patch of wall so beautifully painted in yellow. He felt that he had rashly sacrificed the former for the latter.[17]

With this "wealth of accumulated materials" under our belts, we can now turn, with a "tailor's eye," to Sedgwick's final exhibition.[18]

Hawthorns, or Between Women

The first exhibit in *Works in Fiber, Paper, and Proust* was a book board collage to which Sedgwick applied a rectangle of hand-colored paper, a monochrome photograph of a woman and girl by turn-of-the-twentieth-century German photographer Heinrich Traut, and twenty-four smaller pieces of similar hand-colored paper, with text from volume 5 of *In Search of Lost Time*: "When we speak of the 'niceness' of a woman, we are doing no more perhaps than project outside ourselves the pleasure that we feel in seeing her, like children when they say: 'My dear little bed, my dear little pillow, my dear little hawthorns.'"[19]

Sedgwick lays out Proust's text in two columns, around a central, spinal gutter, the left side right-oriented, and the right side left-oriented (see figure 6.1). She follows Proust's punctuation down to the final period, characteristically capitalizing his text. Her setting does not resemble a single Proustian page, but extends across the *spread* of two, puzzling an initial visual perception that reads across the gutter, expecting a single-page format. Her lineation chops up Proust's multiclause sentence into smaller, bite-size chunks that characteristically emphasize its internal rhymes.

Sedgwick's sentence emerges from a narrative context in which, torn between "desires and fears," "pain and pleasure," the narrator recalls Albertine across hundreds of pages following her sudden death, as she repeatedly metamorphoses in response to his "difference of perspective." He begins flooded "with tender emotion" thinking of her intelligence and kindness; a pleasurable sensation he compares to the "sweetness of a fruit" causing his lips to "instinctively protrude" as he "savour[ed her] memory," just as the child in Sedgwick's photograph opens her mouth with the pleasure of pressing her thumb and fingers into the woman's cheeks to tauten her mouth into a smile.[20] The narrator then juxtaposes Albertine's death with his grandmother's, noticing how differently understood and loved he had been by both. Then comes Sedgwick's sentence:

> My joy at having possessed a little of Albertine's intelligence and of her heart arose not from their intrinsic worth, but from the fact that this possession of Albertine was a stage further toward the complete possession of Albertine, a possession which had been my goal and my chimera ever since the day when I had first set eyes on her. When we speak of the "niceness" of a woman, we are doing no more perhaps than project outside ourselves the pleasure that we feel in seeing her, like children when they say: "My dear little bed, my dear little pillow, my dear little hawthorns." Which explains, incidentally, why men never say of a woman who is not

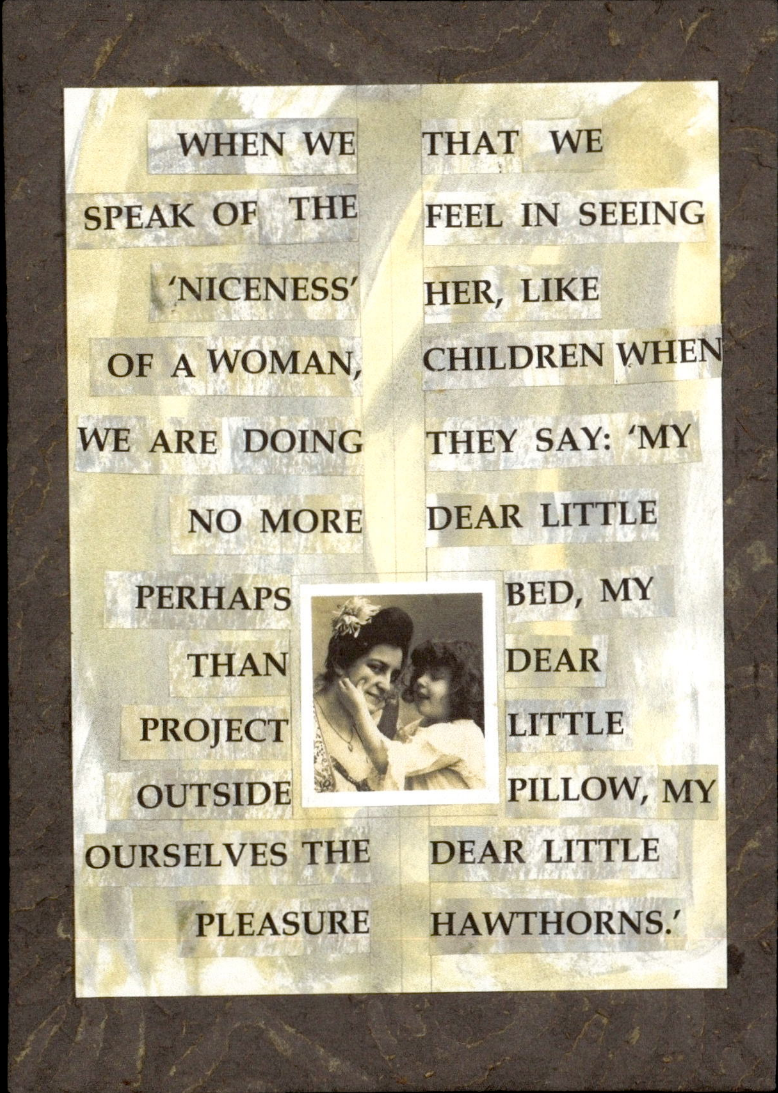

Figure 6.1. Eve Kosofsky Sedgwick, untitled collage, 2005. Photograph: H. A. Sedgwick. Collection of H. A. Sedgwick. © H. A. Sedgwick

unfaithful to them: "She is so nice," and say it so often of a woman by whom they are betrayed.[21]

In the passage, the paranoid-schizoid parts of the narrator's mind triumph; his joy at having possessed a little of Albertine's intelligence and heart diagnosed as arising not from their intrinsic worth, but from his possessiveness. As a result, he interprets Albertine's supposed "niceness" as a projection and generalizes his sensation to the characteristic response of all men over a generically unfaithful woman, an overcompensation stemming from men's sense of abandonment and betrayal.

Sedgwick's emphasis is different. In cutting Proust's generalizing first and third sentences, she diminishes the determining paranoid-schizoid scene of the larger jealous narrative to a single word, "perhaps." This makes it *possible* our sense of a woman's "niceness" is compensating projection, but not *probable*. In its place, Sedgwick emphasizes the sense that the pleasure derived from a woman's appearance, from the point of view of a now-ungendered "we," is akin to a child's pleasure in an abundant world full of "dear little" things—a bed, a pillow, and hawthorns—whose attention we do not have to compete for, but which, given their promiscuous presence, are likely competing for our favor. In short, she recasts the narrator's paranoid-schizoid feelings to make her collage *reparative*.

This is the more healing context of the paragraphs that follow in the text. The narrator next recalls Albertine "seated at her pianola," "pink-faced beneath her dark hair," as Sedgwick's older women is surely seated, given the adjacent heights of the woman and child, both of whom may be pink faced beneath their dark hair. Following this, the narrator describes Albertine's "maternal, incomestible" but still "nutritious, hallowed tongue" as it tried to part his lips, just as Sedgwick's child has her mouth receptively open, perhaps about to stick out her tongue, as the older woman looks knowingly at the viewer, pleasurably triangulating this delicious cross-generational scene. It is important that Albertine's tongue is "incomestible" and yet "nutritious"; it suggests her reassuringly *external* presence in the world rather than her being part of the narrator's fantasy.[22]

Sedgwick's illustration is less eroticized than Proust's description. By transforming his scene of same-generational, cross-gendered, heterosexual adult lovers into an image of cross-generational, same-gendered familial intimacy, Sedgwick makes it harder to imagine her child's tongue as a "secret dewy flame" that will run over the surface of the older woman's body, much of the latter cropped out of the image. Indeed, Traut's photograph does not depict the inside of either figure's mouth, let alone a representation of the child's tongue. Sedgwick is more interested in the tactile brush of finger against skin and fiber, anticipating the narrator's later comparison of Albertine's kisses to those of his "sister" or a "child."[23]

As the exhibition's title indicates, however, Sedgwick's patchworks were not illustrations of *In Search of Lost Time*, but *Works in Fiber, Paper and Proust*. Indeed, her artist's screed insisted that while the pieces emerged from a "decades-long engagement" with Proust, they were not meant to "illustrate the book" or "evoke its time, place, or atmospheres," although her exhibits repeatedly do the latter, as we shall see. Instead, the show reflected her interest in "using Proust's language and thought as a medium, one with texture and materiality comparable to other artistic media, that can be manipulated through various processes to show new aspects." As well as reflecting the "transformative potential of a prolonged immersion in someone else's mental world," of "being 'in Proust,'" her exhibits were "in" Proust in the "same sense that they're 'in' fiber or paper."[24]

As in the collage, the narrator notices that "nothing ever repeats itself exactly, and the most analogous lives which, thanks to kinship of character and similarity of circumstances, we may select in order to represent them as symmetrical, remain in many respects opposed."[25] Viewers find traces of this through the play of rhyme and repetition that Sedgwick's verse establishes, and her mirroring layout. The text on either side of the gutter looks lexically and metrically symmetrical, thanks to the similarly sized pieces of rectangular paper on which she prints Proust's words, and the number of syllables and words she locates on either side of the divide frequently, but don't always, provide mirror images.

Similarly, vertically organized around a central spine, the child is not a mirror image of the woman. They share a family resemblance but are divided by generation and the child's penetrative activity, as it presses its fingers and thumb into the woman's receptive flesh, even as both delight in the pleasure of the breathy intimacy. Indeed, with the photograph in mind, spectators might again recall Sedgwick's account of her formal ambitions in "The Warm Decembers," which gathered instances of "ontological thresholds and of the perverse, desiring energies that alone can move across them: between a person alive and dead; a person and a photograph; a sister and a sister; a present and a past; a person child and adult; people with the same name; a happening and a dream of it; a writer (or a model) and a character; an I and a she or he," with the poem's first person representing an "attempt to make the difference between I and she or he no *more* weighty or unappealable than these other differentials."[26]

In addition, like Clementina Hawarden's photograph on the cover of *Novel Gazing*, viewers might feel inclined to read, in autobiographical terms, the joint portrait Sedgwick pastes into her collage because the left lost-profile of the child's face recalls the portrait of Sedgwick on the cover of *Fat Art*.[27] If so,

Traut's image suggests the range of embodied pleasures that sustained her early and late life, especially since the narrator describes the way his "memory of those hours of sweetness" with Albertine provided him with a "feeling of well-being which the approach of death itself would not have disturbed."[28]

But while the collage hints at the narrator's oral pleasures in his recollections of Albertine's kisses, it more insistently evokes the dear little pillowy, tactile pressures of fingers impressing cheeks; the tickle of hair against skin; the silken sensation of flowers on hair; the metallic weight and temperature of jewelry on a décolletage; and the differential textural sensations of skin against cool lacy cotton, above the older woman's breasts and fitted tightly around the child's upper arms, but hanging more freely about its elbows and chest; as well as the more elaborate and heavy texture of the embroidered fabric weighing over the older woman's shoulders.

In addition, Sedgwick's characteristic palette of pale green, cream, and white recalls the photograph of Sedgwick from her visit to *Bodhisattva Fractal World* (see figure 5.11), and evokes the narrator's comparison of Albertine to "dear little hawthorns," suggesting the again reparative, impersonal color and scent of flowers. One way to describe the photograph's creamy monochrome, and a good way of characterizing the gray-green palette of Sedgwick's hand-colored papers, would be to say they were hawthorn flower colored. The "appeal of the hawthorns" represents one of the most recurrent images in Proust. Indeed, *In Search of Lost Time* is "drenched with the scent of hawthorn."[29] In *The Captive* (in volume 5), the narrator expresses his "desire to go to the country in the early spring to see once again the hawthorns" in blossom; and later evokes the "circumscribed and fixed," "dense oleaginous" scent of flowers that hung "with a certain stability about the hedge."[30]

The appeal of the hawthorns is closely bound up with the "memory of Combray" that gave "hawthorn blossom a greater reality" than other, "unfamiliar flowers."[31] That is because Proust's narrator associates the hawthorns with one of the narrative's key early moments, and poignant misunderstandings between himself and Gilberte. This is his glimpse of her "on the other side of the hedge of pink hawthorn."[32] Sedgwick's triangulated scene—between viewer, happy older woman, and smiling, securely attached child—again represents a reparative recasting of the more paranoid-schizoid, zero-sum triangle the novel presents of the narrator looking longingly at Gilberte, assuming she doesn't desire him; of her looking longingly at him, who fails to recognize her desiring look; and both watched by Gilberte's lover, "or the man who according to Combray gossip occupied that position—studying [him] from behind that same hedge with an air of disapproval."[33]

Perhaps anticipating the end of her own life, her body resting on her "dear little bed," her head on her "dear little pillow," no longer able to move or speak, Sedgwick worked with Proust to anticipate something other than the narrator's paranoid-schizoid scene of relational, physical, and emotional pain, the collage a reminder of the potential tactile and olfactory pleasures that might remain to her: the feel of a hand on her cheek, the scent of "dear little hawthorns" around her bed.

White Flag, or *The Most Exclusive Love*

Earlier in the book, I explored the relationship between Sedgwick's and Andy Warhol's stitched photographs, especially those involving body scans, and suggested the importance of his *Flowers* to her *Reality Is Flowerlike*. In this section, I develop my account of the two artists' interrelation through her *The Most Exclusive Love Is Always a Love for Something Else* (figure 6.2).

The diptych comprises two overlapping rectangular patches of cotton, in landscape orientation, with the cream cloth overlaid on and glued to the black, at the spinal midsection and along the top left. This represents a kind of pictorial half-frame, suggesting that the collage be hung horizontally, as a flag, rather than vertically, despite the orientation of the text. In landscape orientation, the banner prioritizes the portraits of Kuanyin, the left panel recalling Jasper John's 1954 *White Flag*, again suggesting a queer aesthetics of mortal surrender.

Sedgwick screen-printed onto her swatches four images of the now-familiar head of a vandalized crowned, sculpted Kuanyin, with eyes meditatively closed, the same sculpture from *As in Classic Landscapes*. Sedgwick prints the two bodhisattvas on the left in olive green, those on the right in brown. She attaches to the ground a further eight pieces of fabric, which appear pink against the cream ground, and cream against the black. Onto these, she roughly hand-stenciled, with fabric paint in rainbow colors, a sentence from *Within a Budding Grove* (volume 2 of *In Search of Lost Time*):

> THE MOST
>
> EXCLUSIVE
> LOVE FOR
>
> A PERSON
> IS ALWAYS
>
> A LOVE FOR
> SOMETHING
>
> ELSE.[34]

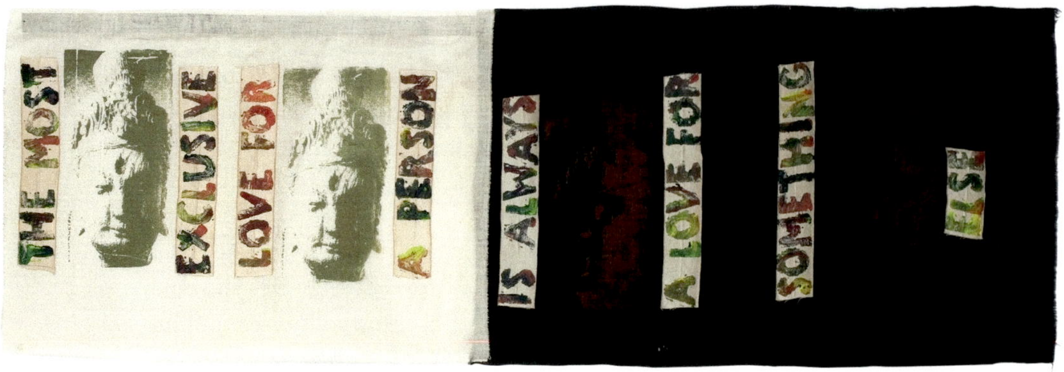

Figure 6.2. Eve Kosofsky Sedgwick, untitled collage, 2005. Photograph: H. A. Sedgwick. Collection of H. A. Sedgwick. © H. A. Sedgwick

In the novel, the meaning of the sentence is complex and various. At the moment it appears, as we have seen, it signals the narrator's simultaneous love for Albertine, her marine companions, and the "mountainous blue undulations of the sea" against which he first saw them.[35] In addition, the narrator evidently has an erotic *type*, revealed by the "course of [his] successive love affairs."[36] The beloveds' "characteristics" also "did not belong only to the girls. They were those of their parents." The broader "influence of culture and fashion" is also propagated in the girls' "identical mannerisms of speech and thought."[37]

In discussing these issues, the narrator shares Sedgwick's photographic idiom. He notes that his perception of his beloved changed thanks to the presence of "pictures taken of them at different moments," with "the difference between the two pictures" representing "a measure of the displacement that they [had] undergone in relation to [him]."[38] He describes how his pleasure was "like photography. What we take, in the presence of the beloved object, is merely a negative, which we develop later, when we are back at home, and have once again found at our disposal that inner darkroom the entrance to which is barred to us so long as we are with other people."[39] The narrator's past was also like a "photographic dark-room encumbered with innumerable negatives which remain useless" until the "intellect could develop them," such that "what one feels is like a negative which shows only blackness until one has placed it near a special lamp and which must also be looked at in reverse."[40] The narrator similarly observes that his mind contained a "strip of memories," like Sedgwick's bodhisattvas, a "series of Albertines, separate from one another, incomplete, a collection of profiles or snapshots" at once "fugitive and fixed."[41]

Like Sedgwick's polarized, solarized images of Kuanyin, Proust also sought to "bring out the opposed facets of each of his characters in order to show its volume," emblematized best by the "strange development" of "inversion."[42] Finally, like Sedgwick, in her late bardo, meditating on Kuanyin, the narrator realized that he had to "traverse an infinite number of successive states of a single face" if he wished to understand the person, up to the "last extremity to which that body could be brought without suffering utter disintegration."[43] "All the successive images" revealed to him the "relationship that existed between the present and the past."[44]

There may also be a relationship between the sloppy, polarized collage and the narrator's description of how Time, "while respecting the unity of the individual and the laws of life," could "introduce bold contrasts in two successive aspects of a single person" such that many people could be "identified immediately, but only as rather bad portraits of themselves hanging side by side in an exhibition," with the effect that "to 'recognize' someone" was to be able "to predicate two contradictory things of a single subject"; all of which was "to apprehend a mystery almost as disturbing as that of death, of which it is, indeed, as it were the preface and the harbinger."[45]

In setting Proust's sentence, Sedgwick characteristically capitalizes it, removes the final period, and colors the font, blending blues, pinks, and greens, with an appropriately pink flush around the first "LOVE." Her sloppily painted text is comparatively illegible, the capitalization encouraging as much emphasis on the letter as the word or sentence. If one reorients the text from vertical to horizontal, the quotation reads up from the bottom, with Sedgwick stretching Proust's words apart, like pairs of legs around each bodhisattva's crowning head; an image of (re)birth to offset the intimations of mortality.

In its poem form, Sedgwick further adds a rhythmic emphasis, with an alternation of iambs and dactyls, as well as a rhyme scheme, with the repetition of "FOR" and loose rhyme of "MOST," "ALWAYS," and "ELSE." Sedgwick also adds more space *between* the lines, with approximately two line spaces where the bodhisattvas appear, with an additional blank space between lines 4 and 5, and between 6 and 7, as if Proust's asthmatic speaker had struggled with the length of his sentence and had to grab some extra breaths to complete the phrase.

As such, Sedgwick's sentence is perhaps initially more difficult to read, but ultimately easier to comprehend, because she offers readers more space to ponder each part, freed from the narrative context of the million-word novel.

Indeed, the patchwork suggests a koan-like exercise, generically signaled by the bodhisattva's four heads, of parsing what the sentence means in *this* context. The first part of the phrase, "THE MOST EXCLUSIVE LOVE FOR A PERSON," feels and sounds, appropriately, sonorously, close, thanks to the "claustral" repetition of the *ve* sounds of "EXCLUSIVE LOVE" and of the *s* sounds of "MOST," "EXCLUSIVE," and "PERSON," a sound that centers, purposively, on the "US" of "EXCLUSIVE."

Then, as the text moves from its cream background into its black ground, the apparent sense of the *surprising* sentence, which maintains its rainbow font, turns on its end. Suddenly, the most monogamously dedicated "EXCLUSIVE LOVE FOR A PERSON," signaled in the twin-like paralleling of the first two, olive green, Kuanyin heads, turns out to be not just once, but "ALWAYS[,] A LOVE FOR" not someone but "SOMETHING ELSE." Sedgwick makes that "SOMETHING ELSE" the direct opposite of the object of "THE MOST EXCLUSIVE LOVE," akin to its photographic negative, black to its white; and hard to grasp visually and conceptually because where there is a strong contrast between the olive-green bodhisattva and her cream ground, in the case of the "MOST EXCLUSIVE LOVE," making that love easy to focus on, in comparison with its black background, the shadowy Kuanyin seems like a retinal afterimage. Viewers thus move through a gestalt shift, from light to dark, as they journey left to right.

In so moving, spectators might recall a moment from Sedgwick's "The Weather in Proust" essay that Jonathan Goldberg singled out. In this, Sedgwick muses over the different responses to the death of the narrator's maternal grandmother, comparing the mother's melancholic "failure to grieve" and "continuing failure to internalize the grandmother in the form of a good object," as a "source of nurturance or possibility," with the narrator's positive ability to employ the idea of his grandmother as a "kind of holding environment" that allows him "to think of something *else*" and move on.[46]

The collage adds affective, aesthetic density to this idea. It acknowledges that viewers might welcome the surprising, comforting ability to think of something else in the wake of someone's death, or in the vicinity of a "MOST EXCLUSIVE LOVE" that, in Proust's later volumes, leads to little satisfaction and plenty of paranoia. But the exhibit also acknowledges that, to make room for "SOMETHING ELSE," spectators must first let fade into darkness the "PERSON" for whom they felt so much. Indeed, the collage's gestalt shift is not, reassuringly, from darkness to light, as if a surprising new light bulb idea emerged, but from creamy light into inky black, from repeated appearance to sudden disappearance, from warm figuration to the earthy-black depth of the ground.

My reading so far leaves two issues unresolved: Sedgwick's reason for employing Kuanyin's head and her Warholian idiom. Viewers might start by noticing that the piece evokes the Zen idea that "if your mind changes, then the color of your face changes."[47] In addition, the patchwork juxtaposes Kuanyin's ability to appear miraculously in different incarnations, temporally and spatially, with a repeated reminder of earthly mortality, in the white left swatch of Buddhist mourning and the dark right swatch of European mourning. In addition, the collage acknowledges the frequent appearance, in Western museums, of mutilated, decapitated heads of Buddha statues, their jeweled assets stripped by trophy hunters, offering a complementary meditation to Osho's encouragement to imagine you don't have a head: Imagine your body has been stolen, as a person with metastatic cancer might well do.

Because Kuanyin's head increasingly fades into the ground, and because of the positive-negative interplay between left and right, Warhol's serial photography also again comes to mind. Sedgwick's montage recalls the way his photographic sequences play with "exposure problems" and employ an "extreme tonal variation," ranging from "nearly white" to "almost black," in a "sequence of over- and under-exposure," here evoking mortality. Like Sedgwick's collage, Warhol's serial photographs "serve to negate their subjects by showing them fading in and out of visual existence."[48]

The dominantly off-white tonality of the left side also recalls Sedgwick's reflections, around the time she was working on the collage, of Warhol's shyness, whiteness, and queer performativity. Certainly, read from left to right, the montage suggests her view that the "people with the most powerful presences are the ones who aren't all there"; and chimes with her interest in divine "*presence*" and the subsequent "withdrawal of a god." According to Sedgwick, such a fragile performativity is likely to generate an "excruciated and rapt audience" experiencing the "poetics, politics, semiotics, and somatics of shame." This results from a situation in which spectators "wishe[d] to look at or commune with" Kuanyin's "loved face" "but suddenly cannot" because she is fading away or has metamorphosed into her perceptual negative.

Read from right to left, however, viewers might, more reparatively, imagine Kuanyin emerging from "shyness to shining," or what Sedgwick describes as the way an "uncanny and unmistakable presence wills itself into existence in the flickering, holographic space"; a "florid religiosity" she characterizes as queer "*flaming*," suggesting the queer as well as Buddhist performativity in any "work of metamorphosis, reframing, refiguration, *trans*figuration, affective and symbolic loading, and deformation," as well as the "work of purgation and deontological closure."[49]

Seen from a critical-race-studies angle, another key aspect of Sedgwick's Warhol essay, the collage may be thinking about the "heuristic of being 'white'" for anyone "involved, at any angle," in "exacerbated race relations," which is to say, for everyone. Kuanyin appears in "white" and "brown" versions, while the montage's cybernetic opposition of binary white and black swatches, juxtaposed with its employment of an analog rainbow spectrum of text, reveals that the semiotics of whiteness are always contextual.[50]

Alternatively, viewers might think about *The Most Exclusive Love* as a meditation on Warhol's elegiac 1962 Marilyn diptych, marking her then-recent death, with its juxtaposition of full color and monochrome, and increasingly faded and solarized, as well as blackly smudged out, Marilyns on the right side; an "incandescent," "unstable" star whose popularity Sedgwick found troubling and whom she replaces with Kuanyin's more reparative form.[51] Finally, Sedgwick's collage also resonates with Warhol's interest in Proust, in his *A la recherché du shoe perdu*; and fondness for making works that would, ultimately, "prepare the stage," and his audience, for his "own last disappearance."[52]

Polyp, or *The Weather in Proust*

Polyp (figure 6.3) is a lightweight, multistrand soft sculpture made up of ten rectangular swatches of harmonious pastel-colored *shibori* silk that can be arranged into different forms. As such, the piece again emphasizes the overlapping, but not identical, experiences of reading and looking in two-, two-and-a-half-, and three-dimensional forms. Sedgwick's swatches hang down, like descending warp threads, with knots at the bottom, bound together into a group at the top, with Sedgwick rubber-stamping half of the pieces with one from a series of five closely related sentences from *Within a Budding Grove*:

> The sun at that moment was scorching the sea topaz-yellow, fermenting it, turning it pale and milky like beer, while now and then there hovered over it great blue shadows which, for his own amusement, some god seemed to be shifting to and fro by moving a mirror in the sky.[53]

> A band of red sky above the sea, compact and clean as a layer of aspic over meat, then, a little later, over a sea already cold and steel-blue, like a grey mullet, a sky of the same pink as the salmon that we should presently be ordering at Rivebelle, reawakened my pleasure in dressing to go out to dinner.[54]

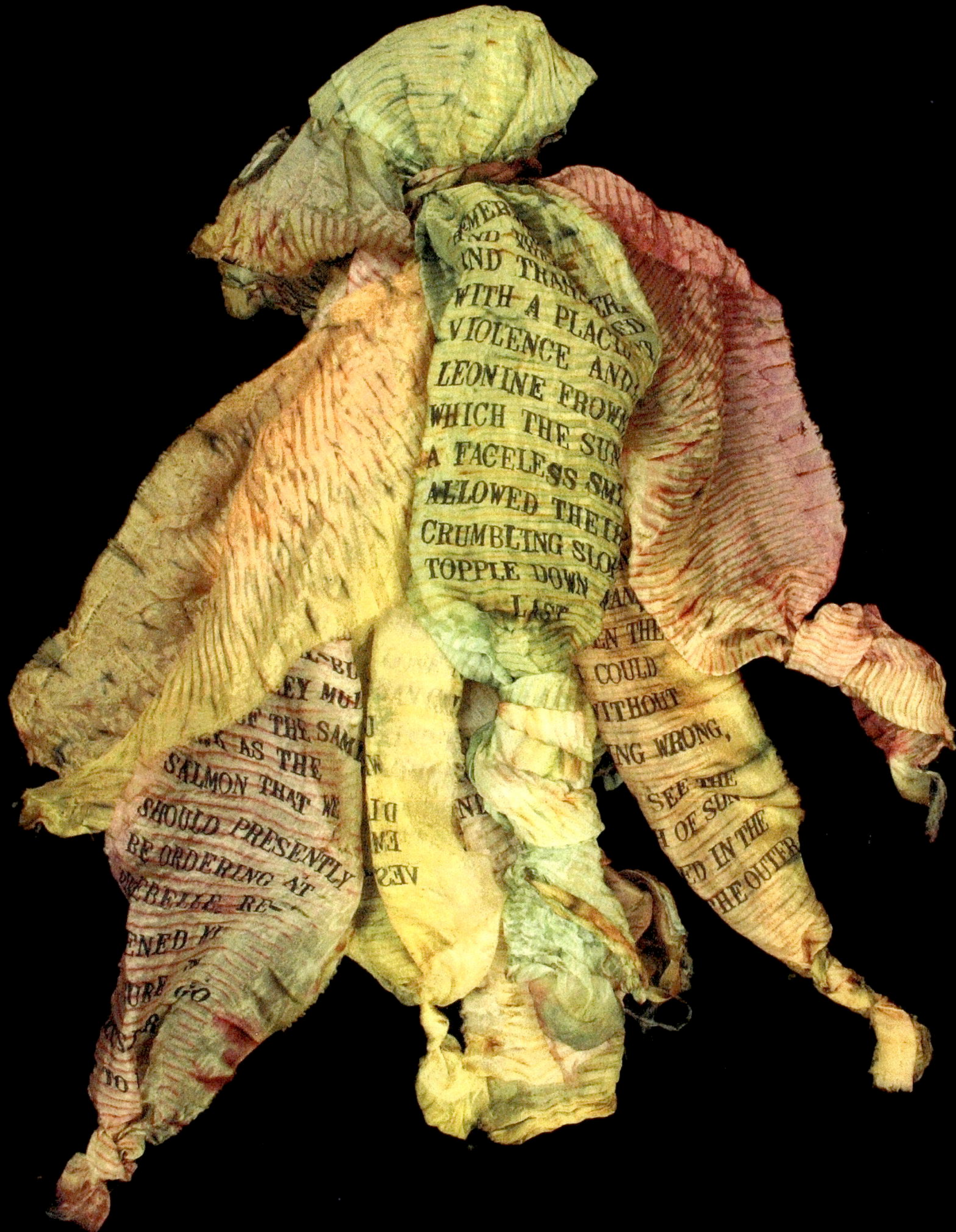

Figure 6.3. Eve Kosofsky Sedgwick, *Polyp*, 2005. Photograph: Kevin Ryan. Collection of H. A. Sedgwick. © H. A. Sedgwick

Emerald waves, here and there polished and translucent, with a placid violence and a leonine frown, to which the sun added a faceless smile, allowed their crumbling slopes to topple down at last.[55]

The weather had been so dazzling and so unchanging that when Françoise came to open the window I could always, without once being wrong, expect to see the same patch of sunlight folded in the corner of the outer wall.[56]

The summer day seemed as dead, as immemorial as a sumptuous millenary mummy from which our old servant had done no more than cautiously unwind the linen wrappings before displaying it, embalmed in its vesture of gold.[57]

Sedgwick rubber-stamped these five translated sentences, letter by letter, in black roman uppercase text, on swatches of ragged, textured, crinkled, and knotted shiny patterned and colored silk, in contrast to Proust's rectilinear, white, matte, flat, published paper ground. Her techniques decrease the contrast between text and ground, making the words more difficult to read, but provide an evocative chromatic, decorative, as well as soft tactile, textural background, whose silk fibers are temperature sensitive; all emblematic, as we shall see, of the littoral weather Proust describes.

Sedgwick makes Proust's sentences more difficult to read in three further ways. Her elastic *shibori* fabric recoils, making individual lines difficult to view; she knots and overlaps her various "pages"; and she encourages readers to shuffle the temporal sequence of sentences depending on the layering. This emphasizes reading as a difficult, partial, and recursive visual and tactile experience, amenable and vulnerable to the queer and reparative, manual and conceptual twists and turns of a viewer's interests and desires.

The specific sentences Sedgwick chose are emblematic of the quotidian mysticism she enjoyed in *Within a Budding Grove* that centered on "simple material metamorphoses" rather than anything systemically "esoteric or occult," although there is nothing simple about the transformations that Proust describes and Sedgwick's forms enact. In her first excerpt, Proust emphasized the temporality of perceptual and conceptual experience, in which everything is only as it is at one "moment" or "now and then." At one instant, the sun might be "scorching the sea topaz-yellow," the color of one of Sedgwick's swatches, "fermenting it," as the scrunched-up textiles appear to be bubbling and frothing, like waves in the wake of a boat. But, at the next moment, the sun can turn the sea "pale and milky" like fermented beer, the chromatic intensity and crystalline clarity of the previous moment replaced by a creamy translucency, recalling milk and beer, which don't especially recall each other: one drunk warm, one cold; one for adults, one for children. At a further moment, the sea is covered by hovering "great blue shadows," reflecting and resembling clouds in the sky. This is a plied, shadowed ocean that Sedgwick's technique approximates with its layers of text over pattern over color, all produced with liquid dyes.

Sedgwick's second sentence continues this marine meditation on the interrelation of sky and sea. In it, there is a "band of red sky above the sea," a sunrise or sunset pink echoed in the dominant tonality of a couple of Sedgwick's swatches, and shot into at least a further two, with individual patches possessing stripes of red we have encountered before. This band of red is "compact and clean as a layer of aspic over meat," suggesting, for carnivores, a delectable pinky flesh, and making sense of, and perhaps palatable, the familiar resemblance of Sedgwick's silk to bloodstained medical gauzes. Proust, however, deliberately confuses things, since aspic is transparent, and meat is red. A "little later," a sea now "already cold and steel-blue" resembles not meat, but fish, a "grey mullet" in fact, also evoking the cold steel-blue knife used to gut or cut it.

The appropriately maritime piscine imagery continues when the narrator describes the sky as being the pink color of salmon; the whole carnivorous description turning out to be as much an account of the scene as of the desires of the man describing it, as he anticipates dressing for dinner and ordering salmon. This human dressing, like the dressing of meat or fish in a sauce, suggests that Sedgwick fashioned *Polyp* to resemble multiple crumpled silk cravats, requiring the iron and attention of the narrator's family servant, Françoise, whom viewers meet again in Sedgwick's fourth quotation. She stamped this description on one of the pinkest, bloodiest swatches, the dead fish and meat finding further mortal resonance in the dead silkworms that generated her swatches.

Sedgwick provided an equally appropriate chromatic background for her next sentences. On a piece of shiny metallic green silk, she printed the description of "emerald waves, here and there polished and translucent," moving with a "placid violence and a leonine frown"; the hard, cold, smooth metal of the first half of the sentence evoked in the sheen of silk, but metamorphosing, in the second, to a soft, textured, warm mammalian furriness.

Again, there is a distorted reflection of sea and sky, matched by the bisymmetrical folding evident in Sedgwick's *shibori* patterns, as the waves' lionlike faces are echoed by the sun's "faceless smile." If there is a repetitive, decorative patterning of sea and sky, the sentence resolves with a more radical metamorphosis when the narrator makes the waves suddenly stony, an avalanche of foam crashing on the shore compared to mountains that "allowed their crumbling slopes to topple down at last," just as the piece of silk Sedgwick stamped it on is scrunched up into a knotty, twisted base, with the knot providing the same pull of gravity that causes the crumbling slopes to fall in the ceaseless attrition of coastal erosion.

So far, Sedgwick has aligned Proust's radically contingent universe with beautiful land- and seascape effects, and the supposedly delicious transformations of flesh into food; perhaps reassuring scenarios given the unwilled metamorphoses her body was undergoing after her diagnosis. All of this suddenly, surprisingly, shifts in her next quotation. Here, the weather has been so consistently "dazzling" and "unchanging" that, when "Françoise came to open the window," to let fresh air into the room of the asthmatic narrator struggling, like Sedgwick, with a chronic illness, he could always "expect to see," "without once being wrong," the "same patch of sunlight *folded* in the corner of the outer wall"; a sentence Sedgwick transcribed onto an orange-yellow shot silk, which she appropriately *folds* into a knot just as the phrase ends.[58]

Sedgwick's final quotation, from the last paragraph of *Within a Budding Grove*, is, perhaps, the most preoccupied with mortality. Here, the summer day seems as "dead" and "immemorial as a sumptuous millenary mummy"; a long-surviving, but millennia-long-dead, corpse-like image emphasizing again the place of the dead silkworms within the cocoons unraveled to make Sedgwick's silk, as mummies were unwound from their "linen wrappings" before being displayed. Indeed, Proust's vocabulary makes Sedgwick's textile ground highly resonant: the word *millenary*, meaning "across a millennium," suggesting *millinery*, the fabric objects made by a milliner, especially in the context of *sumptuous*, suggesting *sumptuary*, again referring to expensive clothes, often made of silk. In the scene, it is Françoise, "our old servant," who is imagined to be unwrapping the mummy. Proust's use of *our* implicates Sedgwick's viewer, who is invited to think about "unwind[ing] the linen wrappings" while being presented with numerous pieces of bound silk that can be unknotted from themselves and unwrapped from each other.

Considered more visually and texturally, rather than textually, and appropriately given the marine-themed quotations, *Polyp* resembles a marine invertebrate, somewhere between a polyp, octopus, and jellyfish, perhaps stranded on the beach and approaching desiccation and death; or swimming through its supportive aqueous medium, in water so deep, in the official photograph, that light cannot penetrate its dark depths.

Polyp, or Proust and the Squid

Partly because of the potential extinction of coral reefs, polyps have recently become the subject of sustained scholarly interest.[59] According to Alfred Kroeber, coral reefs comprise "billions of tiny polyp animals" on their "ocean-fronting" surfaces, their architectural substrate representing the "accumulated precipitate of dead polyps" as well as "affording to millions of living polyps a base" and "place to thrive."[60] Stefan Helmreich, meanwhile, describes coral polyps as "small sedentary creatures" comprising a "tiny ring of gelatinous tentacles floating above an equally small, internally rippled sac." These are "symbiotic with a microscopic form of algae called zooxanthellae, which live inside the polyps and provide them with nutrients derived from photosynthesis," which enable them to put down "layer after layer of calcium carbonate, a form of limestone," which forms a kind of "skeleton, or corallite, at their base, into which the polyp retreats during the day," and which forms the "literal bedrock of the coral reef."[61]

Much about these descriptions would have resonated with Sedgwick as she fashioned *Polyp*. With her late-life bardo in mind, viewers might think about the polyp's complex status between "the living and nonliving" and its symbiotic character in relation to Sedgwick's tumors.[62] Spectators might also consider the polyp's immobility in the context of Sedgwick's spinal degeneration, which would, ultimately, cause paralysis; and, more positively, recent investigations into whether polyps might represent "potential sources for new anticancer drugs" and treatments for HIV.[63]

In addition, viewers might meditate on the polyp as a creature who was, unlike Sedgwick, capable of secreting a new skeletal form, an idea she emphasizes in her evocation of lively "pulpy polyp[s]" rather than the more "sculptural" but "sepulchral forms" of coral.[64] Eva Hayward has also recently paralleled the polyp with the queer-crip identity of the "invert," the first "without backbones," the second "who transpose gender roles."[65] Helmreich also notes that coral is "good to queer with," following Donna Haraway's earlier, reparative meditation on the "generative capacities of marine creatures" and on "non-mammalian replicative doings among marine invertebrates."[66] Like Kuanyin, coral does not conform, in any straightforward sense, to human notions of supposedly binary gender. Polyps are capable of generating and broadcasting eggs and sperm, usually on a full moon, and engage in asexual budding, thus offering a potential "critique of received wisdom about the nature of such things as embodiment and sex."[67] Although, as Elizabeth Wilson has argued, to characterize marine invertebrates, such as polyps, as queer might be "too glib" if we mean that they "simply mimic" the "human, cultural, and social forms now routinely marked as queer."[68]

Sedgwick's clustered *shibori* scarves also visually recall an octopus. Like an octopus, *Polyp* seems to be a soft-bodied, multiarmed invertebrate that can rapidly, radically transform its shape and color, given Sedgwick's stretchy *shibori* fabric and use of orange, red, brown, yellow, and black pigments; all colors octopuses generate for camouflage or communication. Again like an octopus, *Polyp* clusters into a knotty central pucker at the top and knot-like suckers at the tips of its tentacles. The presence of Proust's texts inked on its limbs, meanwhile, suggests the octopus's high IQ and body full of black melanin ink ejected to paralyze predators, with Sedgwick suffering from paralysis in her late life. The fact that most species of octopus are short-lived further indicates that issues of mortality loom large. That said, as a species, octopuses have lived for some 500 million years, a more reparative image of how to live long and prosper.[69]

Like a lone jellyfish, meanwhile, *Polyp* is colorful, soft-bodied, and gathered to a roughly hemispheric body at the top, with trailing tentacles below; the *shibori* patterns, with their suggestions of expansion and contraction, evoking the propulsive pulsation of the jellyfish bell. Despite its Latin name, *Medusa*, recalling the paralyzing, tentacled head of the gorgon in Greek mythology, Sedgwick's jellyfish means us no harm. Its tentacles may be used to capture prey or defend against predators by emitting stinging toxins, but, in the official photograph, *Polyp* is swimming past us, its tentacles knotted at the base, sealing them in.

Jellyfish have been around for some 500 million years, making them the oldest surviving multiorgan animal, again a good totem for someone with a terminal illness. The jellyfish's multiphase life-forms also recall Sedgwick's earlier interest in insects and silkworms that undergo radical bodily transformations. Jellyfish begin with a *planula*, larval stage, before developing into minute *polyps*, often little more than a small stalk with a mouth, in sessile or free-floating forms, which live alone, or, as in the case of Sedgwick's *Polyp*, in groups, where they can collectively share a common stomach cavity, a process known as *strobilation*. Finally, and sometimes after many years, the polyp transforms into an *ephyra*, a free-swimming precursor to the final adult *medusa*; the stage most recognizable as a jellyfish, most like Sedgwick's *Polyp*.

Sedgwick had long been "transfixed" by such marine metamorphoses. "The Warm Decembers" ended with a meditation on "two arts that feed as one," like the polyps' collaborative digestive world. The poem's final lines also visualized a "submerged and wreathy," silent and melancholy "Medusan sister muse," *wreathy* again suggesting mortality. This drew its "breath at the surface," more like an air-breathing marine mammal, such as a whale, since octopuses mostly absorb oxygen through their skins, but an image anticipating the way *Polyp* floats or propels itself toward the top left of the official photograph, before sinking down to feed, indeed "gag . . . on coral"; images signaling, in the poem, a sinking depression and the "buoyant illusion" of "ordinary joie de vivre."[70]

Sedgwick's title, meanwhile, *Polyp*, if not the multipart form of the piece, encourages viewers to attend to the jellyfish's second life stage. This is when it reproduces asexually by budding, suggesting a life-form, like the starfish, that can accommodate loss of significant parts of its body but that, unlike Sedgwick's lost breast, can go on to thrive separately. In rare cases, polyps can also transform into medusae and back again, making them effectively immortal; another reparative trope for Sedgwick, and icon of a kaleidoscope of Kleinian *positions*, rather than teleological Freudian *phases*.

Polyp, however, also simultaneously pulls in the opposite direction, since a polyp is a medical term for an abnormal, tumor-like, but often benign growth of tissue projecting from a mucous membrane. As a result, *Polyp* encourages viewers to think again about Sedgwick's unwilled bodily metamorphosis in the more inspiring form of marine metamorphoses while not forgetting the threats to her bodily integrity and mortality such transformations posed.

Like Sedgwick, Proust was profoundly interested in the regenerative, multiphase life of marine creatures and insects, which exhibited "changes as numerous as the Metamorphosis of Ovid."[71] Especially in the Balbec volumes, with their reigning divinity, "Proteus[,] who cannot remain the slave of any one shape," the narrator described a range of "primitive organisms in which the individual barely exists by itself" and is "constituted by the polypary rather than by each of the polyps that compose it."[72] Indeed, in a passage we have already considered, the narrator noted that he had

> always considered each of us to be a sort of multiple organism or polyp, not only at a given moment of time—so that when a speck of dust passes it, the eye, an associated but independent organ, blinks without having received an order from the mind, and the intestine, like an embedded parasite, can fall victim to an infection without the mind knowing anything about it—but also, similarly, where the personality is concerned and its duration through life, I had thought of this as a sequence of juxtaposed but distinct "I"s which would die one after the other or even come to light alternately, like those which at Combray took one another's place within me when evening approached. But I had seen that these moral cells of which an individual is composed are more durable than the individual himself.[73]

Here, Proust's simultaneous sense of the polyp as the live part of coral and an active part of a cancer becomes poignant, since the narrator later acknowledged that it was the "possession of a body" that posed a "great danger to the mind, to our human and thinking life," which it was "surely less correct to describe as a miraculous entelechy of animal and physical life than as an imperfect essay—as rudimentary in this sphere as the communal existence of protozoa attached to their polyparies."[74]

In addition, Proust's narrator described the poignant fate of a "sterile jellyfish that must perish upon the sand." Initially, he recalled, such appearances "used to revolt" him, but when he "had the eyes to regard them . . . from the standpoint of natural history and aesthetics," he recognized them as akin to an "exquisite blue girandole."[75] He also later noted how, "unlike the knives and forks" that were about to be used to consume it, "some marine monster" that was presented for dinner was "contemporary with the primitive epochs in which the Ocean first began to teem with life, at the time of the Cimmerians." This was a fish whose body with its "blue and pink veins" anticipated Sedgwick's *shibori* swatches. It was also a creature that had been "constructed by nature" according to an "architectural plan, like a polychrome cathedral of the deep"; one of his Proustian paradigms for perfect art that simultaneously preoccupied Sedgwick, as we shall see.[76]

If the narrator's comments emphasize further a Sedgwick coming to terms with her potential degeneration from a more complex to simple form of life, his feelings remained mixed, noting that "after the sponge of sleep" had wiped from his brain the "signs of everyday occupations," he had a life "more inanimate than that of the jellyfish," in which he could "equally well believe that [he] had been drawn up from the depths of the sea."[77] The narrator also noted that "to ask pity of our body," when it was ill, was "like discoursing in front of an octopus, for which our words can have no more meaning than the sound of the tides, and with which we should be appalled to find ourselves condemned to live." And if the "morbid phenomena" of which our bodies were the "theatre remained obscure and beyond the reach" of our minds, they were "clear and intelligible to certain beings belonging to the same natural kingdom as themselves, beings to whom the human mind has learned gradually to have recourse in order to understand what its body is saying to it."[78] *Polyp*'s viewer may no longer be, may never have been, entirely human.

Madeleine Moments, or *The Weather in Proust*

Fashioned from paper, cardboard, and plastic, the *shibori*-like *Weather in Proust* accordion book could be squeezed together and opened out, suggesting that *In Search of Lost Time* was an instrument to be played (see figures 6.4–6.7). In the exhibition, the book was displayed on its back, resting on two of its three spines; abundant, multiple spinal imagery resonating, reparatively, with Sedgwick's physiological predicament. As laid out, the object revealed a pair of parallel book

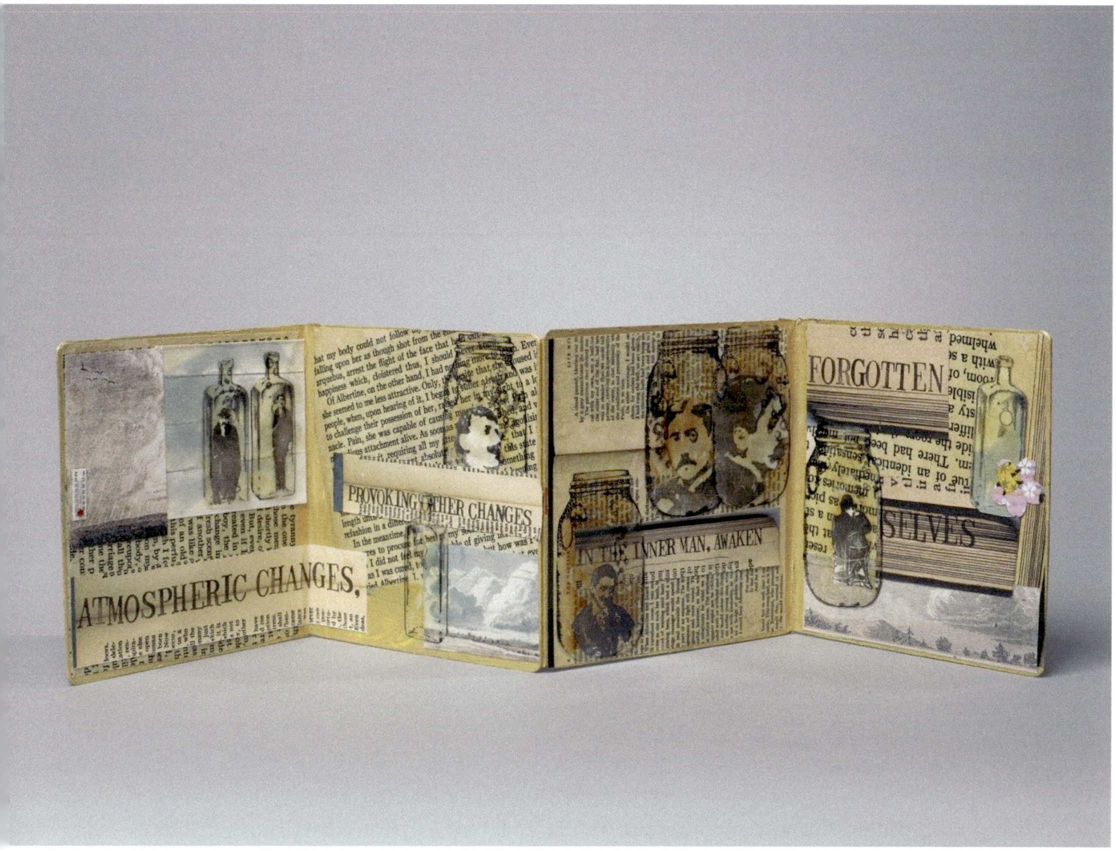

Figure 6.4. Eve Kosofsky Sedgwick, *Accordion Book*, 2005. Photograph: Kevin Ryan. Collection of H. A. Sedgwick. © H. A. Sedgwick

spreads, their inner-page edges joined along a raised central spine. The spread centered on a capitalized newsprint headline from *The Captive*, whose rubber-stamped font size changes as it unfurls:

> ATMOSPHERIC CHANGES,
> PROVOKING OTHER CHANGES
> IN THE INNER MAN, AWAKEN
> FORGOTTEN
> SELVES.[79]

Recalling old, yellowed newsprint, Sedgwick's text reminds us that one of the leading French papers in Proust's period was *Le Temps*; old news emblematizing forgotten selves.[80]

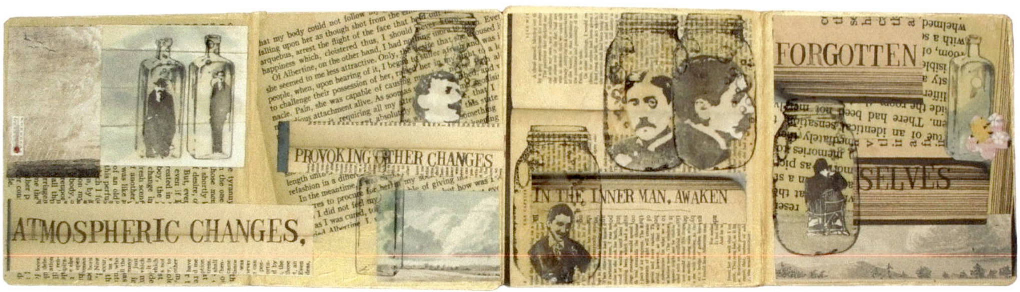

Figure 6.5. Eve Kosofsky Sedgwick, *Accordion Book*, 2005. Photograph: Kevin Ryan. Collection of H. A. Sedgwick. © H. A. Sedgwick

Sedgwick pastes Proust's sentence on a collaged background of other, faded pages from the novel, and prints of the author, along with a five-petaled pink-and-yellow Japanese paper flower. This alludes to the famous end of chapter 1 in *Swann's Way* (volume 1 of *In Search of Lost Time*):

> As in the game wherein the Japanese amuse themselves by filling a porcelain bowl with water and steeping in it little pieces of paper which until then are without character or form, but, the moment they become wet, stretch themselves and bend, take on color and distinctive shape, become flowers or houses or people, permanent and recognizable, so in that moment all the flowers in our garden and in M. Swann's park, and the water-lilies on the Vivonne and the good folk of the village and their little dwellings and the parish church and the whole of Combray and its surroundings, taking shape and solidity, sprang into being, town and gardens alike, from my cup of tea.[81]

Within the pink flower's main body are smaller white flowers-within-flowers that have already unfolded. In addition, like paper flowers, Sedgwick's Proust portraits seem submerged in water in their glass storage jars, just as Sedgwick steeped herself in the environment of *In Search of Lost Time*. The flower's

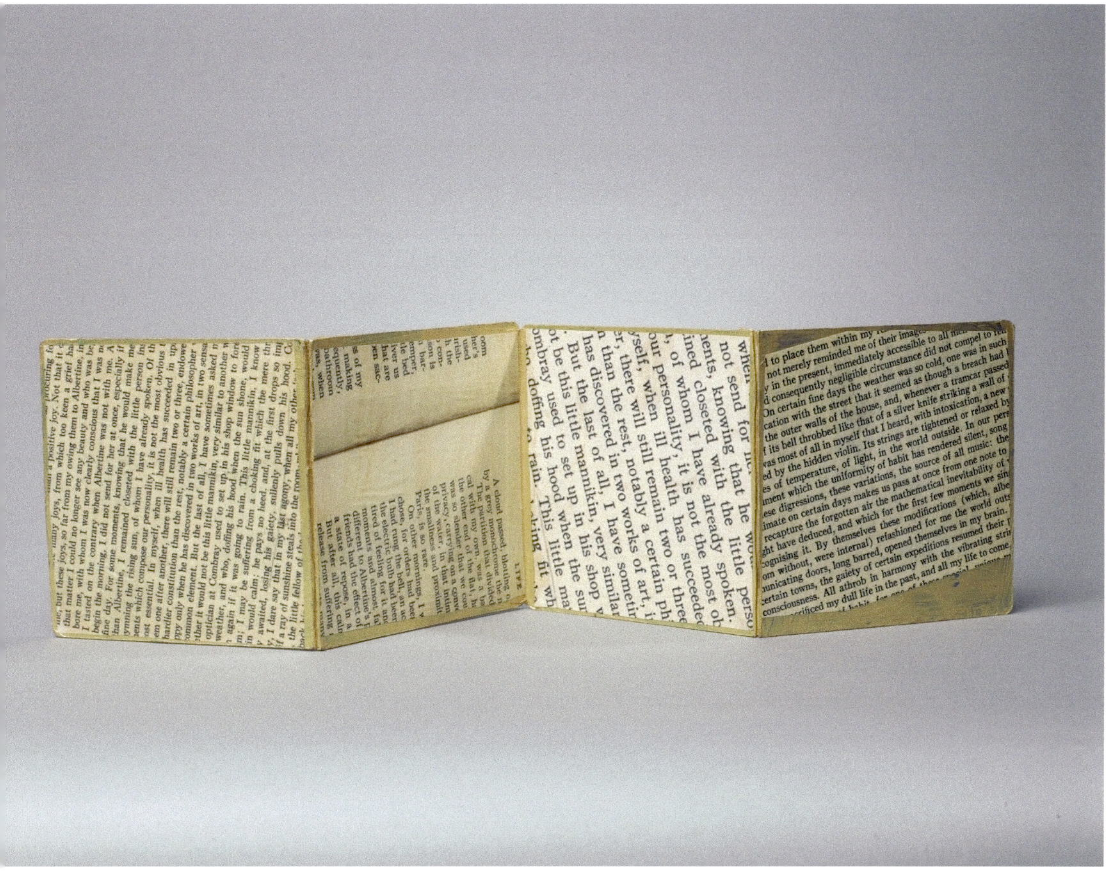

Figure 6.6. Eve Kosofsky Sedgwick, *Accordion Book* (back), 2005. Photograph: Kevin Ryan. Collection of H. A. Sedgwick. © H. A. Sedgwick

silhouette, meanwhile, recalls the shape of that "little scallop-shell of pastry" soaked in a "decoction of lime blossoms": the only more famous madeleine moment immediately before this, which sets off Proust's novel.

Viewers in Sedgwick's archive first encounter the book closed and must unfold it for themselves. The book's exterior comprises a roughly, thickly painted gold "ground," evoking a lo-fi Byzantine icon, with some traces of Sedgwick's self-consciously sloppy gluing process visible. Above, Sedgwick affixes various pages of *In Search of Lost Time*, cut without respect for the integrity of individual sentences. Unlike quotations from Proust in her published essays, these appear without footnotes. Readers must recall or source them, offering the pleasures and frustrations of remembering, that most Proustian of activities.

The front cover incorporates a passage about the weather, cut on the bias, to be read on a lower-left to upper-right diagonal, when the book is closed and laid on its back. Here is the passage transcribed *straight*:

> I took my share of the pleasures of the new day; the arbitrary desire—the capricious and purely spontaneous inclination to taste them would not have sufficed to place them within my reach, had not the peculiar state of the weather not merely reminded me of their images in the past but affirmed their reality in the present, immediately accessible to all men whom a contingent and consequently negligible circumstance did not compel to remain at home. On certain fine days the weather was so cold, one was in such full communication with the street that it seemed as though a breach had been made in the outer walls of the house, and, whenever a tram car passed, the sound of its bell throbbed like that of a silver knife striking against a wall of glass. But it was most of all in myself that I heard, with intoxication, a new sound rendered by the hidden violin. Its strings are tightened or relaxed by mere changes of temperature, of light, in the world outside. In our person, an instrument which the uniformity of habit has rendered silent, song is born of these digressions, these variations, the source of all music: the change of climate on certain days makes us pass at once from one note to another. We recapture the forgotten air the mathematical inevitability of which we might have deduced, and which for the first few moments we sing without recognizing it. By themselves these modifications (which, albeit coming from without, were internal) refashioned for me the world outside. Communicating doors, long barred, opened themselves in my brain. The life of certain towns, the gaiety of certain expeditions, resumed their place in my consciousness. All athrob in harmony with the vibrating string, I would have sacrificed my dull life in the past, and all my life to come, erased with the India-rubber of habit, for a state so unique.[82]

With Proust's passage in mind, the book's accordion-like structure obviously echoes the narrator's account of a violin. Just as the exhibit can be stretched open or compressed shut, the violin's strings can be "tightened or relaxed" by the instrument's screws and by "changes of temperature, of light, in the world outside." In addition, just as the narrator's consciousness is "born of . . . digressions" that stretch his sentences' syntax, so the accordion's structure is elastic. If viewers want more aesthetic experience, they can unfold the "quadriptych" with a "mathematical inevitability," like the "communicating doors" that, "long barred, opened themselves" in the narrator's brain.

In addition to Sedgwick's dis- and reorienting changes in text direction, font size, and resolution, emphasizing the queer embodied phenomenology of reading, the text on the second panel from the left is a photocopy from across a double spread, complete with the gutter, emphasizing further the idea of spines, by adding a virtual example. Given its importance to Sedgwick in several contexts, it is worth quoting the long passage she repeatedly cites in full:

> A cloud passed, blotting out the sun; I saw extinguished and replaced by a grey monochrome the modest, screening foliage of the glass.
>
> The partition that divided our two dressing-rooms (Albertine's, identical with my own, was a bathroom which Mamma, who had another at the other end of the flat, had never used for fear of disturbing my rest) was so slender that we could talk to each other as we washed in double privacy, carrying on a conversation that was interrupted only by the sound of the water, in that intimacy which, in hotels, is so often permitted by the smallness and proximity of the rooms, but which, in private houses in Paris, is so rare.
>
> On other mornings, I would remain in bed, drowsing for as long as I chose, for orders had been given that no one was to enter my room until I had rung the bell, an act which, owing to the awkward position in which the electric bulb had been hung above my bed, took such a time that often, tired of feeling for it and glad to be left alone, I would lie back for some moments and almost fall asleep again. It was not that I was wholly indifferent to Albertine's presence in the house. Her separation from her girlfriends had the effect of sparing my heart any fresh anguish. She kept it in a state of repose, in a semi-immobility which would help it recover. But after all, this calm which my mistress was procuring for me was a release from suffering rather than a positive joy. Not that it did not enable me to taste many joys from which the intensity of my anguish had debarred me, but, far from my owing them to Albertine, who in any case I no longer found very pretty and with whom I was bored, with whom I was indeed clearly conscious that I was not in love, I tasted these joys on the contrary when Albertine was not with me. And so, to begin the morning, I did not send for her at once, especially if it was a fine day.
>
> For some moments, knowing that he would make me happier than Albertine, I remained closeted with the little person inside me, the melodious psalmist of the rising sun, of whom I have already spoken. Of the different persons who compose our personality, it is not the most obvious that are the most essential. In myself, when ill health has succeeded

> in uprooting them one after another, there will still remain two or three endowed with a hardier constitution than the rest, notably a certain philosopher who is happy only when he has discovered between two works of art, between two sensations, a common element. But I have sometimes wondered whether the last of all might not be this little mannequin, very similar to another whom the optician at Combray used to set up in his shop window to forecast the weather, and who, doffing his hood when the sun shone, would put it on again if it was going to rain. I know how selfish this little manikin is; I may be suffering from an attack of breathlessness which only the coming of rain could assuage, but he pays no heed, and, at the first drops so impatiently awaited, all his gaiety forgotten, he sullenly pulls down his hood. Conversely, I dare say that in my last agony, when all my other "selves" are dead, if a ray of sunshine steals into the room while I am drawing my last breath, the little barometric manikin will feel a great relief, and will throw back his hood to sing: "Ah, fine weather at last."[83]

Much about the passage resonates in the context of the exhibit and Sedgwick's late life. The book's numerous actual and virtual gutters share their name with the architectural feature designed to carry off rainwater, thus recalling the way the pair's conversations were "interrupted only by the sound of the water," of taps, showers, baths running. Also evocative for a Sedgwick who was married but maintained her own apartment, the narrator emphasizes the masturbatory, meteorological possibilities of his solitude.[84] Like Sedgwick in her late bardo, Proust's narrator also wonders which of the "different persons" who composed his personality would survive the longest. The narrator's speculation was that when ill health had uprooted most of his character traits, a certain philosopher would remain, happy only on discovering a common element between two sensations or works of art; a late-life incarnation the accordion book honors through the manifold ways it responds to, and overlaps with, Proust's text. Proust's philosopher is particularly enamored of the sun, even though his asthmatic body prefers the cool rain. Sedgwick helpfully provides both environments. The accordion book's gold ground represents fine weather around a Proust depicted repeatedly with his head uncovered, emphasizing Sedgwick's delight in his "gaiety," while the inside of the exhibit incorporates four prints of cloudy skies.

Once opened, the accordion book reveals four leaves. On the left, Sedgwick pastes in a passage so fragmentary I could not source it. Over this, she pastes the first two words of "ATMOSPHERIC CHANGES" in line with the reader's

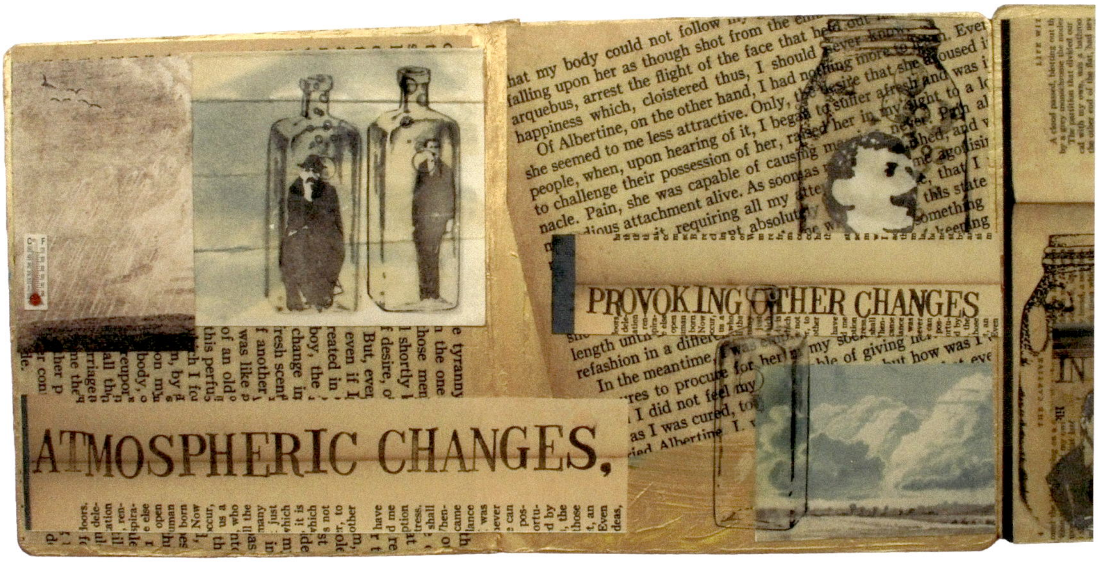

Figure 6.7. Eve Kosofsky Sedgwick, *Accordion Book* (detail), 2005. Photograph: Kevin Ryan. Collection of H. A. Sedgwick. © H. A. Sedgwick

rectilinear requirements, but stamps the words *across* the photocopied gutter of a two-page spread. Above this, she pastes her first two cloudscapes. The gray-brown left example depicts clouds condensing into rain falling on the sea, with four gulls floating high in the sky. The scene represents the water cycle's remarkable, quotidian transformations, dependent on atmospheric pressure and temperature, with saltwater present in the metamorphic form of the sea and freshwater in the similarly changing form of clouds and falling rain.

The image recalls again the Guermantes fountain that preoccupied Sedgwick. Like the fountain, her seascape is "seen from a distance" and gives the "impression of art" as much as the "sensation of water." There is a "moist cloud . . . gathering at its summit," with the "exhausted drops" of rain seen "falling back" down; or, if we conceive the image as a scientific illustration of evaporation, then "on the way up" to the sky. Viewers are "teased with their hesitations," as they try to establish, from the gestalt, whether the flow is downward or "in the opposite direction." Either way, the seascape is "seemingly painted in an unchanging golden brown."[85]

To the image Sedgwick affixes a working thermometer that registers, in real time, the changing temperature. This recalls how, according to Proust's narrator, "fine weather" caused the "mercury in a thermometer" to "dart . . . upwards in the heat."[86] Poignant, in the context of Sedgwick's late life, and its various missed diagnoses and misdiagnoses, is the narrator's description of how, when Dr. Cottard told the family to take the dying grandmother's temperature, "a thermometer was fetched," but in the context of a broader discussion of hit-and-miss medical efficacy that represented a "compendium of the successive and contradictory mistakes of medical practitioners," such that "when we summon the wisest of them to our aid the chances are that we may be relying on a scientific truth the error of which will be recognized in a few years' time. So that to believe in medicine would be the height of folly, if not to believe in it were not a greater folly still, for from this mass of errors a few truths have in the long run emerged."[87] To the right is a piece of gray-blue washed paper, marked with three approximately parallel horizontal lines, perhaps representing telegraph wires cutting across a rainy sky or indicating horizon lines on a cloudy blue seascape. Sedgwick has rubber-stamped two glass bottles on top, each glass closet containing a portrait of Proust, with several air bubbles or empty thought bubbles rising from his head. This is a scene of quiet drowning that resonates with the asthmatic narrator's difficulty breathing; an apparently carceral condition Sedgwick emphasizes by the three barring horizontal lines. The passage Sedgwick reproduces at the lowest level is concerned precisely with the pleasures and problems of asthmatic confinement:

> It often happens that the pleasure which everyone takes in turning over the keepsakes that memory has collected is keenest in those whom the tyranny of bodily ill-health and the daily hope of recovery prevent, on the one hand, from going out to seek in nature scenes that resemble those memories, and, on the other hand, leave so convinced that they will shortly be able to do so that they can remain gazing at them in a state of desire, of appetite, and not regard them merely as memories, as pictures. But even if they were never to be anything more than memories to me, even if I, as I recalled them, saw merely pictures, immediately they re-created in me, of me as a whole, by virtue of an identical sensation, the boy, the youth who had first seen them. There had been not merely a change in the weather outside, or, inside the room, the introduction of a fresh scent, there had been in myself a difference of age, the substitution of another person. The scent, in the frosty air, of the twigs of brushwood, was like a fragment of the past, an invisible floe broken off from the ice of an old winter that stole into my room, often variegated moreover with this perfume or that light, as though with a sequence of different years, in

> which I found myself plunged, overwhelmed, even before I had identified them, by the eagerness of hopes long abandoned. The sun's rays fell upon my bed and passed through the transparent shell of my attenuated body, warmed me, made me as hot as a sheet of scorching crystal. Whereupon, a famished convalescent who has already begun to batten upon all the dishes that are still forbidden him, I asked myself whether marriage with Albertine would not spoil my life, as well by making me assume the burden, too heavy for my shoulders, of consecrating myself to another person, as by forcing me to live in absence from myself because of her continual presence and depriving me, forever, of the delights of solitude.[88]

Sedgwick's Victorian scrapbook form deftly evokes Proust's turned-over keepsakes, memories of his nineteenth-century youth—he is seen without a mustache on the right. Her modernist collage aesthetic, meanwhile, suggests that youth as recalled by his invalid, mustache-sporting, early twentieth-century self on the right. In addition, given that Proust's passage is begun by Françoise throwing a handful of twigs into an empty fireplace, to light a fire, Sedgwick's use of layered paper and cardboard implies that the accordion book is kindling and also suggests her repeated identification with the much-loved, much-maligned family servant.

Sedgwick leads the spectator's eye to the far side of this first diptych, by the way she bleeds, across the gutter, the main horizontal, organizing phrase, "ATMOSPHERIC CHANGES." This ascends from the bottom right to meet the next part of the phrase, "PROVOKING OTHER CHANGES," a clause similarly buffeted by changing barometric conditions, or the increase in hot air attendant on the narrator's paranoid-schizoid feelings in the passage Sedgwick cites below:

> Of Albertine, on the other hand, I had nothing more to learn. Every day, she seemed to me less attractive. Only, the desire that she aroused in other people, when, upon hearing of it, I began to suffer afresh and was impelled to challenge their possession of her, raised her in my sight to a lofty pinnacle. Pain, she was capable of causing me; joy, never. Pain alone kept my tedious attachment alive. As soon as my pain vanished, and with it the need to soothe it, requiring all my attention, like some agonizing distraction, I felt that she meant absolutely nothing to me, that I must mean absolutely nothing to her. It made me wretched that this state should persist, and, at certain moments, I longed to hear of something terrible that she had done, something that would be capable of keeping us at arm's-length until I was cured, so that we might then be able to be reconciled, to refashion in a different and more flexible form the chain that bound us.[89]

In front of the main, irregular-pentagon-shaped passage, Sedgwick included a third portrait of Proust; a severed head recalling Kuanyin's in *The Most Exclusive Love*. Proust's containing glass jar is a rounder, fatter example with a screw-top lid, to complement the thinner-art cork-able bottles opposite, all four jars open to the environment at the top. In the bottom-right corner, meanwhile, Sedgwick includes a third, soft aqua cloudscape, above parched, flat, arable land that would welcome some rain from the gathering, condensing cumulonimbus above. When laid out, the accordion book's central spine represents the highest summit of its peak-and-trough, wavelike, undulating form, suggesting, through its hills and valleys, a microbarometric system; its atmospheric shifts provoke changes "IN THE INNER MAN" and "AWAKEN FORGOTTEN SELVES," a phrase Sedgwick underlines with images of cut page edges.

In the third panel, viewers find a further three variant Proust busts. He is smiling at bottom left, in lost right profile. He is face on in the center, making eye contact. He is in right profile at top right and, so, more available to the objectifying view of the spectacle of his closet.[90] Sedgwick's three Prousts represent the standard European portrait genres, a generically constrained variety of images, emphasizing a trinity of selves, as well as a point-of-view effect central to his poignant social comedy and Sedgwick's account of reader relations.

The passage Sedgwick chose as her ground describes the narrator's pleasure in the light seen through his and Albertine's bathroom windows, on the rare mornings he was up early. These windows were "not smooth and transparent," like Sedgwick's glass jars, but "crinkled with an artificial and old-fashioned hoar frost" to protect the pair's modesty. "All of a sudden," however, the narrator notes, "the sun would colour this muslin glass, gild it," as the glass surrounding Sedgwick's Proust takes on the colors of her faded pink pages and painted gold ground.[91]

In the final panel, Sedgwick's Proust has regained his privacy. Seated in a wicker chair, his back turned, his eye is appropriately caught by the Japanese paper flower located above another cloudy, arable monochrome landscape as the "ATMOSPHERIC CHANGES" that began at the start of the book, having awoken parallel changes in the inner man across the middle spread, now awaken "FORGOTTEN SELVES" and recall "the heart of the country amidst golden foliage." Sedgwick repeatedly underlines these last "FORGOTTEN SELVES" in the now-familiar form of page edges, encouraging spectators to ponder further their own growing and cut edges, and to close the accordion book to feel the texture of its compressed spine, just as they have explored its expansively open, fat art incarnation.

Not Like a Cathedral, or The Silence of the Silkworms

The textile ground of *Not Like a Cathedral* first appeared in *In the Bardo*, where it graced the back of one of Sedgwick's soft sculptures. She reincarnated the abbreviated ghost of the earlier piece, having initially crafted the exhibit by tearing a larger sheet of textured handmade mulberry paper into the approximate shape of a human torso with its extremities removed. She then folded it vertically, to produce the bilaterally symmetrical pattern, and tied it with string, before dyeing it blue, leading to the thin, scalelike lines (see figures 6.8 and 6.9).

Onto the fabric substrate, Sedgwick printed a phrase from volume 6 of *In Search of Lost Time*. In her capitalized version, it reads:

NOT	MORE
LIKE	SIMPLY
A	LIKE
CATHEDRAL,	A
BUT	DRESS

In the longer passage that Sedgwick's quotation is sourced from, the narrator refers to his characteristic compositional technique:

> And—for at every moment the metaphor uppermost in my mind changed as I began to represent to myself more clearly and in a more material shape the task upon which I was about to embark—I thought that at my big deal table, under the eyes of Françoise, who like all unpretentious people who live at close quarters with us would have a certain insight into the nature of my labors (and I had sufficiently forgotten Albertine to have forgiven Françoise anything that she might have done to injure her), I should work beside her and in a way almost as she worked herself (or at least as she had worked in the past, for now, with the onset of old age, she had almost lost her sight), and pinning here and there an extra page, I should construct my book, I dare not say ambitiously like a cathedral, but quite simply like a dress.[92]

Sedgwick condenses Proust's multiclause sentence into a punchier poem, its two-column layout echoing the swatch's bisymmetrical shape. The poem's meter similarly possesses a certain symmetry, with Sedgwick's staccato lines beginning and ending with three single-syllable phrases. Her recasting characteristically emphasizes Proust's internal rhyme, with only "CATHEDRAL" and "DRESS" failing to find a rhyme, evoking their ontological difference.

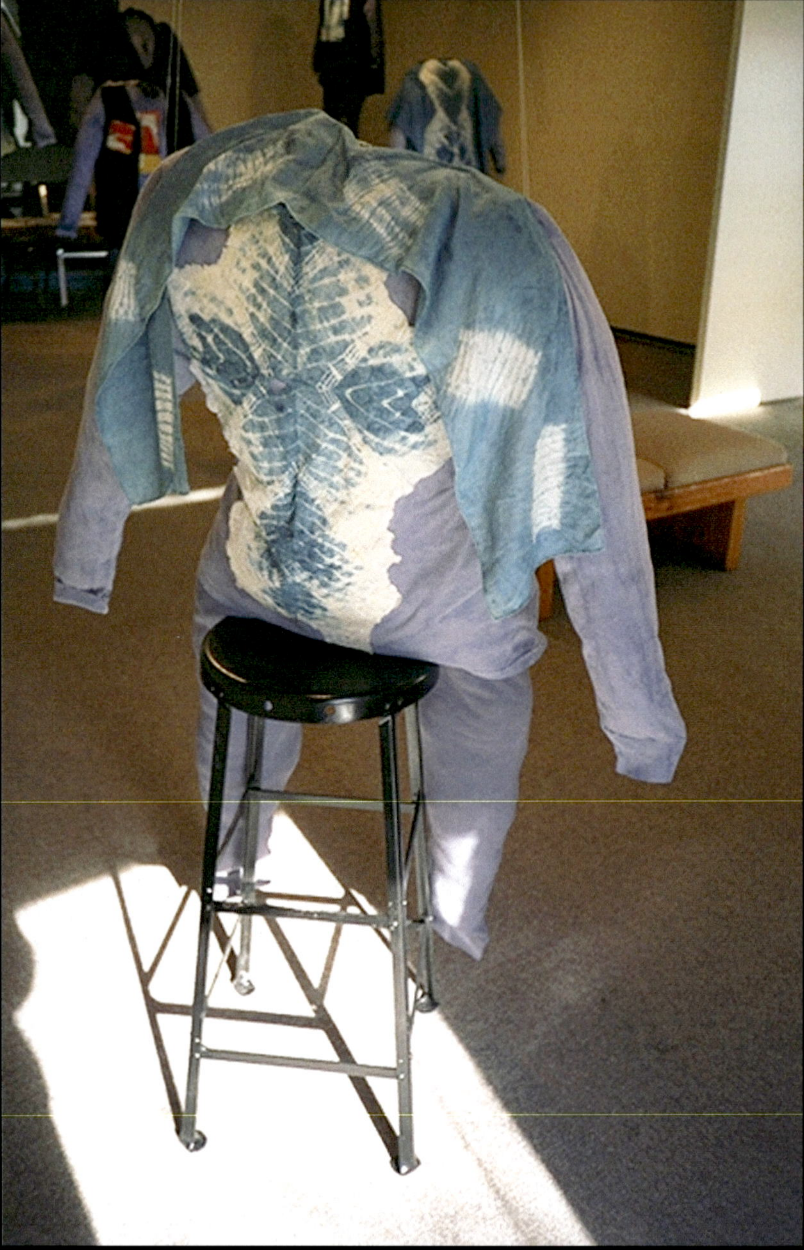

Figure 6.8. Eve Kosofsky Sedgwick, mannequin from *In the Bardo*, 2002. Photograph: H. A. Sedgwick. Collection of H. A. Sedgwick. © H. A. Sedgwick

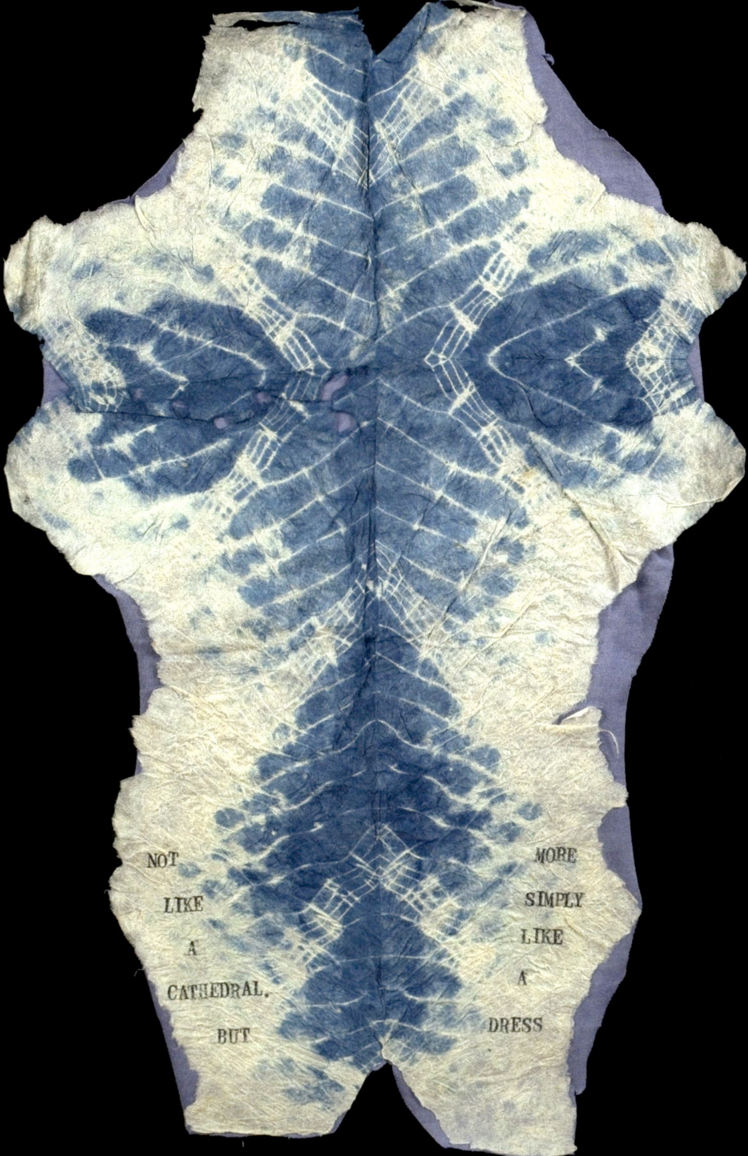

Figure 6.9. Eve Kosofsky Sedgwick, untitled collage, ca. 2002–5. Photograph: Kevin Ryan. Collection of H. A. Sedgwick. © H. A. Sedgwick

Sedgwick typically includes a punctuation point, after the first part of Proust's phrase, but leaves the sentence without a final period to indicate the narrator's acknowledgment that "at every moment the metaphor" for the construction of his novel "changed."

Sedgwick printed the poem on textured, fat, rather than flat, artisanal matte paper, with the phrases mostly set against a creamy white ground. She laid out by hand the bumpy, wobbly black stamped lettering; a sloppy craft evident in the uneven lineation and inconsistent ink. As seen against its textural, ground, Sedgwick's poem suggests she was evoking the start of the narrator's conceptual process, as he began to represent "in a more *material* shape the task upon which [he] was about to embark."[93] This phase represents the sustained moment of *Time Regained* (volume 6 of *In Search of Lost Time*), as he moves to begin his long-*precipitated* novel, the descending zigzag line of Sedgwick's columns perhaps suggesting rain falling through barometric currents. There is, as Sedgwick knew, always weather in Proust.

Sedgwick's swatch makes concrete her identification with the narrator and Françoise. Sedgwick sat at her table crafting the piece, as if imaginatively beside them, working unpretentiously, with scraps of old projects and Proust's prose. She signals her self-conscious lack of pretension by her sloppy craft, offsetting Proust's high canonical status, eliding the multisyllabic "ambitiously" from her quotation.

Like a Françoise almost blind "with the onset of old age," and a narrator conscious of his mortality and "how many great cathedrals remain unfinished," Sedgwick might have felt an urgency while fashioning the piece, as she faced her own mortality.[94] The swatch, however, emphasizes a quiet, slow absorption, in the form of the savored syllables of Proust's prose, printed laboriously letter by letter across the dress-pattern-like paper substrate.

In making her collage, Sedgwick avoids "pinning here and there an extra page," instead gluing the paper onto the fabric ground. This represented a characteristic avoidance of needles in preference for a queer, cross-class, cross-gender Whitmanian adhesion among Sedgwick, Françoise, and the narrator's "paperies," the thick, textured expensive mulberry paper making it more difficult to consign to a background than the smoothly regular, uniformly rectangular paper employed in the pages of the mass-produced novel.[95] In addition, like the narrator, Sedgwick seeks to "execute the successive parts of [her] work in a succession of different materials," with the mulberry paper *layered* on a brushed cotton ground.[96]

Mulberry paper is made from the same substrate, and in the same way, as silk, and so its unfolding after the *shibori* process was complete would have again recalled silkworms boiled to death within, and unwrapped from, their silk cocoons, with all their intimations of transformation and mortality. In addition, the patchwork's overall shape and patterning recalls a death's-head hawk moth, a pinned-out specimen seen from above. This had long functioned as a naturally occurring memento mori, given the skull-like pattern on its upper thorax. It was used to famous effect in the iconography of Jonathan Demme's 1991 film *The Silence of the Lambs*, and so evoked, in the period, both intimations of mortal female vulnerability and Clarice Starling's determination to survive the mortal threat posed by Hannibal Lecter.[97]

We Alone, by Our Belief: Memorial Rags, or The Ties That Bind

Sedgwick's sixth exhibit was a ribbon banner, formed of joined strips of beige, mustard, and rust-colored *shibori*, with text from *Within a Budding Grove* (figure 6.10). The quotation concerned the narrator's account of the "composite, heterogeneous" form of Swann, Odette, and Gilberte's living room, which, as a result of the narrator's memory, and the association of the objects and images with the Swanns, gave the room a "cohesion," "unity," and "individual charm." Indeed, the narrator declared that the room and its contents felt "alive and stamped with the imprint of a living personality," Swann and Odette's idioms having been "distributed" and "amalgamated" through the "arrangements of the furniture," "thickness of the carpets," and "position of the windows."[98]

Perhaps importantly, given the materiality of Sedgwick's patchwork, fabric and especially silk loom large in the narrator's memory, cocooning him there. These include "vaporous tapestries" hanging in the room, the "swarm of little chairs," "stools," and "things draped in old Louis XVI silks," and "the silk-covered [foot] stool" that Odette pushes toward him, a "defenseless cushion" he was "almost reluctant to set [his] feet on," since the family's "personality" and "soul was latent there." In the scene, Odette also sports a "marvelous garment of crepe-de-Chine or silk, old rose, cherry-colored, Tiepolo pink, white, mauve, green, red or yellow, plain or patterned."[99] This causes the narrator to observe:

> WE ALONE BY OUR
> BELIEF THAT THEY HAVE
> AN EXISTENCE
> OF THEIR OWN, CAN GIVE
> TO CERTAIN THINGS WE SEE

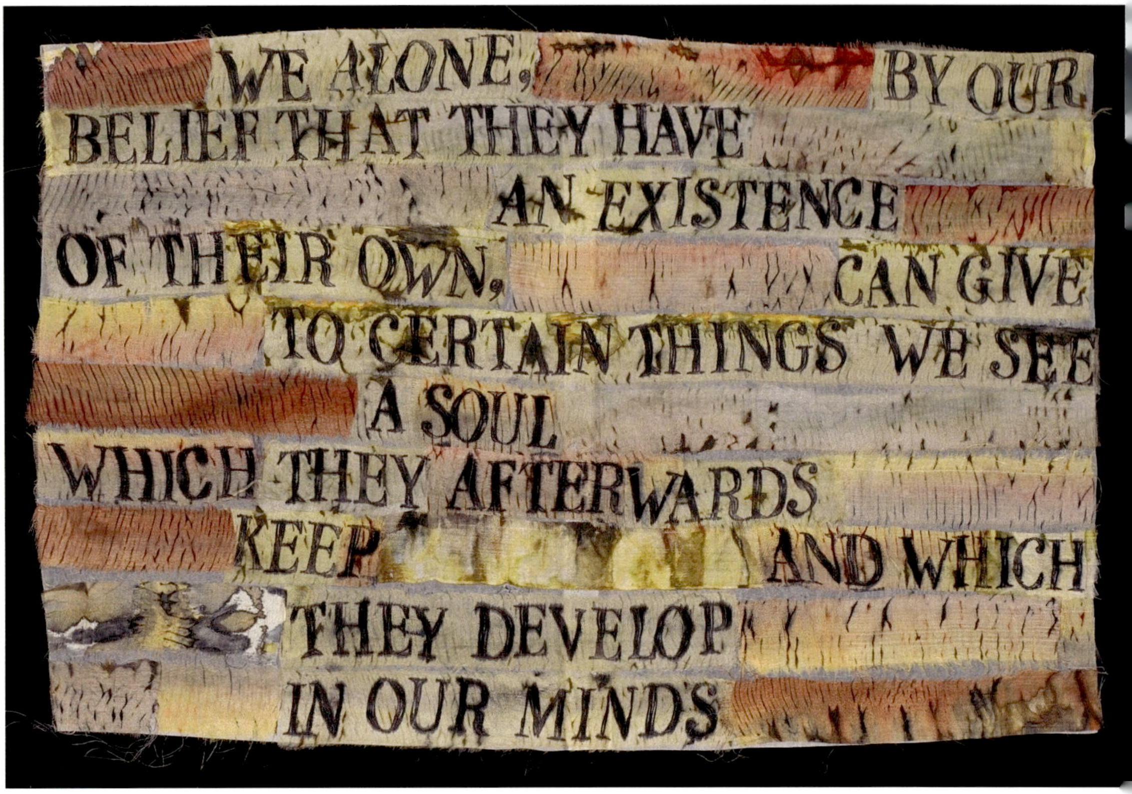

Figure 6.10. Eve Kosofsky Sedgwick, untitled collage, 2005. Photograph: Kevin Ryan. Collection of H. A. Sedgwick. © H. A. Sedgwick

A SOUL
WHICH THEY AFTERWARDS
KEEP AND WHICH
THEY DEVELOP
IN OUR MINDS[.][100]

Sedgwick characteristically refashions Proust's prose to her own reparative, poetic, visual, and material ends. She omits the first word, "for," and maintains the mid-sentence punctuation, but not the final period, so the sentence remains live in the present tense of the narrator's, her own, and "OUR MINDS." She enjambs his part-sentence into a ten-line verse with multisyllabic lines, the line breaks picking up the internal rhymes. The poem's capitalization evokes the overall "cohesion" and "unity" the narrator's mind gives to Swann, Odette, and Gilberte's aesthetic idiom; its lineation and internal spacing recalling the reality of the room as "composite" and "heterogeneous," "distributed" and "arranged."

Because of the melodic rise and fall of the lines, thanks to Sedgwick's buckling ribbons, her fabric feels "alive." It also appears to be "stamped with the imprint of [her] living personality" because she has rubber-stamped, rather than stenciled, the individual letters, as viewers can detect from the repeating ink gaps. Sedgwick's internal spacing is also akin to the idiomatic "position of the windows" at Swann and Odette's, and recalls the "vaporous" tapestries moth-eaten with time. Sedgwick's two-and-a-half-dimensional ribbons additionally evoke the "thickness of the carpets."

Sedgwick's palette, meanwhile, recalls the colors of Odette's "old rose, cherry colored, Tiepolo pink" crepe-de-chine gown.[101] Spectators might also remember the narrator's tentative foot, as it extends toward the "silk-covered stool" Odette "pushes towards him," which evoked the family's latent "personality" and "soul," making the narrator think he is playing collective footsy with Swann, Odette, and Gilberte. This scene, of course, echoes Sedgwick's autobiography, wherein she and Shannon Van Wey's feet were often "delicately poised" at the opposite corners of a shared footstool; Sedgwick, unlike the shy narrator, delighting at her immersion in Van Wey's textural idiom and physical proximity.[102]

In addition to recalling Odette's silk gown, spectators might ponder Sedgwick's bloodred ribbons in relation to the AIDS crisis, given the importance of the blood transmission of HIV, red-ribbon days, and the queer "Memorial Rags" her friend Michael Moon discussed in a 1995 essay, in a volume dedicated to the memory of Sedgwick's friend Michael Lynch.[103] Moon focused on the "superabundance of wounds and ragged bandages" in Whitman's war poetry, among a range of queer fabrics including "rags, bandages, torn garments, and blankets that cover the dead and enfold them for burial." Moon's description of the poet's "ragged strips of bloody cloth" seems particularly resonant in this context. For Moon, Whitman's rags were important because the "care-giving" activity of "undressing, bathing, drying, and dressing" the "wounds" of friends and loved ones who were "patients" could be "erotically charged." This was a sexy caretaking crucial for queer people's erotic identity during the AIDS crisis. In addition, Moon emphasized that the resulting fabrics, the "remnants," "remainders, and reminders" of the loved one's body, need not be shamefully put away, but might be displayed and worked with, to resist the "sexist, heterosexist, and homophobic trajectory of Freud's account" of mourning and melancholia, which had a "fundamentally normalizing" effect in the context of the crisis.[104]

For Moon and Sedgwick, such memorial medical cloths were not a shameful secret to be discarded. They were to be cherished and displayed, as proudly perhaps as "the cloth of [a] banner" or flag.[105] Indeed, in this context, Proust's sentence emphasizes memorialization, with its belief that we can give to, or recognize in, certain people and objects a "soul" that might outlive them, that we can keep safely cocooned in our minds. There is also a passing resemblance between Sedgwick's banner and the US flag. Her hanging may not have a rectangle of stars at top left, but its text, read from the left, zigzags down the banner, as the lines of stars are laid out, in alternating left-justified and then tabbed-in form. Her red-striped hanging, with its ten lines, again alternating, at the left side, between text and color, red and gray patches, also recalls the thirteen red stripes of the star-spangled banner.

This particular blood-and-urine flag may have gotten ragged around the edges, revealing the queer "open mesh" of its silk weave. It has also gotten buckled in the middle, and the individual pieces of fabric contain some "gaps," in the top left where the *shibori* is clearly torn. In addition, individual ribbons are layered on top of each other, revealing their queer "overlaps," rather than being tessellated. But Sedgwick was never interested in straight rectilinearity, a fact reflected in the piece's silhouette and the shape of its poetic lines, preferring a fat, queer art of curvaceous swelling and soft rippling. This is, therefore, another textile in which Proust's lines "aren't made (or *can't* be made) to line up," neatly, or to "signify monolithically," as the collage evokes simultaneously the manifold contexts of its reparative craft production, the specific contexts of Proust's novel and the AIDS crisis, and the red stripes of her pornographic poetry.

Marionettes, or Asthmatic Paranoia and Coronary Reparation

In *The Fugitive* (in volume 5 of *In Search of Lost Time*), the narrator describes one of his favorite artworks, Giotto's Arena Chapel, and spectators might think about Sedgwick's seventh exhibit as a kind of lo-fi, queer craft approximation, with its sky similarly "blue-washed" and "peopled with flying angels" (figure 6.11). "Watching the flight of these angels," the narrator had an "impression of actual movement, literally real activity":

> For all the celestial fervor, or at least the childlike obedience and application, with which their miniscule hands are joined, they are represented in the Arena Chapel as winged creatures of a particular species that had really existed, that must have figured in the natural history of biblical and

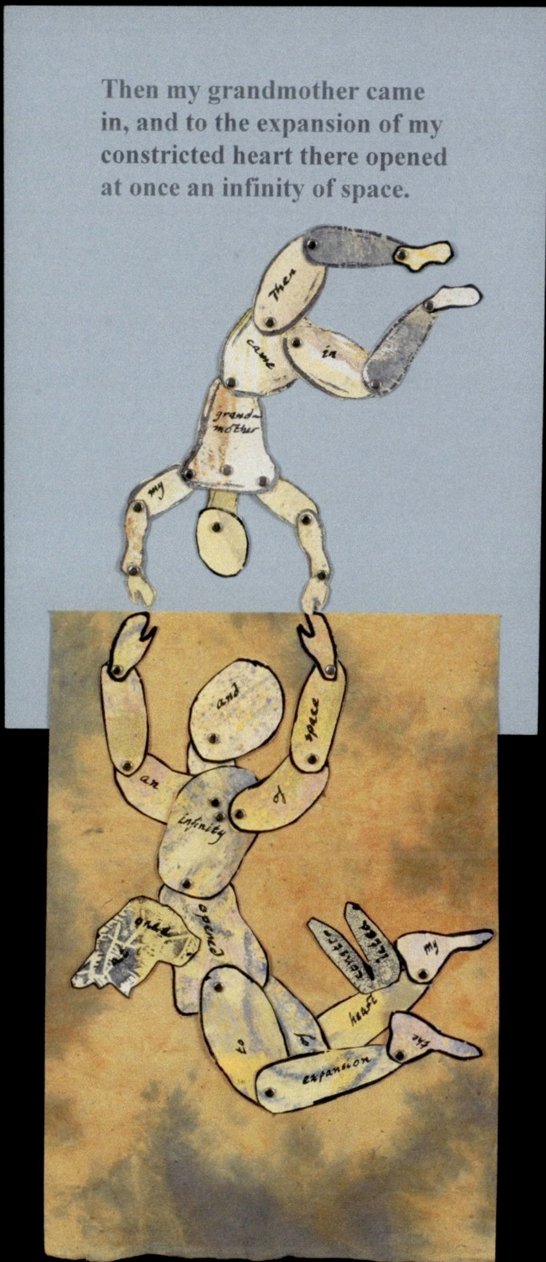

Figure 6.11. Eve Kosofsky Sedgwick, *Marionettes*, 2005. Photograph: Kevin Ryan. Collection of H. A. Sedgwick. © H. A. Sedgwick

> apostolic times. Constantly flitting about above the saints whenever the latter walk abroad, these little beings, since they are real creatures with a genuine power of flight, can be seen soaring upwards, describing curves, "looping the loop," diving earthwards head first, with the aid of wings which enable them to support themselves in positions that defy the laws of gravity, and are far more reminiscent of an extinct species of bird, or of young pupils of Garros practicing gliding, than of the angels of the Renaissance and later periods whose wings have become no more than emblems and whose deportment is generally the same as that of heavenly beings who are not winged.[106]

The text Sedgwick employed in her collage, however, derived from *Within a Budding Grove*. The collage comprised a pair of marionettes made from hand-colored papers, mounted on overlapping card, backed by book board, on which she handwrote the passage; the same sentence is also printed at the top:

> Then my grandmother came
> in, and to the expansion of my
> constricted heart there opened
> at once an infinity of space.[107]

Sedgwick excerpted the sentence from the famous scene in which the narrator, feeling unwell on his arrival at Balbec, is nearly overcome by the strange situation, before his grandmother's arrival improves his mood. The piece's twin marionettes, surrounded by different colors, speak to the way the narrator formed "an impression of the reality of the external world." Comparing his "vague and timorous" expectations of the staff with the reality he encountered, he noted how "a whole frieze of puppet-show characters" issued from that "Pandora's box which was the Grand Hotel, undeniable, irremovable, and, like everything that is realized, jejune"; Sedgwick's schematic figures emphasizing the "jejune" character of the disappointingly real.[108] Sedgwick's collage also evokes the positive transformations the narrator's grandmother worked in his mind; the result of changes that he did "nothing to bring about" but that proved "something had happened which was external" to himself. "Half dead with exhaustion," "burning with [the] fever" of the paranoid-schizoid, and on the "vigilant defensive," the narrator finds nothing familiar to make him feel comfortable. Sedgwick's marionettes, falling through their different, sky-like backgrounds, suggest a twice-described aspect of the room the narrator first experiences: its "high" and "lofty ceiling."[109] In this mood, he struggles to recognize, and take comfort in, his reflection in the "large cheval-glass." Sedgwick evokes this mirror reflection of two similar, but not identical figures in her two marionettes fashioned in the same idiom, but different in scale and spatial orientation, as well as in the color of the surrounding space; a variant chromatic ground that does not represent the "extensions of [the narrator's] organs" or an "enlargement of [him]self."[110]

But just as the narrator feels he has "no world, no room, no body that was not menaced" by "enemies thronging round" him, and felt "alone and longed to die," his grandmother "came in, and to the expansion of [his] constricted heart there opened at once an infinity of space"; the sentence Sedgwick cites. As a result, he is led into a different internal and external world, as if "personally conducted by one of Thomas Cook's guides," just as Sedgwick's marionettes ascend from a stormy to a sublime aerial blue.[111]

The terminally ill Sedgwick probably found evocative the narrator's description because of the way he associated his grandmother with a return to well-being. He acknowledged that "everything that was mine, my cares, my wishes, would be buttressed, in my grandmother, by a desire to preserve and enhance my life that was altogether stronger than . . . my own." As a result, he feels as if his thoughts were "continued and extended in her without undergoing the slightest deflection, since they passed from my mind into hers without any change of atmosphere or of personality."[112]

Sedgwick's collage evokes this passage equivocally. The two marionettes, the smaller narrator at the top and the larger grandmother at the bottom, continue and extend one another, but there is a chromatic change in the surrounding "atmosphere." As a result, Sedgwick's marionettes recall the narrator's earlier discussion of a baffled man who "tries to fasten his tie in front of a glass and forgets that the end which he sees reflected is not on the side to which he raises his hand," as the lower figure raises its hands to its mirror image; "or like a dog that chases along the ground the dancing shadow of an insect in the air," since both figures seem to fly through the sky.[113]

Like her upper marionette, however, the narrator "threw [him]self into the arms of [his] grandmother and pressed [his] lips to her face" as though he were "gaining access to that immense heart which she opened" to him. When he felt his "mouth glued to her cheeks, to her brow," as the two marionettes are securely glued to their colored paper, he "drew from them something so beneficial, so nourishing, that [he] remained as motionless, as solemn, as calmly gluttonous as a babe at the breast." Or, as Sedgwick's two acrobatic figures, freeze-framed in midair, where the narrator, the smaller top puppet, "gazed inexhaustibly" at his grandmother's "large face," "outlined," as the marionettes are, "like a beautiful cloud, glowing and serene, behind which I could discern the radiance of her tender love"; a sensation Sedgwick captures in the cloudy orange glow of her bottom panel.[114]

The two figures remain apart in the collage, their mittens close to touching, but located on either side of a layered, chromatic paper divide. That step recalls the "quite thin" partition wall of the hotel rooms dividing and connecting the narrator and his grandmother. Across this they tap out a series of Morse Code–like communications, in the form of SOS-like messages comprising "three knocks" or "three little taps, timidly, faintly, but for all that distinctly," particularly in the morning before the grandmother brings milk to the narrator; a milky palette Sedgwick employs for the inside of the upper marionette's body.

The upper panel of Sedgwick's text, meanwhile, with its letters clearly stamped on the blue ground, further alludes to the grandmother's reassuring and health-bringing three knocks, "stamped with a calm authority" and "in a different tone" from the narrator's more tremulous taps, perhaps signaled by the shakier character of Sedgwick's handwritten text within the marionettes. But since the grandmother's knocks are "repeated twice over so that there should be no mistaking," perhaps both fonts represent the grandmother's reassuring presence.[115]

The narrator characterizes his grandmother's knocks as "singing like [an] angelic choir," "steeped in love and joy" and "grown melodious, incorporeal," which "contrived to waft to [him] the soul of [his] grandmother, whole and perfect, and the promise of her coming, with the swiftness of an annunciation." As a result, Sedgwick's marionettes may be both falling fearfully through empty space and calmly descending from the heavens, with a divine message.[116]

But if Proust's text articulates the reparative scene of heartfelt relation, expansion, and coronary cure, and a release from chronic-asthmatic contraction, anxiety, and breathlessness, the narrator reminds readers that the stakes remain mortally high. He wonders if his fear of "sleeping in a strange room" represented the "most humble, obscure, organic, almost unconscious form of that great and desperate resistance put up by the things that constitute the better part of our present life against our mentally acknowledging the possibility of a future in which they are to have no part."[117]

Sedgwick's collage, by contrast, seems less bleak, honoring the frequently more reparative scenes in Proust where apparent death forms the prelude to an impossible-to-imagine metamorphosis. This would represent a "survival" in which the narrator would not be allowed to take with him his "memories," "frailties," and "character"; a transformation into an "eternity" in which he "would have no part," "so that it would be in a real sense the death of the self, a death followed, it is true, by resurrection, but in a different self."[118]

Perhaps because Sedgwick felt kindly toward the narrator and herself, or because she was conscious of the difficulty of escaping the "clinging scenes of karma" at the point of rebirth, her scene of ascension and resurrection is into a body different only in chromatic, atmospheric environment and scale and accessories.[119] For example, the lower figure, unlike the upper, has a patch of fabric billowing out from their crotch and a winged right Achilles heel, even as the basic, articulated form of the body, with its sixteen parts, remains the same.[120]

At the top, meanwhile, Sedgwick's enjambment breaks Proust's sentence into a four-line poem, without a rhyme scheme:

> Then my grandmother came
> in, and to the expansion of my
> constricted heart there opened
> at once an infinity of space.

As a result of the infectious jouissance of the joyful grandmother, Sedgwick visually indicates the expansion of the narrator's heart through the line break between "my" and "constricted heart" as well as between "opened" and "at once an infinity of space"; an overall aeration that might account for the reparative currents of air that keep the marionettes high in the sky.

Sedgwick's earlier account of the beaten thighs and buttocks of enjambment, meanwhile, hovers around her handwritten version of the narrator's sentence scribed onto the marionettes' limbs, torso, and other body parts. The upper marionette hosts the words "then my grandmother came in," but not in any spatially adjacent, easy-to-read order. The textual sequence in the lower marionette is even more difficult to get a handle on. Indeed, Sedgwick makes it peculiarly hard to make sense of the sentence as viewers first hunt the words across the marionettes' two bodies and then try to read them given the different angles at which they are written in Sedgwick's handwriting.

This was a scene of acrobatic reading familiar to Proust's narrator, who described how a "writer who had taken Bergotte's place in [his] affections wearied [him] not by the incoherence but by the novelty—perfectly coherent—of associations which [he] was unaccustomed to following." "The point, always the same, at which [he] felt [him]self falter indicated the identity of each renewed feat of acrobatics that [he] must undertake. Moreover, when once in a thousand times [he] did succeed in following the writer to the end of his sentence, what [he] saw there always had a humour, a truthfulness, and a charm similar to those which I had found long ago in reading Bergotte, only more delightful."[121] Like the paranoid-schizoid narrator in the early part of the hotel scene, Sedgwick's readers are disoriented, struggling to locate and recognize individual words and things in an initially unfamiliar outside world, where nothing is where it should be. Given the way the different parts of the marionettes' bodies are bolted together onto the page, however, she invites viewers to think about reorienting, to their own preferences, the narrator's text, moving the position of an arm, leg, or foot, and changing its overall spatial orientation, to work *with* Proust's words as she had done. This was a scene of active puppetry she frequently invited her readers and viewers to consider in her later career, as we have seen in *In the Bardo*, and to which we shall return.

In her circa 2004–5 "The Weather in Proust" essay, for example, Sedgwick discusses the "puppet theatre" of Greek modernist poet Constantin Cavafy's poem "The Footsteps," and the Handspring Puppet Theater of South Africa's Bunraku contribution to William Kentridge's then-recent production of Claudio Monteverdi's *Il ritorno d'Ulisse in patria* (*The Return of Ulysses to His Homeland*). Here, as we have seen, Sedgwick documented that "near-life-size puppets" were "manipulated by dark-clad but quite visible onstage puppeteers," who "gave an almost unbearable immediacy to the sense at once of [their] complete power over the puppets" and their "radical subordination to them."[122]

Sedgwick compared this theatrical scene to the "humility and absolute absorption of a *stabat mater*" who "devoted every atom" of her attention to "maintaining the tenuous threads of the dying man's illusory life," although in the case of the collage, spectators might think about the viewer as a kind of Proustian *stabat grand-mater*, which is to say offering a hymn to the suffering grandmother.[123] Spectators might be offered the "somber absorption in the exercise" of tracking down the narrator's various words. But Sedgwick's manipulable puppet forms can also "become expressive of the emotion" viewers want to "convey to the insentient body of the puppet," with spectators again reminded of their affinity to the "fates in the image of a medieval 'Death' controlling every movement of the 'man-puppet,'" with hands that can be "fond or vindictive" in a "play of absolute dependency with power, tenderness, and envy unfolded in many dimensions."[124]

Spectators might additionally think about the viewer as akin to Proust's aged narrator, at the final party in the novel, where he sees

> a puppet-show, yes, but one in which, in order to identify the puppets with the people whom one had known in the past, it was necessary to read what was written on several planes at once, planes that lay behind the visible aspect of the puppets and gave them depth and forced one, as one looked at these aged marionettes, to make a strenuous intellectual effort; one was obliged to study them at the same time with one's eyes and

> with one's memory. These were puppets bathed in the immaterial colors of the years, puppets which exteriorized Time, Time which by habit is made invisible.[125]

This was an "epiphanic, extravagantly reparative" late-life scene Sedgwick had earlier drawn attention to in *Touching Feeling*, in which she and Proust's narrator are both "assailed . . . by a climactic series of joy-inducing 'truths' about the relation of writing," and here crafting, "to time"; a "temporal disorientation that initiates [them] into [a] revelatory space" of the "brutal foreshortening" of their own and "so many [other] queer life spans," and within it, the "related practices of reparative knowing."[126]

The *Loom Book*(s), or A Text Is Being Beaten

Works in Fiber, Paper, and Proust contained two pieces titled *Loom Book* (figures 6.12 and 6.13). Sedgwick fashioned the smaller, about half the size of a pencil, from gold-painted book board, woven with five gold wefts, recalling a musical stave, which pierce through a piece of hand-marbled, pastel-on-gold paper, accordion-folded into four peaks and three troughs. On this, she wrote by hand, in purple ink, a sentence we have already pondered:

> Then my grandmother came in,
> and to the expansion of my
> constricted heart there opened
> at once an infinity of space.

In addition, on three rectangular pieces of transparent acetate that float on the troughs, she printed in black capitals: "FOR WITH THE PERTURBATIONS OF MEMORY ARE LINKED THE INTERMITTENCIES OF THE HEART."

The loom's gold ground again recalls a Byzantine icon-like mystery that, combined with Sedgwick's modestly small-scale, lo-fi technique, suggests the quotidian mysticism she identified with Proust. The transparency of the floating acetate sentence reveals the color below while the palette of the purple prose of the partially concealed lower text combines the pastel pink and sky blue marbling below, so the words risk becoming part of its decorative effect.

Sedgwick characteristically represents Proust's sentences in two overlapping, perpendicular short-poem-like structures. These interrupt each other, with readers having to reorient their vision through ninety degrees or rotate the object, depending on which sentence they want to read. Keen to emphasize issues of transformation and variation, she divides up Proust's sentence differently on

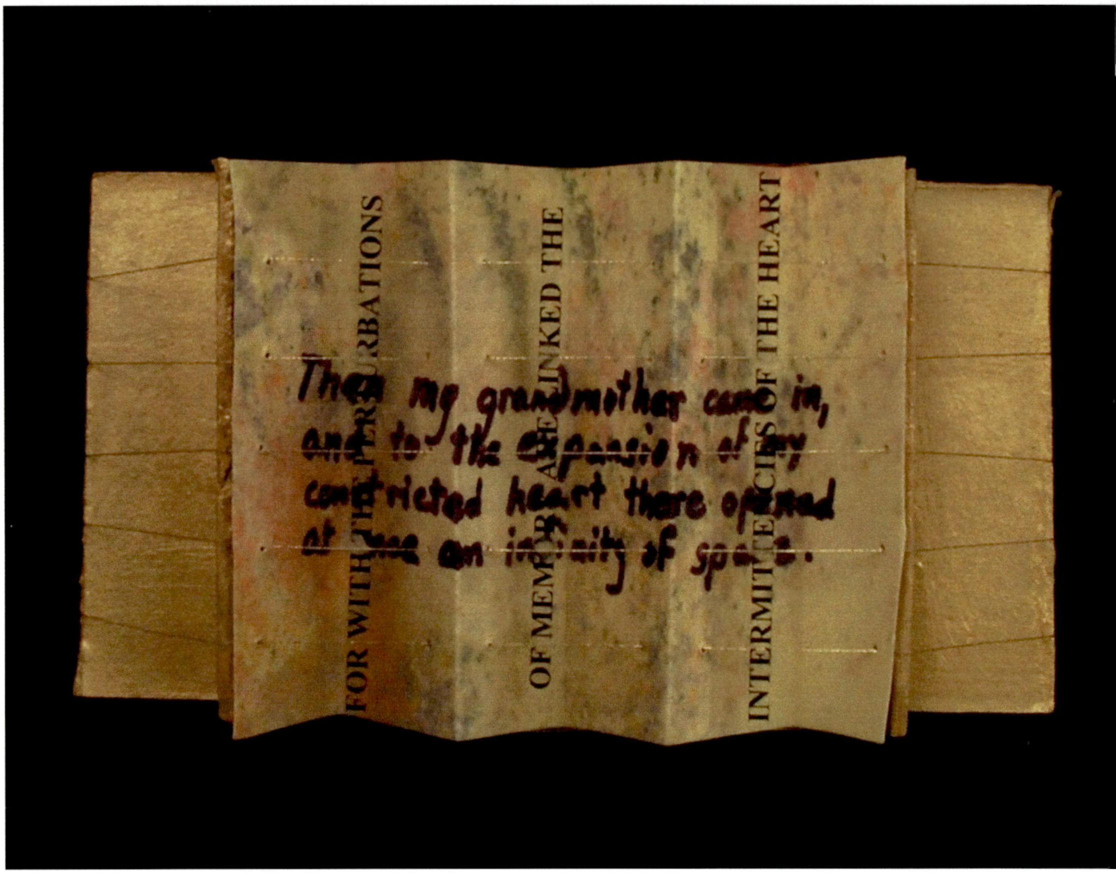

Figure 6.12. Eve Kosofsky Sedgwick, *Loom Book*, 2005. Photograph: Kevin Ryan. Collection of H. A. Sedgwick. © H. A. Sedgwick

the two loom books, centering his original, like a heart within a body, on the small loom, thus:

> FOR WITH THE PERTURBATIONS
> OF MEMORY ARE LINKED THE
> INTERMITTENCIES OF THE HEART

Sedgwick fashions the sentence into an uppercase, unrhymed, metrically irregular three-line form. Her enjambment emphasizes the "PERTURBATIONS" through the pause after the word and before "INTERMITTENCIES," the irregular syllabics only resolving into a more even heartbeat in the last line, but with the sentence left floating, by the missing period.

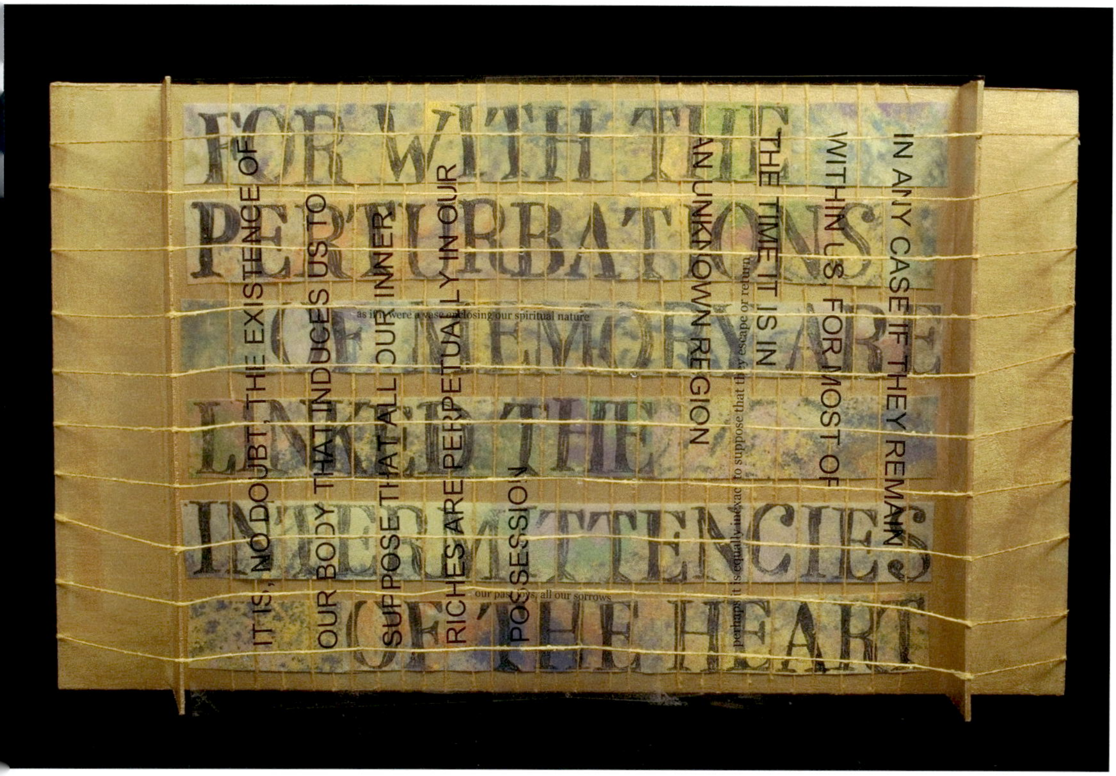

Figure 6.13. Eve Kosofsky Sedgwick, *Loom Book*, 2005. Photograph: Kevin Ryan. Collection of H. A. Sedgwick. © H. A. Sedgwick

Sedgwick refashions Proust's second sentence into a lowercase four-line poem, with an again irregular meter, and the hint of a rhyme between "in" and "opened":

> Then my grandmother came in,
> and to the expansion of my
> constricted heart there opened
> at once an infinity of space.

In Proust's original, the passage moves from a deathly moment where the narrator, like Sedgwick at moments in her late life, felt terribly ill, fearing he had "no world, no room, no body that was not menaced by the enemies thronging round" him, as he was "penetrated to the very bones by fever," or in her case cancer, and "longed to die." She evokes this sense of being trapped by the bar-like wefts crossing the loom book, keeping spectators from the dawn- or dusk-like heaven on the pastel paper behind. She uses this also five-rib-like structure to evoke being penetrated to the bones.[127]

At this trying moment, the narrator's grandmother arrives, and "to the expansion of [his] constricted heart there opened at once an infinity of space." Like the ventricles of a heart, the accordion-like form of the folded paper on which the quotation appears can be contracted and expanded. Here the accordion-heart appears, depressively, somewhere in the middle, but Sedgwick emphasizes the reparative expansion toward an infinity of space through her sky-like marbling.

If the first line break follows the narrator's punctuation, the second introduces some much-needed space before viewers get to the more tightly bunched "constricted heart," a space Sedgwick expands after the word "opened" at the third line end. She finishes her sentence with a period, suggesting a final peace.

There may be perturbations, and the heart may beat irregularly, the body might be pierced with pain, and flesh and bones both penetrated by needles and threads, suturing together something that had been torn apart or taken away, but there is always the possibility of expansively "fine weather at last."

Accordion Book, or Beauty in the Cybernetic Fold

The exhibition's third vitrine contained what Sedgwick described as a "folding screen," a polyptych stretching the codex format further still than the loom books, elaborating a sentence we have repeatedly encountered: "FOR BEAUTY IS A SERIES OF HYPOTHESES." Fashioned from card and overlapping pieces of multicolored marbled paper, the accordion book, like Proust's heart and memory, can again contract and expand to reveal ten unnumbered pages (see figures 6.14–6.16). Sedgwick's quotation runs horizontally across the five spreads, beginning on the top left of the first page and concluding on the bottom right of the last. She characteristically translates the sentence into uppercase and disaggregates it into a short two-line rhyming poem:

> FOR BEAUTY IS A SERIES
> OF HYPOTHESES

While Sedgwick largely respects the integrity and clarity of Proust's individual letters, giving mostly pairs of them their own pages, she emphasizes the sense of something cut short, in an ugly rather than beautiful fashion, by sloppily allowing letters to run over the gutter or edge of a page. This encourages the

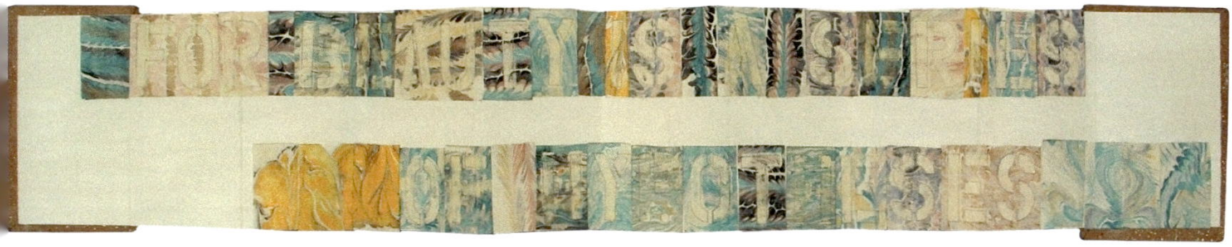

Figure 6.14. Eve Kosofsky Sedgwick, *Accordion Book* (interior), 2002. Photograph: Kevin Ryan. Collection of H. A. Sedgwick. © H. A. Sedgwick

left-to-right flow of the text across the undulating structure but makes reading individual letters difficult.

For clarity, Sedgwick respects the spaces between words by introducing a thin column of marbled paper, but a colored surface that paradoxically suggests a continuity of pattern as much as a separation of words. Adding to the complexity and confusion, spectators are invited to think about the overall patterning of both lines, where many of the letters, but not their background patterns, repeat. Sedgwick's D-Day font also resonantly disaggregates many letters into multiple parts. Only three words retain their integrity on the page: "IS," "A," and "OF." By contrast, "FOR," "BEAUTY," "SERIES," and "HYPOTHESES" bleed across multiple pages or spreads. As a result, the reading of individual letters, words, and the overall phrase is more hypothetical and surprising than its source text.

Like the adjacent loom books, the *Accordion Book* suggests that *In Search of Lost Time* is an instrument to be creatively performed and transformed rather than a text to be iterated silently, here squeezed shut and stretched open to make music. In addition, the *Accordion Book* reminds spectators that every turn of a page leads to the expansion of a new spread, and that the experience of reading is a constant folding together and opening out, a movement between the implicate and explicate orders, in David Bohm's terms.[128] As such, the *Accordion Book* is also useful for thinking further about fat and thin art. While Sedgwick's poetic chapbook is comparatively svelte when closed, its ten pages, including endpapers, taking up little space on the archive shelf, when unfolded it expands to an elastic, fat horizontality way beyond the codex book's comparatively svelte spread.

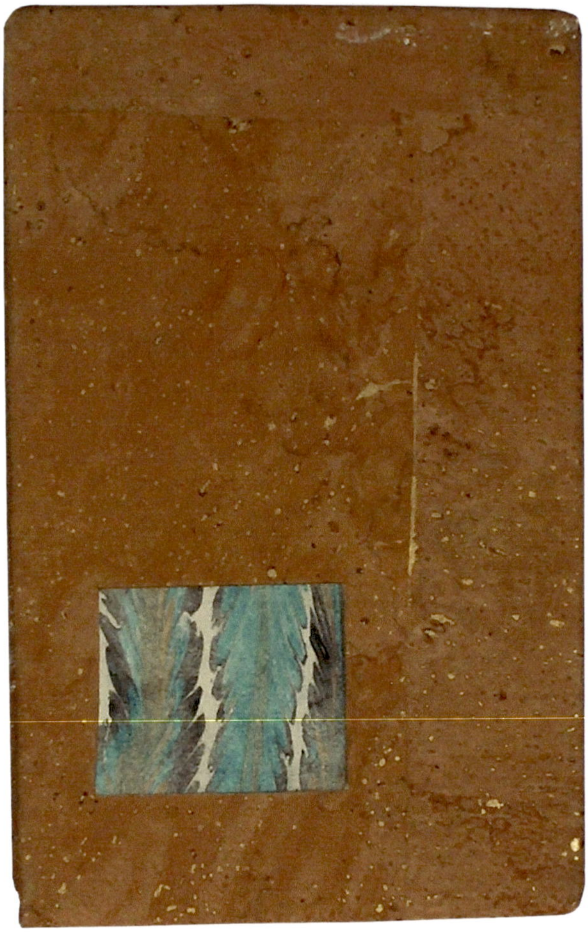

Figure 6.15. Eve Kosofsky Sedgwick, *Accordion Book*, 2002 (cover). Photograph: Kevin Ryan. Collection of H. A. Sedgwick.

Spectators might also again characterize, as somehow *spinal*, the feather-like forms of many of Sedgwick's *suminagashi* patterns, as well as the overall two-line form of the text. After all, extended vertically rather than horizontally, the *Accordion Book*'s pages recall segmented adjacent vertebrae, especially given the hollow white line that runs down the center, reversing the polarity of Sedgwick's

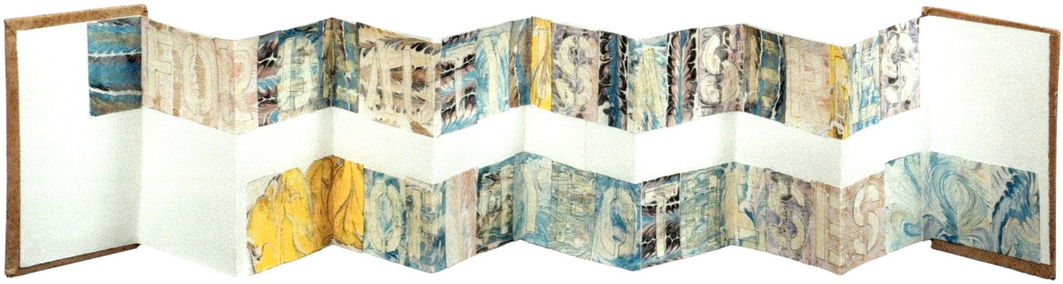

Figure 6.16. Eve Kosofsky Sedgwick, *Accordion Book*, 2002 (interior). Photograph: Kevin Ryan. Collection of H. A. Sedgwick. © H. A. Sedgwick

earlier spinal body scans, with their white bone extremities and colorful spinal columns.

In so doing, the *Accordion Book* encourages viewers to think about the expanded and contracted, implicate and explicate, vertical and horizontal, upright spine and supine, as well as their structural interrelation, in the cybernetic folds of an object that can be displayed and photographed both standing up, on its zigzag lower edges, as if in the midst of life, or laid out, on its back, like a corpse.

Adjective Game, or *Wordplay in Proust's Closet*

Sedgwick fashioned her *Adjective Game* from book board, handmade paper, fabric, and Velcro (figures 6.17 and 6.18). At Harvard, spectators encountered it open, with its insides laid bare, while visitors to the archive first meet the closed form. Like several exhibits examined so far, the game has a closet- and triptych-like structure, with a pair of outer wings folded over a central panel, attached to it by four pieces of landscape-oriented, roughly marbled swatches of rectangular tape, located one-third from the top and bottom of the doors. Sedgwick cut the tapes from larger pieces of marbled paper, which share a Giotto palette of sky blues, yellow golds, shell grays, and pastel pinks and more saturated tones of pink. Indeed, the tapes resemble microfragments of the Arena Chapel frescoes, reduced to small-scale abstract-expressionist color fields, hinting at the religious character of the Proustian passage inside.[129]

Sedgwick covered the wings and panel back in pale-wood-colored paper striated with organic rhizomatic, branching green lines. These recall *shibori*

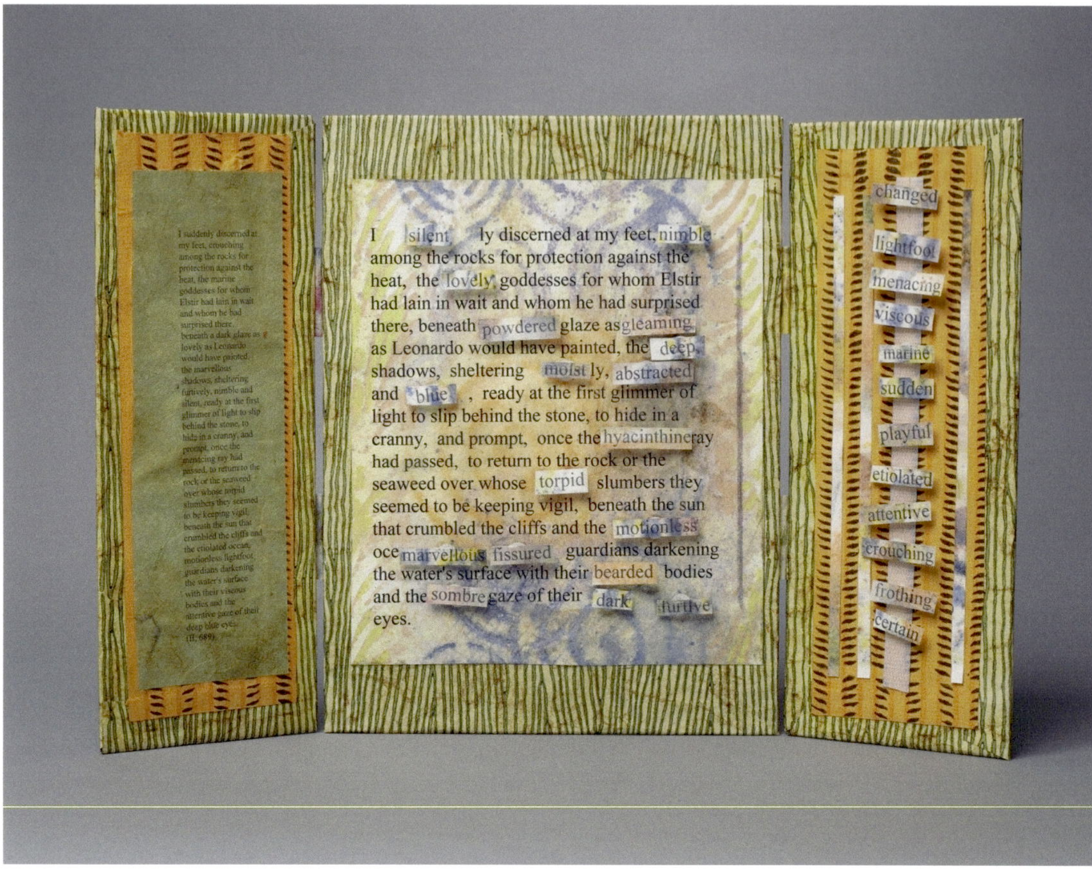

Figure 6.17. Eve Kosofsky Sedgwick, *Adjective Game* (front), 2005. Photograph: Kevin Ryan. Collection of H. A. Sedgwick. © H. A. Sedgwick

patterns and are weft-like across the back of the central panel, as if woven with green thread against a tightly packed gold warp, and warp-like down its wings, with the intersecting horizontal tapes resembling weft patches. Weaving evidently remained in Sedgwick's mind, even if her disintegrating spine meant she could no longer sit at her loom.

The overall organic, woody pattern further evokes the interactive devotional aesthetics of a wood-paneled medieval triptych. In addition, the horizontal lines of the central panel anticipate the wefts of Proustian text that spectators discover on the flip side; the interrupting tapes anticipate the word-patches players will encounter on the inside wings to be inserted into Proust's sentences.

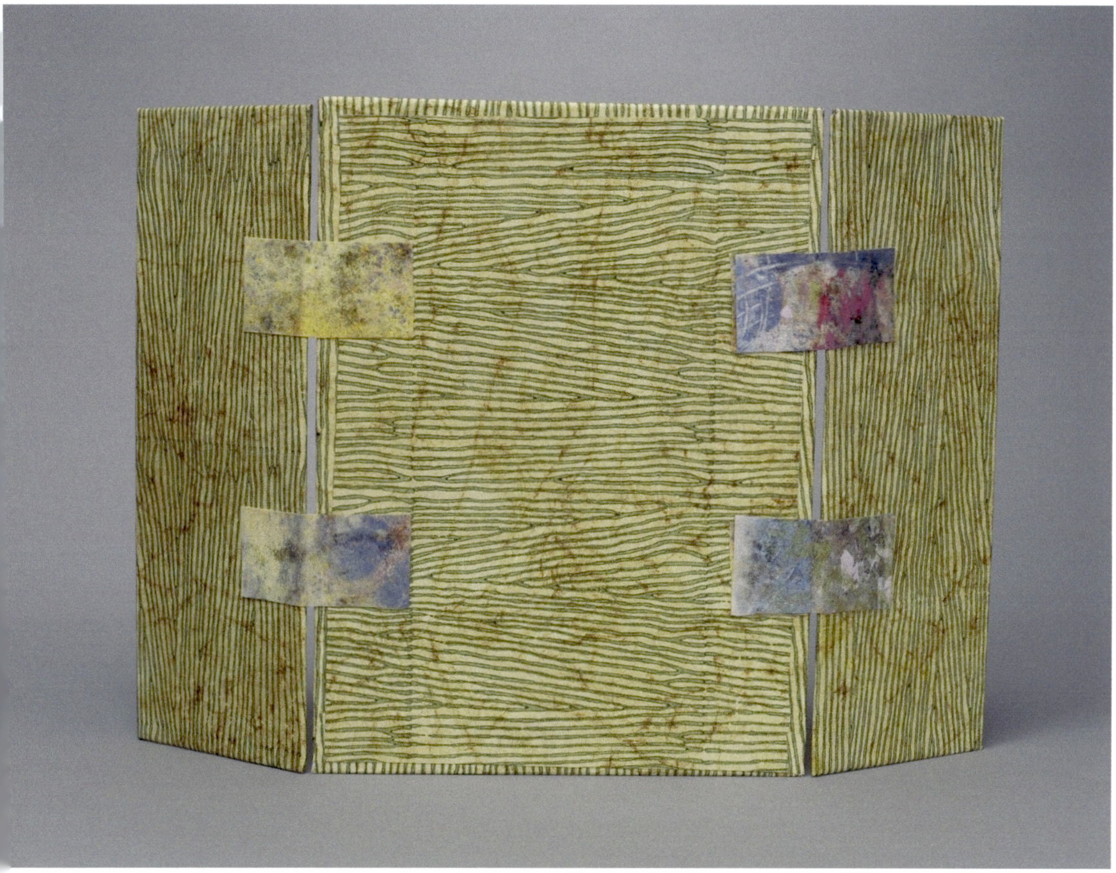

Figure 6.18. Eve Kosofsky Sedgwick, *Adjective Game* (back), 2005. Photograph: Kevin Ryan. Collection of H. A. Sedgwick. © H. A. Sedgwick

Sedgwick's external patchwork aesthetic derives from the nonidentical swatches of tape; the way she applies those patches over the ground, to suture it together and give it strength; and the way she seems, at first glance, to have constructed the branching pattern using smaller patches of paper cut and layered diagonally one over the other, especially in the central panel. This again anticipates what viewers find inside the box, which offers a patch-*word* game, with similar possibilities for sympathetic or interruptive swatches, given the way the top-left tape blends into its patterned background, sharing a similar "shot" green over gold tonality, while the top-right swatch is more dissonant.

Once opened, *Adjective Game* can either be stood up, to emphasize its triptych form, with its weight resting on the partially opened wings, or laid flat, as in the exhibition, like a codex book, with three differently scaled pages; two hollow spines or gutters; or a single central page, with generous margins for commentary. Sedgwick lines the inside of the triptych with the same paper as the outside. On the inside, the pattern runs vertically and recalls bamboo branches, nutritious foodstuff for a panda lover, like Sedgwick.

Sedgwick glues to each wing a piece of patterned orange paper, its horizontal green stripes organized into five floating columns or warps. If the rectangular orange paper emphasizes the rectilinear, door-like character of the wings, the internal pattern suggests that those panels are columns, evoking a gestalt shift between conceiving of *Adjective Game* as a closet and a small-scale classical domestic temple, with *In Search of Lost Time* functioning as the habitat of the queer little gods spectators will encounter in the text panels.

On the left wing, layered on top of the orange paper, is a further piece of green paper on which Sedgwick printed a short passage from *Within a Budding Grove*. On the right door, in addition to the central Velcro strip, she added three further, again spinal-column-like strips of paper, cut from a roughly marbled larger sheet. Spectators might read each strip of paper as representing a spinal cord running down between, and protected by, the surrounding vertebrae suggested by the diagonal green lines on either side of them on the patterned paper below. But, except for the central Velcro column, the pieces of paper she employs do not cover the distance between the two columns of vertebrae, suggesting her dissolving spine in three out of four cases.

The Velcro column, by contrast, is twice the width of the outer columns, and to this more secure spine Sedgwick sticks twelve adjectives, resembling vertebrae. In the official photograph, these are "menacing," "powdered," "marvelous," "marine," "crouching," "attentive," "motionless," "playful," "torpid," "lovely," "etiolated," and "frothing." They represent a subset of some thirty words viewers can play with, all printed against the same pastel ground. Other adjectives Sedgwick included, and toyed with, were "silent," "blue," "somber," "viscous," "gleaming," "bearded," "moist," "furtive," "menacing," "lightfoot," "sudden," "hyacinthine," "certain," "fissured," "changed," "nimble," "dark," and "abstracted."

On the left wing, she printed the passage she again invited spectators to make their own; a sentence translated from Proust's French into English, given a ragged right margin, and characteristically made into a poem:

I suddenly discerned at
my feet, crouching
among the rocks for

protection against the
heat, the marine
goddesses for whom
Elstir had lain in wait
and whom he had
surprised there,
beneath a dark glaze as
lovely as Leonardo
would have painted,
the marvelous
shadows, sheltering
furtively, nimble and
silent, ready at the first
glimmer of light to slip
behind the stone, to
hide in a cranny, and
prompt, once the
menacing ray had
passed, to return to the
rock or the seaweed
over whose torpid
slumbers they seemed
to be keeping vigil,
beneath the sun that,
crumbled the cliffs and
the etiolated ocean,
motionless lightfoot
guardians darkening
the water's surface
with their viscous
bodies and the
attentive gaze of their
deep blue eyes.[130]

Sedgwick refashions Proust's long, multiclausal sentence into thirty-six lines, employing the original punctuation mark only five times as a cue for a line break, characteristically enjambing the quotation to emphasize the narrator's rhymes, without employing a systematic scheme. Indeed, with only one exception—line 17's "slip"—every word finds a rhyme or half rhyme.

In the main panel, Sedgwick enjambs the sentence differently, into half the number of lines, although again quietly emphasizing the sentence's internal rhymes at line ends, without deferring to any traditional rhyme scheme:

> I silently discerned at my feet, blue
> among the rocks for protection against the
> heat, the sombre goddesses for whom Elstir
> had lain in wait and whom he had surprised
> there, beneath a viscous glaze as gleaming
> as Leonardo would have painted, the bearded
> shadows sheltering moistly, furtive
> and deep, ready at the first glimmer of
> light to slip behind the stone, to hide in a
> cranny, and prompt, once the lightfoot ray
> had passed, to return to the rock or the
> seaweed over whose sudden slumbers they
> seemed to be keeping vigil, beneath the sun
> that crumbled the cliffs and the hyacinthine
> ocean, certain fissured guardians darkening
> the water's surface with their changed bodies
> and the nimble gaze of their dark abstracted
> eyes.

The aqueous theme of Proust's sentence in part explains the pattern of the paper ground Sedgwick chose for this section. This is covered with a range of perhaps potato-printed or stamped marks washed over with a thin layer of water, or applied to an already wet sheet, since the colors bleed from their edges. Sedgwick's palette of pastel pinks, blues, and pale greens again recalls Giotto and resonates with the sunny marine scene Proust describes, with an off-central area of dusky solar pink surrounded by sky and sea blue. This evokes Proust's description of how the fictional impressionist painter Elstir—part Claude Monet, part James McNeill Whistler—looks down toward the rocks at his feet and encounters there several diminutive "marine goddesses" whom he had awaited. The watery eddies of Sedgwick's surface evoke the goddesses' surprised trembling as they try to remain invisibly still or seek a "nimble and silent" escape. Her medium, however, is watercolor, rather than oil, so pulls against Proust's description of how the scene appears shadowy "beneath a dark glaze as lovely as Leonardo would have painted." In so doing, she again works *with* Proust rather than subordinate her aesthetic *to* his.

Except for the "attentive gaze of their deep blue eyes," whose circular blue irises Sedgwick's outer pattern suggests, Proust's goddesses are nowhere to be seen, having presumably slipped "behind the stone, to hide in a cranny." Sedgwick is more characteristically preoccupied with the behaviors of water, focusing on the traces left behind by these "motionless lightfoot guardians darkening the water's surface with their viscous bodies," like the long-legged flies she evoked in *Floating Columns*. Sedgwick's green-striated back papers also resonate with Proust's passage, now resembling flat, desiccating bladderwrack spread across a sunny beach, with the text describing how "once the menacing ray had passed," the goddesses returned to the "seaweed over whose torpid slumbers" they had "seemed to be keeping vigil." In addition, the falling diagonal green lines on the vertical orange wings gain new resonance from Proust's sun that "crumble[s] the cliffs"; collapsing, geologically striated cliffs that *Adjective Game* recalls when stood up, resembling a cliff face with three-dimensional verbal outcrops that can be dislodged.

Sedgwick encourages viewers to play further with Proust's adjectives, having already inserted new descriptive words into his sentence. In so doing, the game registers the narrator's description of how, in "too rapid readings," readers, "on the basis of a single syllable and without waiting to identify the rest," replaced "the word that is in the text with a wholly different word" their "memory supplie[d]."[131] For the narrator, the charm of Elstir's pictures also "lay in a sort of metamorphosis of the objects represented, analogous to what in poetry we call metaphor," such that "if God the Father had created things by naming them, it was by taking away their names or giving them other names that Elstir created them anew," the "names which designate[d] things correspond[ing] invariably to an intellectual notion, alien to our true impressions, and compelling us to eliminate from them everything that is not in keeping with that notion."[132]

Sedgwick's characteristically idiomatic interventions sometimes blend the narrator's prose into her colorful background, as in the case of "silent" and "blue," its palette, cut from similarly marbled paper, dissolveing into the tones below. At other moments, she shifts the palette of his prose, in the interruptive colors of words including "viscous," "moist," "deep," "lightfoot," and "sudden." Sedgwick's scene also begins more peacefully and relationally than Proust's. Where the narrator "suddenly" and disturbingly discerns the goddesses, Sedgwick and the viewer's "I" *silently* find them. The narrator's goddesses crouch down for protection; Sedgwick's less figurative idiom reduces them to a patch of color, "blue amongst the rocks." Proust's divinities are redundantly "marine," obvious given the location; Sedgwick makes them "sombre." The narrator finds blandly "lovely" Leonardo's shadowy glaze; Sedgwick, preoccupied with texture and more of an impressionist, makes her scene "gleaming" and "viscous" rather than "dark." Her trans goddesses are "bearded" and shelter "moistly, furtive and deep," rather than Proust's again blandly "marvelous" "nimble and silent" prototypes. If Proust's solar rays are "menacing," Sedgwick, ever the foot fetishist, emphasizes their "lightfoot" quality, encouraging viewers to think further about the eddies of her central artwork as the delicious product of a goddess's balletic toe, dipped in the water, causing it to radiate out, recalling the ballerina cover of *Performativity and Performance* (1995).[133]

In Proust, the divinities return to a "torpid" sleep, once recovered from being disturbed. Sedgwick's more roused bladderwrack falls, suggestively, into a "sudden slumber," as if satisfied, postcoital. Sedgwick encourages this eroticized reading by making the ocean not "etiolated," as in Proust, but, in a world more full of light, "hyacinthine," resembling Hyacinthus, Apollo's hothouse-flower boy lover. Proust's waters again run stiller than Sedgwick's: His "motionless" ocean guardians become her "certain fissured" figures; a fissuring the *Adjective Game* encourages, given its dis/aggregating triptych character, the two versions of Proust's text Sedgwick employs, and the way the added adjectives split up otherwise two-dimensional sentences into more layered, *two-and-a-half-dimensional* forms. Finally, if Proust's marine goddesses predictably have "deep blue eyes," Sedgwick's are more mysteriously "dark" and "abstracted." And, always emphasizing the quotidian metamorphoses of experience in her late work, the goddess's bodies are not "viscous," but "changed" one more time.

The Final Scene: *Scroll Book*, or Proust and the Spectacle of the Closet

Some change in the atmosphere or in my own state of health brought to the surface of my consciousness some forgotten scroll on which were recorded impressions of other days.

—Marcel Proust, *In Search of Lost Memory*, volume 3

Scroll Book (Yellow/Gold/Gratitude) was the final exhibit viewers encountered at Harvard and is the final object I explore in this book (see figures 6.19–6.21). Fashioned from sewn paper and cardboard, employing rubber stamps and gloss paint, the triptych incorporated text from *Swann's Way*, *Within a Budding Grove*, and *The Captive* (volumes 1, 3, and 5 of *In Search of Lost Time*), its form again offering spectators the "delights of extension after those of contraction."[134] In choosing passages, Sedgwick's was again a strong, condensing editorial hand. She cut phrases from the beginnings, middles, and ends of her quotations, without signaling her elisions, working *with* Proust rather than quoting him verbatim. The decade or so after 1996 had been a period when Sedgwick

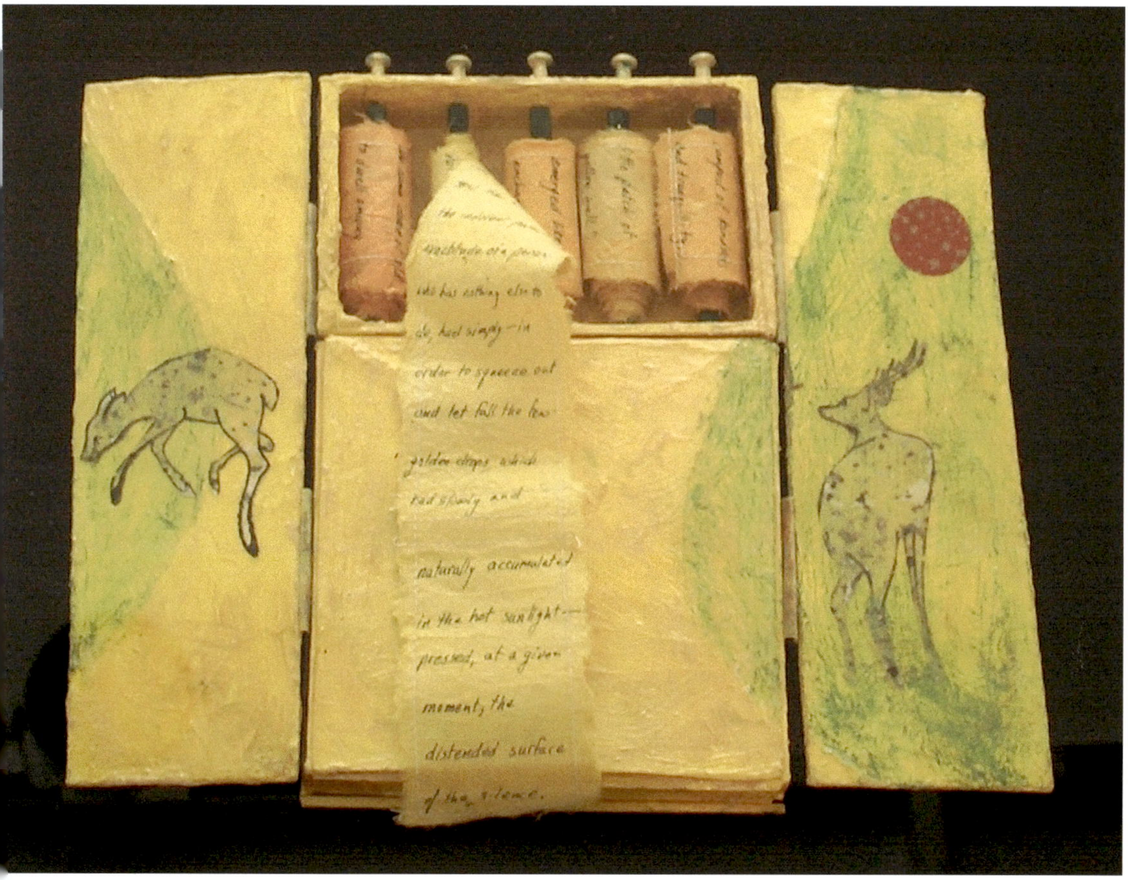

Figure 6.19. Eve Kosofsky Sedgwick, *Scroll Book (Yellow/Gold/Gratitude)*, 2005. Photograph: Kevin Ryan. Collection of H. A. Sedgwick. © H. A. Sedgwick

had become an increasingly experienced editor, publishing volumes of the work of Gary Fisher and Silvan Tomkins, and collections on the queer novel, performativity, and performance.

At Harvard, the *Scroll Book* was open to reveal its internal contents, with one scroll unfurled, but viewers encountering the object in Sedgwick's archive are again presented with a different first view. They are invited to open the leaves of a small cardboard box painted thickly and roughly, in multiple apparently random, overlapping directions, with yellow-gold paint. Sedgwick again attaches four roughly pastel-painted swatches, to secure the two wings covering the front, their palettes correlating diagonally: dominantly blue and salmon-pink tape at the upper left and bottom right; a sky blue found, with less intensity, on the alternating pieces of paper, at the upper right and lower left. Running

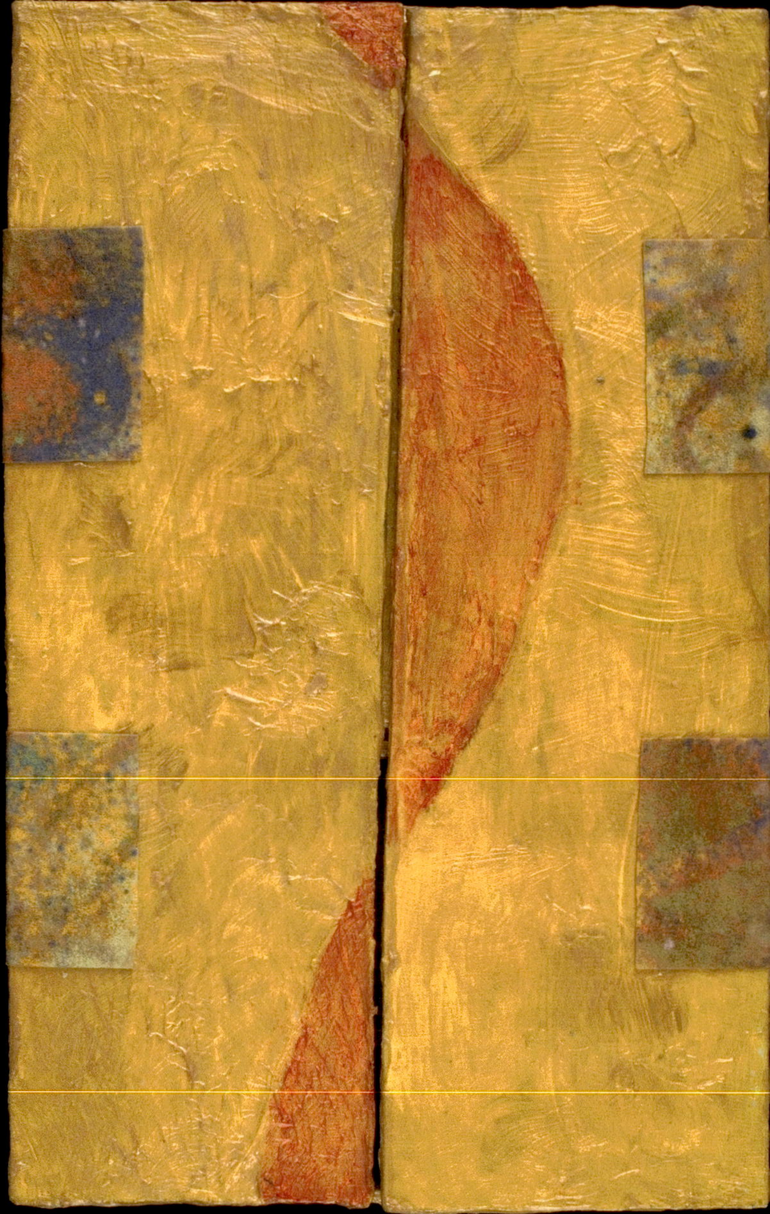

Figure 6.20. Eve Kosofsky Sedgwick, *Scroll Book (Yellow/Gold/Gratitude)*, 2005. Photograph: Kevin Ryan. Collection of H. A. Sedgwick. © H. A. Sedgwick

vertically across the dividing line of the two doors is an orange sinewave starting at top left, moving across the right wing, and curving down to the bottom left. Taken as a whole, the box's exterior suggests decorative orders of two, in its bilateral symmetry; three, in the patches of orange paint within the sine curve; and four, in the adjoining tape strips.

Opening the leaves of the box recalls religious practices of unveiling sacred objects; the erotics of undressing items with vertical bilateral symmetry, such as shirts or blouses; the parting of bodily exteriors, such as buttocks or labia, to engage in anilingus or cunnilingus, fingering or fisting; and, perhaps most resonantly, the title of Sedgwick's first (ca. 1990) essay on Proust: "Proust and the Spectacle of the Closet."[135]

Once opened, the object again forms a triptych, with two side panels and a larger central image space. Sedgwick depicts on the left wing a painted, dappled rubber-stamped fawn juxtaposed with a green half circle. This is a freshwater pond, perhaps, from which the deer might be leaning down to drink; a green pond bisected and cropped by the outer edge of the left door. Sedgwick's cubist perspective effects are again multiple and contradictory. Read from the top or bottom, the green circle seems to be flat and decorative like the yellow paint it is figured against. But read from the right side, the fawn, in left profile, seems to have stepped *into* green water with some depth and recession. If so, then it seeks relief for its hot feet as well as from its thirst in this cool oasis, green against the hot desert sand. This is an image of infantile bodily nourishment that Sedgwick associated with reading Proust's more reparative volumes and that she signaled by the resemblance between the oasis and a breast seen in right profile. The box's desert-like scene, meanwhile, had preoccupied her from her adolescence, as revealed by her early poetic fascination with the Old Testament Saul, David, and Jonathan as well as imperial adventurers Richard Burton and T. E. Lawrence, among other queer desert dwellers.[136]

On the right wing, Sedgwick depicts a related scene: a more mature spotted stag, seen from the rear, stood again in a green lake or patch of shadow, perhaps cast from a nearby wood to the right, but whose decorative flatness again refuses an easy perspectival reading. Above the stag, or perhaps reflected in the water, is a deep-red sun, while the stag's attention seems to have been caught by both the fawn, perhaps its offspring, perhaps the object of its desire, and the central scrolls, evoking perhaps the potential gustatory pleasures of mulberry paper. The swelling abdominal green patch that extends beyond the right wing again suggests the stag in utero, the red circle a comfortingly adjacent nipple or placenta. Taking the wings together, Sedgwick encourages viewers to imagine again the close relation between being inside a box, book,

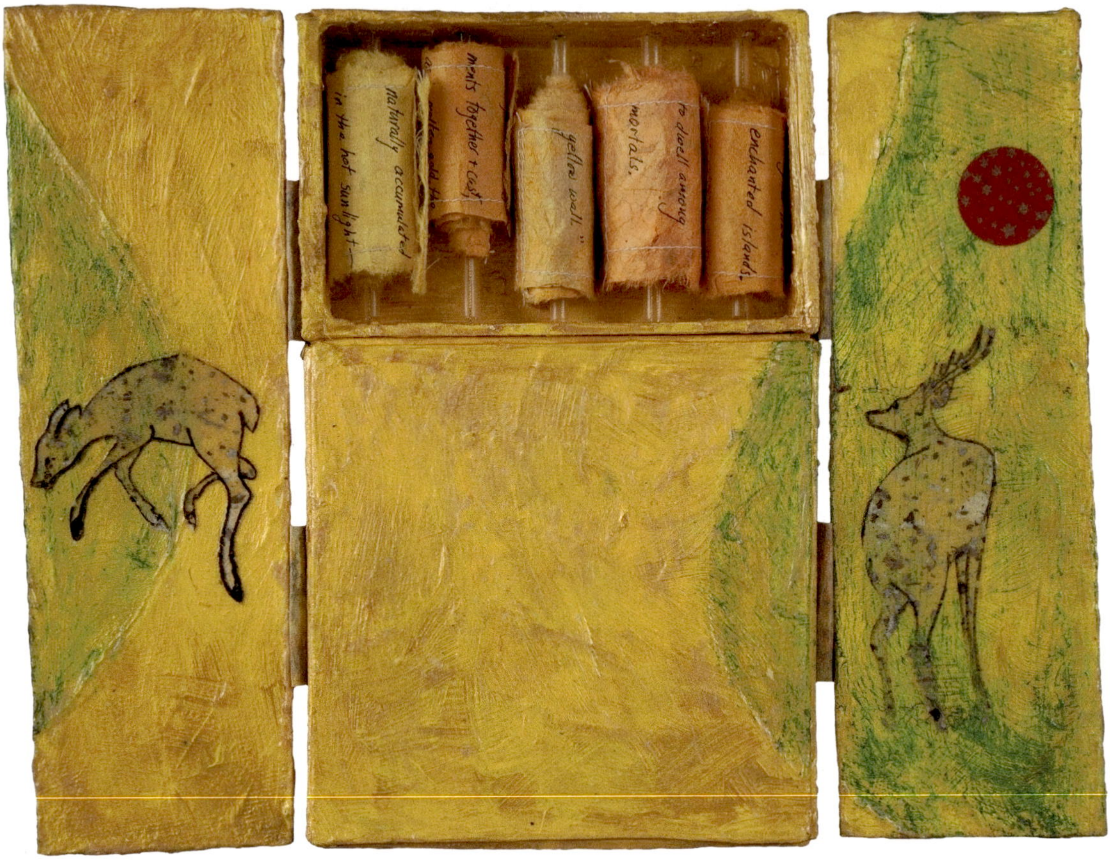

Figure 6.21. Eve Kosofsky Sedgwick, *Scroll Book (Yellow/Gold/Gratitude)*, 2005. Photograph: Kevin Ryan. Collection of H. A. Sedgwick. © H. A. Sedgwick

closet, and maternal body; reparative, claustral, containing experiences of being within the "kind of skin that sheer textual attention can weave around a reading body."[137]

Sedgwick locates in the upper niche of the central section five scrolls fashioned from thick, textured handmade mulberry paper in pale yellow green, orange, and orange gold, its ragged edges unusually hemmed with white cotton to prevent tearing. Sedgwick inscribes Proust's text on these in dark ink by hand. As a result, the box brings into relation two different religious traditions: the familiar golden ground of Byzantine icons and Buddhist scroll paintings, although here she employs text, rather than imagery, on her scrolls, locating the *animalier* imagery on the wings.

If the location of Proust's text on the upper shelves of this closet recalls Sedgwick's first 1990 essay on the author, as in the essay she does not make objectifying him straightforward. To read his words, viewers first must get access to the scrolls, impossible behind the vitrine glass of the Harvard display, where only a fraction of the different sentences were visible, requiring a reader with an encyclopedic, verbatim knowledge of Proust to recognize the quotations without accompanying footnotes. On opening the box in the archive, meanwhile, spectators are actively implicated in its queer unveiling.

Rather than reproduce Proust's text in standardized, "invisible" block print, Sedgwick orients it perpendicular to the viewer's visual plane and copies it out in her idiomatic hand, against textured, colored paper that characteristically reduces the contrast of text and ground. Unlike the pages of a codex, where multiple paragraphs are laid out across the spread, in *Scroll Book* Sedgwick limits the spectator's access to Proust's words to the unrolled area, the shortness of the phrases she employs for individual lines maximizing the interruptive, disciplining, erotic enjambment she delighted in.

The scroll form also pulls in a further familiar corporeal direction, nodding back to the epistemology of the water closet.[138] The generous supply of toilet paper–like scrolls identifies Proust's text with various forms of urethrality and anality; a urination that informed the imagery of the first passage Sedgwick transcribed from *Swann's Way*: "When an hour struck, you would have said not that it broke upon the calm of the day, but that it relieved the day of its superfluity, and that the steeple, with the indolent, painstaking exactitude of a person who has nothing else to do, had simply—in order to squeeze out and let fall the few golden drops which had slowly and naturally accumulated in the hot sunlight—pressed, at a given moment, the distended surface of the silence."[139] Several things point to Sedgwick's thalassic interests, including the fact that this was the only passage unrolled from the scroll at Harvard, clearly legible from "in order to squeeze" until the end. Readers might think of the vocabulary of *relief*, as in *relieving yourself*; and *painstaking*, not a million miles from *piss-taking*; as well as the excretion of a "superfluity," with its conjuring of *fluidity*. There is also a urethra-like steeple "squeeze[ing] out and let[ting] fall the few golden drops which had slowly and naturally accumulated," which had "pressed" the "distended surface" of the bladder-like silence. These piss-golden drops seem to have stained the box and dyed the usually white toilet-roll scrolls in colors that range across a urinary orange-yellow spectrum. As read through Sedgwick's corpus, Proust's scene again recalls her "Bathroom Song" and Beatrix's moonlight flit to London, where, en route to see the equally welcoming "dome of St. Paul's spread silvery," she urinates in the broads.[140]

The text on Sedgwick's second scroll also derived from *Swann's Way*. This time, in addition to eliding the start of Proust's sentence, she removed some of his middle clauses and phrases between the sentences she was working with/in. "She would push back her hair with both hands, and her forehead, her whole face would seem to grow larger; then, suddenly, some ordinary human thought . . . would flash from her eyes like a ray of gold. . . . These moments did not occur in vain. By the process of memory, Swann joined the fragments together and cast, as in molten gold, the image of an Odette compact of kindness and tranquility."[141] In employing this passage, Sedgwick suggests a parallel between Odette's pushing back her hair to reveal her face and the viewer opening the box to display its two-story golden interior, with the scrolls at the height of the forehead; a surface that similarly flashes out rays of glossy yellow paint. In addition, the *Scroll Book* evokes Sedgwick's Swann-like procedure of quotation as, like him, she joined fragments together on a scroll within a box whose gloss paint still seems liquid, and molten, like Odette's image. Again like Swann's fantasy of Odette, the box's imagistic environment is tranquil enough that deer can peacefully drink; the stag interested in, not startled by, what is surrounding him.

We have already encountered the third passage Sedgwick chose, from *The Captive*, the famous sentences in which Bergotte has a fatal heart attack in front of Vermeer's *View of Delft*: "He noticed for the first time some small figures in blue, that the sand was pink, and finally, the precious substance of the tiny patch of yellow wall. His dizziness increased, he fixed his gaze on the precious little patch of wall. . . . 'That's how I ought to have written,' he said. 'My last books are too dry, I ought to have gone over them with a few layers of color, made my language precious, in itself, like this little patch of yellow wall.'"[142] While Vermeer's sand is pink, Bergotte's thoughts of sand perhaps explain the sandy-yellow palette of the *Scroll Book*. Hung vertically, spectators might also experience the box itself, with its wardrobe-like form, as a parallel patch of yellow against a wall.

Sedgwick's fourth scroll returns the viewer to *Swann's Way* and brings back to life an earlier Bergotte, folding back on itself Proust's complex reflective temporal scheme and suggesting his reincarnation through the successive Buddhist scroll format. "If she should ask her parents whether anyone were coming to dinner, she would be answered by those two syllables, radiant with light, by the name of that golden guest who was to her no more than an old friend of the family, Bergotte, . . . and above all, when she went to visit other towns, he would be walking by her side, unrecognized and glorious, like the gods who came down of old to dwell among mortals."[143] Again viewers find the radiant gold light saturating the box, suggesting, perhaps, a similarly glorious two-syllabled "Marcel" inspiring Sedgwick's daily mystical devotion, especially since the *Scroll Book* characteristically recalls a modestly fashioned homemade altar, with Proust appearing, in scroll form, as a kind of divinity, or multiple minidivinities, akin to the intermittently luminous *lares* that preoccupied Sedgwick's circa 2007 artist's book, *Last Days of Pompei*.[144]

The final sentence Sedgwick employed derived from *Within a Budding Grove*: "A personality, a soul was latent there which linked it secretly to the afternoon light, so different from any other light in the gulf which spread beneath our feet its sparkling tide of gold out of which the bluish sofas and vaporous tapestries emerged like enchanted islands."[145] Here, Sedgwick's eroticized-desert aesthetics again come to mind in the idea of a latent, T. E. Lawrence–like personality somehow secreted within the afternoon light of the gulf and revealing as a "sparkling tide" the water from which her beached deer drink. Finally, the passage returns to mind the quietly sublime, Virgilian vision Sedgwick has toward the end of her autobiography, where, like Aeneas, she "encounter[s] a stranger / Venus" and guesses

> just from the rosy
> glow of [her] neck and [her] feet,
> and [her] stately step,
>
> though too late, "Surely,
> stranger, you are a goddess.
> Surely my mother."[146]

The queerly erotic, maternal, and grand-maternal, gently but powerfully reparative aesthetic of Proust, then, its color, texture, energy, language, images, idiom, syntax, and structure, everywhere inspired Sedgwick's *Scroll Book* and late work more generally, just as her ongoingly, generously fat, divinely reparative craft has inspired this book.

Refusing again Freudian developmental teleology in favor of a kaleidoscopic Kleinian positionality, Sedgwick's last exhibition, *Works in Fiber, Paper, and Proust*, in many ways brought her, and brings us, full circle, its patchwork title recalling the subtitle of her first show, *Floating Columns: Works in Silk, Paper, and Soie Mariée*. In her last Proustian works, Sedgwick continued to be fascinated by the creatively metamorphic life of silkworms, and, inspired by their silken productions, she characteristically thickened up the flat two-dimensionality of codex book paper to the fatter *two-and-a-half-dimensionality* of her mulberry papers while also increasingly stretching out the comparatively svelte codex book into more three-dimensional loom, scroll, and accordion books. The complex, multipart forms of these exhibits also simultaneously returned to the *cybernetic* warps and wefts of Sedgwick's earlier weavings, to encourage a richer, queerer, more embodied, and *reparative* phenomenology of reading that was as visual and tactile as it was verbal; that was less argumentative, critical, and propositional and more Buddhist or Taoist metamorphic, cubist multiperspectival

The earlier Buddhist texts may have given way to an apparently more exclusive love for Proust, but Sedgwick's selections from *In Search of Lost Time* revealed a similarly rich and reparative, polytheistic divinity-scape. The queer little sculptural gods of *Floating Columns* remained a source of reparative reflection. The weathered, ravaged, damaged, decapitated Buddhas, somehow still surviving, magnetic, were joined in the last show again by Kuanyin, alongside a new *trans* arrival: Proust's bearded goddesses, reminding us that one of the rejected titles for Sedgwick's last monograph was *Proust and the Queer Little Gods*.

Sedgwick may have had ongoingly mixed feelings about the NAMES quilt, but its patchwork aesthetic nevertheless continued to haunt productively her own reparative craft. Complex, unpredictable, radically transformative life cycles, marine now as well as insect, coupled with the metamorphic water and weather cycles, also continued to feed Sedgwick, whose soft sculptural and puppet interests, as evidenced in *In the Bardo*, reappeared in her later *Polyp* and marionettes. With so many sources of queer nourishment, Sedgwick's craft remained a shamelessly *fat* art to the end.

Sedgwick may have gotten increasingly less interested in her own autobiographical first person, at least as it manifested verbally, after her 1999 autobiography, but her structural, textural, and chromatic idiom continued to be everywhere present in her later life, surrounding and infusing the quotations she delighted in recontextualizing.

CODA

"An Inward Accumulation of a Wealth of Materials"

For several reasons, *The Weather in Proust* (2005) would prove to be Eve Kosofsky Sedgwick's final exhibition, ending a roughly decade-long intense engagement with textiles that had begun around the time of her diagnosis with metastatic breast cancer in 1996. Her interest in fiber art began, as we have seen, with a sustained passion for scraps of secondhand kimono silk, which she carried back from her travels in Asia; their comforting materiality and metamorphic genealogy within the cocooned bodies of silkworms were both of interest to her as she began to experiment with *patchworking*.

In these early experimental pieces, Sedgwick employed a basic orthogonal warp and weft–like structure of overlapping swatches, in a color palette she shared with her then recently deceased friend, writer and painter Gary Fisher, perhaps in memory of him, certainly in identification with him; and stitched, sloppily, in drool-like lines that recalled her younger brother David's childhood comfort pillow. Sedgwick had early intuited, as we have seen, from her deep knowledge of Victorian literary, visual, and material culture that the "monstrous," "strange," and "terrible" practice of embroidery, involving "tedious labor" and "sheer wastage of (typically female) eyesight," was not for her.[1]

Sedgwick's "left-over" or "waste" silk patches were, nevertheless, central to her early attempts, as we learn from her autobiography, to think and feel through her painful discovery, in 1996, that her breast cancer had metastasized to her spine. Sedgwick would keep these early patchworks safely tucked away, returning to at least one in her subsequent exhibition, *Floating Columns*.

Picking up on the warp and weft–like structure of the early patchworks, Sedgwick next turned her increasingly skilled hand to *weaving*, to which she devoted more of her time and in which she developed more of an expertise; taking classes, buying looms, and even, for a while, contemplating becoming a professional weaver. In her weaving practice, Sedgwick again employed swatches of secondhand kimonos as her weft, continuing her explorations of the phenomenology of silk, imagining her weavings both as forms of self-decoration and as more conceptual craft objects through which to practice thinking in a conceptual domain that she was becoming increasingly interested in, thanks to her discovery of mid-twentieth-century affect theorist Silvan Tomkins: the one where *n > 2 but < infinity*, the *cybernetic* zone, as she and Adam Frank would frame it in their writing at the time.[2] As she sought to push her thinking in this analog, nondualistic direction, the binary combination of warp and weft, and almost endlessly different textures and tones of threads and swatches, represented an excellent example of a repertoire of possibility, a "color wheel of different" possibilities in fact, a "periodic table of infinitely recombinable elements," both analog and digital, that she was increasingly eager to explore.[3]

Silk would also prove central to Sedgwick's third project, and her first public, group exhibition, *Floating Columns*, which involved works in handmade mulberry paper, silk, and *soie mariée*, all again involving the earlier metamorphic labors of the silkworm, which Sedgwick largely fused together with heat. After the patterned, chromatic, and decorative preoccupations of her earlier work, the exhibition was Sedgwick's first foray into figuration, involving sewn photographs of mutilated Thai Buddha statues, frequently decapitated and missing other body parts. Sedgwick employed these alongside short, sentence-length texts from a range of popular anglophone Buddhist sources; an emerging interest in Buddhism that would color and aerate her thinking for the remainder of her life.

Sedgwick's passion for sewn photographs likely derived, as we have seen, from her sustained interest, in this period, in Andy Warhol, on whom she had been working, in the mid-1990s, with several of her friends and students at Duke. The iconography of *Floating Columns* also included a second metamorphic icon, in addition to the fibrous products of the silkworm: the dragonfly; an interest in forms of life undergoing unwilled bodily changes that would again recur in her later work on Marcel Proust.

The Buddhism first seen in *Floating Columns* was at the heart of Sedgwick's fourth project, and the subject of her first solo exhibition, *In the Bardo*. The show involved a range of suspended lightweight and soft decapitated Sedgwick-like sculptures, dressed in clothes she had made for them, floating in midair, and set in motion by passing breezes and spectators. Both the scale and the number of exhibits were significantly greater than anything Sedgwick had attempted before. The show combined her early penchant for making her own clothes, often because she was unable to find anything she desired in her size, with her increasingly sustained thinking about the pregnant, poignant time periods, the *bardo*s, between life and death, and between lives, and about how to navigate them most skillfully. The exhibition incorporated a number of Sedgwick's early silk patchworks, as well as fused silk components, a sign of her sustained habit of repurposing earlier experimental works in her later exhibitions, another example of her interest in metamorphosis; interests also present in the show's incorporation of some of her own body scans.

Sedgwick's penultimate exhibition, *Bodhisattva Fractal World*, returned to her earlier interest in wall-mounted patchwork, fusing together a more diverse array of components and at a significantly larger scale of individual exhibits. These included examples of Japanese death haiku, a poetic form that had long interested Sedgwick because of its centrality to the 1993 autobiography of her favorite poet, James Merrill's *A Different Person*. There were also further kimono silk swatches and more of Sedgwick's body scans as well as cyanotypes—an early, feminist form of camera-less blueprint photography—of statues and conservation X-rays of the Chinese bodhisattva Kuanyin and her masculine Indian predecessor, Avalokiteshvara.

Bodhisattva Fractal World also featured a further lo-fi craft form dear to Sedgwick's heart, rubber stamps, employed for the letters of many of the texts, alongside two more complex Asian textile techniques: *shibori*, or tie-dyeing, and *suminagashi*, or floating ink on water, a marbled form providing the background to the cover of Sedgwick's third book, *Epistemology of the Closet*. The *Reality Is Flowerlike* collage, from the same period as *Bodhisattva Fractal World*, suggested that Warhol continued to loom large in Sedgwick's thinking.

Sedgwick's final exhibition, *The Weather in Proust*, featured a number of her favorite passages from *In Search of Lost Time*, recontextualized by new cyanotypes of Kuanyin statues and Warholian screen prints, as well as printed on mulberry scrolls and on a variety of book-like structures, some resembling accordions, others looms. Also patchworked into the mix were popular prints of Proust himself; photocopies of pages from his books; and *shibori* silk scarfs bearing passages from *In Search of Lost Time*. Sedgwick also again resurrected and metamorphosed a piece of *shibori* from *In the Bardo*, whose new incarnation was as the bearer of a further passage from Proust.

The Weather in Proust proved to be Sedgwick's final show, although she continued to run an amateur studio art course, How to Do Things with Words and Other Materials, for her graduate students at CUNY, where students thought about experimental artists' books and were encouraged to make their own, at Sedgwick's home studio apartment in Manhattan and in her CUNY office, both then treasure troves of tools and materials she made generously available for use.

After a sustained period of comparative well-being in which Sedgwick could largely treat herself at home, her range of medical options began to diminish. In summer 2008, Sedgwick's condition worsened, and, in winter 2009, the cancer in her spine began to impinge on her spinal cord, meaning that she ultimately required a wheelchair. In April 2009, Sedgwick entered the Beth Israel Medical Center hospice in Lower Manhattan, whose gift shop panda had, earlier, poignantly appeared in one of Sedgwick's *Panda Alphabet Valentines*. Sedgwick died at the medical center on April 12, 2009.

Twice in her published writings, Sedgwick returned to a passage (ca. 1905) from Henry James's notebooks that she made deliciously notorious. In her first analysis, in a footnote within *Epistemology of the Closet*, she characterized the passage as James's "rich . . . , pregnant" address to his "male muse" and as an "invocation of 'fisting-as-*écriture*.'"[4] Sedgwick's second meditation on the passage occurred in her circa 1995–96 essay "Shame, Theatricality, and Queer Performativity: Henry James's *The Art of the Novel*," ultimately collected in *Touching Feeling*. There, she characterized the passage as the "best condensation" of what James's late prefaces "press us to recognize as his most characteristic and fecund relation to his own anal eroticism." This was a "scene of fisting," according to Sedgwick, ripe with intertexts including Alexander Pope's *The Dunciad* (1728–43), with its "obstetric hand feeling for wealth in the rectum," and William Shakespeare's *The Tempest* (1610–11), to which we have often had recourse, with Sedgwick noting that Ariel's song and Pope's poem both here "undergo . . . a sea-change to become a virtually absolute symbol of imaginative value."[5]

Since Sedgwick's passing, I have often returned to this passage and found it deeply comforting, as well as queerly sexy, increasingly recognizing that if the fat excesses of this melancholy book have worked hard to keep Sedgwick alive in my mind, I could never return her to life, no matter how hard I have tried, for nearly fifteen years. And yet, more happily, so much remains to be felt and thought, discovered and done, within Sedgwick's curiosity cabinet of an archive down in Durham, North Carolina, and so much remains, not just inside me and this book, of her life and work.

> I sit here, after long weeks, at any rate, in front of my arrears, with an inward accumulation of material of which I feel the wealth, and as to which I can only invoke my familiar demon of patience, who always comes, doesn't he? when I call. He is here with me in front of this cool green Pacific—he sits close and I feel his breath, which cools and steadies and

inspires, on my cheek. Everything sinks in: nothing is lost. Everything abides and fertilizes and renews its golden promise, making me think with closed eyes of deep and grateful longing when, in the full summer days of L[amb] H[ouse], my long dusty adventure over, I shall be able to [plunge] my hand, my arm, *in*, deep and far, and up to the shoulder—into the heavy bag of remembrance—of suggestion—of imagination—of art—and fish out every little figure and felicity, every little fact and fancy that can be to my purpose. These things are all packed away, now, thicker than I can penetrate, deeper than I can fathom, and there let them rest for the present, in their sacred cool darkness, till I shall let in upon them the mild still light of dear old L[amb] H[ouse]—in which they will begin to gleam and glitter and take form like the gold and jewels of a mine.[6]

ACKNOWLEDGMENTS

Reparative Craft has been nearly twenty years in the making. Thanks to everyone who has persevered with me as this book metamorphosed. At Duke, I am grateful to the readers, for their transformative suggestions; and to Ken Wissoker, Ryan Kendall, Lisa Lawley, and Alejandra Mejía, as well as the late Lauren Berlant, for their ongoing enthusiasm. That neither Lauren nor Jonathan Goldberg is here to see this book in print is a source of deep regret to me.

In the book's long gestation, I discovered I was carrying monographic twins. Thanks to Vincent W. J. van Gerven Oei and Eileen Joy at Punctum Press for bringing out the sister volume, *Queer and Bookish: Eve Kosofsky Sedgwick as a Book Artist*; as well as an older sibling, *Bathroom Songs: Eve Kosofsky Sedgwick as a Poet*, including Eve's uncollected poetry. I see now that these three books form a kind of memorial tryptic.

This book would have been impossible without the support of the Eve Kosofsky Foundation, which subsidized its publication and commissioned its suite of color photographs. At the foundation, I am indebted to Hal A. Sedgwick and Sarah McCarry, especially in the early days of this project, when they gave me sustained access to Eve's archive at a moment when we were all in mourning and long before it was publicly available. For more on the archive (which is now at the Sallie Bingham Center for Women's History and Culture, at Duke), the foundation, and Kevin Ryan's photographs of Eve's artworks, visit https://evekosofskysedgwick.net/art/artworks.

Over the course of writing this book, I co-organized several Sedgwick memorial conferences at York, Manchester, and the CUNY Graduate Center. For help in those three locations, I am indebted to Angus Brown, Joshua Wilner, and Jackie Stacey. To all the participants, thank you for your intelligence, creativity, generosity, kindness, openness, and willingness to travel. In addition, I gave several talks of material that ended up in the book, and for invitations I'm grateful to the late Jutta Vincent at the University of Birmingham; to Ariane Mildenberg at the University of Kent; and to Carol Mavor, formerly at the University of Manchester.

At the University of York, I would like to thank my colleagues in the Art History Department. Wot Larks we have. I'm grateful to my former fellow travelers in the Complexity Theory Reading Group, especially Leo Caves, Jeanne Nuechterlein, Susan Stepney, Elizabeth Tyler, and Richard Walsh, who regularly blew my mind with their smarts and tolerated my awkward, well-intentioned splashing around in their pool. To my former and current PhD students, I can't tell how much I've learned from Team Jason(!).

Many of Eve's former chums are now, somehow, magically, also mine. Thank you to Mary Baine Campbell, Jonathan Flatley, Adam Frank, Katy Hawkins, Katie Kent, Joseph Litvak, Douglas Martin, Ti Meyerhoff, Michael Moon, Simon Watney, and Carolyn Williams for letting me join your gang. I always feel like a cool kid in your company.

I've said it before, and I'll say it again. (In fact, I'll quote Ani DiFranco again.) We owe our lives to the people that we love. For me, indispensable are Charlotte Anderson, Connor Anderson, Meg Boulton, Nicole Devarenne, Christine Edwards, Coen Edwards, Dylan Edwards, Mike Edwards, Paul Edwards, Tracy Edwards, Alison Farrell, Helen Finch, Adam Frost, Rose B. Ganim, Sarah Haessler, Amy Kapzcinsky, Kate Lewis, Beth Linklater, Nicola McDonald, Mary McFarlane, Ariane Mildenberg, Sarah Monks, James Nash, Neko, Diane Nelson, Ben Nichols, Melanie Patrick, Monica Pearl, Jacki Piper, Sophie Raudnitz, Sara Salih, Tamsin Silver, Stuart Taberner, Stephanie Taylor, Elizabeth Tyler, and Clare Westall.

This book is dedicated to Eve Kosofsky Sedgwick. The world without you feels like Memphis after Elvis. I probably got almost everything wrong, but I hope you'd have got a kick out of this. Here's to more iced tea and fries for breakfast, in another time and place.

NOTES

Introduction. Reparative Craft

1. For the discussion so far, see Miller, "All about Eve" and "Reviewing Eve." See also K. Hawkins, "Woven Spaces" and "Re-Creating Eve"; Nelson, "In the Bardo"; Cvetkovich, "Utopia of Ordinary Habit"; Edwards, "Introduction: *Bathroom Songs*?," 68–74, and "For Beauty." For a more recent assessment, see Goldberg, *Come as You Are*, 85–124.

2. Some of the later textiles were likely made for an "experimental seminar/studio workshop" Sedgwick taught at the CUNY Graduate Center, "How to Do Things with Words and Other Materials," in 2004 and 2008. This invited students to conceptualize and practice different ways of combining written text and other visual media, making unconventional use of the materiality of the written word and its support, with students creating a portfolio "exploring different aspects of the complex relations among language, materiality, and visuality." Quoted in Herring, "Sedgwick's 'Other Materials,'" 5.

3. For Sedgwick's aversion to a developmental psychology of *stages*, in favor of a theorization of alternating affective *positions*, see *Touching Feeling*, 93–123; and *Weather*, 123–43. In the book I use, interchangeably, ideas of collage, assemblage, patchwork, and quilting, despite their different art historical genealogies and conceptions. For example, while collage has the highest art historical status, as a form of modernist, masculinist self-referentiality, quilting boasts a proud African American genealogy, and assemblage has been recently understood as a model for queer and trans self- and world-making. Sedgwick's preferred term was *patchwork*, but, in mixing up the vocabularies, and their traditions, I want to insist on the Black/feminist craft origins and queer and trans implications of collage, and the high-modernist, complex semiotics of quilting. For more on trans assemblage, see Stryker, "My Words to Victor Frankenstein" and "More Words."

4. In postponing a critique of Sedgwick's "cross-cultural perspective," I have been, to quote Sedgwick and Adam Frank on Silvan Tomkins, "conscious of wishing to defer a certain amount of accounting, not only out of protectiveness for [Sedgwick], but out of a sense that, if the deferral proved possible, the terms of that accounting might be richly

altered." Sedgwick and Frank, "Shame in the Cybernetic Fold," in Sedgwick *Touching Feeling*, 117.

5. For more *loving* reader relations to Sedgwick, see Kelleher, "If Love Were All"; and Allan, "Falling in Love." Heather Love suggests that "to read Sedgwick *always* reparatively is to miss the energizing force of paranoia in her work" and "reduces the kinds of relations we might now cultivate with her." In this book, I leave Love to her "hard work of deidealisation." Love, "Truth and Consequences," 240. For more on the need to deidealize queer theory, see Amin, *Disturbing Attachments*.

6. Hoffmann, *Japanese Death Poems*. In a recent discussion of Sedgwick, Cassie Westwood describes this as an "ardent reading" practice in which "even the most devoted of readers . . . tend to remember parts" of a text "rather than the whole thing," "fragments" to be "turned round in our memories like the melody from a music box." Westwood, "Queer Art," 50. For more on Sedgwick's encounters with Proust, see Goldstein, "Some Scenes in Proust"; Litvak, "*The Weather in Proust* (Review)"; and Butler, "Proust at the End."

7. For more on Sedgwick's emergence as a textile artist in the mid-1990s, see her "Making Things, Practicing Emptiness," in *Weather*, 69–122; and my *Queer and Bookish*, 169–212, 213–58.

8. Sedgwick, *Touching Feeling*, 149. For other experiments with reparative reading, see Bradway, *Queer Experimental Literature*; Johnson, *Cultural Memory*; and K. Hawkins, *Thinking Feelingly*.

9. Sedgwick, *Weather*, 104–5. For more on Kuanyin, see Blofeld, *Bodhisattva of Compassion*; Karcher, *Kuan Yin Oracle*; Palmer and Ramsay, *Kuan Yin Chronicles*; and especially Yu, *Kuan-yin*.

10. Sedgwick, *Fat Art*, 67–68.

11. Sedgwick, *Between Men*, 196–97.

12. For example, in her 1985 essay "A Poem Is Being Written," Sedgwick noted that "in among the many ways" she identified "as a woman, the identification as a gay person is a firmly male one, identification 'as' a gay man." *Tendencies*, 209.

13. Sedgwick, "Response to C. Jacob Hale"; and its draft (ca. 1997), "Comments on Judith Halberstam and Jacob Hale Papers," in the Sedgwick archive. This is now located in the Sallie Bingham Center for Women's History and Culture at Duke University.

14. Sedgwick, "Queerer than Fiction."

15. Sedgwick, *Touching Feeling*, 123–52, 149–50. For a range of responses to the essay, see my "Reparative Reading at 21."

16. Sedgwick, *Touching Feeling*, 149.

17. Sedgwick, *Touching Feeling*, 149–50. For more on "sloppy" and amateur craft, see Paterson and Surette, *Sloppy Craft*; and Holroyd, "Review of *Amateur Craft*."

18. Sedgwick, *Touching Feeling*, 150.

19. For more on the so-called New Formalism and the return to decontextualized close reading, see Gallop, "Ethics of Reading"; Wolfson, "Reading for Form"; and Levinson, "What Is New Formalism?" For related musings on languorous reading, see Hanson, "Languorous Critic."

20. Sedgwick, *Touching Feeling*, 150–51.

21. For more, see *Tendencies*, 52–72; and *Weather*, 123–43.

22. Sedgwick, *Weather*, 208.

23. Sedgwick, *Touching Feeling*, 8.

24. Sedgwick, *Tendencies,* 187. For the *locus classicus* of these interests, see Sedgwick's notorious 1985 essay "A Poem Is Being Written," with its account of *spanking* meter, enjambment as *stretching*, arousing scenes of sadomasochistic punishment, and female anal eroticism. *Tendencies*, 177–214. For a poignant recent account of the risks of Sedgwick-inspired queer pedagogy in the (in some ways) very different context of the post-#MeToo moment, see Doyle, *Shadow of My Shadow*, especially 123–35.

25. Sedgwick, *Tendencies*, 15–16.

26. For the essay, see *Tendencies*, 73–103. For a fuller account of my inaugural encounter with Sedgwick, see Edwards, *Eve Kosofsky Sedgwick*, 2–3.

27. Sedgwick, *Gary in Your Pocket*. For discussion, see Haye and Sedgwick, "All About Eve"; Arthur Frank, "Bodies, Sex, and Death"; Reid-Pharr, "Shock of Gary Fisher"; Hanson, "Future's Eve"; and Muñoz, "Race, Sex"; as well as Edwards, *Queer and Bookish*, 89–134.

28. The early poems are from Sedgwick, *Fat Art*, 74–79, 83–85; the late poems are collected in Edwards, *Bathroom Songs*, 209–10, 234–36. (My *Bathroom Songs* is a collection of essays on Sedgwick's poetry along with previously unpublished poems. The poems will be cited via the book throughout.) For more on Sedgwick's urethral eroticism, see Edwards, *Bathroom Songs*, 31–37. For more on Sedgwick's interest in James's anality, see *Epistemology*, 182–212; and *Touching Feeling*, 27–35; and on Charles Dickens's anality, *Between Men*, 161–79.

29. For more on the phenomenology of reading, see Iser, "Reading Process." For a bravura account of queer phenomenology, see Ahmed, *Queer Phenomenology*.

30. Sedgwick, *Tendencies*, 5.

31. Sedgwick, *Touching Feeling*, 84. For a recent "descriptive turn" in literary studies, see Marcus et al., "Building a Better Description"; Best and Marcus, "Surface Reading"; and Love, "Close but Not Deep."

32. Sedgwick, "Teaching 'Experimental Critical Writing.' "

33. Sedgwick, "Teaching 'Experimental Critical Writing.' "

34. Sedgwick, "Teaching 'Experimental Critical Writing.' "

35. Sedgwick, "Teaching 'Experimental Critical Writing,'" 113.

36. Sedgwick, *Fat Art*, 20. For more on close reading as "a way of listening," see Gallop, "Ethics of Reading," 12; and my "Reparative Reading at 21."

37. Sedgwick, *Touching Feeling*, 105–6. For more on Tomkins, see Sedgwick and Frank, "Shame" and *Shame*.

38. For more, see Butler, "Capacity."

39. Sedgwick, *Fat Art*, 152.

40. Sedgwick and Moon, "Divinity: A Dossier, a Performance Piece, a Little Understood Emotion," in *Tendencies*, 215–51. For an alternate *thin* aesthetics, presuming that less is more, see Berlant, "Two Girls" and "Pedagogies"; and Crawford, "Slender Trouble."

41. Sedgwick, *Fat Art*, 15.

42. Sedgwick, *Fat Art*, 35.

Chapter 1. The First Four Pages of a Texture Book (ca. 1996–99)

1. Parker, *Subversive Stitch*. For a recent reappraisal, see McBrinn, *Queering the Subversive Stitch*.

2. Sedgwick, *Epistemology*, 174–75

3. Sedgwick, *Epistemology*, 174–75.

4. Stoller, *Stitch 'n Bitch*, *Stitch 'n Bitch Nation*, *Stitch 'n Bitch Crochet*, *Son of Stitch 'n Bitch*, and *Stitch 'n Bitch Superstar*.

5. For more, see Moon, *Disseminating Whitman*, 12–13, 50, 156.

6. Sedgwick, *Fat Art*, 29. Sedgwick employed the apocryphal Freudian phrase in one of her advice columns for *MAMM* magazine, a journal for those living with breast cancer. For more, see Sedgwick, "Scar."

7. For Sigmund Freud's and Sedgwick's differing experiences of cancer, see Lin, *Freud's Jaw*, especially 82–114.

8. For more on Sedgwick's S/M fantasy life, see Tsoukala, "Reading *A Poem*." For a related poem in which Sedgwick imagines looking back, with pleasure, on an earlier painful scene, see Sedgwick, "Forsan et haec olim meminisse juvabit," in Edwards, *Bathroom Songs*, 208.

9. Sedgwick, *Dialogue*, 48.

10. Sedgwick, *Dialogue*, 218.

11. Sedgwick, *Dialogue*, 218–19.

12. Sedgwick, *Dialogue*, 219. For Sedgwick's "tender buttons," see Kent, "'Excreate a No Sense'" and "'Surprising Recognition'"; and my *Bathroom Songs*, 58–61.

13. For more on the culture of the kimono, see Hayao and Nobuhiko, *Robes of Elegance*; Milhaupt, *Kimono*; and Jackson, *Kimono*.

14. For more on the *Panda Alphabet Valentines*, see Edwards, *Queer and Bookish*, 259–306.

15. Sedgwick, *Tendencies*, 9.

16. For more, see Kopplin et al., *Flickwerk*; and Keulemans, "Geo-Cultural Conditions of *Kintsugi*."

17. Sedgwick, *Touching Feeling*, 149–50.

18. Sedgwick, *Touching Feeling*, 150.

19. Sedgwick, *Dialogue*, 206.

20. Quite different from this random stitching is the *nuihaku* embroidery found on traditional kimonos.

21. Sedgwick, *Dialogue*, 206. For Sedgwick's interest in anality, see *Between Men*, 161–202; *Epistemology*, 182–212; *Tendencies*, 73–104, 177–214; *Touching Feeling*, 35–66; and *Weather*, 166–82.

22. Chandler, *Learning to Weave*, 205.

23. Sedgwick, *Dialogue*, 206.

24. The dating of Sedgwick's patchworks is difficult. While we might be tempted to date them ca. 2000, given her documented trip to Japan, she was employing kimono silk as early as the *Panda Alphabet Valentines* (ca. 1996), as we have seen. *A Dialogue on Love* also suggests a date before 1999.

25. Derrida, "Silkworm," 3, 5.

26. Derrida, "Silkworm," 6, 28.

27. Derrida, "Silkworm," 49.

28. Derrida, "Silkworm," 49–50. For more on late style, see Said, *On Late Style*.

29. For more, see Vincentelli, "Japanese Sashiko Textiles."

30. Sudo, *East Quilts West*, 9–10, 20. For more, see Stevens and Wada, *Kimono Inspiration*, 160, 195; and Shin-ichiro and Williams, *Riches from Rags*.

31. Stevens and Wada, *Kimono Inspiration*, 177.

32. Milhaupt, *Kimono*, 141, 148, 158, 219, 237; Stevens and Wada, *Kimono Inspiration*, 109.

33. Milhaupt, *Kimono*, 83, 126.

34. Sedgwick, *Dialogue*, 207.

35. For more, see P. Hawkins, "Naming Names"; Moon, "Memorial Rags"; Pearl, "American Grief"; and Bryan-Wilson, *Fray*, 181–250.

36. Sedgwick, *Tendencies*, 264. For a related discussion, see *Epistemology*, 141–50.

37. Sedgwick, *Tendencies*, 264. For a related discussion, see *Dialogue*, 213–14.

38. Sedgwick, *Tendencies*, 264.

39. Sedgwick, *Tendencies*, 264.

40. Sedgwick, *Tendencies*, 264.

41. Sedgwick, *Tendencies*, 264.

42. Sedgwick, *Tendencies*, 264.

43. Sedgwick, *Epistemology*, 243, 244n33.

44. Sedgwick, *Tendencies*, 264; *Fat Art*, 15.

45. Sedgwick, *Tendencies*, 264.

46. Sedgwick, *Tendencies*, 264–65.

47. Sedgwick, *Tendencies*, 265. For more, see Crimp, "Mourning and Militancy" and *Melancholia and Moralism*.

48. Sedgwick, *Tendencies*, 265. For a fuller discussion on how this relates to the Gettysburg Address, see Sedgwick, *Touching Feeling*, 67

49. For more on the film, see Lawrence, "AIDS"; a text Sedgwick knew, since it was published adjacent to her "Response to C. Jacob Hale," a text we have already encountered.

50. For more on ACT UP T-shirts in the context of the 1992 gay pride parade in New York City, see *Tendencies*, xi. On the textile overlaps between ACT UP and the quilt, see Bryan-Wilson, *Fray*, 218–19.

51. Sedgwick, *Tendencies*, 264–65.

52. For more on Sedgwick's relation to Fisher, see Sedgwick, *Gary in Your Pocket*. For discussion, see Haye and Sedgwick, "All About Eve"; Arthur Frank, "Bodies, Sex, and Death"; Reid-Pharr, "Shock of Gary Fisher"; Hanson, "'Future's Eve'"; and Muñoz, "Race, Sex"; as well as Edwards, *Queer and Bookish*, 89–134.

53. Sedgwick, *Gary in Your Pocket*, 290–91.

54. For more, see Sedgwick, *Touching Feeling*, 93–122. For Frank's later reflections on Tomkins, see Frank and Wilson, *Silvan Tomkins Handbook*.

Chapter 2. A Weft Is Being Beaten, or Weaving in the Cybernetic Fold (ca. 1996–99)

1. Sedgwick, *Fat Art*, 73.

2. Sedgwick, *Fat Art*, 73.

3. Sedgwick, *Weather*, 71, 75.

4. Cohen, "Lit Critics."

5. Sedgwick, *Gary in Your Pocket*, 279.

6. For Sedgwick's interest in queer homonyms, see *Tendencies*, 52–73.

7. Sedgwick, *Touching Feeling*, 93–94.

8. Sedgwick, *Touching Feeling*, 114–15.

9. Sedgwick, *Touching Feeling*, 95–96.

10. Sedgwick, *Touching Feeling*, 98–100.

11. Sedgwick, *Touching Feeling*, 100, 104.

12. Sedgwick, *Touching Feeling*, 101.

13. Sedgwick, *Touching Feeling*, 100–101, 110.

14. For example, see figure 1 in Sedgwick, *Epistemology* (30); and *Touching Feeling*, 101, 103, 105–6.

15. For more, see Dimmock, "Weak Theory."

16. Sedgwick, *Touching Feeling*, 105–6.

17. Sedgwick, *Touching Feeling*, 108, 112.

18. Sedgwick, *Touching Feeling*, 114, 117.

19. Sedgwick, *Touching Feeling*, 114, 117.

20. Sedgwick, *Touching Feeling*, 117.

21. For more, see Albers, *On Weaving*; Coxon et al., *Anni Albers*; Smith, "Architectonic" and *Bauhaus Weaving Theory*.

22. Krauss, "Grids," 50.

23. Sedgwick, *Dialogue*, 207.

24. Krauss, "Grids," 57, 60; Sedgwick, *Tendencies*, 8.

25. Krauss, "Grids," 60, 63–64. For a more materialized reading of Piet Mondrian's grids, see Bois, "Piet Mondrian."

26. Sedgwick, *Touching Feeling*, 117.

27. Sedgwick, *Dialogue*, 188–89; Merrill, *Collected Poems*, 361. Merrill bought his kimono on his first trip to Japan. He liked to wear it and was buried in it. Hammer, *James Merrill*, 488–90. For more on Sedgwick's relation to Merrill, see Sedgwick, "1001 Seances"; and Edwards, Introduction: *Bathroom Songs?*, 37–53.

28. For Sedgwick's earlier interest in blueprints as a book artist, see my *Queer and Bookish*, 81–88.

29. Merrill, *Collected Poems*, 560.

30. Merrill, *Collected Poems*, 560.

31. For more, see Halberstam, *Queer Art of Failure*.

32. For more on *suminagashi*, see Grunebaum, *How to Marbleize Paper*; Chambers, *Suminagashi*; and A. Brown, "Look with Your Hands," 77–80. For more on *shibori*, see Wada et al., *Shibori*; and Wada, *Memory on Cloth*.

33. Sedgwick, *Fat Art*, 12.

34. Albers, *On Weaving*, 13, 24–25, 38–39.

35. Albers, *On Weaving*, 39–40, 48, 65, 68, 70, 78.

36. Sutton and Sheehan, *Ideas in Weaving*, 10, 14–15, 32, 37, 39, 107.

37. Sutton and Sheehan, *Ideas in Weaving*, 10, 14–15, 32, 37, 39, 107.

38. Albers, *On Weaving*, 20, 47, 50, 74.

39. For examples, see R. Brown, *Weaving, Spinning, and Dyeing*; Mayer, *Clothing from the Hands*; and Chandler, *Learning to Weave*.

40. On Sedgwick's foot fetishism, to which we shall return, see *Tendencies*, which describes the foot as the "most universally repressed and mutilated of pleasure-taking organs" (205).

41. Sedgwick, *Weather*, 75.

42. For more, see Liz Williamson's website, https://lizwilliamson.com.au (accessed August 9, 2024); and that of the Penland School of Craft, https://penland.org (accessed August 9, 2024).

Chapter 3. *Floating Columns* (1999–2000)

1. Sedgwick first gave the talk at SUNY Stony Brook in November 1999 and then again at the CUNY Graduate Center in March 2000. For more, see Goldberg, *Come as You Are*, 85. The book is available as a free download at https://punctumbooks.com/titles/come-as-you-are-after-eve-kosofsky-sedgwick/ (accessed October 9, 2025).

2. Sedgwick, *Weather*, 106.

3. Sedgwick, *Weather*, 106. For more, see Barker, *Tibetan Prayer Flags*; and Wise, *Blessings on the Wind*.

4. Sedgwick, *Dialogue*, 207.

5. For more on the visual iconography of health and sickness in the Buddhist tradition, see Avedon et al., *Buddha's Art of Healing*.

6. For more on the floating world, see Kita, "Reconsidering Ukiyo-e."

7. The piece might recall so-called Japanese *yukata* quilts, made from pieces of blue-and-white traditional cotton, traditionally associated with summer and, in informal kimono form, worn to and from bathing; a bathing perhaps signaled by the "floating" context of the exhibition.

8. For Sedgwick's essay, see *Tendencies*, 109–29.

9. Derrida, "Silkworm," 3, 7, 28, 37–38, 49–51. In the context of Sedgwick's late-life bardo, viewers might also recall Michel de Montaigne's "On Solitude" essay, which argued that, at the "tail-end of life," when "our powers are failing," it is better to live "for ourselves," bringing our "thoughts and reflections back to ourselves and our own well-being" in readiness "for our departure," loving this or that but "marry[ing] nothing but ourselves" (266, 272–73).

10. For more, see Irigaray, "When Our Lips Speak."

11. For more, see Nichols, *Same Old*.

12. For more, see Delaney, *Times Square*; and Warner, *Trouble with Normal*, 149–94. For a more recent reflection, see Schulman, *Gentrification of the Mind*.

13. For more on *thangkas* and other key forms of Tibetan art, see Rhie and Thurman, *Wisdom and Compassion*; Behrendt, *How to Read Buddhist Art*; and Pal, *Himalayas*.

14. For more, see Tucci, *Tibetan Painted Scrolls*.

15. Schumann, *Historical Buddha*, 139; Rinpoche, *Tibetan Book*, 91. For more on Sedgwick's relation to Rinpoche, see *Touching Feeling*, 157–71, 177; and *Weather*, 210.

16. According to Zen commentator Seung Sahn, whom Sedgwick was reading, understanding karma is "simple"; each moment your "mind makes your next moment," and "all of this makes your life, like pearls strung together on a necklace." Sahn, *Compass of Zen*, 193.

17. First founded in 1350, Ayutthaya quickly became the capital of Buddhist Thailand, before it was conquered and destroyed by the Burmese in 1767.

18. Sedgwick, *Weather*, 75, 79, 102, 104, 120n3.

19. Fickle, *Images of the Buddha*, 1, 6.

20. Sedgwick, *Weather*, 77, 79.

21. For more, see Sedgwick, *Tendencies*, xii, 13n12; Lorde, *Cancer Journals* and *Burst of Light*.

22. Fickle, *Images of the Buddha*, 29, 32.

23. Birasri, *Thai Buddhist Sculpture*, 12, 18, 20.

24. Birasri, *Thai Buddhist Sculpture*, 15, 27.

25. Fickle, *Images of the Buddha*, 7.

26. Sedgwick, *Epistemology*, 208.

27. Sedgwick, *Fat Art*, 39.

28. Sedgwick, *Weather*, 83–84.

29. Sedgwick, *Weather*, 83–84.

30. Sedgwick, *Weather*, 75.

31. Ganis, *Warhol's Serial Photography*, 21–22.

32. Ganis, *Warhol's Serial Photography*, 21–22.

33. Ganis, *Warhol's Serial Photography*, 24; Sedgwick, "Queer Performativity," 134.

34. Ganis, *Warhol's Serial Photography*, 67, 73, 106, 119. For more on the *punctum*, see Barthes, *Camera Lucida*.

35. Ganis, *Warhol's Serial Photography*, 116.

36. Sedgwick, *Touching Feeling*, 100–101.

37. Sedgwick, *Fat Art*, 20.

38. For more on such picturesque conventions, see Tiffin, *Southeast Asia in Ruins*.

39. For Sedgwick's interest in Hockney photomontages, see my *Queer and Bookish*, 126–31.

40. Sedgwick, *Weather*, 102, 104.

41. Ganis, *Warhol's Serial Photography*, 23–24, 31. Sedgwick's use of body scans might also recall Warhol's portrait of Philip Niarchos, which, as Trevor Fairbrother documents, made "use of a CAT scan of the subject's head," an unrecognizable "form of portraiture," as "momentary as an X-ray." Fairbrother, "Skulls," 110.

42. Sedgwick, *Fat Art*, 48.

43. Sedgwick, *Touching Feeling*, 123–52.

44. Yeats, "Long-Legged Fly," 327.

45. Yeats, "Long-Legged Fly," 327.
46. Proust, *In Search*, 6:305.
47. Proust, *In Search*, 6:299–300, 305.

Chapter 4. *In the Bardo* (1999–2000), or Epistemology of a Different Closet

1. Sedgwick, *Fat Art*, 95.

2. In "Teaching 'Experimental Critical Writing,'" Sedgwick had encouraged her students to think about the relationship of asthma to speech, voice, and performance (113).

3. Sedgwick, *Fat Art*, 95, 97–98, 139, 145.

4. For more, see Sedgwick, *Weather*, 210–12, 213n1

5. For more, see Sedgwick, "1001 Seances."

6. Sedgwick, *Fat Art*, 129.

7. Sedgwick, *Fat Art*, 130.

8. Trollope, *Autobiography*, 18.

9. Sedgwick, *Fat Art*, 150–51. For the original context of Sedgwick's "left by his mother in the mother's place / his murderous father's bloated punching bag," see Trollope, *Autobiography*, 15.

10. Nancy K. Miller described the poignant latter scenario, noting how, after the exhibition, Sedgwick's snuffed, "stuffed forms" were taken down "from the ceiling" where they "brightly constellated" the room. Their "polyester fiberfill insides were neatly stuffed into large trash bags up against the walls outside [Sedgwick's] office, waiting patiently to be removed." Miller did not feel "happy about the bags." She wanted to "remember them full and suspended, bearing signs of a journey across boundaries; beckoning to all who pass, urging us to make an effort of the imagination, or maybe the heart." Miller, "Reviewing Eve," 221–22, 224.

11. For more on the CUNY installation, see Nelson, "In the Bardo." Nelson recalled that when the show opened, Sedgwick gave a talk, accompanied by a short handout and slideshow featuring images from her first Asian trip. Rather than speak at the front, she spoke "from a podium in the rear," as if from a "strangely suspended place," as the images, "mostly of statues, prayer flags, and temples," which she did not much refer to, drifted by as she spoke, as if a dream. Nelson also recalled Sedgwick's interest in certain "strand[s]" of Tibetan Buddhism, which had "suddenly become very personal to her," and while Nelson was trying to look at Sedgwick's slides, her view was "obscured and framed" by the dozen or so "large stuffed bodies" "hanging from the ceiling," "clothed in different kinds of cloth, paper, and *soie mariée*, in varying shades of indigo." Nelson could also see Sedgwick's torso, but a "translucent blue shawl hanging from one of the figures covered her face." According to Nelson, Sedgwick suggested that these figures represented aspects of her experience in the bardo of dying, documenting the "disorienting and radically denuding bodily sense generated by medical imaging processes and illness" and "material urges" to "dress," "mend," "ornament," "re-cover, and heal." In addition, latecomers to the talk "bumped into the figures on their way to sit down," an effect

"comic and eerie," as the "swinging figures seemed both alive and . . . lifeless," recalling "lynched" bodies (9).

12. Shantideva, *Bodhisattva's Way of Life*, 41, 68.

13. Palmer and Ramsey, *Kuan Yin Chronicles*, 170.

14. Sahn, *Compass of Zen*, 43, 61–62, 65, 67, 99. "Pile" is Thurman's translation, in *The Central Philosophy of Tibet*, 157.

15. Thurman, *Essential Tibetan Buddhism*, 25, 103, 141, 186, 273, 310–11.

16. Sedgwick, "Artist's Screed," quoted in Miller, "Reviewing Eve," 222. The full statement has recently been reprinted in Goldberg, *Come as You Are*, 109–11.

17. Sedgwick, *Touching Feeling*, 157.

18. Sedgwick, *Touching Feeling*, 157, 173–74.

19. For a history of the book's unlikely genesis and development, see Lopez, *Tibetan Book*.

20. Sedgwick, *Touching Feeling*, 174. Rinpoche acknowledged he knew a number of people who had died from AIDS and had "seen how often they were treated as outcasts, even by their friends"; the "stigma attached to the disease reduc[ing] them to despair" and making them "feel their life was disgusting and had in the eyes of the world already ended." This prompted him to observe that "we need a fundamental change in our attitude to death and dying." Rinpoche, *Tibetan Book*, 9–10.

21. Sedgwick, *Fat Art*, 28; *Weather*, 104–5.

22. Sedgwick, *Touching Feeling*, 174; *Fat Art*, 28. While the patch resembles a pocket in both scale and location, none of the clothes Sedgwick makes for the mannequins have pockets, perhaps reminding us that, in Sahn's words, "the shroud has no pockets." Sahn, *Compass of Zen*, 48.

23. Sedgwick, *Touching Feeling*, 174–77, 179.

24. Sedgwick, *Touching Feeling*, 177–78, 180.

25. Thurman, *Tibetan Book*, 24.

26. Thurman, *Tibetan Book*, xvii, xix, 14, 24.

27. Thurman, *Tibetan Book*, 18, 20, 137.

28. Thurman, *Tibetan Book*, 24, 27, 72.

29. Thurman, *Tibetan Book*, 27, 29, 171.

30. Thurman, *Tibetan Book*, 168–69, 176, 192.

31. Thurman, *Tibetan Book*, 45, 56, 61, 112, 157, 171, 196–97.

32. Thurman, *Central Philosophy of Tibet*, 25, 103.

33. Sedgwick, "Artist's Screed," quoted in Miller, "Reviewing Eve," 222.

34. Rinpoche, *Tibetan Book*, 91.

35. Rinpoche, *Tibetan Book*, 11, 18–19.

36. Miller, "Reviewing Eve," 224.

37. Rinpoche, *Tibetan Book*, 19–20, 22.

38. Rinpoche, *Tibetan Book*, 23, 25, 36, 41–42.

39. Rinpoche, *Tibetan Book*, 54, 104, 125, 164, 242, 251.

40. Rinpoche, *Tibetan Book*, 288, 299.

41. Rinpoche, *Tibetan Book*, 45.

42. Sedgwick, *Fat Art*, 67–68.

43. Sedgwick, *Fat Art*, 68.

44. Sedgwick, *Touching Feeling*, 119.

45. Anderson, *Mythology*, 6, 13, 17.

46. Sedgwick, *Weather*, 21–22.

47. Sedgwick, *Weather*, 21–22.

48. Anderson, *Mythology*, 23, 35–37, 43, 103. For more on the *punåkawan*, see 42–43, 47–48, 64–67, 72, and 79. For illustrations, see Sedgwick, "Trace at 46."

49. Sedgwick, *Weather*, 71.

50. Rinpoche, *Tibetan Book*, ix, 309.

51. Sedgwick, *Tendencies*, 215, 229.

52. Hoffmann, *Japanese Death Poems*, 267.

53. Sedgwick, *Weather*, xiv–xv.

54. For the variant translation, see Hoffmann, *Japanese Death Poems*, 267.

55. Sedgwick, *Fat Art*, 113.

56. Sedgwick, *Weather*, 124.

57. Sedgwick, *Weather*, 125–26.

58. For more, see Lacan, "Mirror Stage."

59. For more on Sedgwick's use of fragmentary classical sculpture in her artist's book, *The Last Days of Pompeii* (ca. 2007), see my *Queer and Bookish*, 384–89.

60. Sedgwick, *Dialogue*, 93–94.

61. Sedgwick, *Weather*, 9. In describing the "heat/water/steam machine we call *weather*," Sedgwick is quoting Rodney Farnsworth's *Mediating Order and Chaos*. Her posthumously published essay does not include a page number for the quotation.

Chapter 5. *Bodhisattva Fractal World* (2002)

1. Sedgwick, "Artist's Statement" (2002), *Boddhisattva Fractal World,* Eve Kosofsky Sedgwick website, http://www.evekosofskysedgwick.net/art/bodhisattva-fractal-world-exhibition.html (accessed May 14, 2018).

2. Sedgwick, "Artist's Statement."

3. For more on Taoism, see Bachelor, *Tao Te Ching*; Cleary, *Essential Tao*; and Mitchell, *Tao Te Ching*.

4. Sedgwick, *Fat Art*, 139.

5. Sedgwick, "Artist's Statement." For more on *wabi-sabi*, see Koren, *Wabi-Sabi for Artists;* for more on Gandharan sculpture, see Abe, "Inside the Wonder House."

6. Sedgwick, "Artist's Statement."

7. For more, see "Zero, Infinity, Chaos, Sublimity" (after 1998), Eve Kosofsky Sedgwick website, http://www.evekosofskysedgwick.net/teaching/zero-infinity.html (accessed May 14, 2018).

8. Sedgwick, *Weather*, 90.

9. Sedgwick, *Weather*, 100–101. For more, see Bohm, *Wholeness*; and Campbell, "Shyly," 143–44.

10. For more, see Falconer, *Fractals*, xi–xii, 3.

11. Falconer, *Fractals*, 1–2, 5, 8, 17–35, 120.

12. Falconer, *Fractals*, 94, 101, 108, 109, 115. For more on the iconography of extended arms in Sedgwick's corpus, see my *Bathroom Songs*, 63–65.

13. Koren, *Wabi-Sabi*, 21–23, 28, 31, 72.

14. Koren, *Wabi-Sabi*, 31, 33, 68.

15. Koren, *Wabi-Sabi*, 71, 87.

16. Wada et al., *Shibori*, 7.

17. Wada et al., *Shibori*, 13, 55.

18. Wada et al., *Shibori*, 22–23.

19. Edwards, *Bathroom Songs*, 229–30, 232, 235. For more on flogging, see Vincent, "Flogging Is Fundamental."

20. Wada et al., *Shibori*, 18, 67, 116, 221–22, 259.

21. Hoffmann, *Japanese Death Poems*, 286–87.

22. For more, see Crill, *Indian Ikat Textiles*.

23. Sedgwick, *Fat Art*, 111.

24. Sedgwick, *Touching Feeling*, 101.

25. Sudo, *East Quilts West*, 9, 13.

26. Sudo, *East Quilts West*, 9–10, 13.

27. Sudo, *East Quilts West*, 26.

28. Sudo, *East Quilts West*, 36, 71, 78, 114, 119.

29. Watts, *Way of Zen*, 43, 153, 315–16.

30. Hayao and Nobuhiko, *Robes of Elegance*, 79, 121, 127, 143, 155, 233.

31. For more, see Dillenberger, *Religious Art*, 27, 32; Warhol, *Flowers, Flowers, Flowers*; and Lobel, *Andy Warhol Flowers*. See also Flatley, *Liking Andy Warhol*; and Doyle et al., *Pop Out*, where Simon Watney notes that, across the 1970s, critics became more interested in the *Flowers* (21).

32. Auther, *String, Felt, Thread*, 115, 118.

33. Lobel, *Andy Warhol Flowers*, n.p. [1–11]. There are close resemblances between Warhol's nasturtiums and Sedgwick's collages in the examples given as plates 12, 15–17, 19 and 21, and 45 of Lobel, *Andy Warhol Flowers*, and 13, 24, and 74 of Warhol, *Flowers, Flowers, Flowers*.

34. Proust, *In Search*, 4:301.

35. Proust, *In Search*, 3:165, 314.

36. Proust, *In Search*, 2:610.

37. Sedgwick, "Artist's Statement."

38. Sedgwick and Frank, *Shame*, 20–21.

39. For more, see Fried, *Absorption and Theatricality*. For Sedgwick's relation to Fried, see my *Queer and Bookish*, 40–44.

40. Sedgwick, *Weather*, 96. For more on Sedgwick's relation to Atkins, see my *Queer and Bookish*, 84.

41. For Sedgwick's reading of the submarine presence of *The Tempest* in James's *Notebooks*, see *Epistemology*, 208; and *Touching Feeling*, 47–48.

42. Shakespeare, *The Tempest*, 178.

43. For Sedgwick's discussion of Odetta, see "Queer Performativity," 134.

44. Larson and Kerr, *Guanyin*, 21–22.

45. Hoffmann, *Japanese Death Poems*, 154.

46. For more, see Sedgwick, *Tendencies*, 252–66.

47. For more on coral, see Helmreich, "How Like a Reef." For related trans theoretical meditations on marine life with regenerative powers, see Hayward, "Lessons from a Starfish" and "More Lessons."

48. For more on the semiotics of the photographic positive and negative, see Batchen, *Negative/Positive*. For more in the specific context of HIV/AIDS, see Joselit, "Mark Morrisoe's Photographic Masquerade."

49. Sedgwick's love of three-line stanza forms is also apparent in her early "From an Ending for *The Triumph of Life*," in Edwards, *Bathroom Songs*, 263–71.

50. Rexroth, *One Hundred Poems*, lvi. While this is not the translation Sedgwick employs, which I have been unable to source, for more, see *Tales of Ise*, 158.

51. *Tales of Ise*, 52.

52. H. Jay Harris, translator's introduction to *Tales of Ise*, 12.

53. *Tales of Ise*, 158.

54. *Tales of Ise*, 158.

55. H. Jay Harris, translator's notes to *Tales of Ise*, 228.

56. Sedgwick, *Weather*, 210.

57. *Tales of Ise*, 158; Sedgwick, *Weather*, 210.

58. Sedgwick, *Touching Feeling*, 178.

59. Sedgwick, *Weather*, 211–12.

60. Sedgwick, *Weather*, 211–12.

61. Sedgwick, *Weather*, xv.

62. For more, see Mitter, *Much-Maligned Monsters*.

63. Sedgwick, *Weather*, 138.

64. Sedgwick, *Dialogue*, 219–20.

65. Sedgwick, *Dialogue*, 219.

66. Sedgwick, *Dialogue*, 219–20.

67. Sedgwick, *Fat Art*, 72. For more, see A. Brown, "Look with Your Hands."

68. Sedgwick, *Dialogue*, 219–20.

69. For more, see Hoffmann, *Japanese Death Poems*, 273.

70. For illustrations, see Garner, "About That Ouija Board."

71. For more, see Kosofsky and El-Baz, *Moon*.

72. Ryokan quoted in Mitchell, *Enlightened Heart*, 162.

73. Hoffmann, *Japanese Death Poems*, 271.

74. Hoffmann, *Japanese Death Poems*, 271.

75. Bashō, *Narrow Road*, 120. For more on Sedgwick's thalassic aesthetics, see my *Bathroom Songs*, 31–36; and *Queer and Bookish*, 68–72. For more on urethrality, see Ferenczi, *Thalassa*.

76. Hoffmann, *Japanese Death Poems*, 238.

77. Hoffmann, *Japanese Death Poems*, 238.

78. Hoffmann, *Japanese Death Poems*, 237–38.

79. We might think about Sedgwick's stamps as akin to the stamp of a foot, given her pedo-eroticism.

80. For more on the parallels between architectural and literary forms, see Travares, *Anatomy of the Architectural Book*.

81. James, *Notebooks*, 318, quoted in Sedgwick, *Epistemology*, 208.

82. For Sedgwick's engagements with Klein, see Sedgwick, *Touching Feeling*, 123–52; and *Weather*, 123–43.

83. For more on indigo and Indian yellow, see Eaton, *Colour, Art, and Empire*.

84. Yu, *Kuan-yin*, 431.

85. Palmer et al., *Kuan Yin*, 92.

86. Shantideva, *Bodhisattva's Way of Life*, 34–35, 41.

87. For a vegan theoretical reading of Sedgwick's poetry, see Westwood, "Abject Animal Poetics."

88. Yu, *Kuan-yin*, 257–58.

89. Here Sedgwick may also be cross-pollinating Buddhism with Proust, whose narrator recalled one of the Balbec girls holding "on her lap a bowl full of fish" and who wished he had been "able for a moment to metamorphose [him]self into a fish that sleeps in the sea, carried along in its slumber by the currents and the waves." Proust, *In Search* 2:267, 341. The narrator also reminds us that "you're as ignorant as a carp" was idiomatic in turn-of -the-century French. Proust, *In Search*, 5:344.

90. Shantideva, *Bodhisattva's Way of Life*, 121.

91. For more, see chapter 8 of Yu, *Kuan-yin*.

92. Yu, *Kuan-yin*, 432.

93. Yu, *Kuan-yin*, 432.

94. On the importance of ambivalence in reparative reading, see Stacey, "Wishing Away Ambivalence."

95. Hoffmann, *Japanese Death Poems*, 164–65. On what it might mean to be a "real" man, see Sedgwick, "Gosh, Boy George."

96. Hoffmann, *Japanese Death Poems*, 165.

97. As Jennifer Doyle has recently documented, ice was a similarly key metaphor for Sedgwick when it came to her own reparative *writing* practice. In a letter to her brother David of May 15, 1983, for example, Sedgwick acknowledged that "what I most importantly ask of the work is so very little (just to keep me off the ice)" of depression. Doyle, *Shadow*, 127–28.

98. The English translation, calligraphic original, and drawing are reproduced in Ueda, *Bashō*, 346–47.

99. Ueda, *Bashō*, 11, 67.

100. For example, Bashō documented "the solitary voice of a toad / Beneath [a] silkworm nursery" and described how he would go as far as he could, "deep as the snow" was, until he stumbled and fell, "viewing the white landscape." *Narrow Road*, 54, 76, 97, 104, 122.

101. Ueda, *Bashō*, 11.

102. For more on Sedgwick's relation to Dickinson, see my *Bathroom Songs*, 54–58; and *Queer and Bookish*, 101–11.

103. Sedgwick, *Touching Feeling*, 28–29.

104. Sedgwick, *Touching Feeling*, 29.

105. Hoffmann, *Japanese Death Poems*, 267.
106. Hoffmann, *Japanese Death Poems*, 267.
107. Sedgwick, *Weather*, 1–3.
108. Hoffmann, Japanese Death Poems, 275.
109. Hoffmann, *Japanese Death Poems*, 275.
110. Sedgwick, *Fat Art*, 109–12, 147.
111. Sedgwick, *Fat Art*, 109–12.
112. Sedgwick, *Weather*, xv; Goldberg, *Come as You Are*, 103, 108.
113. Hoffmann, Japanese Death Poems, 154.
114. Hoffmann, *Japanese Death Poems*, 154.
115. Neck pain was what caused Sedgwick's metastasis to be first diagnosed. For an illustration of her neck brace and discussion, see Lin, *Freud's Jaw*, 103. For a discussion of their chronic neck pain, see Sedgwick and Snediker, "Queer Little Gods"; and Snediker, *Contingent Figure*.
116. Proust, *In Search*, 5:679 (emphasis mine).
117. For Sedgwick's and Michael Moon's relation to Waters, see *Tendencies*, 215–51.
118. Sedgwick, *Fat Art*, 67.
119. Sedgwick, *Fat Art*, 67–69.
120. Sedgwick, *Fat Art*, 70.
121. For more, see "Dazu Rock Carvings," World Heritage Convention, UNESCO, https://whc.unesco.org/en/list/912/ (accessed September 11, 2024).
122. Proust, *In Search*, 5:679.
123. Proust, *In Search*, 6:291.
124. Proust, *In Search*, 4:308, 433; 5:561.
125. Proust, *In Search*, 4:464–65.
126. Proust, *In Search*, 1:766.
127. Sedgwick, *Fat Art*, 158.
128. Proust, *In Search*, 3:337–38.
129. Sedgwick, *Dialogue*, 217.
130. Sedgwick, *Dialogue*, 216–17.
131. Sedgwick, *Dialogue*, 219. For more on the "security of the womblike recesses of a pocket" in *Dialogue* and the title of *Gary in Your Pocket*, see Lin, *Freud's Jaw*, 107–8.
132. Sedgwick, *Epistemology*, 1.
133. Sedgwick, *Fat Art*, 156–57.
134. Flatley, "Like," 78. See also Flatley, "Unlike Eve Sedgwick." For longer meditations on sameness and similarity, see Flatley, *Liking Andy Warhol*; Nichols, *Same Old*; and Menon, *Indifference to Difference*.
135. Flatley, "Like," 78.
136. Proust, *In Search*, 2:476–77.
137. Proust, *In Search*, 2:565.
138. Proust, *In Search*, 5:163, 6:112.
139. Proust, *In Search*, 6:306.
140. Foucault, quoted in Sedgwick, *Tendencies*, 264.
141. Sedgwick, *Weather*, 96.

142. Sedgwick, *Touching Feeling*, 114.

143. Emphasis mine.

144. Proust, *In Search*, 2:337–38.

145. While scholars have emphasized Sedgwick's late interest in tactility, thanks to the title of *Touching Feeling*, scent was also emerging as a key sense in her writing and artwork, one central to her engagement with sculpture. She described how the "beat-up Buddha statues from Thailand" offered a "radically open pelvis, and frequently an open armpit," so that "if the statue were a person, you'd know their smell as well as their look." *Weather*, 104.

146. Sedgwick, *Touching Feeling*, 149–51.

147. Proust, *In Search*, 3:47.

148. For Sedgwick's queer meditation of Racine's *Esther* (1689), see *Epistemology*, 78–82.

149. Proust, *In Search*, 3:46–48.

150. Proust, *In Search*, 1:4.

151. Proust, *In Search*, 1:3.

152. For more, see my *Queer and Bookish*, 307–400.

153. Proust, *In Search*, 1:4.

154. Proust, *In Search*, 1:4–5.

155. Proust, *In Search*, 1:5.

Chapter 6. *Works in Fiber, Paper, and Proust* (2005)

1. Litvak, "*The Weather in Proust* (Review)." For Litvak's engagements with Proust, see Litvak, "Strange Gourmet" and *Strange Gourmets*. For Litvak's engagement with Sedgwick, see Litvak, "Sedgwick's Nerve."

2. Karpeles, *Paintings in Proust*, 10, 14, 16–17, 19.

3. Proust, *In Search*, 6:431.

4. Proust, *In Search*, 5:23, 599. I owe the phrase to McDonald, *Proustian Fabric*.

5. Proust, *In Search*, 5:11, 82, 497.

6. Proust, *In Search*, 3:235.

7. Proust, *In Search*, 3:51.

8. Proust, *In Search*, 4:77.

9. For Sedgwick as a book artist, see my *Queer and Bookish*.

10. Proust, *In Search*, 3:42, 66, 166.

11. Proust, *In Search*, 5:556, 589, 652.

12. Proust, *In Search*, 3:179, 421; 6:292.

13. Proust, *Days of Reading*, 52, 55–56. For more on the ideal textile environment for reading Sedgwick, see Boulton, "Waiting in the Dark."

14. Proust, *In Search*, 6:222; Karpeles, *Paintings in Proust*, 32.

15. Proust, *In Search*, 3:47, 324; 5:63, 76, 281; Karpeles, *Paintings in Proust*, 100.

16. Proust, *In Search*, 6:428; 5:94, 266.

17. Proust, *In Search*, 5:207–8.

18. Proust, *In Search*, 2:463, 4:112.

19. Proust, *In Search*, 5:568. I am grateful to Carol Mavor for helping me identify Traut. There at least three images depicting the woman and girl. In the other two, they look at viewers or each other. Sedgwick characteristically chose the variant in which the woman addressed viewers, triangulating the scene.

20. Proust, *In Search*, 5:566–67.

21. Proust, *In Search*, 5:568.

22. Proust, *In Search*, 5:569. For a bravura reading of the pederasty at the heart of twentieth-century canonical French gay literature, see Amin, *Disturbing Attachments*.

23. Proust, *In Search*, 5:570.

24. Sedgwick, "Artist's Statement" (2005) (Sedgwick archive). The archive is contained within the Sallie Bingham Center for Women's History and Culture at Duke University. Sedgwick's early kimono collages were similarly *in* Gary Fisher's idiom, as we have seen.

25. Proust, *In Search*, 5:570.

26. Sedgwick, *Fat Art*, 157.

27. For more on the possible autobiographical contexts of the cover of *Novel Gazing*, see my *Queer and Bookish*, 159–67.

28. Proust, *In Search*, 5:571.

29. Proust, *In Search*, 4:214, 6:377.

30. Proust, *In Search*, 5:90, 470.

31. Proust, *In Search*, 5:633.

32. Proust, *In Search*, 5:633.

33. Proust, *In Search*, 6:351.

34. Proust, *In Search*, 2:563.

35. Proust, *In Search*, 2:476–77.

36. Proust, *In Search*, 2:475.

37. Proust, *In Search*, 2:565, 6:300.

38. Proust, *In Search*, 4:486.

39. Proust, *In Search*, 2:522.

40. Proust, *In Search*, 6:254–55, 273.

41. Proust, *In Search*, 5:163, 513.

42. Proust, *In Search*, 6:112, 431.

43. Proust, *In Search*, 6:288.

44. Proust, *In Search*, 6:292.

45. Proust, *In Search*, 6:306, 310–11.

46. Sedgwick, *Weather*, 31; Goldberg, "Eve of the Future," 376.

47. Sahn, *Compass of Zen*, 79.

48. Ganis, *Warhol's Serial Photography*, 80–82.

49. Sedgwick, *Tendencies*, 9; and "Queer Performativity," 134, 137–38, 142.

50. Sedgwick, "Queer Performativity," 138–39.

51. Sedgwick, *Dialogue*, 76–77.

52. For more, see Dillenberger, *Religious Art*; and Lamoureux, "Ending Myths."

53. Proust, *In Search*, 2:291.

54. Proust, *In Search*, 2:443.

55. Proust, *In Search*, 2:289.
56. Proust, *In Search*, 2:618.
57. Proust, *In Search*, 2:618.
58. Emphasis mine.
59. I derive my section title from Wolf, *Proust and the Squid*.
60. Kroeber, *Anthropology*, 255–56.
61. Helmreich, "How Like a Reef," 9.
62. Helmreich, "How Like a Reef," 3.
63. Helmreich, "How Like a Reef," 14.
64. Helmreich, "How Like a Reef," 7.
65. Hayward, "Fingereyes," 589.
66. Helmreich, "How Like a Reef," 12; Haraway, foreword, xi–xii.
67. Helmreich, "How Like a Reef," 9.
68. Wilson, "Biologically Inspired Feminism," 284.
69. For more on the natural and cultural history of octopuses, see Sweid, *Octopus*.
70. Sedgwick, *Fat Art*, 152.
71. Proust, *In Search*, 2:386.
72. Proust, *In Search*, 5:221, 2:466.
73. Proust, *In Search*, 6:299–300.
74. Proust, *In Search*, 6:435.
75. Proust, *In Search*, 4:31.
76. Proust, *In Search*, 2:315–16.
77. Proust, *In Search*, 5:131–32.
78. Proust, *In Search*, 3:341–42.
79. Proust, *In Search*, 5:561.
80. The butler is instructed to "bring *Le Temps*" in *In Search*, 6:125.
81. Proust, *In Search*, 1:54–55.
82. Proust, *In Search*, 5:19–20.
83. Proust, *In Search*, 5:4–5.
84. For a parallel reading of the meteorological pleasures of being single, see Cobb, *Single*.
85. Proust, *In Search*, 4:75–76, quoted in Sedgwick, *Weather*, 1–2.
86. Proust, *In Search*, 5:468.
87. Proust, *In Search*, 3:342.
88. Proust, *In Search*, 5:21–22.
89. Proust, *In Search*, 5:23.
90. For "Proust and the Spectacle of the Closet," see Sedgwick, *Epistemology*, 213–52.
91. Proust, *In Search*, 5:2–3.
92. Proust, *In Search*, 6:432.
93. Emphasis mine.
94. Proust, *In Search*, 6:431.
95. Proust, *In Search*, 6:432.
96. Proust, *In Search*, 6:222.

97. In *Touching Feeling*, Sedgwick worried that she had made Henry James's *Prefaces* "sound too much like *Silence of the Lambs*" (59).

98. Proust, *In Search*, 2:130.

99. Proust, *In Search*, 2:129–31.

100. Proust, *In Search*, 2:130.

101. Karpeles, *Paintings in Proust*, 261.

102. Sedgwick, *Dialogue*, 94.

103. For more on Sedgwick's relation to Lynch, see Sedgwick, *Tendencies*, 252–66; my *Queer and Bookish*, 102–11; and Lynch, "Terrors of Resurrection."

104. Moon, "Memorial Rags," 238–39.

105. Moon, "Memorial Rags," 238.

106. Proust, *The Fugitive*, vol. 5, quoted in Karpeles, *Paintings in Proust*, 280. Another intertext may be Sedgwick's still-unpublished circa 1997 essay "Flying with Samuel Delaney," the introduction she gave when he was awarded the CLAGS Kessler Award, and a figure she described as an "intimate inner interlocuter" and "authorial ego-ideal for many, many years." The brief talk, in part, focused on what she called the "ravishing," "often highly eroticized image of flying that animates so much of Delaney's fiction: a momentum that's propelled by and along the invisible but knowable fault lines of the difference between one air pressure, air temperature, air direction, and another, and propelled too by the skilled aerodynamic *resistance* through which the flyer learns to tap into the latent energy of such differentials." Such flying adventures, Sedgwick observed, constituted "sexuality" itself at some moments, an experience "where desire and excitement might live"; where wind "stroked" "arms," "back," and "buttocks"; where the sun might warm a neck, wind chill a face, arms, fingers; an "excitement of flight" making the "heart hammer," the stomach "contract."

107. Proust, *In Search*, 2:281–87.

108. Proust, *In Search*, 2:281.

109. Proust, *In Search*, 2:281–83.

110. Proust, *In Search*, 2:281–83.

111. Proust, *In Search*, 2:282–83.

112. Proust, *In Search*, 2:283–84.

113. Proust, *In Search*, 2:283–84.

114. Proust, *In Search*, 2:284.

115. Proust, *In Search*, 2:284–85.

116. Proust, *In Search*, 2:286.

117. Proust, *In Search*, 2: 286.

118. Proust, *In Search*, 2:286.

119. Sedgwick, *Weather*, xv.

120. Proust, *In Search*, 2:286–88.

121. Proust, *In Search*, 3:377.

122. *Touching Feeling* also discusses the "animation of character by reaching a hand up its backside," or, to put it another way, "the puppet theater" of James's fisted golden bowl (60).

123. In Sedgwick's late poem "Bathroom Song," it is, tellingly, the recollection of the "flushed and handsome face" of her "Grandma" that brings Sedgwick comfort. *Weather*, xv.

124. Sedgwick, *Weather*, 21–22, 66.

125. Proust, *In Search*, 6:291.

126. Sedgwick, *Touching Feeling*, 147–49.

127. Proust, *In Search*, 2:281–87.

128. See Bohm, *Wholeness and the Implicate Order*.

129. For a semiotic reading of Giotto's color patches, see Kristeva, "Giotto's Joy." For more on Proust's relation to Giotto, see Karpeles, *Paintings in Proust*, 37, 68, 76, 122, 150, 280.

130. Proust, *In Search*, 2:583–84.

131. Proust, *In Search*, 2:436.

132. Proust, *In Search*, 2:479.

133. Sedgwick and Parker, *Performativity and Performance*. For more on the balletic cover, see my *Queer and Bookish*, 135–53.

134. Proust, *In Search*, 3:89.

135. Sedgwick, *Epistemology*, 213–53.

136. For more, see Edwards, *Bathroom Songs*, 193–97, 272–73, 275–76, 281–84, and 287–90.

137. Sedgwick and Frank, *Shame*, 21.

138. For more, see Edelman, "Tearooms and Sympathy."

139. Proust, *In Search*, 1:146.

140. Sedgwick, *Fat Art*, 109–12.

141. Proust, *Swann's Way*, 1:378.

142. Proust, *In Search*, 5:207.

143. Proust, *In Search*, 1:86.

144. For more, see Edwards, *Queer and Bookish*, 307–400.

145. Proust, *In Search*, 2:131.

146. Sedgwick, *Dialogue*, 217.

Coda. "An Inward Accumulation of a Wealth of Materials"

1. Sedgwick, *Epistemology*, 174–75.

2. Sedgwick, *Touching Feeling*, 93–122.

3. Sedgwick, *Touching Feeling*, 114. In the same quotation, Sedgwick compared Tomkins's cybernetic thinking to a "complex, multi-layered phyllo dough" (114), reminding us that while this book has explored her textile works, Sedgwick's simultaneous work in ceramics and glass, now in the Duke archives, remains to be explored. Sedgwick's archive is located in the Sallie Bingham Center for Women's History and Culture at Duke University.

4. Sedgwick, *Epistemology*, 208.

5. Sedgwick, *Touching Feeling*, 47–48.

6. James, *Notebooks of Henry James*, 318.

BIBLIOGRAPHY

Abe, Stanley K. “Inside the Wonder House: Buddhist Art and the West.” In *Curators of the Buddha: The Study of Buddhism Under Colonialism*, edited by Donald S. Lopez Jr., 63–107. Chicago: University of Chicago Press, 1995.

Ahmed, Sara. *Queer Phenomenology: Orientations, Objects, Others*. Durham, NC: Duke University Press, 2006.

Albers, Anni. *On Weaving*. 1965. Middletown, CT: Wesleyan University Press, 1974.

Allan, Jonathan A. “Falling in Love with Eve Kosofsky Sedgwick.” *Mosaic: A Journal for the Interdisciplinary Study of Literature* 48, no. 1 (March 2015): 1–16.

Amin, Kadji. *Disturbing Attachments: Genet, Modern Pederasty, and Queer History*. Durham, NC: Duke University Press, 2017.

Anderson, Benedict. *Mythology and the Tolerance of the Javanese*. 1965. Jakarta: Equinox, 2009.

Auther, Elissa. *String, Felt, Thread: The Hierarchy of Art and Craft in American Art*. Minneapolis: University of Minnesota Press, 2010.

Avedon, John F., Tamdin Sithar Bradley, Fernand Meyer, N. D. Bolsokoeva, and K. M. Gerasimova, eds. *The Buddha's Art of Healing: Tibetan Paintings Rediscovered*. New York: Rizzoli, 1988.

Bachelor, Stephen, trans. *Tao Te Ching*. San Francisco: HarperPerennial, 1992.

Barber, Stephen M., and David L. Clark, eds. *Regarding Sedgwick: Essays on Queer Culture and Critical Theory*. London: Routledge, 2002.

Barker, Diane. *Tibetan Prayer Flags*. London: Connections, 2003.

Barthes, Roland. *Camera Lucida*. 1981. London: Vintage, 2000.

Bashō, Matsuo. *The Narrow Road to the Deep North and Other Travel Sketches*. Translated by Nobuyuki Yausa. London: Penguin, 1966.

Batchen, Gregory. *Negative/Positive: A History of Photography*. London: Routledge, 2021.

Behrendt, Kurt. *How to Read Buddhist Art*. New York: Metropolitan Museum, 2019.

Berlant, Lauren. “The Pedagogies of ‘Pedagogy of Buddhism.’” *Supervalent Thought*, March 18, 2010. https://supervalentthought.wordpress.com/2010/03/18/after-eve-in-honor-of-eve-kosofsky-sedgwick/.

Berlant, Lauren, ed. *Reading Sedgwick*. Durham, NC: Duke University Press, 2019.
Berlant, Lauren. "Two Girls, Fat and Thin." In Barber and Clark, *Regarding Sedgwick*, 71–108.
Best, Stephen, and Sharon Marcus. "Surface Reading: An Introduction." *Representations* 108, no. 1 (Fall 2009): 1–21.
Birasri, Silpa. *Thai Buddhist Sculpture*. 1954. Bangkok: National Culture Institute, 1956.
Blofield, John. *Bodhisattva of Compassion: The Mystical Tradition of Kuan Yin*. Boston: Shambala, 2009.
Bohm, David. *Wholeness and the Implicate Order*. London: Routledge, 1980.
Bois, Yve-Alain. "Piet Mondrian, *New York City*." In *Painting as Model*, 157–83. Cambridge, MA: MIT Press, 1993.
Boulton, Meg. "Waiting in the Dark: Some Musings on Sedgwick's Performative(s)." In Edwards, *Bathroom Songs*, 169–76.
Bradway, Tyler. *Queer Experimental Literature: The Affective Politics of Bad Reading*. London: Palgrave, 2017.
Brown, Angus Connell. "Look with Your Hands." In Edwards, *Bathroom Songs*, 77–83.
Brown, Rachel. *The Weaving, Spinning, and Dyeing Book*. New York: Knopf, 1983.
Bryan-Wilson, Julia. *Fray: Art and Textile Politics*. Chicago: University of Chicago Press, 2017.
Butler, Judith. "Capacity." In Barber and Clark, *Regarding Sedgwick*, 109–20.
Butler, Judith. "Proust at the End." In Berlant, *Reading Sedgwick*, 63–71.
Campbell, Mary Baine. "'Shyly / as a Big Sister I Would Yearn / to Trace Its Avocations,' or Who's the Muse?" In Edwards, *Bathroom Songs*, 139–50.
Chambers, Anne. *Suminagashi: The Japanese Art of Marbling—A Practical Guide*. London: Thames and Hudson, 1991.
Chandler, Deborah. *Learning to Weave*. Loveland, CO: Interweave, 1995.
Cleary, Thomas. *The Essential Tao*. San Francisco: Harper, 1993.
Cobb, Michael. *Single: Arguments for the Uncoupled*. New York: New York University Press, 2012.
Cohen, Patricia. "Lit Critics Who Peer Under the Covers." *New York Times*, April 18, 2009.
Coxon, Ann, Bryony Fer, and Maria Muller-Schareck, eds. *Anni Albers*. London: Tate, 2018.
Crawford, Lucas. "Slender Trouble: From Berlant's Cruel Figuring of Figure to Sedgwick's Fat Presence." *GLQ* 23, no. 4 (October 2017): 447–72.
Crill, Rosemary. *Indian Ikat Textiles*. London: V&A, 1998.
Crimp, Douglas. *Melancholia and Moralism: Essays on AIDS and Queer Politics*. Cambridge, MA: MIT Press, 2002.
Crimp, Douglas. "Mourning and Militancy." *October*, no. 51 (Winter 1989): 3–18.
Cvetkovich, Ann. "The Utopia of Ordinary Habit: Crafting, Creativity, and Spiritual Practice." In *Depression: A Public Feeling*, 154–202. Durham, NC: Duke University Press, 2012.
Delaney, Samuel R. *Times Square Red, Times Square Blue*. New York: New York University Press, 1999.

Derrida, Jacques. "A Silkworm of One's Own (Points of View Stitched on the Other Veil)." *Oxford Literary Review* 18, no. 1 (1996): 3–66.
Dillenberger, Jane Daggett. *The Religious Art of Andy Warhol*. New York: Continuum, 1998.
Dimmock, Wai Chi. "Weak Theory, Henry James, Colm Toibin, and W. B. Yeats." *Critical Inquiry* 39, no. 4 (Summer 2013): 732–53.
Doyle, Jennifer. *Shadow of My Shadow*. Durham, NC: Duke University Press, 2024.
Doyle, Jennifer, Jonathan Flatley, and José Esteban Muñoz, eds. *Pop Out: Queer Warhol*. Durham, NC: Duke University Press, 1996.
Eaton, Natasha. *Colour, Art, and Empire: Making and Breaking the Imperial Palette*. London: I. B. Taurus, 2013.
Edelman, Lee. "Tearooms and Sympathy; or, The Epistemology of the Water Closet." In *Homographesis: Essays in Gay Literary and Cultural Theory*, 148–72. London: Routledge, 1994.
Edwards, Jason. "Introduction: *Bathroom Songs*? Eve Kosofsky Sedgwick as a Poet." In *Bathroom Songs,* 17–76.
Edwards, Jason, ed. *Bathroom Songs: Eve Kosofsky Sedgwick as a Poet*. Santa Barbara, CA: Punctum, 2017.
Edwards, Jason. *Eve Kosofsky Sedgwick*. Routledge Critical Thinkers. London: Routledge, 2009.
Edwards, Jason. "For Beauty Is a Series of Hypotheses? Sedgwick as Fiber Artist." In Berlant, *Reading Sedgwick*, 72–91.
Edwards, Jason. *Queer and Bookish: Eve Kosofsky Sedgwick as Book Artist*. Santa Barbara, CA: Punctum, 2021.
Edwards, Jason. "Reparative Reading at 21." Paper presented at Reparative Reading at 21 symposium, University of York, February 14, 2017. https://evekosofskysedgwick.net/conferences/rr21.
Fairbrother, Trevor. "Skulls." In *The Work of Andy Warhol*, edited by Gary Garrels, 93–114. Seattle: Bay, 1989.
Falconer, Kenneth. *Fractals: A Very Short Introduction*. Oxford: Oxford University Press, 2013.
Farnsworth, Rodney. *Mediating Order and Chaos: The Water-Cycle in the Complex Adaptive Systems of Romantic Culture*. Amsterdam: Rodopi, 2001.
Ferenczi, Sandor. *Thalassa: A Theory of Genitality*. London: Karnac, 1989.
Fickle, Dorothy H. *Images of the Buddha in Thailand*. Oxford: Oxford University Press, 1989.
Flatley, Jonathan. "Like: Collecting and Collectivity." *October*, no. 132 (Spring 2010): 71–98.
Flatley, Jonathan. *Liking Andy Warhol*. Chicago: University of Chicago Press, 2018.
Flatley, Jonathan. "Unlike Eve Sedgwick." *Criticism: A Quarterly for Literature and the Arts* 52, no. 2 (Spring 2010): 225–34.
Frank, Adam, and Elizabeth A. Wilson. *A Silvan Tomkins Handbook: Foundations for Affect Theory*. Minneapolis: University of Minnesota Press, 2020.
Frank, Arthur W. "Bodies, Sex, and Death." *Theory, Culture, and Society* 15, nos. 3–4 (August 1998): 417–25.

Fried, Michael. *Absorption and Theatricality: Painting and Beholder in the Age of Diderot*. Berkeley: University of California Press, 1980.

Gallop, Jane. "The Ethics of Reading: Close Encounters." *Journal of Curriculum Theorising* 32, no. 1 (Fall 2000): 7–17.

Ganis, William V. *Andy Warhol's Serial Photography*. Cambridge: Cambridge University Press, 2004.

Garner, Dwight. "About That Ouija Board: How Langdon Hammer Summoned a Poet's Spirit." *New York Times*, August 29, 2016.

Goldberg, Jonathan. *Come as You Are: After Eve Kosofsky Sedgwick*. Santa Barbara, CA: Punctum, 2021.

Goldberg, Jonathan. "On the Eve of the Future." *PMLA* 125, no. 2 (March 2010): 374–77.

Goldstein, Bill. "Some Scenes in Proust." *Criticism: A Quarterly for Literature and the Arts* 52, no. 2 (Spring 2010): 263–70.

Grunebaum, Gabriele. *How to Marbleize Paper: Step-by-Step Instructions for 12 Traditional Patterns*. New York: Dover, 1984.

Gunn, Thom. *The Man with the Night Sweats*. London: Faber and Faber, 1992.

Halberstam, Jack. *The Queer Art of Failure*. Durham, NC: Duke University Press, 2011.

Hammer, Langdon. *James Merrill: Life and Art*. New York: Knopf, 2015.

Hanson, Ellis. "'The Future's Eve': Reparative Readings After Sedgwick." *South Atlantic Quarterly* 110, no. 1 (Winter 2011): 101–19.

Hanson, Ellis. "The Languorous Critic." *New Literary History* 43, no. 3 (Summer 2012): 547–64.

Haraway, Donna. Foreword to *Women Writing Culture*, edited by Gary A. Olson and Elizabeth Hirsh, xi–xii. Albany: State University of New York Press, 1995.

Hawkins, Katy. "Re-Creating Eve: Sedgwick's Art and the Practice of Renewal." *Criticism: A Quarterly for Literature and the Arts* 52, no. 2 (Spring 2010): 271–82.

Hawkins, Katy. *Thinking Feelingly: Somatic Approaches to Poetry*. Self published, 2022.

Hawkins, Katy. "Woven Spaces: Eve Kosofsky Sedgwick's *Dialogue on Love*." *Women and Performance: A Journal of Feminist Theory* 16, no. 2 (July 2006): 251–67.

Hawkins, Peter S. "Naming Names: The Art of Memory and the NAMES Project AIDS Quilt." In *Thinking About Exhibitions*, edited by Reesa Greenberg, Bruce W. Ferguson, and Sandy Nairne, 133–56. London: Routledge, 1995.

Hayao, Isimura, and Maruyama Nobuhiko. *Robes of Elegance: Japanese Kimonos of the 16th–20th Centuries*: Raleigh: North Carolina Museum of Art, 1988.

Haye, Christian, and Eve Kosofsky Sedgwick. "All About Eve." *Frieze*, May 6, 1997, 1–4.

Hayward, Eva S. "Fingereyes." *Cultural Anthropology* 25, no. 4 (2010): 577–99.

Hayward, Eva S. "Lessons from a Starfish." In *The Transgender Studies Reader 2*, edited by Susan Stryker and Aren Z. Aizura, 178–88. London: Routledge, 2013.

Hayward, Eva S. "More Lessons from a Starfish: Prefixial Flesh and Transspeciated Selves." *Women's Studies Quarterly* 36, nos. 3–4 (Fall–Winter 2008): 64–85.

Helmreich, Stefan. "How Like a Reef: Figuring Coral, 1839–2010." *Party Writing for Donna Haraway!*, https://partywriting.blogspot.com (accessed April 12, 2018).

Herring, Scott. "Eve Sedgwick's 'Other Materials.'" *Angelaki* 23, no. 1 (2018): 5–18.

Hoffmann, Yoel, ed. *Japanese Death Poems Written by Zen Monks and Haiku Poets on the Verge of Death*. Boston: Tuttle, 1986.
Holroyd, Amy Twigger. "Book Review: *Amateur Craft: History and Theory*." *Journal of Modern Craft* 9, no. 3 (2016): 367–69.
Irigaray, Luce. "When Our Lips Speak Together." *Signs* 6, no. 1 (Autumn 1980): 69–79.
Iser, Wolfgang. "The Reading Process: A Phenomenology of Reading." *New Literary History* 3, no. 2 (Winter 1972): 279–99.
Jackson, Anna. *Kimono: Kyoto to Catwalk*. London: V&A, 2020.
James, Henry. *Notebooks of Henry James*. Edited by F. O. Matthiessen and Kenneth B. Murdock. Oxford: Oxford University Press, 1947.
Jarman, Derek, dir. *Blue*. UK: Zeitgeist Films, 1993. 79 min.
Jarman, Derek, dir. *The Tempest*. UK: Kino Lorber, 1979. 92 min.
Johnson, Erica L. *Cultural Memory, Memorials, and Reparative Writing*. London: Palgrave, 2018.
Joselit, David. "Mark Morrisoe's Photographic Masquerade." In *The Passionate Camera: Photography and the Bodies of Desire*, edited by Deborah Bright, 195–204. London: Routledge, 1998.
Karcher, Stephen. *The Kuan Yin Oracle: The Voice of the Goddess of Compassion*. London: Piatkus, 2001.
Karpeles, Eric. *Paintings in Proust*. London: Thames and Hudson, 2008.
Kelleher, Paul. "If Love Were All: Reading Sedgwick Sentimentally." In Barber and Clark, *Regarding Sedgwick*, 143–65.
Kent, Kathryn R. "'Excreate a No Sense': The Erotic Currency of Gertrude Stein's Tender Buttons." In *Making Girls into Women: American Women's Writing and the Rise of Lesbian Identity*, 139–66. Durham, NC: Duke University Press, 2003.
Kent, Kathryn R. "'Surprising Recognition': Genre, Poetic Form, and Erotics from Sedgwick's *1001 Seances* to *A Dialogue on Love*." *GLQ* 17, no. 4 (2011): 497–510.
Keulemans, Guy. "The Geo-Cultural Conditions of *Kintsugi*." *Journal of Modern Craft* 9, no. 1 (2016): 15–34.
Kita, Sandy. "Reconsidering Ukiyo-e." In *A Hidden Treasure: Japanese Prints from the Carnegie Museum of Art*, 15–33. Pittsburgh: Carnegie Museum, 1996.
Kopplin, Monika, Christy Bartlett, James Henry Holland, and Charlie Iten. *Flickwerk: The Aesthetics of Mended Japanese Ceramics*. New York: Cornell University Herbert F. Johnson Museum of Art; Munster: Museum für Lackkunst, 2008.
Koren, Leonard. *Wabi-Sabi for Artists, Designers, Poets, and Philosophers*. Point Reyes, CA: Imperfect, 2008.
Kosofsky, L. J., and Farouk El-Baz. *The Moon as Viewed by Lunar Orbiter*. Washington, DC: NASA, 1970.
Krauss, Rosalind. "Grids." *October*, no. 9 (Summer 1979): 50–64.
Kristeva, Julia. "Giotto's Joy." In *Desire in Language: A Semiotic Approach to Art*, 383–408. Paris: Seuil, 1977.
Kroeber, Alfred L. *Anthropology: Race, Language, Culture, Psychology, Prehistory*. New York: Harcourt, Brace, 1948.

Lacan, Jacques. "The Mirror Stage as Formative of the Function of the I as Revealed in Psychoanalytic Experience." 1949. In *Écrits: A Selection*, 1–7. London: Tavistock, 1977.

Lamoureux, Johanne. "Ending Myths and the Catholic Outing of Andy Warhol." In *Precarious Visualities: New Perspectives on Identification in Contemporary Art and Visual Culture*, edited by Olivier Asselin, Johanne Lamoureux, and Christine Ross, 100–119. Montreal: McGill-Queen's University Press, 2008.

Larson, John, and Rose Kerr. *Guanyin: A Masterpiece Revealed*. London: V&A, 1985.

Lawrence, Tim. "AIDS, the Problem of Representation, and Plurality in Derek Jarman's *Blue*." *Social Text*, nos. 52–53 (Autumn–Winter 1997): 241–64.

Levinson, Marjorie. "What Is New Formalism?" *PMLA* 122, no. 2 (March 2007): 558–69.

Lin, Lana. *Freud's Jaw and Other Lost Objects: Fractured Subjectivity in the Face of Cancer*. New York: Fordham University Press, 2017.

Litvak, Joseph. "*The Weather in Proust* (Review)." *Modernism/Modernity* 19, no. 4 (November 2012): 805–7.

Litvak, Joseph. "Sedgwick's Nerve." *Criticism: A Quarterly for Literature and the Arts* 52, no. 2 (Spring 2010): 253–62.

Litvak, Joseph. "Strange Gourmet: Taste, Waste, Proust." In Sedgwick, *Novel Gazing*, 74–93.

Litvak, Joseph. *Strange Gourmets: Sophistication, Theory, and the Novel*. Durham, NC: Duke University Press, 1997.

Lobel, Michael, ed. *Andy Warhol Flowers*. New York: Eykyn Maclean, 2012.

Lopez, Donald S. *The Tibetan Book of the Dead: A Biography*. Princeton, NJ: Princeton University Press, 2011.

Lorde, Audrey. *A Burst of Light*. Ithaca, NY: Firebrand, 1988.

Lorde, Audrey. *The Cancer Journals*. San Francisco: Spinsters Ink, 1988.

Love, Heather. "Close but Not Deep: Literary Ethics and the Descriptive Turn." *New Literary History* 41, no. 2 (Spring 2010): 371–91.

Love, Heather. "Truth and Consequences: On Paranoid Reading and Reparative Reading." *Criticism* 52, no. 2 (Spring 2010): 235–42.

Lynch, Michael. "Terrors of Resurrection 'By Eve Kosofsky Sedgwick.'" In *Confronting AIDS Through Literature*, edited by Judith Laurence Pastore, 79–83. Chicago: University of Chicago Press, 1993.

Mandelbrot, Benoit B. *The Fractal Geometry of Nature*. San Francisco: W. H. Freeman, 1982.

Marcus, Sharon, Heather Love, and Stephen Best. "Building a Better Description." *Representations* 135, no. 1 (2006): 1–21.

Mayer, Anita Luvera. *Clothing from the Hands That Weave*. Battleboro, VT: Echopoint, 1984.

McBrinn, Joseph. *Queering the Subversive Stitch: Men and the Culture of Needlework*. London: Bloomsbury, 2021.

McDonald, Christie. *The Proustian Fabric: Associations of Memory*. Lincoln: University of Nebraska Press, 1991.

Menon, Madhavi. *Indifference to Difference: On Queer Universalism*. Minnesota: University of Minnesota Press, 2015.

Merrill, James. *The Changing Light at Sandover*. New York: Athenaeum, 1984.
Merrill, James. *Collected Poems*. New York: Knopf, 2002.
Merrill, James. *A Different Person: A Memoir*. In *Collected Prose*, edited by J. D. McClatchy and Stephen Yenser, 457–684. 1993. New York: Alfred A. Knopf, 2004.
Milhaupt, Terry Satsuki. *Kimono: A Modern History*. London: Reaktion, 2014.
Miller, Nancy K. "All About Eve." *Women's Review of Books* 17, no. 2 (November 1999): 21–22.
Miller, Nancy K. "Reviewing Eve." In Barber and Clark, *Regarding Sedgwick*, 217–28.
Mitchell, Stephen, ed. and trans. *The Enlightened Heart: An Anthology of Sacred Poetry*. London: Harper, 2011.
Mitchell, Stephen, trans. *Tao Te Ching: A New English Version*. New York: Harper Perennial, 1988.
Mitter, Partha. *Much-Maligned Monsters: A History of European Reactions to Indian Art*. Oxford: Clarendon, 1977.
Montaigne, Michel de. "On Solitude." In *The Complete Essays*, edited and translated by M. A. Screech, 266–79. London: Penguin, 2003.
Moon, Michael. *Disseminating Whitman: Revision and Corporeality in "Leaves of Grass."* Cambridge, MA: Harvard University Press, 1991.
Moon, Michael. "Memorial Rags." In *Professions of Desire*, edited by George E. Haggerty and Bonnie Zimmerman, 233–40. New York: MLA, 1995.
Muñoz, José Esteban. "Race, Sex and the Incommensurate: Gary Fisher with Eve Kosofsky Sedgwick." In Berlant, *Reading Sedgwick*, 152–65.
Nelson, Maggie. "In the Bardo with Eve Sedgwick: A Buddhist 'Art of Dying' (and Dyeing)." *CUNY Matters*, Summer 2000, 9.
Nichols, Ben. *Same Old: Queer Theory, Literature, and the Politics of Sameness*. Manchester: Manchester University Press, 2020.
Pal, Pratapaditya, ed. *Himalayas: An Aesthetic Adventure*. Chicago: Art Institute of Chicago, 2004.
Palmer, Martin, and Jay Ramsay with Man-Ho Kwok. *The Kuan Yin Chronicles: The Myths and Prophecies of the Chinese Goddess of Compassion*. Charlottesville, VA: Hampton Roads, 2009.
Parker, Rozsika. *The Subversive Stitch: Embroidery and the Making of the Feminine*. New York: Routledge, 1989.
Paterson, Elaine Cheasley, and Susan Surette, eds. *Sloppy Craft: Postdisciplinarity and the Crafts*. London: Bloomsbury, 2015.
Pearl, Monica. "American Grief: The AIDS Quilt and Texts of Witness." *Gramma: Journal of Theory and Criticism* 16 (2008): 251–72.
Proust, Marcel. *Days of Reading*. Translated by John Sturrock. London: Penguin, 2008.
Proust, Marcel. *In Search of Lost Time*. Translated by Terence Kilmartin and C. K. Scott Moncrieff. Revised by D. J. Enright. 6 vols. London: Vintage, 1996–2002.
Reid-Pharr, Robert F. "The Shock of Gary Fisher." In *Black Gay Men: Essays*, 134–49. New York: New York University Press, 2001.
Rexroth, Kenneth. *One Hundred Poems from the Japanese*. New York: New Directions, 1964.

Rhie, Marilyn M., and Robert A. F. Thurman. *Wisdom and Compassion: The Sacred Art of Tibet*. London: Royal Academy/Abrams, 1991.
Rinpoche, Sogyal. *The Tibetan Book of Living and Dying*. 1992. London: Rider, 1998.
Sahn, Seung. *The Compass of Zen*. Boston: Shambala, 1997.
Said, Edward. *On Late Style: Music and Literature Against the Grain*. New York: Pantheon, 2006.
Schulman, Sarah. *The Gentrification of the Mind: Witness to a Lost Imagination*. Berkeley: University of California Press, 2012.
Schumann, H. W. *The Historical Buddha*. London: Arkana, 1989.
Sedgwick, Eve Kosofsky. *Between Men: English Literature and Male Homosocial Desire*. New York: Columbia University Press, 1985.
Sedgwick, Eve Kosofsky. *A Dialogue on Love*. Boston: Beacon, 1999.
Sedgwick, Eve Kosofsky. *Epistemology of the Closet*. Los Angeles: University of California Press, 1990.
Sedgwick, Eve Kosofsky. *Fat Art, Thin Art*. Durham, NC: Duke University Press, 1994.
Sedgwick, Eve Kosofsky. "Flying with Samuel Delany." Introduction to Samuel Delaney's Center for LGBTQ Studies (CLAGS) Kessler Award, CUNY Graduate Center, New York, 1997.
Sedgwick, Eve Kosofsky, ed. *Gary in Your Pocket: Stories and Notebooks of Gary Fisher*. Durham, NC: Duke University Press, 1996.
Sedgwick, Eve Kosofsky. "Gosh, Boy George, You Must Be Awfully Secure in Your Masculinity." In *Constructing Masculinity*, edited by Maurice Berger, Brian Wallis, and Simon Watson, 1–10. New York: Routledge, 1995.
Sedgwick, Eve Kosofsky, ed. "Introduction: Queerer than Fiction." Special issue, *Studies in the Novel* 28, no. 3 (Fall 1996): 277–80.
Sedgwick, Eve Kososfky. *The Last Days of Pompeii* (Unique artist's book, ca. 2007).
Sedgwick, Eve Kosofsky, ed. *Novel Gazing: Queer Readings in Fiction*. Durham, NC: Duke University Press, 1997.
Sedgwick, Eve Kosofsky. "The 1001 Seances." *GLQ* 17, no. 4 (2011): 457–83.
Sedgwick, Eve Kosofsky. "Queer Performativity: Warhol's Shyness/Warhol's Whiteness." In *Pop Out: Queer Warhol*, edited by Jennifer Doyle, Jonathan Flatley, and José Esteban Muñoz, 134–43. Durham, NC: Duke University Press, 1996.
Sedgwick, Eve Kosofsky. "A Response to C. Jacob Hale." *Social Text*, nos. 52–53 (Autumn–Winter 1997): 237–39.
Sedgwick, Eve Kosofsky. "A Scar Is Just a Scar: Approaching the First Postmastectomy Tryst." *MAMM*, June/July 1998, 27.
Sedgwick, Eve Kosofsky. "Teaching 'Experimental Critical Writing.'" In *The Ends of Performance*, edited by Jill Lane and Peggy Phelan, 105–15. New York: New York University Press, 1998.
Sedgwick, Eve Kosofsky. *Tendencies*. Durham, NC: Duke University Press, 1993.
Sedgwick, Eve Kosofsky. *Touching Feeling: Affect, Pedagogy, Performativity*. Durham, NC: Duke University Press, 2003.
Sedgwick, Eve Kosofsky. "Trace at 46." *Diacritics* 10, no. 1 (Spring 1980): 3–20.

Sedgwick, Eve Kosofsky. *The Weather in Proust*. Edited by Jonathan Goldberg. Durham, NC: Duke University Press, 2011.
Sedgwick, Eve Kosofsky, and Adam Frank, eds. *Shame and Its Sisters: A Silvan Tomkins Reader*. Durham, NC: Duke University Press, 1995.
Sedgwick, Eve Kosofsky, and Adam Frank. "Shame in the Cybernetic Fold: Reading Silvan Tomkins." *Critical Inquiry* 21, no. 2 (Winter 1995): 496–522.
Sedgwick, Eve Kosofsky, and Adam Frank. "Shame in the Cybernetic Fold: Reading Silvan Tomkins," in Sedgwick, *Touching Feeling*, 93–122.
Sedgwick, Eve Kosofsky, and Andrew Parker, eds. *Performativity and Performance*. London: Routledge, 1995.
Sedgwick, Eve Kosofsky, and Michael D. Snediker. "Queer Little Gods: A Conversation with Michael D. Snediker." *Massachusetts Review* 49, nos. 1–2 (2008): 194–218.
Sedgwick, H. A. "A Note on the 1001 Seances." Special section on Eve Kosofsky Sedgwick, edited by Annamarie Jagose and Ann Cvetkovich, *GLQ* 17, no. 4 (2011).
Shakespeare, William. *The Tempest*. Edited by Virginia Mason Vaughan and Alden T. Vaughan. London: Thomas Nelson and Sons, 1999.
Shantideva. *A Guide to the Bodhisattva's Way of Life*. Translated by Stephen Batchelor. New Delhi: Library of Tibetan Works and Archives, 1993.
Shin-ichiro, Toshida, and Dai Williams. *Riches from Rags: Sakiori and Other Recycling Traditions in Japanese Rural Clothing*. San Francisco: San Francisco Craft and Folk Art Museum, 1994.
Smith, Tai. "Architectonic: Thought on the Loom." *Journal of Modern Craft* 4, no. 3 (2011): 269–94.
Smith, Tai. *Bauhaus Weaving Theory: From Feminine Craft to Mode of Design*. Minneapolis: University of Minnesota Press, 2014.
Snediker, Michael D. *Contingent Figure: Chronic Pain and Queer Embodiment*. Minneapolis: University of Minnesota Press, 2021.
Stacey, Jackie. "Wishing Away Ambivalence." *Feminist Theory* 14, no. 1 (2014): 39–49.
Stevens, Rebecca, and Yoshiko Wada. *Kimono Inspiration: Art and Art-to-Wear in America*. Washington, DC: Textile Museum, 1996.
Stoller, Debbie. *Son of Stitch 'n Bitch: 45 Projects to Knit and Crochet for Men*. New York: Workman, 2007.
Stoller, Debbie. *Stitch 'n Bitch: The Knitter's Handbook*. New York: Workman, 2003.
Stoller, Debbie. *Stitch 'n Bitch Crochet: The Happy Hooker*. New York: Workman, 2006.
Stoller, Debbie. *Stitch 'n Bitch Nation*. New York: Workman, 2004.
Stoller, Debbie. *Stitch 'n Bitch Superstar: Go Beyond the Basics*. New York: Workman, 2010.
Stryker, Susan. "More Words About 'My Words to Victor Frankenstein.'" *GLQ* 25, no. 1 (2019): 39–44.
Stryker, Susan. "My Words to Victor Frankenstein Above the Village of Chamonix: Performing Transgender Rage." *GLQ* 1, no. 3 (1994): 237–54.
Sudo, Kumiko. *East Quilts West*. Gualala, CA: Quilt Digest, 1995.
Sutton, Ann, and Diane Sheehan. *Ideas in Weaving*. London: B. T. Batsford, N.D.

Sweid, Richard. *Octopus*. London: Reaktion, 2013.
The Tales of Ise. Translated by H. Jay Harris. Tokyo: Charles E. Tuttle, 1972.
Thurman, Robert A. F. *The Central Philosophy of Tibet: A Study and Translation of Jey Tsong Khapa's Essence of True Eloquence*. Princeton, NJ: Princeton University Press, 1984.
Thurman, Robert A. F. *Essential Tibetan Buddhism*. San Francisco: Harper San Francisco, 1995.
Thurman, Robert A. F., trans. *The Tibetan Book of the Dead: Liberation Through Understanding the In Between*. 1994. San Francisco: HarperCollins, 2011.
Tiffin, Sarah. *Southeast Asia in Ruins: Art and Empire in the Early 19th Century*. Singapore: University of Singapore Press, 2016.
Travares, André. *The Anatomy of the Architectural Book*. Zurich: Lars Müller/Canadian Centre for Architecture, 2016.
Trollope, Anthony. *An Autobiography*. 1883. New York: Dodd, Mead, 1905.
Tsoukala, Philomila. "Reading *A Poem Is Being Written*: A Tribute to Eve Kosofsky Sedgwick." In "A Tribute from Legal Studies to Eve Kosofsky Sedgwick," edited by Janet Halley. Special issue, *Harvard Journal of Law and Gender* 33, no. 1 (Winter 2010): 339–56.
Tucci, Guiseppe. *Tibetan Painted Scrolls*. Rome: La Libreria Della Stato, 1949.
Ueda, Makoto. *Bashō and His Interpreters: Selected Hokku with Commentary*. Stanford, CA: Stanford University Press, 1992.
Vincent, John. "Flogging Is Fundamental: Applications of the Birch in Swinburne's *Lesbia Brandon*." In *Novel Gazing: Queer Readings in Fiction*, edited by Eve Kosofsky Sedgwick, 269–98. Durham, NC: Duke University Press, 1997.
Vincentelli, Moira. "Japanese Sashiko Textiles." *Journal of Modern Craft* 4, no. 1 (2011): 99–103.
Wada, Yoshiko Iwamoto. *Memory on Cloth: Shibori Now*. Tokyo: Kodansha, 2002.
Wada, Yoshiko Iwamoto, Mary Kellogg Rice, and Jane Barton. *Shibori: The Inventive Art of Japanese Shaped Resist Dyeing*. Tokyo: Kodansha, 1999.
Warhol, Andy. *Flowers, Flowers, Flowers*. Boston: Bulfinch, 1996.
Warner, Michael. *The Trouble with Normal: Sex, Politics, and the Ethics of Queer Life*. Cambridge, MA: Harvard University Press, 1999.
Watts, Alan. *The Way of Zen*. 1957. New York: Vintage, 1989.
Westwood, Cassie. "The Abject Animal Poetics of *The Warm Decembers*." In Edwards, *Bathroom Songs*, 85–110.
Westwood, Cassie. "The Queer Art of Ardent Reading." *Raritan* 41, no. 1 (Summer 2021): 50–71.
Wilson, Elizabeth. "Biologically Inspired Feminism." *Australian Feminist Studies* 17, no. 39 (2002): 283–85.
Wise, Tad. *Blessings on the Wind: The Mystery and Meaning of Tibetan Prayer Flags*. San Francisco: Chronicle, 2002.
Wolf, Maryanne. *Proust and the Squid: The Story and Science of the Reading Brain*. Thriplow, UK: Icon, 2008.

Wolfson, Susan J. "Reading for Form." *MLA* 61, no. 1 (March 2000): 1–16.
Yeats, W. B. "Long-Legged Fly." In *Collected Poems*, 327. London: Macmillan, 1951.
Yu, Chun-Fang. *Kuan-yin: The Chinese Transformation of Avalokiteshvara*. New York: Columbia University Press, 2001.

INDEX

Note: Page numbers in *italics* refer to illustrations.